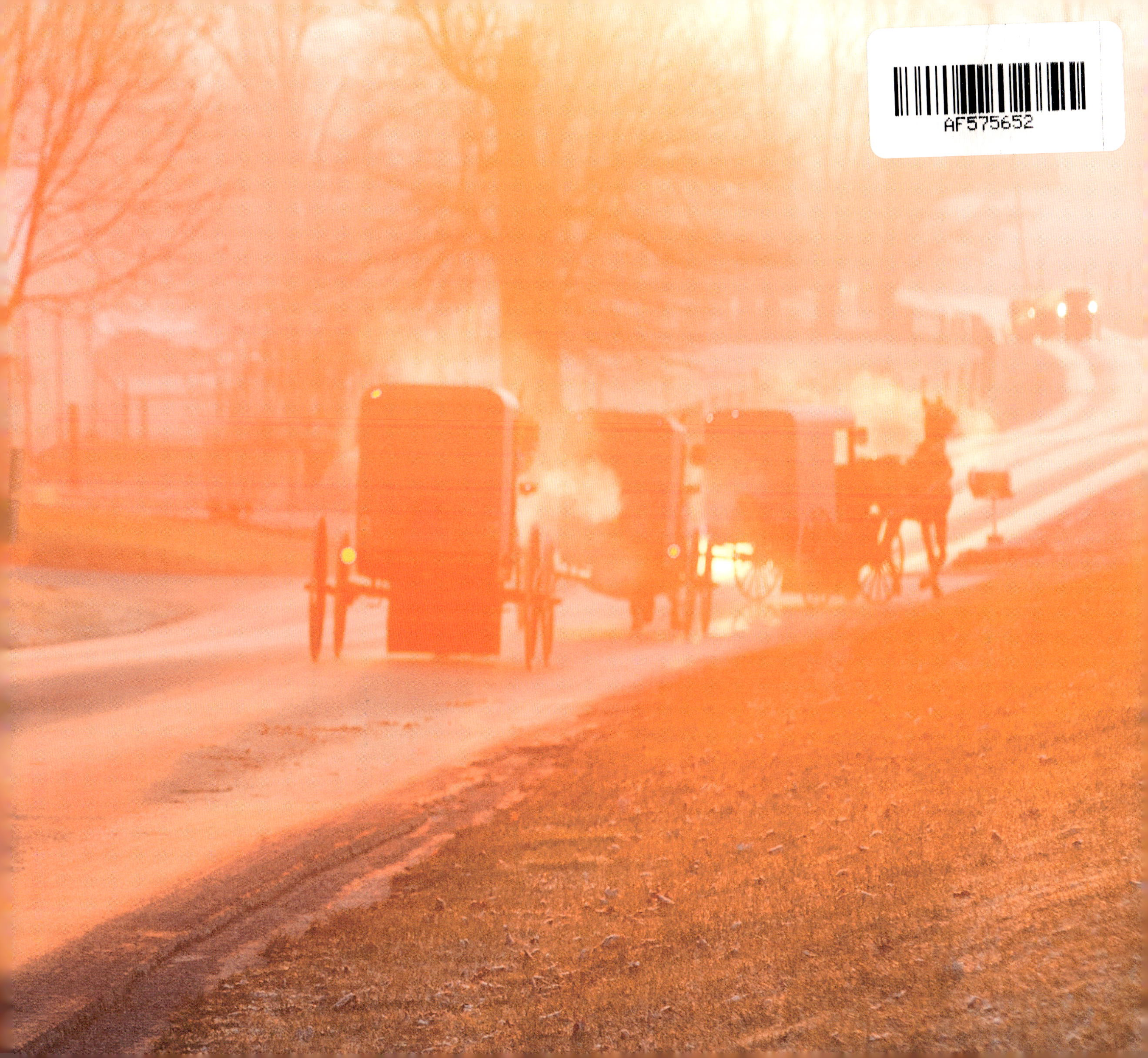

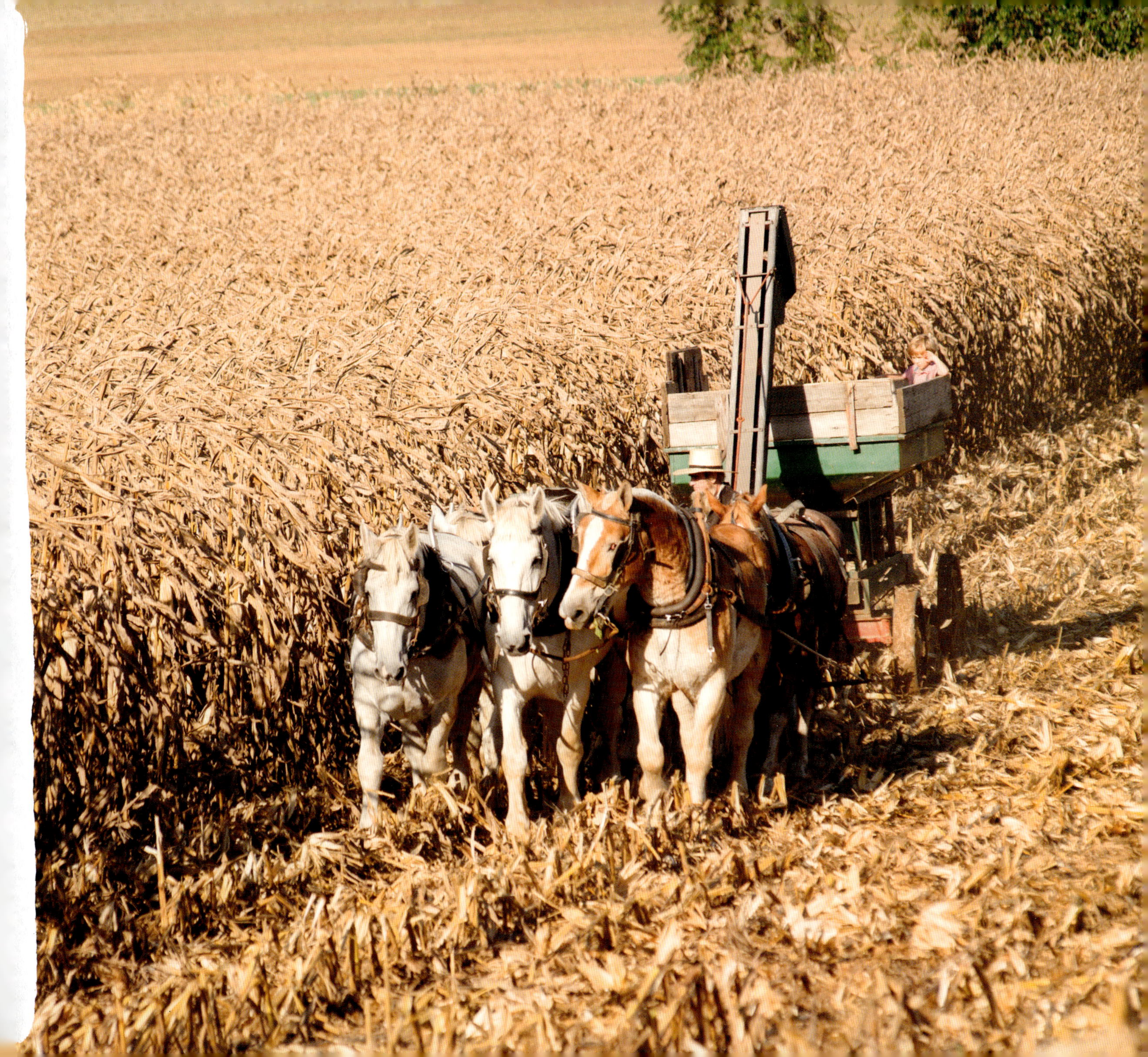

Other Schiffer Books by Beth Oberholtzer and John Herr
Plain Meetinghouses: Old Order Lancaster County Mennonites Gather to Worship, 978-07643-5301-7

Library of Congress Control Number: 2020943546

Designed by Beth Oberholtzer
Cover design by Beth Oberholtzer

Type set in Arno Pro
ISBN: 978-0-7643-6161-6
Printed in India
Published by Schiffer Publishing, Ltd.
4880 Lower Valley Road
Atglen, PA 19310
Phone: (610) 593-1777; Fax: (610) 593-2002
E-mail: Info@schifferbooks.com
Web: www.schifferbooks.com

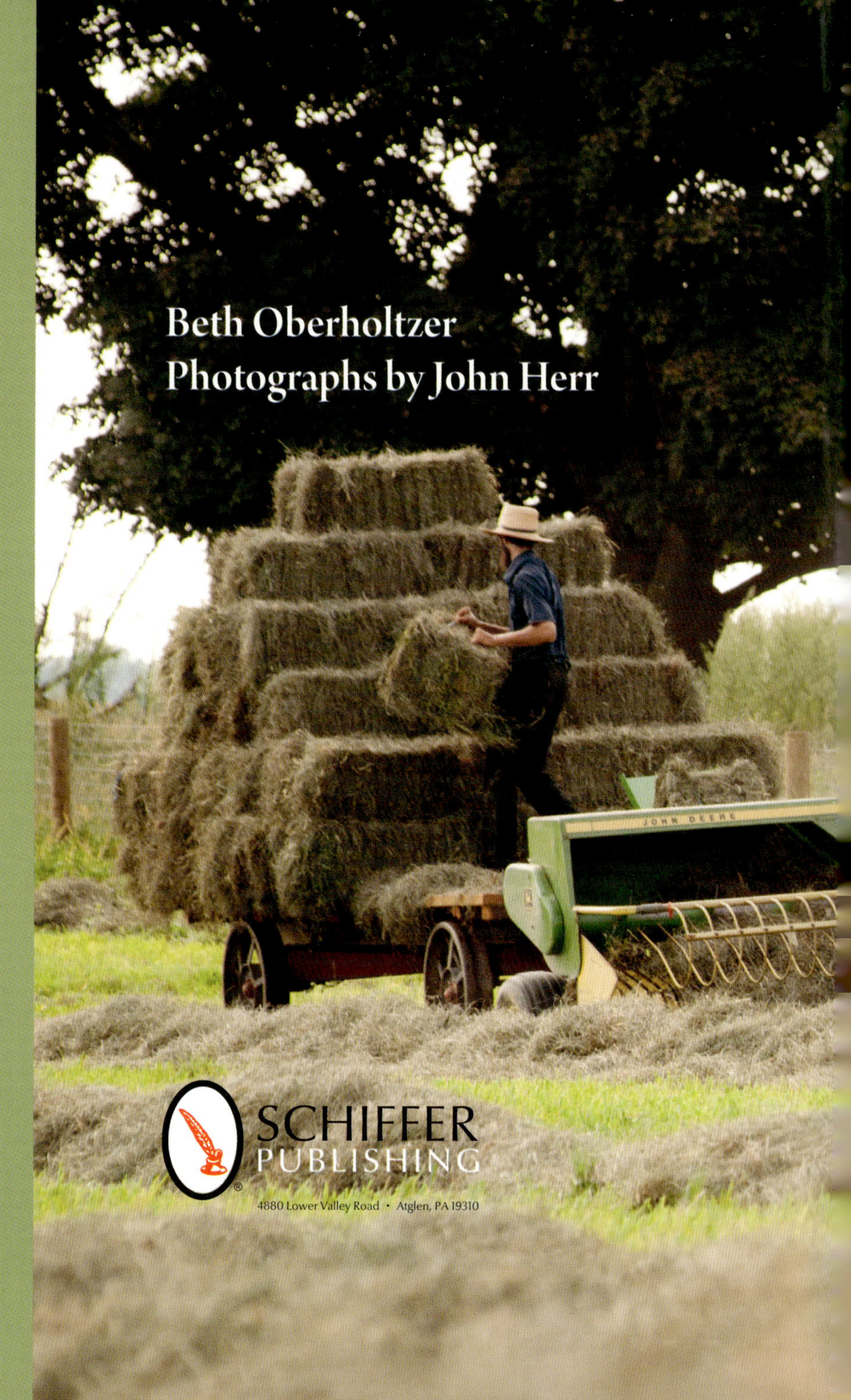

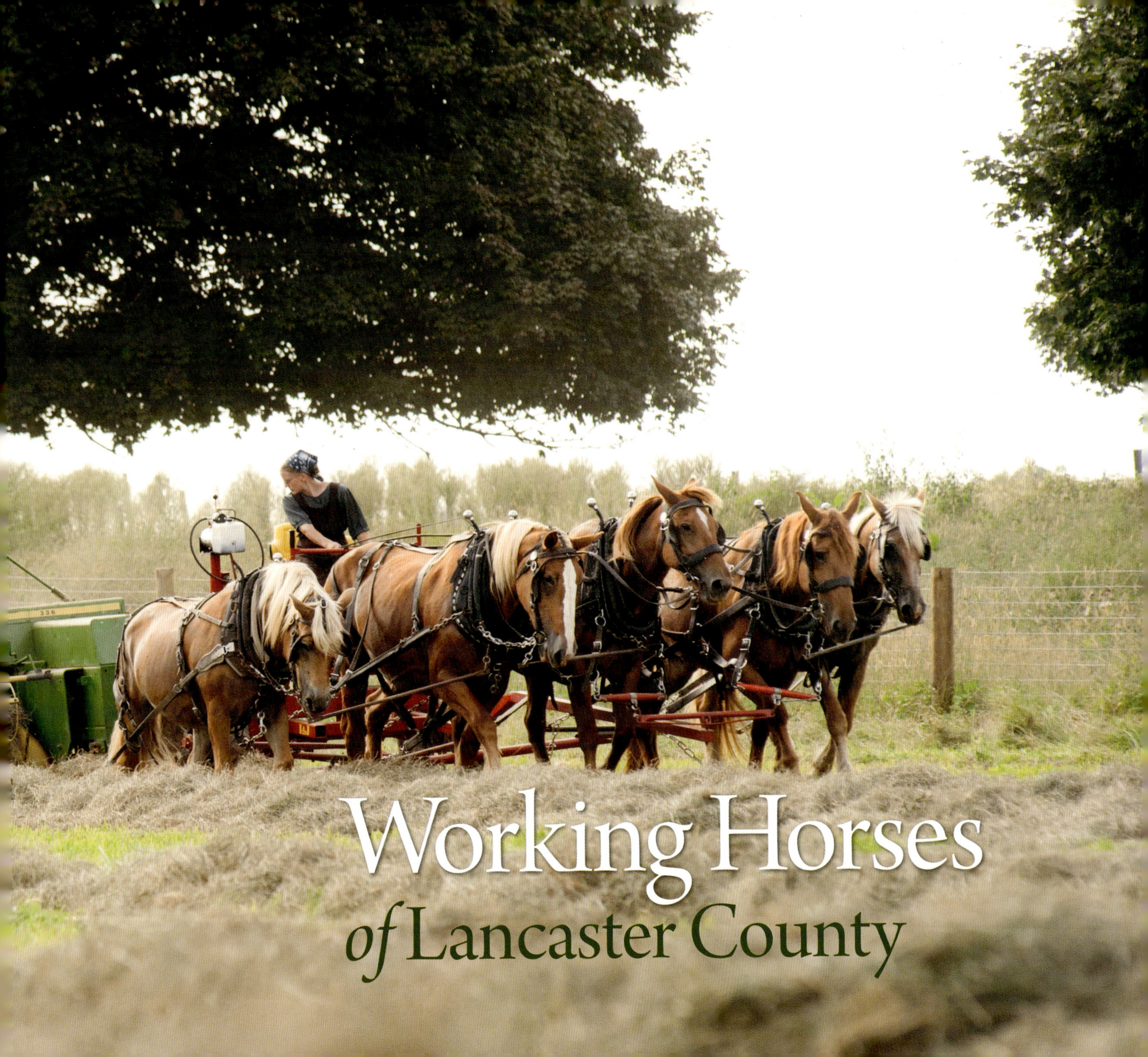
Working Horses
of Lancaster County

To my father and grandfather, John Jacob Oberholtzer and Elmer Oberholtzer, who inspired my love of horses.
—Beth Oberholtzer

To my father, Paul Witmer Herr, who passed on to me his interest in photography and respect for the Old Order community.
—John Herr

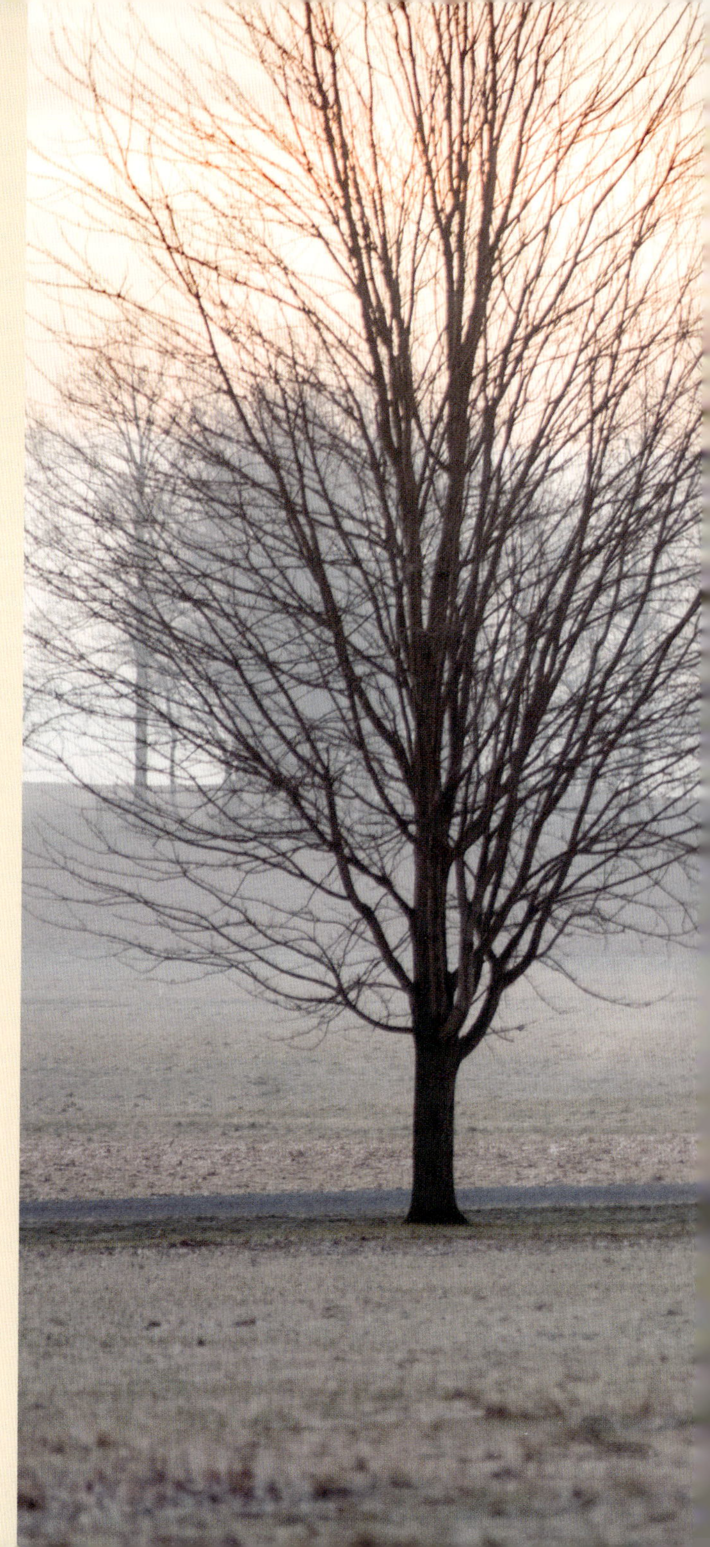

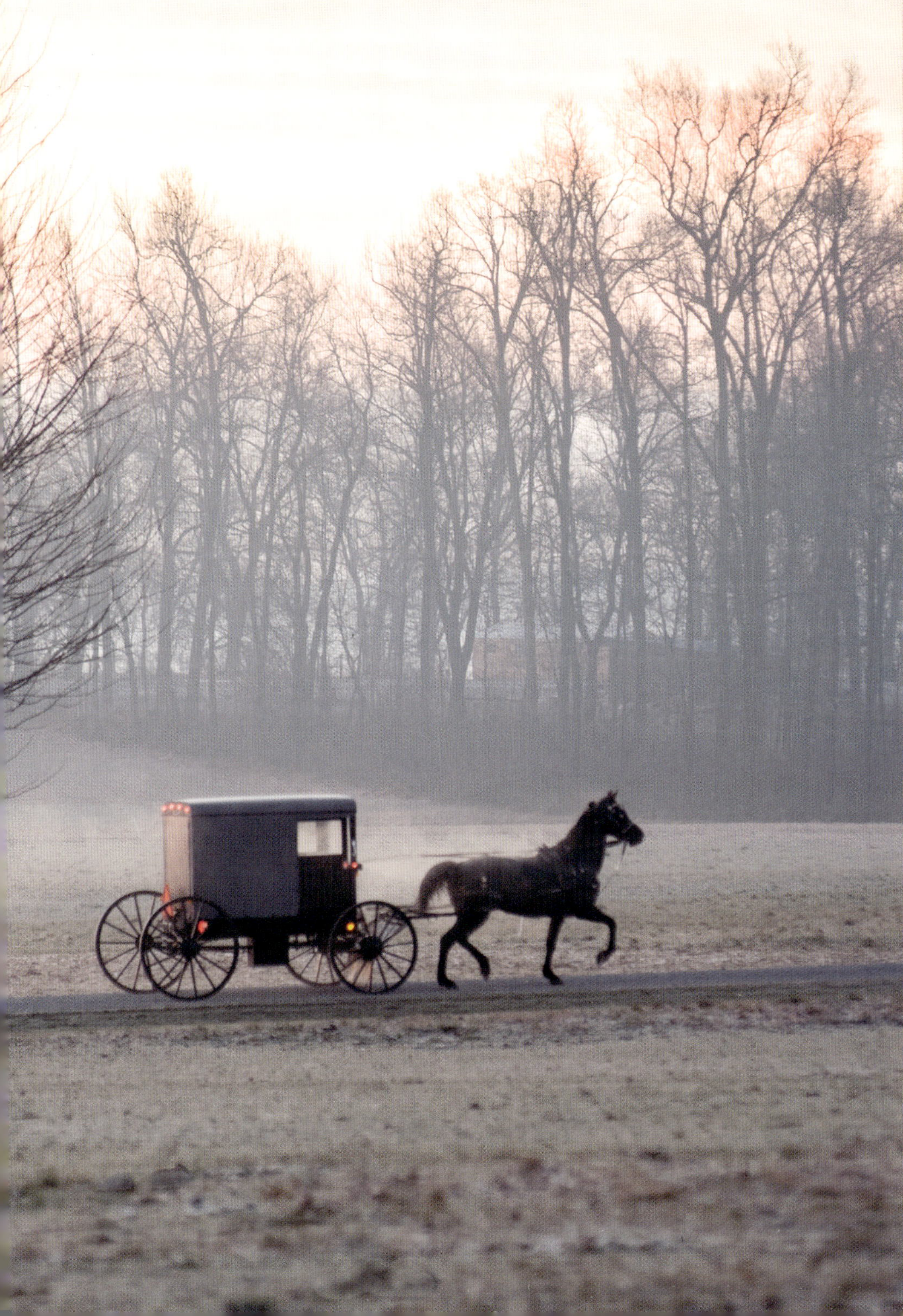

Contents

Foreword

By Dale K. Stoltzfus

Hundreds of nonfiction books have been written about Lancaster County's Plain People; however, *Working Horses of Lancaster County* is undoubtedly the most comprehensive look to date at this crucial aspect of the Amish and Old Order Mennonite way of life. The decision Plain leaders made at the beginning of the twentieth century to keep using horses instead of cars and tractors has come to define this religious sect. They are the horse-and-buggy people, drawing curious visitors from around the globe.

Although my cousins and I are four generations removed from Plain people, I have an abiding love for horses—an interest fed and watered by the opportunities I have had to manage two major events: Horse Progress Days (www.horseprogressdays.com) and the Pennsylvania Draft Horse Sale, now known as the Keystone Draft Horse Sale (www.keystonedhs.com). Those who fully understand the emotional and physical needs of horses know that, like their human counterparts, they're at their best when they have a sense of purpose. A heavy draft horse working alongside teammates to accomplish a task, a well-fed buggy horse moving briskly down the road—transporting its family to the store, the doctor's office, a family reunion, a wedding, to church, to a funeral—completely understands the value of its task. Horses and people feel better when they work, exercising their muscles.

A 2017 US Department of Agriculture survey of southeastern Pennsylvania counted 21,599 horses in Lancaster County—more than twice the number of neighboring Chester County, which has the second-largest horse population and many bucolic horse farms (*East Coast Equestrian,* November 2017). This isn't surprising, given that Lancaster County has the largest Amish population in the US. It is apparent that writer Beth Oberholtzer and photographer John Herr spent countless hours driving back roads and talking in-depth with the horses' owners. This makes the book authentic. The photos are gorgeous but not glamour shots. They show horses at work in real time.

The fourteen pages devoted to Standardbreds is representative of the fact that it is the most popular carriage horse breed. The book also captures a relatively new phenomenon—the impact of Plain young people breeding and training horses. While some horses are sold for the race track or used for show, most of these horses end up on working family farms. The economic impact of the exchange of horses and mules and their ancillary products and services—buggies, harnesses, farm equipment, feed, hay, straw, farrier work, veterinarian care—is difficult to measure, but it is huge.

What's also satisfyingly clear in this book is the pride and joy that the owners and trainers feel for their horses. Herr's photographs capture the power and beauty of these equine workers and the bond between human and animal, while Oberholtzer's narrative offers a rare insider view of Old Order farming methods and the role of horses in fostering a deep sense of family and community.

—Dale K. Stoltzfus is a lifelong resident of Lancaster County, Pennsylvania. Since 1988 he has been raising and training Belgian draft horses and the occasional Percheron. His articles have been published in the *Draft Horse Journal,* Waverly, Iowa; *Farming Magazine,* Mt. Hope, Ohio; and the annual "Horse Progress Days Program Guide."

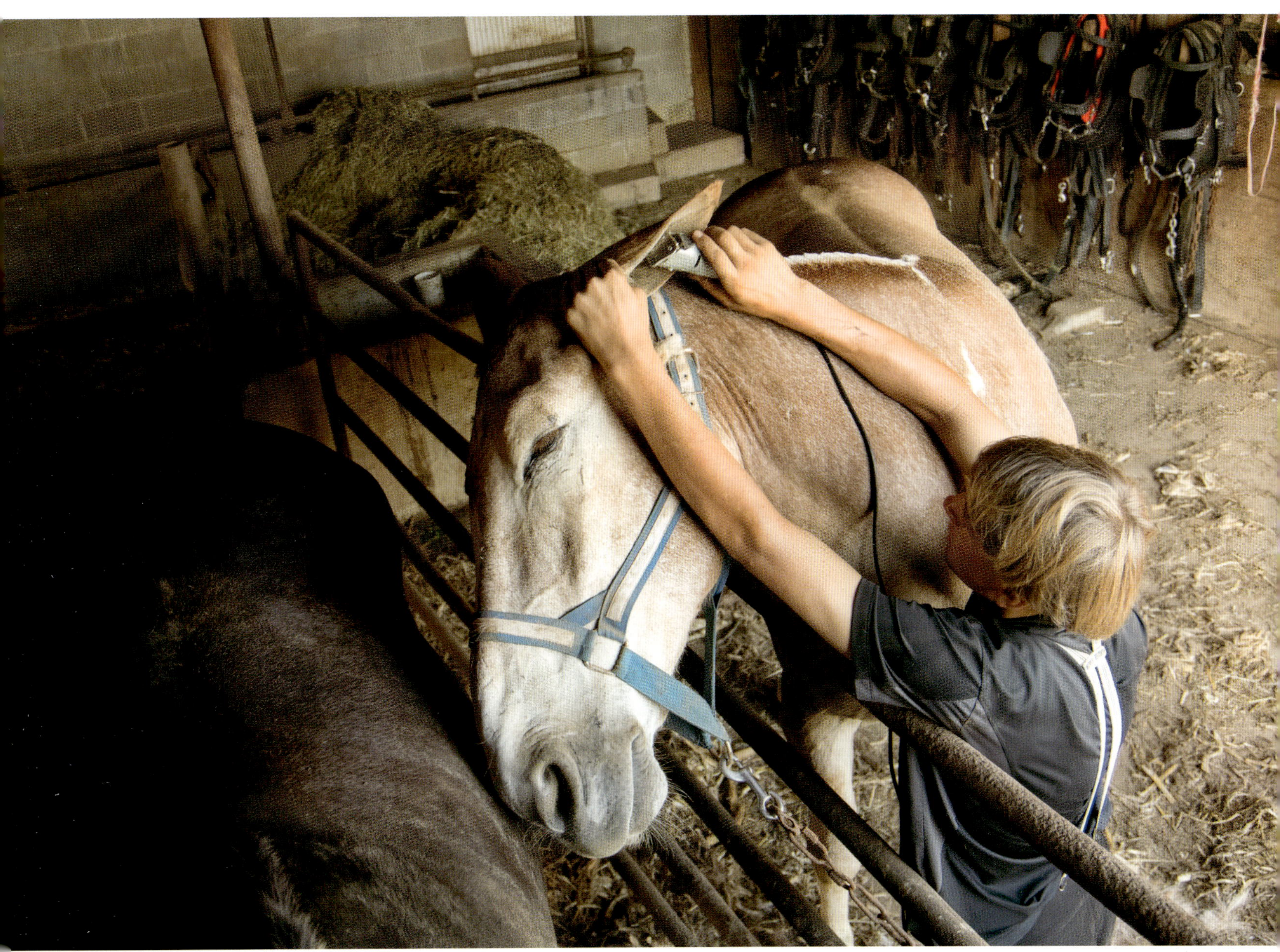

Preface

This book would not have been possible without the generous and gracious help from many working-horse enthusiasts who shared their time and passion with us. The people we met were not interested, however, in receiving attention themselves. Amish and Old Order Mennonites are members of collective societies in which the community is more important than the individual.

We spoke with breeders, trainers, and farmers and photographed their horses. Virtually all the photos were taken at working farms and stables in Lancaster County, though a few were just over the line to the east in Chester County.

We were granted permission to photograph the horses; every photo was approved for publication by the horse owners (except several photos shot at a public venue). Owners also reviewed and approved the written information. When names were used, participants chose whether to use their first, middle, or last names; nicknames; or pseudonyms.

The featured quotes on the pages, though unattributed, were drawn from actual conversations.

The breed facts at the beginning of each chapter were gleaned from breed-specific websites and publications that are listed in the sources section at the end of the book.

We have placed the variety of working-horse breeds in Lancaster County within two categories: draft horses and carriage horses. Though not considered horses, mules are included in the draft horse section because they are offspring of draft horse mares and donkey sires.

Many farmers and breeders estimated that mules compose up to half of the working draft animals in the county.

The horses we saw were treated well. They recognized, responded to, and often showed affection for their owners. Like many animals, horses thrive when they have companionship and a job to do.

We were fortunate to have such good-hearted guides, both human and equine, in our journey through fields and farms of Lancaster County.

Beth Oberholtzer
John Herr

"If you want to build on yourself, forget it. It's not about the individual; it's about working together."

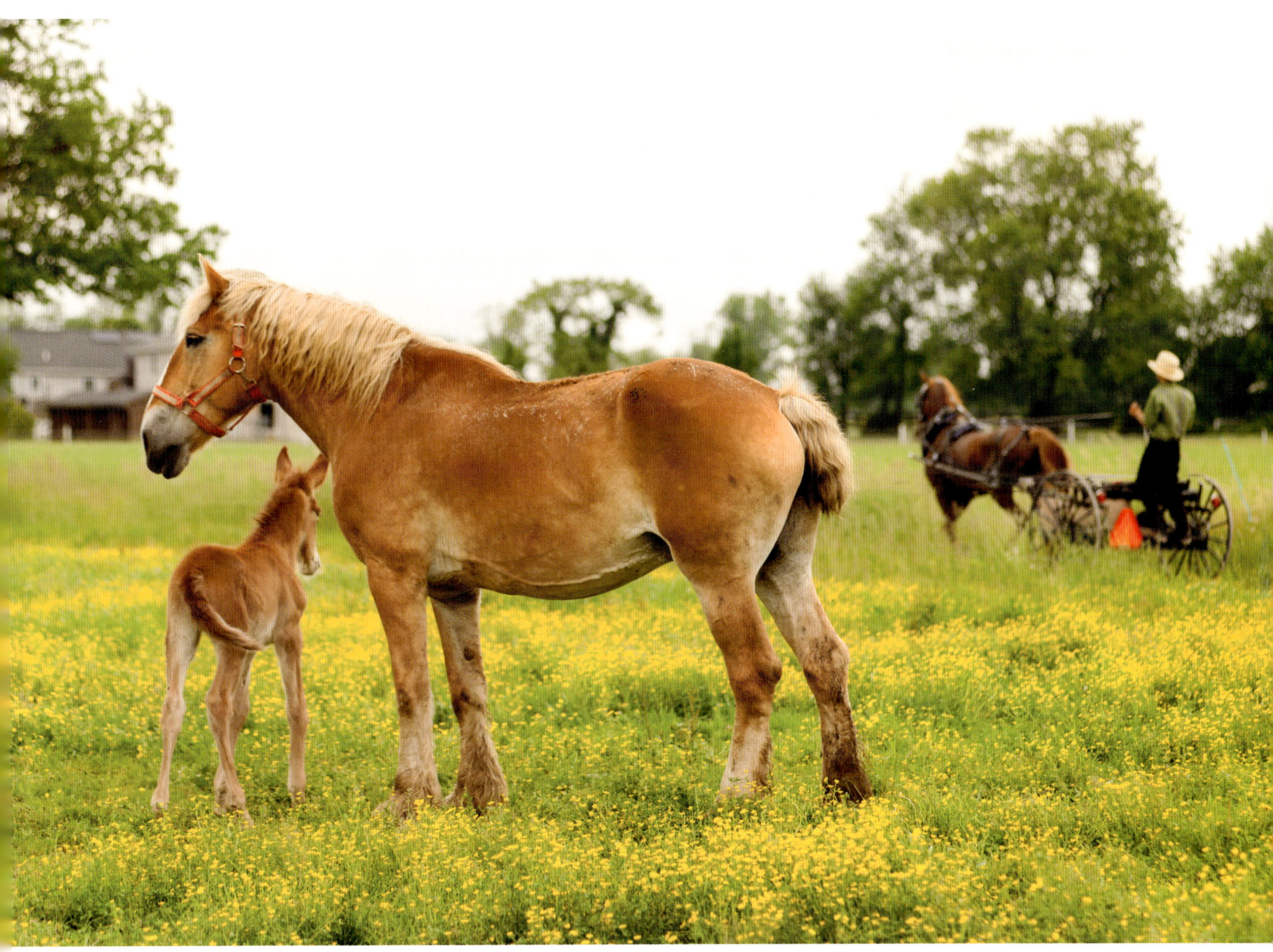

Introduction

Farming has long been a way of life in Lancaster County, and horses have been used to work the land from the beginning. In the early 1700s, settlers came to Lancaster County looking for religious freedom and good farmland. They found both. Even after the tractor became the power of choice for their English neighbors in the 1920s and 1930s, Old Order farmers continued to maintain the old traditions and avoid modern transportation. They plowed with draft horses, and their horse-drawn carriages shared the roads with cars. Amish and Old Order Mennonites still strive to live in a way that is consistent with a faith that calls for loyalty to God and community and remaining "separate" from the broader world.

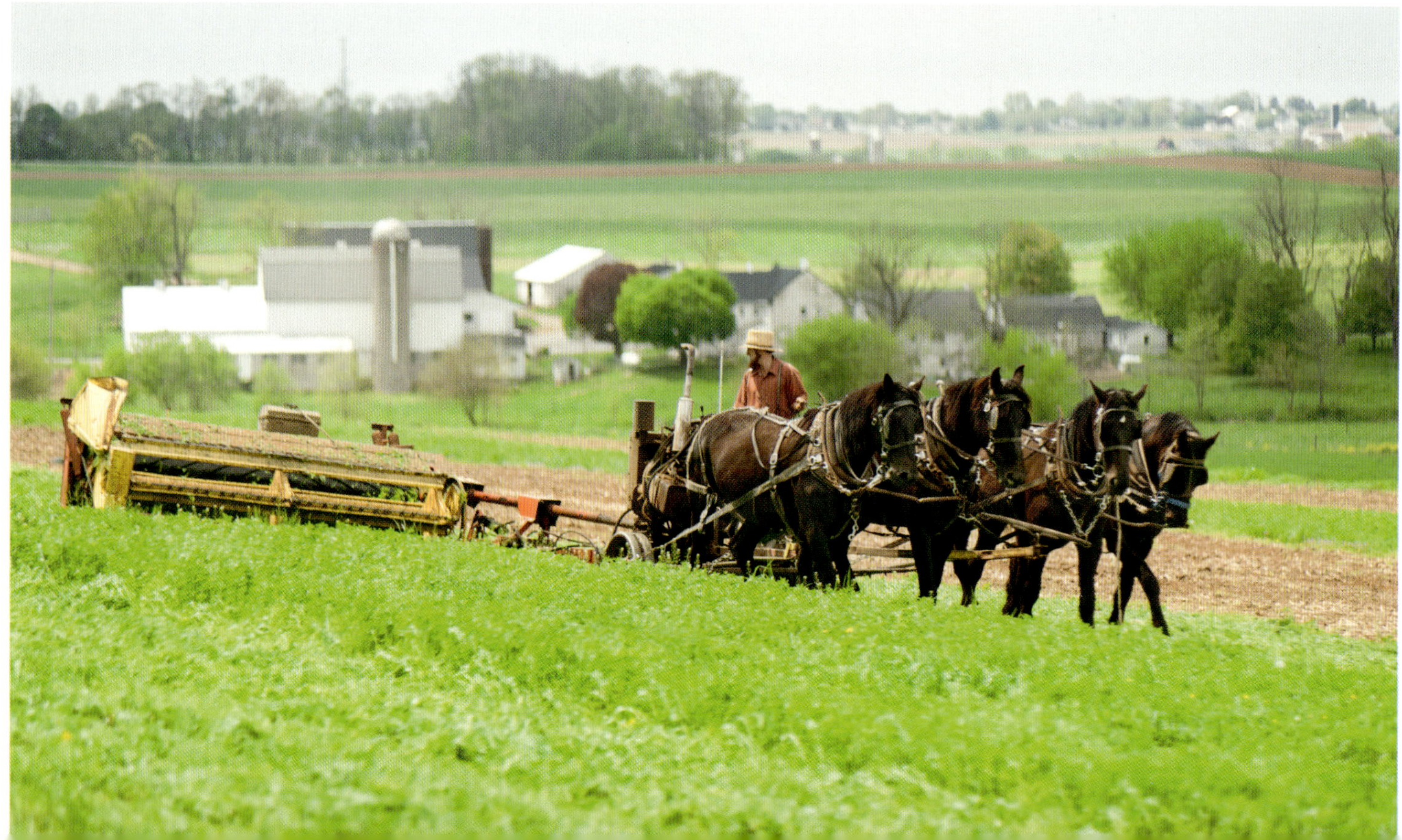

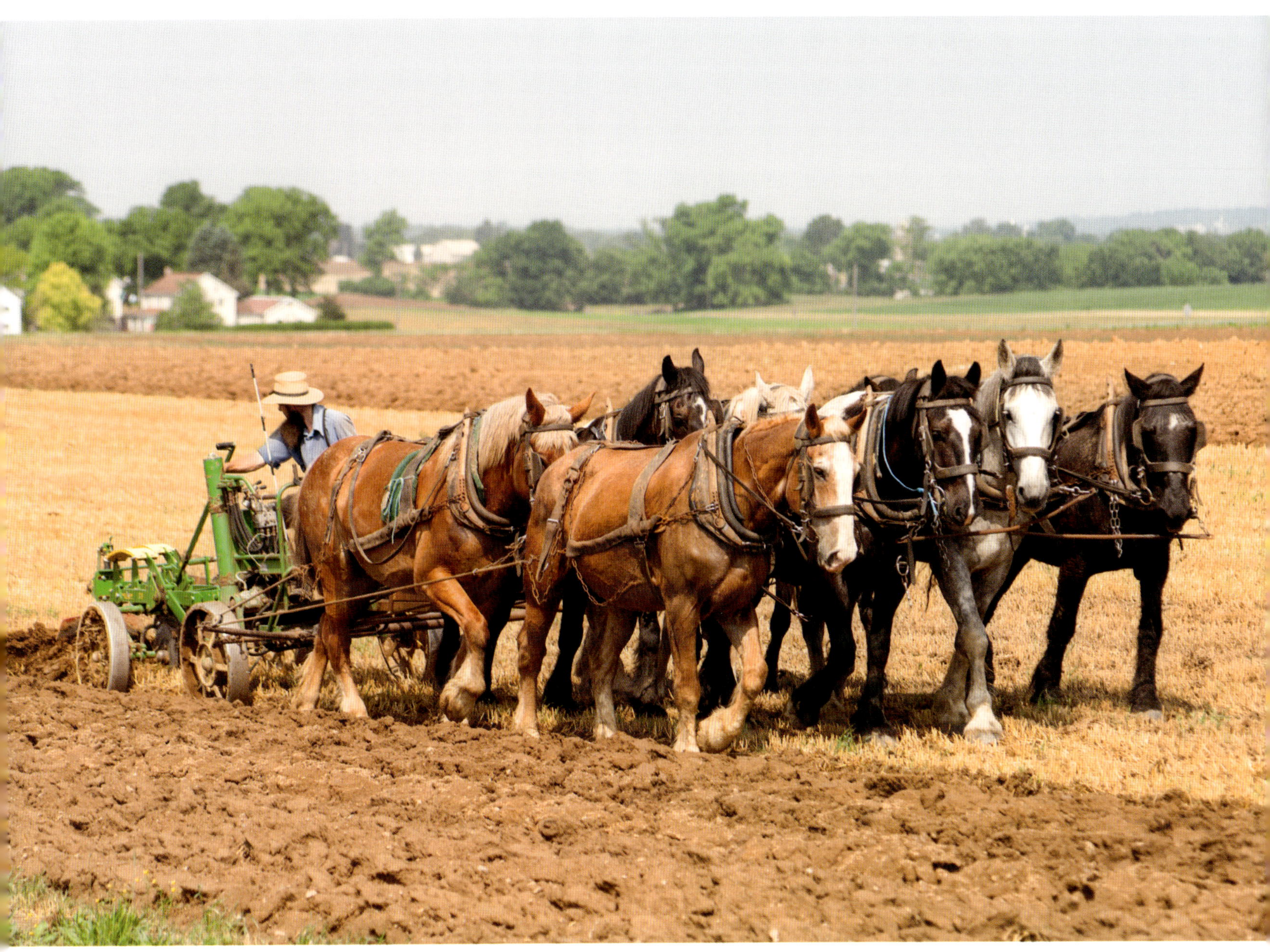

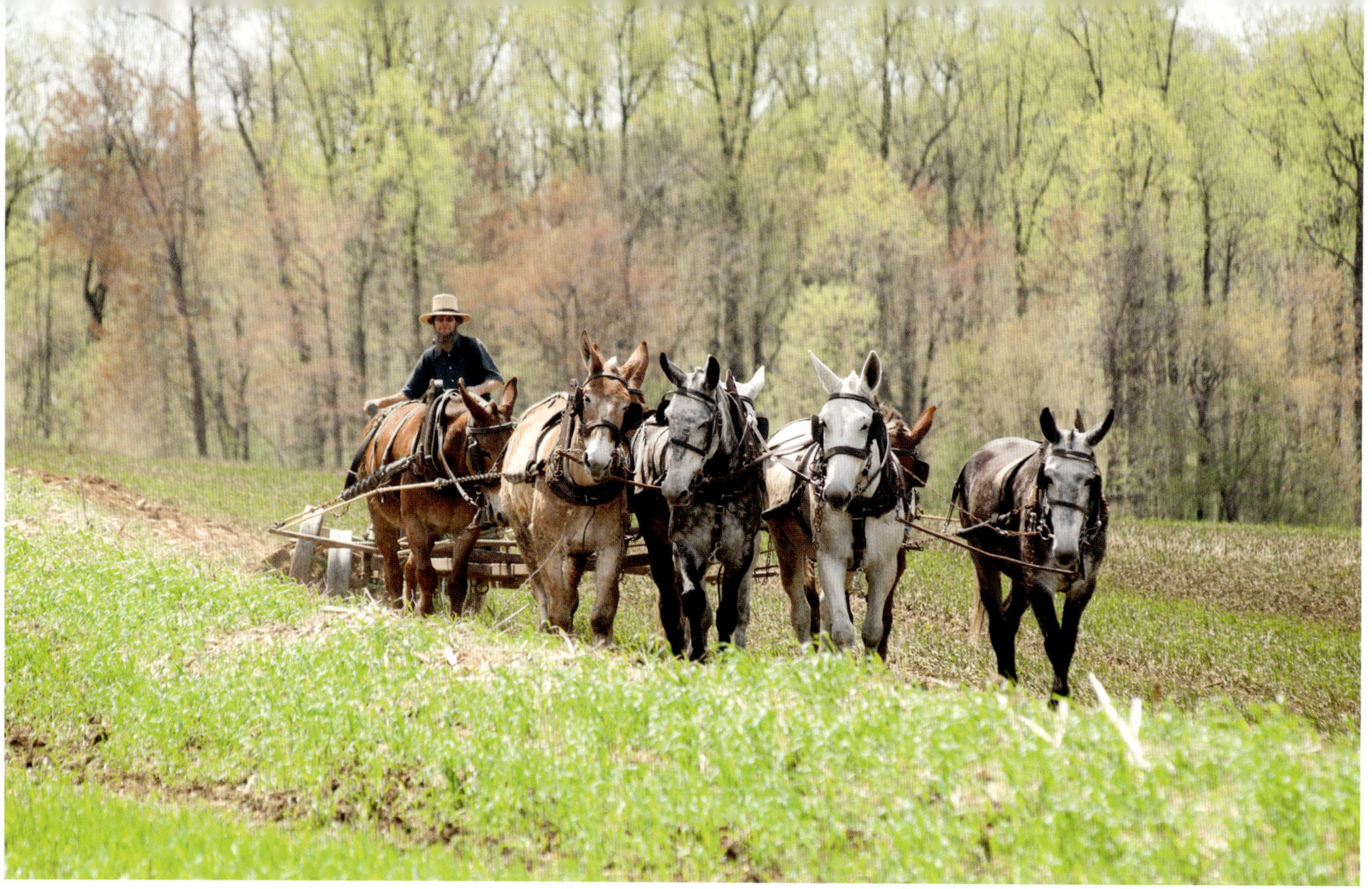

More than 33,000 Amish and 5,000 Old Order Mennonites live in Lancaster County and travel by horse and buggy. While Old Order Mennonites typically farm with steel-wheeled tractors, the Amish use draft animals to pull their farm machinery. But they do not ignore progress. Some horse-drawn equipment is reimagined and manufactured for the "modern" farmer. Other equipment and methods remain as they have been for generations.

The majority of farms worked with horse-drawn equipment occur in an arc along the northern, eastern, and southern parts of Lancaster County. In some places, suburban sprawl bumps up against the farmland.

The sight of an especially fine horse specimen has always turned heads, and by the 1960s and 1970s, the market was growing for handsome, well-trained horses with good bloodlines. Some members of the Old Orders began to buy and breed registered horses. At first, church leaders eyed this practice with skepticism. Registered horses were more expensive than others, and the act of registration itself could invite government notice of a people who wished to separate themselves from mainstream society. After conversations exploring the acceptability of registering horses, breeders decided to move ahead with caution.

Some farmers added horse breeding to their other work of growing crops and tending cattle and poultry. Breeding a prize mare and selling the foal each year could bring in extra money, and the model could scale according to resources and demand. Though the ideal is to produce a horse for show or racing, in reality most of the stock is used for fieldwork or to pull a carriage.

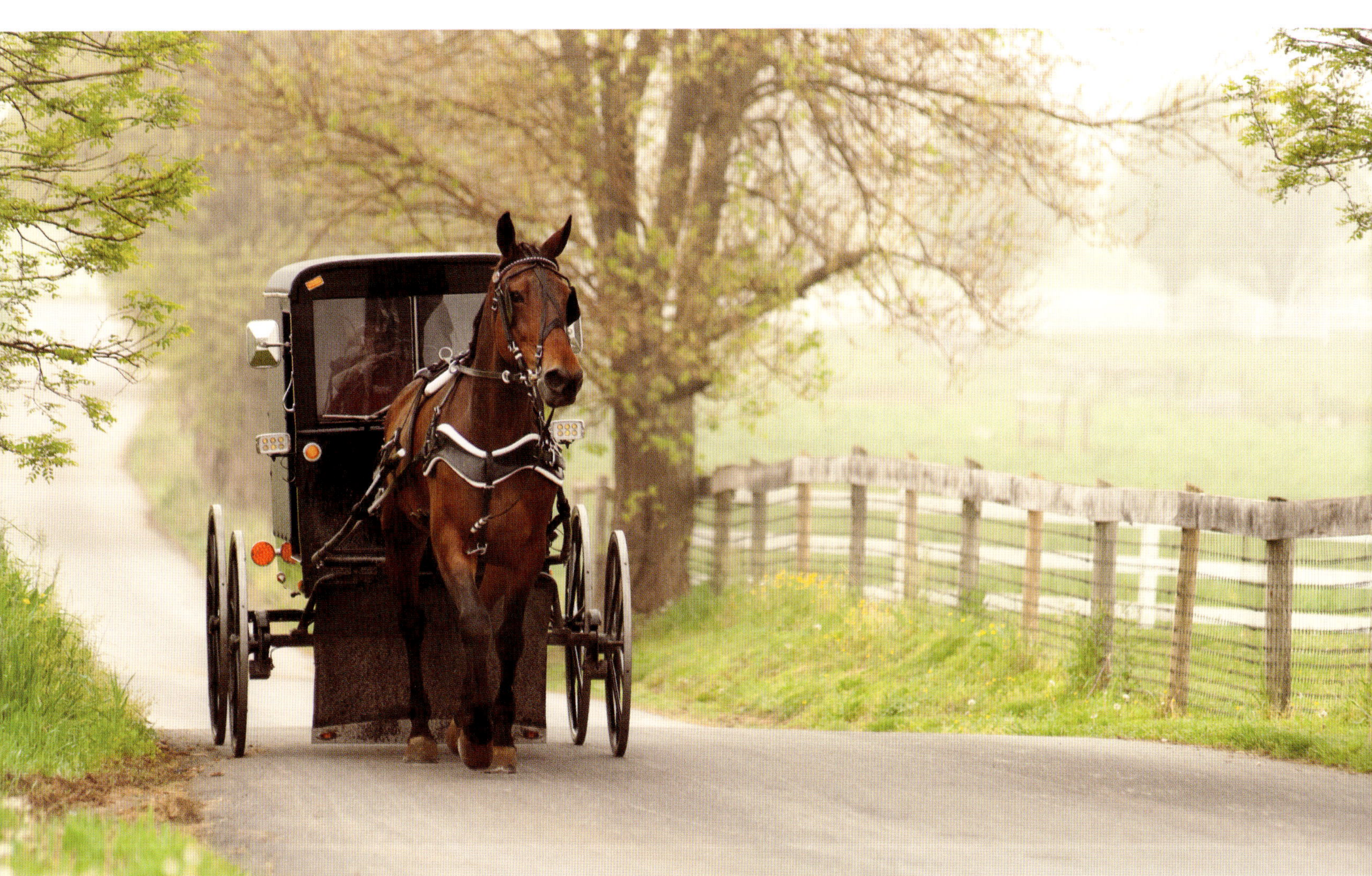

The use of horses reinforces the Amish and Old Order way of life. Traveling by horse and buggy limits the distance people can cover and keeps them close to their neighbors, who are often members of their church or extended family. Family and church provide a social life and safety net. And using horses for fieldwork keeps Amish boys engaged in wholesome work at home rather than finding employment off the farm. Farms remain small enough to be managed by one family—and in a pinch, help with the harvest is just a field or two away.

Fathers and sons, or brothers, often go into business together. They can pool their capital and each shoulder a part of the work. It's not unusual to find two or three brothers living on separate farms but breeding and raising horses under the same stable name, each owning a number of mares with stallions in common.

Younger family members see a model of cooperative work and naturally follow the path that best suits their interests and abilities.

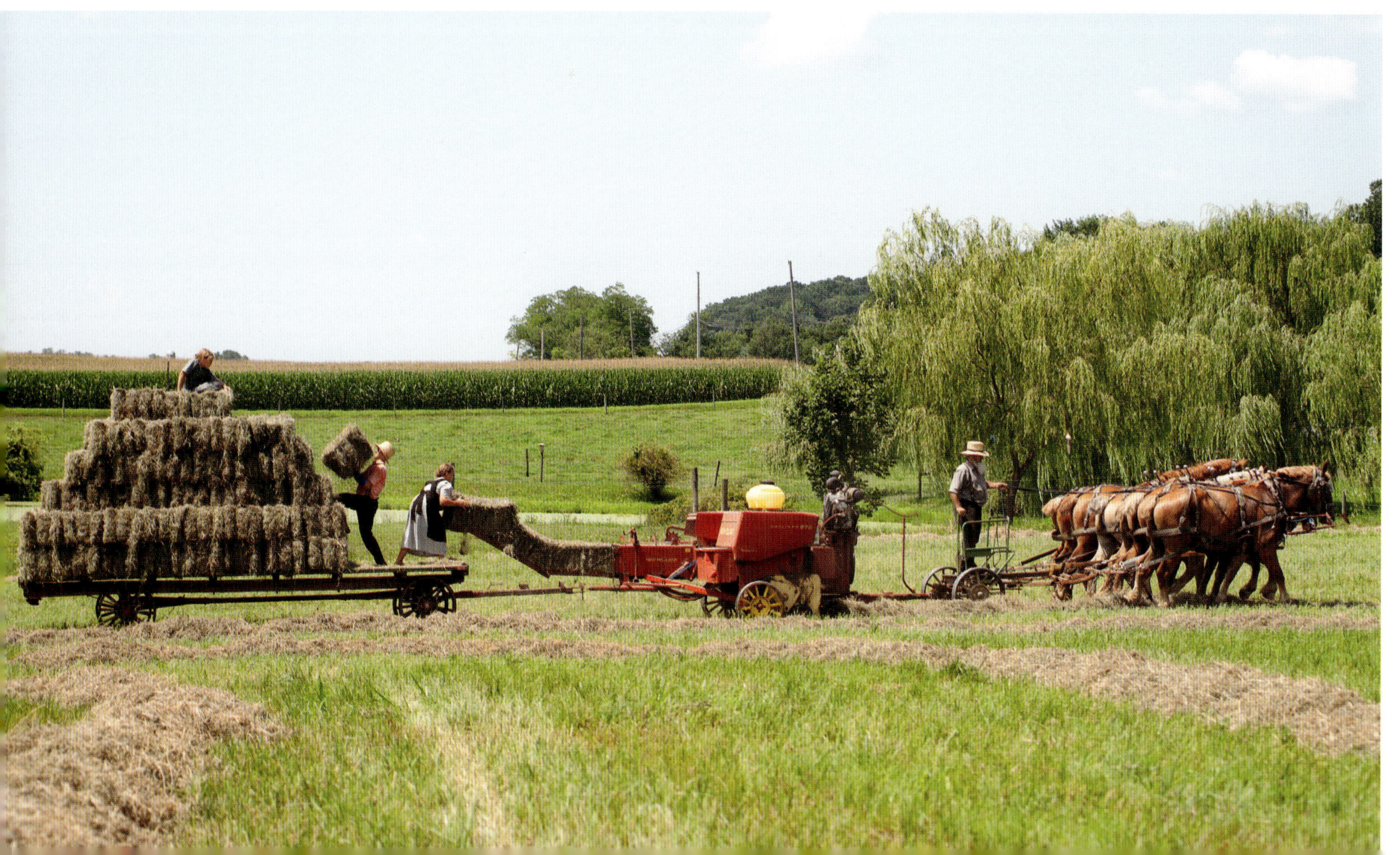

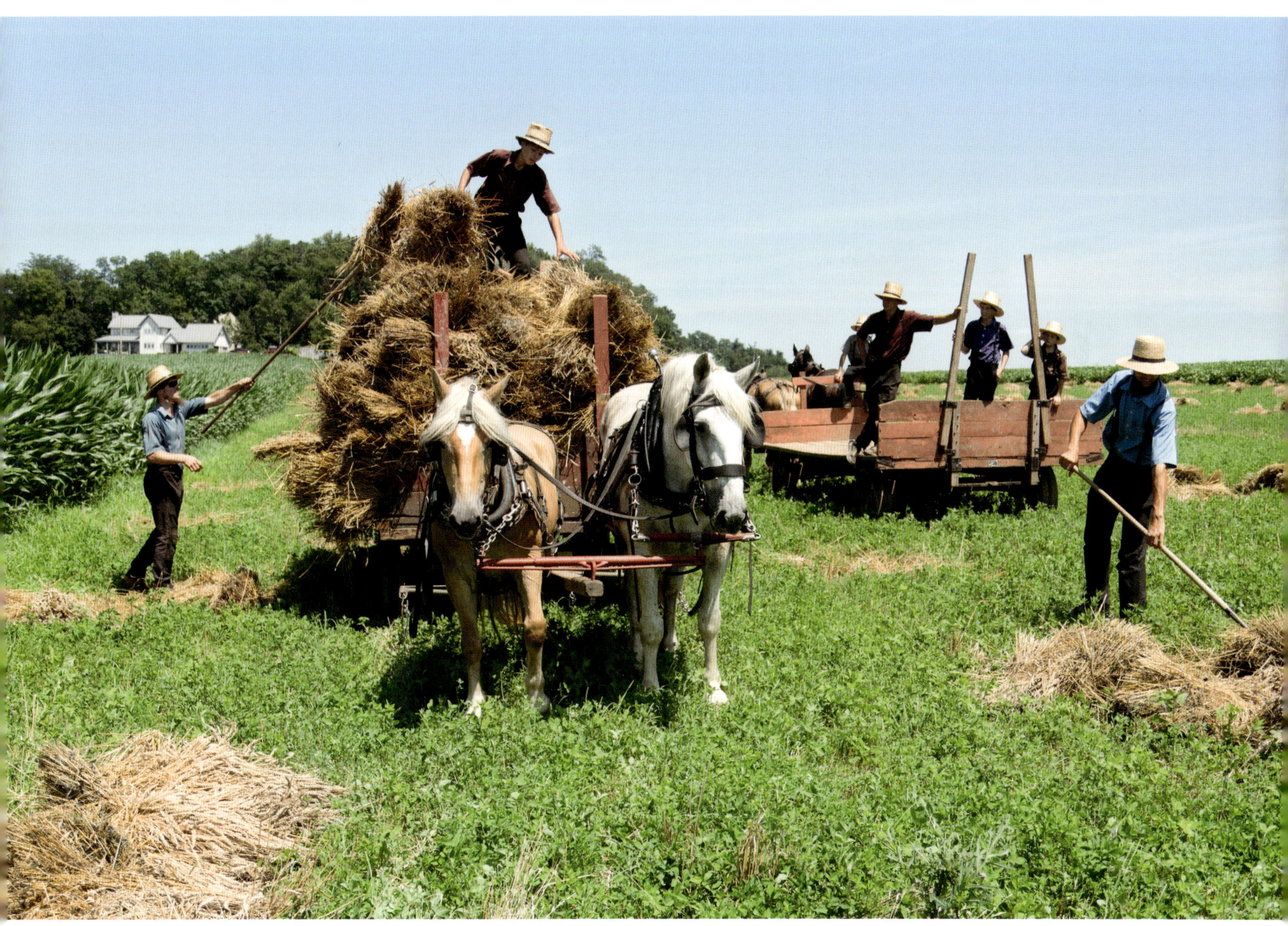

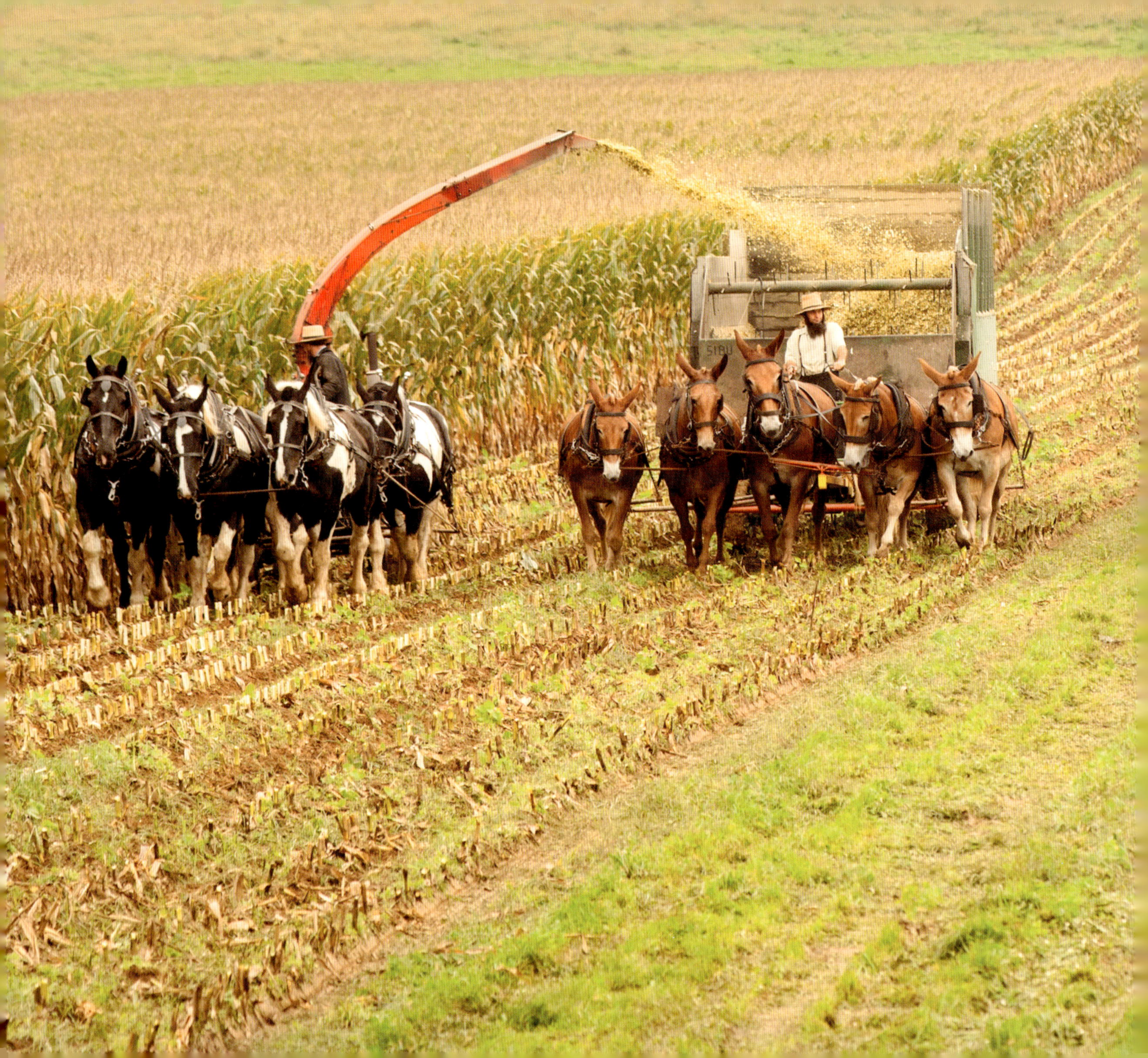

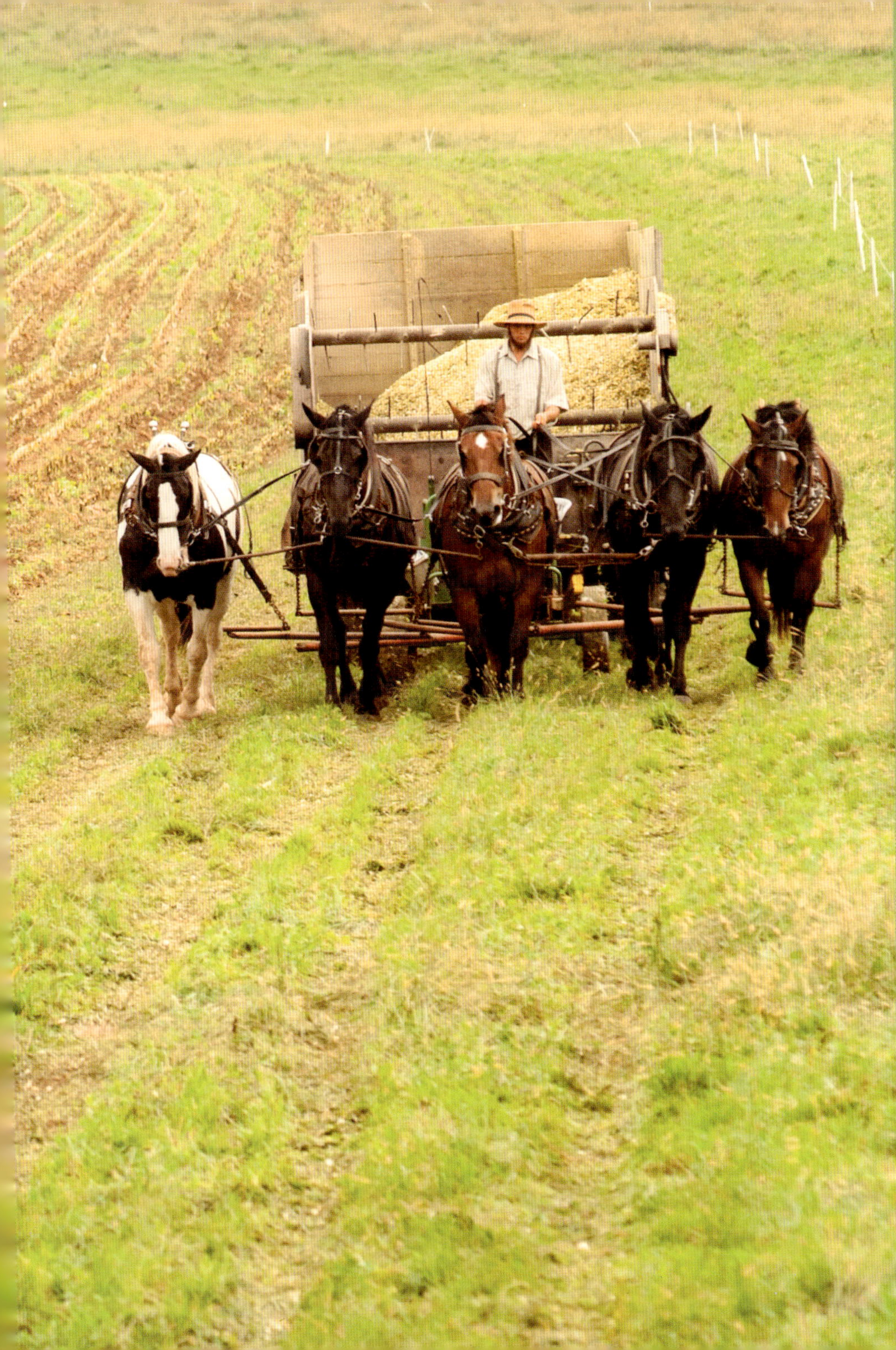

Draft Horses *of* Lancaster County

Belgian

Percheron

Mule

Suffolk

Spotted Draft

Shire

Clydesdale

Haflinger

It had been a rainy summer. The family needed to work quickly in the two-day window of sunshine to cut, rake, and bale the hay. Mark, ten, had just finished the raking and helped his dad get ready to bale. Another storm was due that afternoon.

Of the six draft horses in the barn, they needed only four. They chose their go-to quartet of mares Peppermint, Katelyn, Kayla, and Lori, *right*.

The younger children stayed well out of the way while their father performed the routine of harnessing up the team. Mark expects that he'll be helping harness them in a few years, when he's tall enough to throw the harnesses over the Belgians' backs—no small feat, since each horse is around 17 hands (68 inches) tall at the withers and weighs nearly a ton.

Peppermint is smart and quickly understands the messages passed along the reins. As lead horse, she went to her usual spot on the team at the center left, where her actions guide the other horses. At thirteen she is experienced and strong, but still young enough to have plenty of get-up-and-go. Mark's dad, Gideon, bought Peppermint at an auction five years ago, mainly because she was in foal, but he also liked the look of her head. It turned out she was a natural leader in the harness.

Katelyn is learning the reins, with help from Peppermint and the other horses—and the driver. She took her place to Peppermint's right at center right in the team. She's been in this spot for only six months, but it's clear that in a few years Katelyn will be ready to lead.

Kayla and Lori, the two other horses on the team, are strong and willing but still green—they haven't been worked as much as the others. They stepped into the outside positions. Some workhorses stay steady on the outside for many years; others are ready to move up to the reins quickly. As in a job, they can work toward becoming the foreman or stay contentedly in place as laborers.

Four-year-olds Katelyn and Kayla and three-year-old Lori were born and raised on the farm. Though Gideon generally sells his stud colts as yearlings, he keeps his fillies to serve as brood mares and to work in the field.

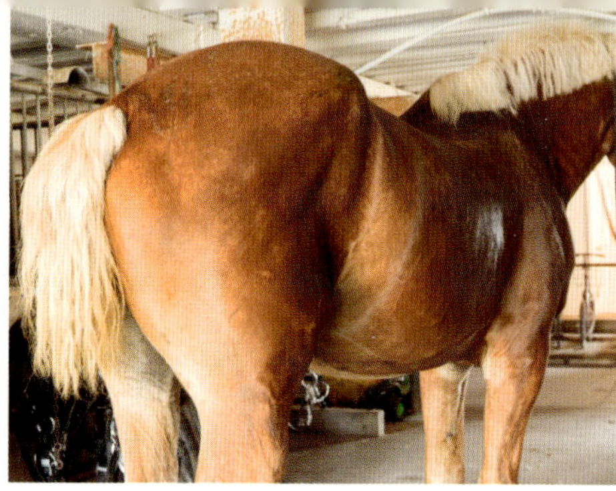

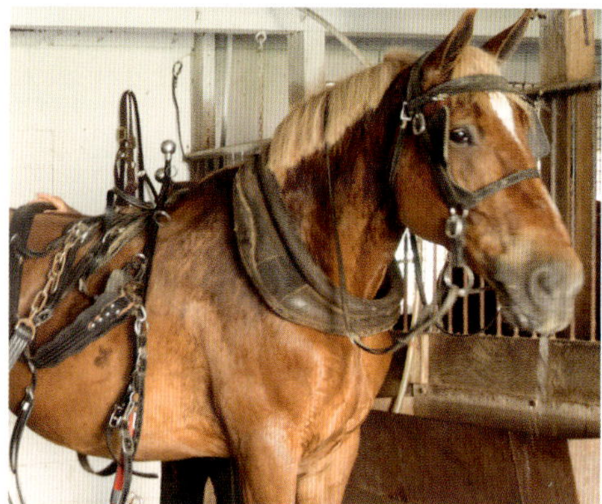

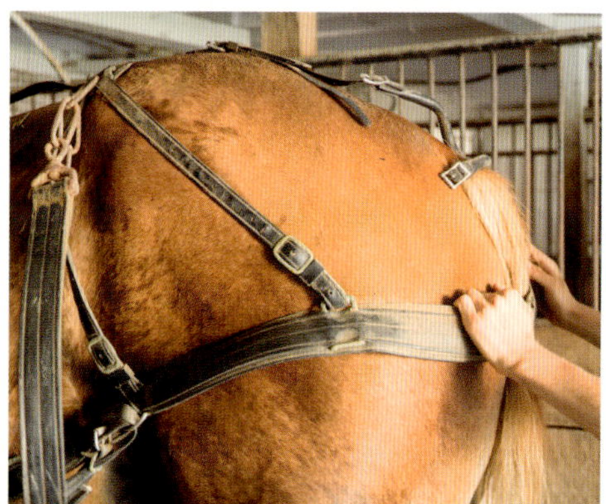

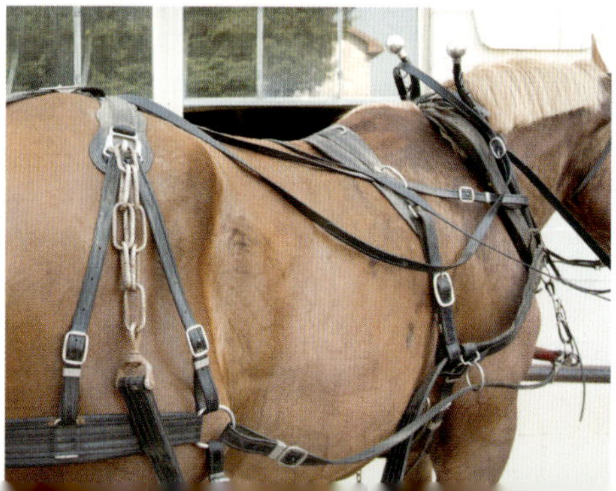

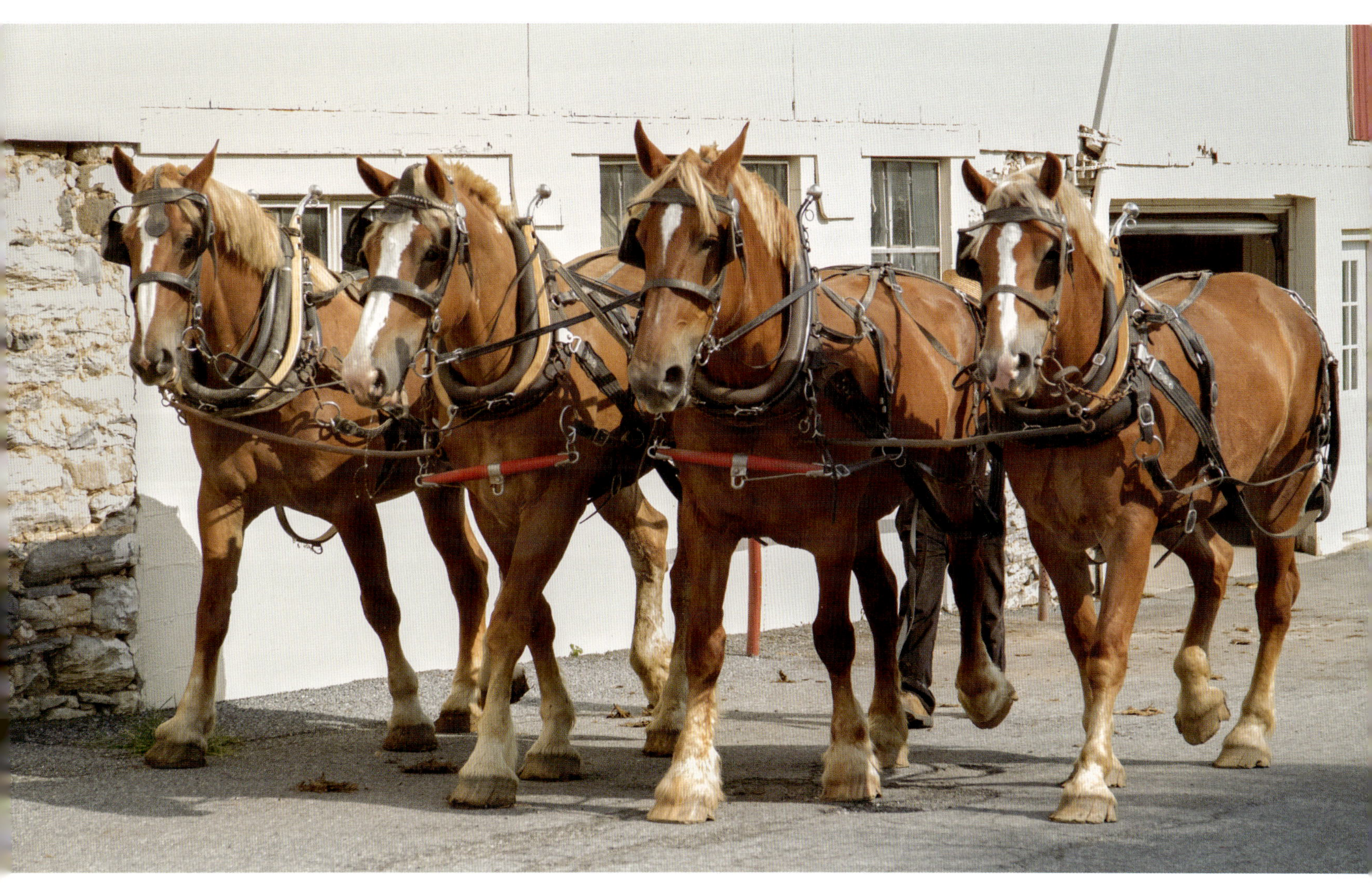

"Like at a job, they can work themselves into the foreman position."

Most draft breeds working in Lancaster County today were originally developed in Europe for warfare. The huge, muscled horses carried warriors in full armor for hand-to-hand combat and hauled military supplies. The advent of guns and long-range artillery brought an end to the use of horses in battle. This made more heavy horses available for rural agricultural work and to pull wagons hauling goods in towns and cities.

When tractors and trucks came into use in Europe and the United States, draft horses were relegated to advertising for companies in the form of multihorse hitch teams, and to recreation, such as riding, showing, pulling wagons for hay rides, and demonstrating strength in horse pulls.

Prior to WWII, companies, including many breweries, transported goods with horses and advertised on their wagons. Some of today's multihorse hitch teams, such as the Budweiser team, carry on the tradition in parades and demonstrations. Other teams are owned, trained, and shown by smaller companies or families and participate in draft shows or hitch classics.

Four-, six-, and eight-horse hitches are hugely popular in parades and at state fairs. Driving competitions are held throughout the United States, in which the drivers complete docking maneuvers such as backing up and turning that would have been practiced unloading goods in cities in years past.

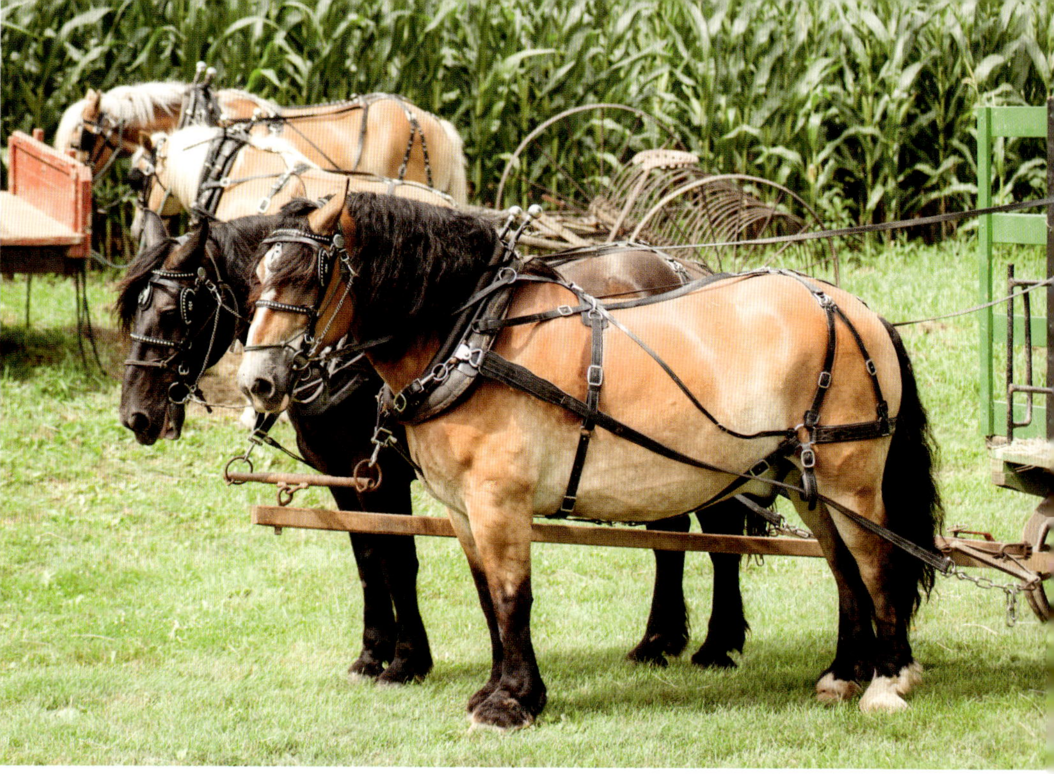

Typically, a hitch horse of any draft breed is tall and leggy, holds its head high, and is well proportioned. It is more spirited than its farming counterparts and has a more animated gait.

Draft horses used for agricultural tasks in modern times in the United States or Europe are in many cases worked by hobbyists on small, sustainable farms, or in historical demonstrations.

An exception to that are the areas in the United States, including Lancaster County, where there are settlements of Old Order Amish and Mennonites who have farmed with draft horses for generations.

Most of the draft animals used in Lancaster County are either Belgian horses or mules. Percherons, Suffolks, and Spotted Drafts are also used, but less often. Some may be crossbred within that group or with other working breeds such as Shire or Clydesdale. Many draft breeds today carry Belgian lineage in their bloodlines.

Though Haflingers are officially categorized as ponies because of their relatively small stature, many are taller than 14.2 hands (maximum pony height) and can do the work of a larger horse.

Many farmers raise and train their own working horses from foal to fully grown. They match their favored mares to carefully chosen stallions, aiming for foals that have a particular build and temperament. It is an investment of time, feed, and pasture that pays off in satisfaction.

The farmers who train their own horses have the advantage of knowing their horses' strengths, weaknesses, and personality quirks—and can work with them.

Rather than training their own, some farmers buy their draft horses fully trained and ready to work.

Preliminary training of a young draft horse begins with halter-breaking as a weanling (around six months old). These large animals must be acclimated to handling, particularly to having their feet trimmed and cleaned. For the first few years, the main job of a working horse is to eat and grow strong. Once trained to the harness at age three or four, a draft horse may be a good worker for eighteen or twenty years.

Teams usually consist of mares or geldings or a mix of the two. Both work equally well and get along with each other. Stallions are occasionally hitched for work, but they're more temperamental.

Draft horses' hooves are trimmed and cleaned regularly for good foot health. The horses do not wear shoes unless they need to travel a distance on the road or their front hooves are worn down late in the summer. Then the farrier nails keg shoes

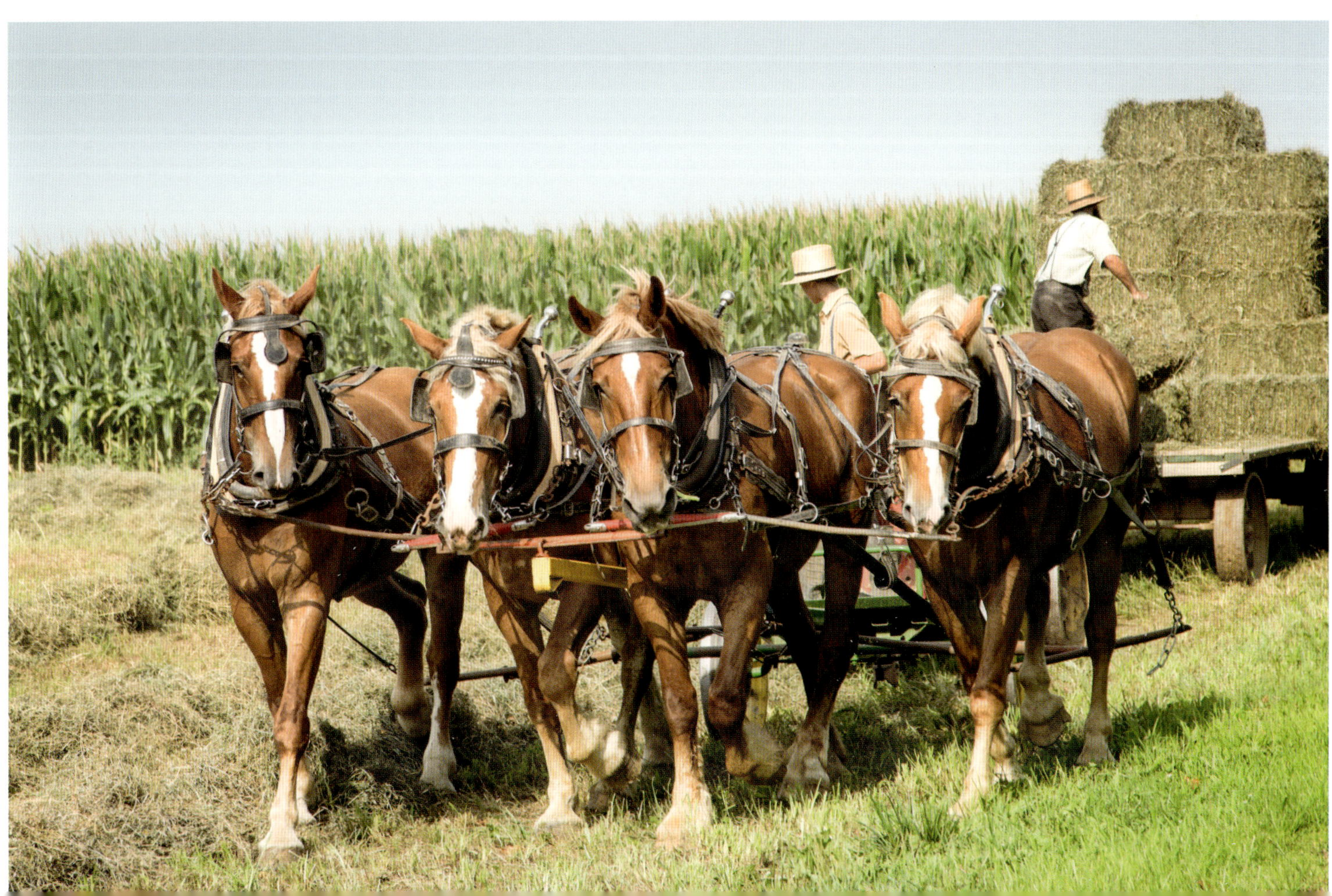

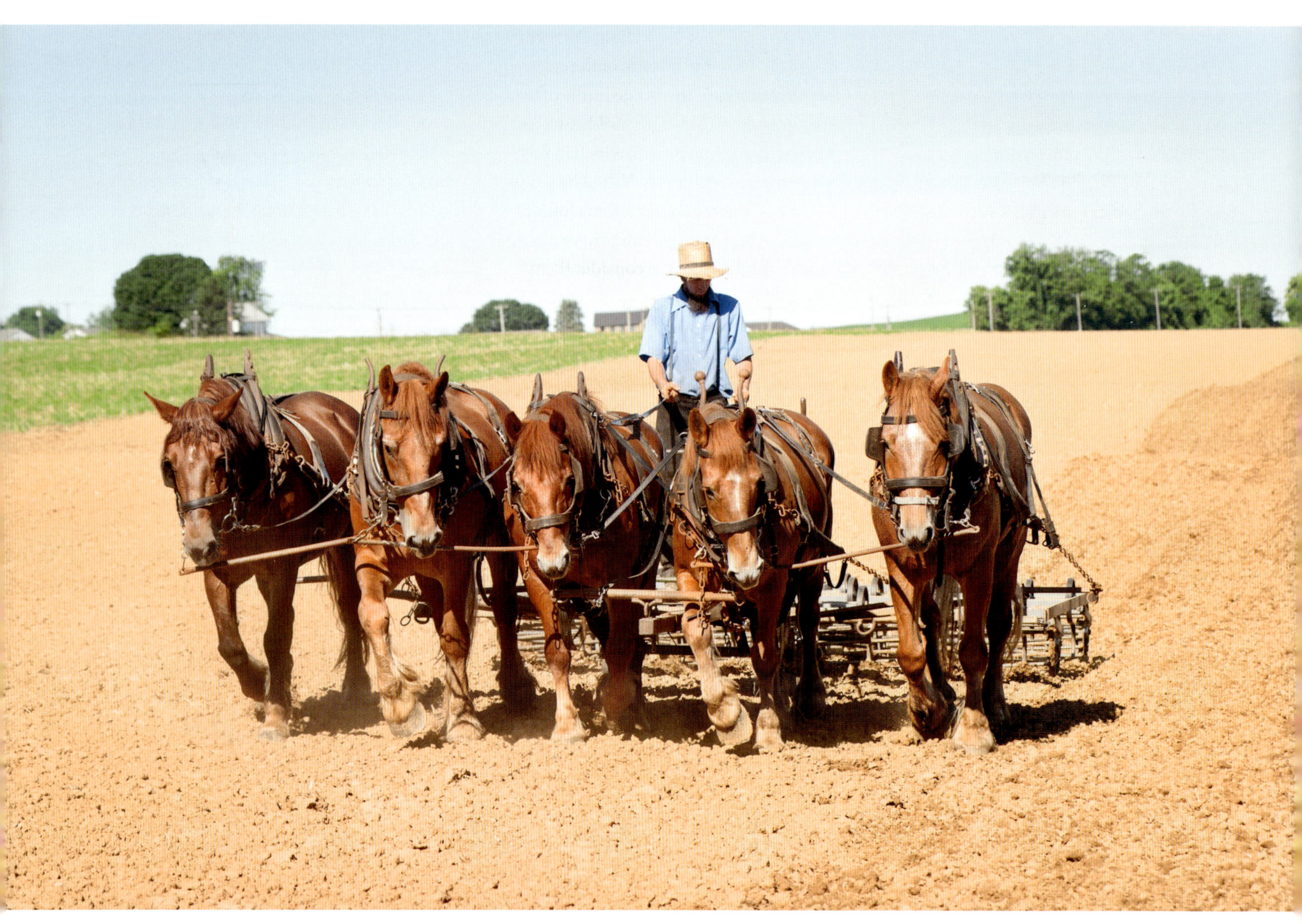

"Drive the two in the center, and the others follow."

(a basic flat shoe) in place to be worn for the remainder of the working season.

When hitching a team, two "line horses" are placed in the center, with the lead horse at center left. The reins from the right side of each of the two line horses' bridles are buckled together into a single rein that is held in the driver's right hand; the reins from the left side of the bridles are buckled together and held in the driver's left hand.

The yoke across the chests of the two line horses is hooked to the tongue of the wagon or cart they are pulling. A jockey stick goes from the outside of the collar of each line horse to the inside bridle of the next horse out. The driver holds two reins that guide the line horses, which in turn guide the outside horses. When he drives the two in the center, the others follow.

Lancaster County farmers have a deep respect for the land and consider themselves stewards for future generations. They take advantage of scientific research to protect the land and increase yields. Some farmers prepare the ground to plant by plowing and harrowing, while many plant no-till, a system of planting in slit trenches on unplowed ground that maintains moisture and nutrients and decreases the need for herbicides.

Alert to market forces, some farmers make the investment to go organic, an endeavor that takes years to complete. They grow organic crops to feed their cows to produce organic milk, or grow organic produce to sell.

Crop Schedule

Crop/Month	April	May	June	July	August	September	October	November
Corn	plow, disk, harrow, and plant, or plant no-till		spray and fertilize at 2 feet tall		chop ears and stalks for silage	pick ears to shell	chop dry stalks for bedding	
Tobacco		plant seedlings	cultivate	spray to stop pollination	harvest and hang in barn to dry			strip leaves and bale them for sale
Alfalfa	sow seeds; crops grow from single planting for three years		cut, ted, rake, and bale on a roughly five-week cycle depending on the weather; plan for four or five cuttings throughout the season				harvest final crop of the season	
Orchard grass	seed for multiyear yields or plant in with alfalfa at end of alfalfa cycle for softer feed for horses			harvest at 4–6 week intervals				
Wheat			thresh grain that was planted in fall; bale straw				sow seeds after tobacco or corn harvest	
Meadows and yards	mow as needed throughout the summer, let grass lie to compost							
Produce and family garden	plow and disk, plant and harvest from early spring through fall; plant first crop of peas in early spring						harvest last batch of squash and pumpkins just prior to first frost	
Cover crop: Oats						plant where early corn or tobacco were harvested		harvest if grows before first frost
Cover crop: Rye grass	harvest crop that was planted in the fall before it seeds to maintain protein in the grass				plant where corn or tobacco was harvested; can be planted into November depending on the weather		continues to grow off and on throughout the winter and early spring	
Manure	chicken litter, cow manure, horse manure			spread on the fields throughout the year				

Wheat on the Stoltzfus farm is cut in the field and propped in sheaves to dry. Two brothers-in-law fork the sheaves onto a wagon, *below,* while the younger boys stack it. The horses haul the wheat to an in-field tractor-powered thresher that also bales.

An uptick in the price of grain and straw makes the labor-intensive planting and harvesting of wheat with horse-drawn equipment a bit more worthwhile than it had been in the last few decades.

On another farm, Mark grows wheat each year that comes from heirloom seed. He drives an antique combine, *right,* that threshes the wheat in the field, collecting the grain in a bin and depositing the straw on the ground. After he rakes the straw into rows and allows it to dry, he drives his same quartet of horses, *facing page,* pulling a baler equipped with a bale tosser to load the wagon. He sells the grain each year to a mill where he then buys flour for the family's bread.

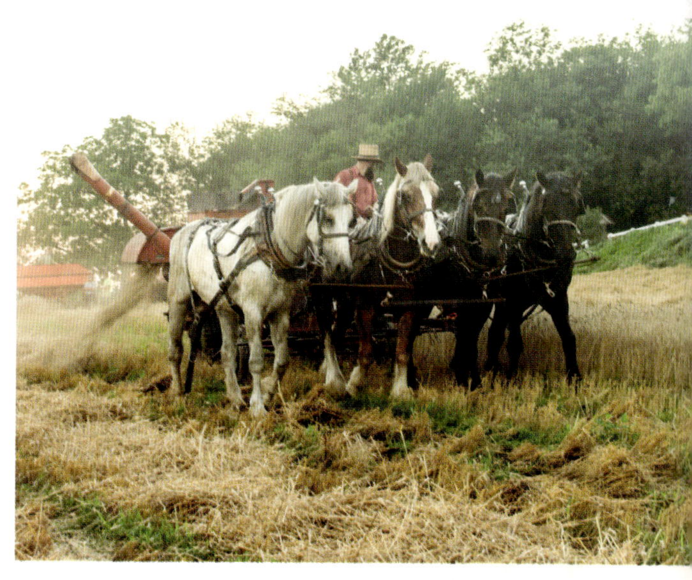

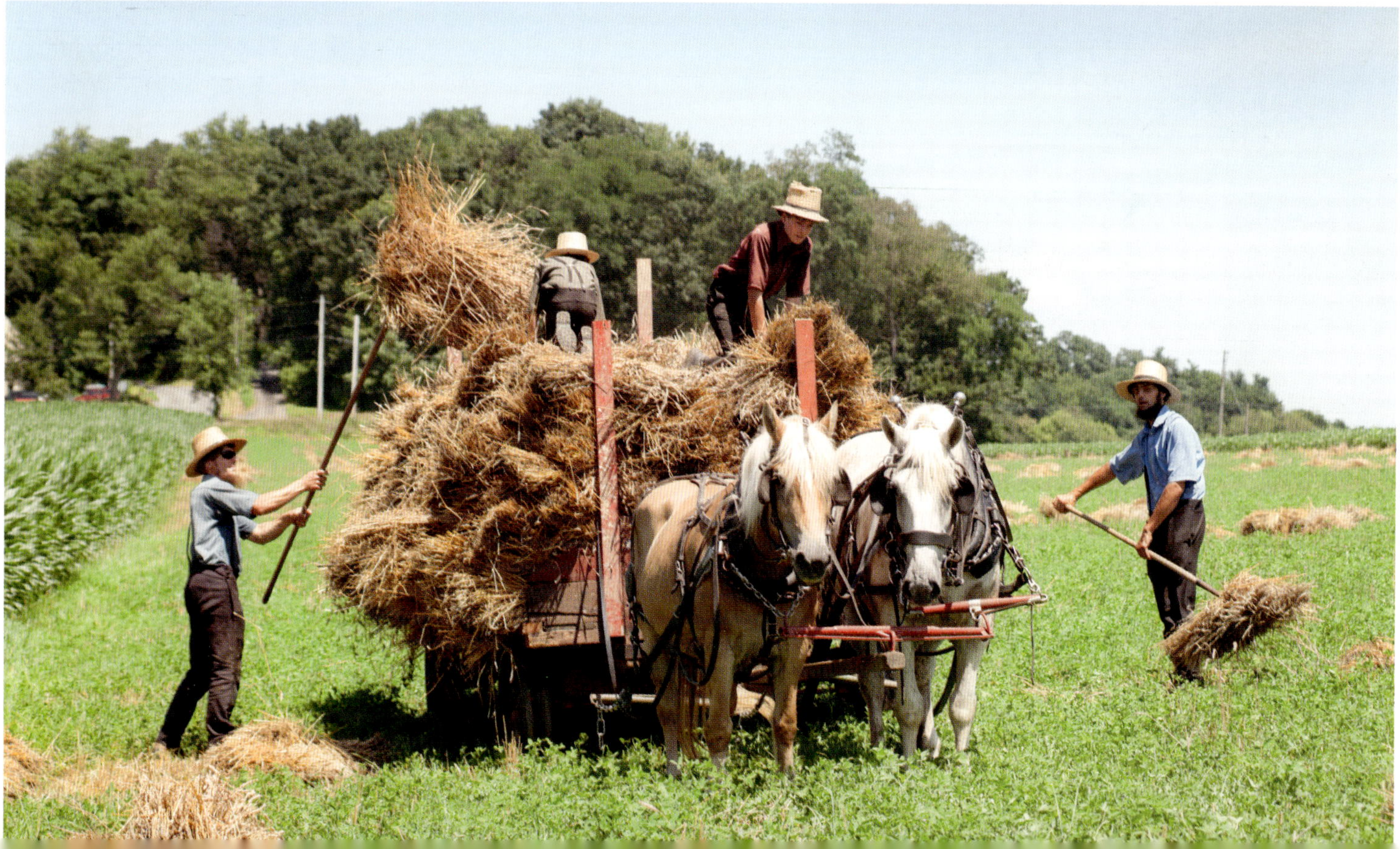

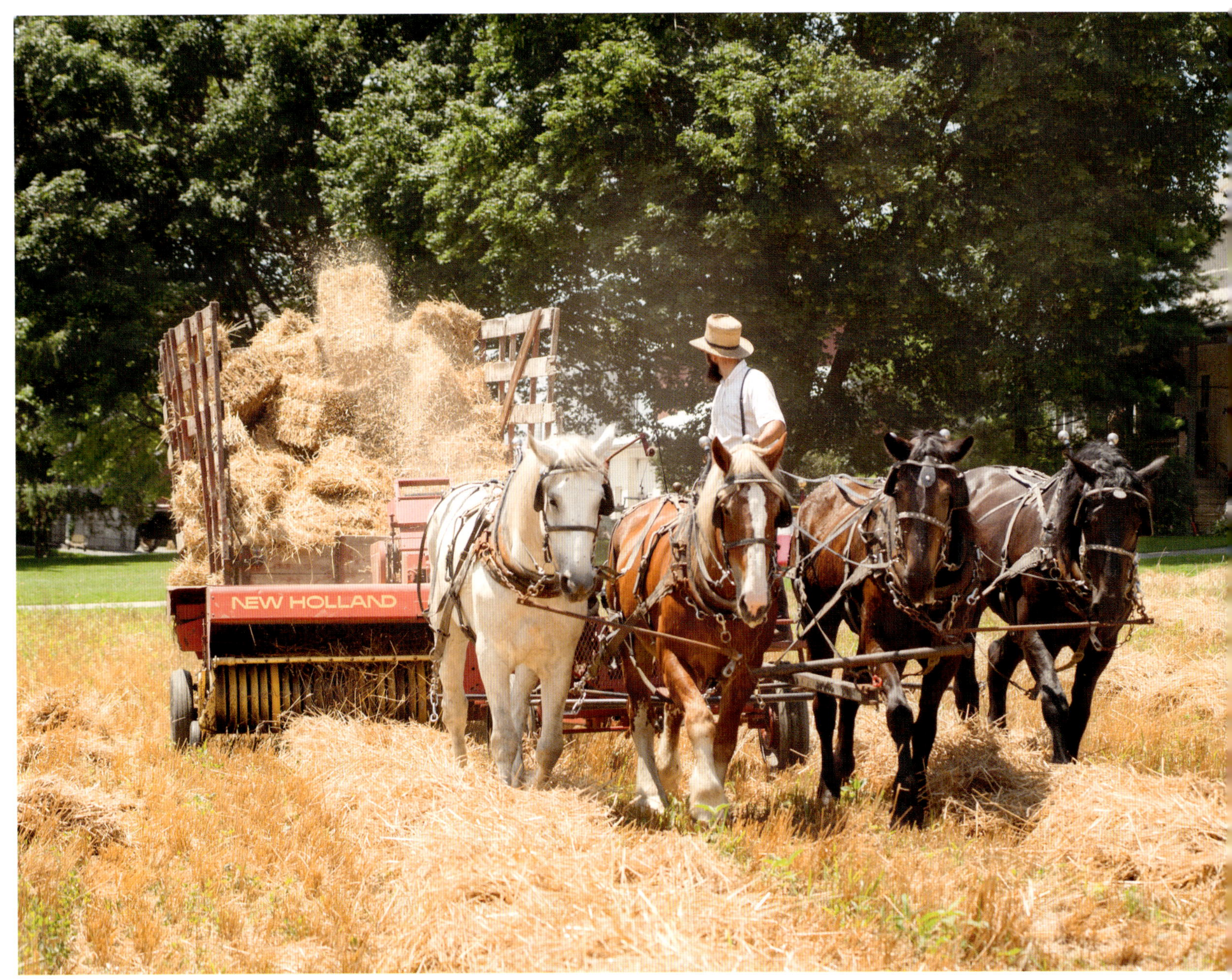
NEW HOLLAND

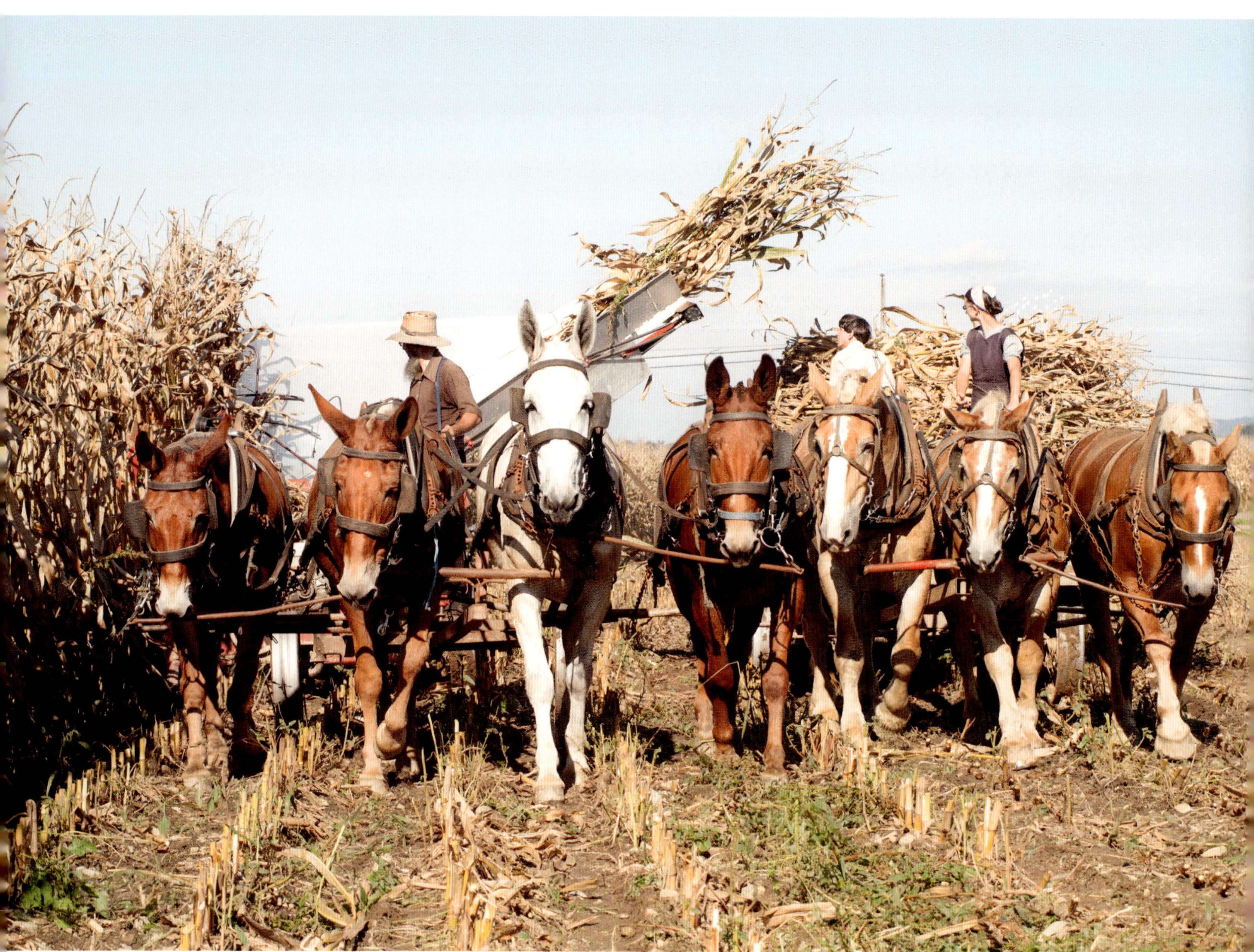

Jacob, *left*, drove his team of four mules to cut corn while his daughter guided the neighbor's three Belgians pulling a wagon and his son loaded the bundled stalks.

All hands pitch in at harvest. Neighbors or members of the extended family frequently help each other in turn. If young women are in the field, they generally drive the horses while the boys and men do the heavier work. Children are assigned tasks according to their abilities.

Farmers usually work with all mules or all horses rather than mixing them in a team. One farmer may take pleasure in a nicely matched single-breed team while another will employ multiple breeds or crosses depending on price and availability.

There is often a broad streak of breed loyalty—particularly a preference for working with either horses or mules—within a family, but neighbors easily join forces when there is work to be done. The horses and mules know their jobs and accept direction from any competent hands on the reins.

Marble, *below*, a Spotted Draft, and Rudy, a Percheron, walked easily between the rows. They followed simple verbal commands to start and stop, waiting patiently as laths of tobacco were stacked on the wagon.

Multiple family members harvested the tobacco on a hot August afternoon, working quickly to beat the coming thunder storm. Two sisters and their dad cut the tobacco and speared the stalks, stacking six on each lath. Their brothers loaded the wagons and ferried the cargo to the tobacco barn. After five months of drying in the barn, the workers will strip the leaves from the stalks and bale the leaves for sale.

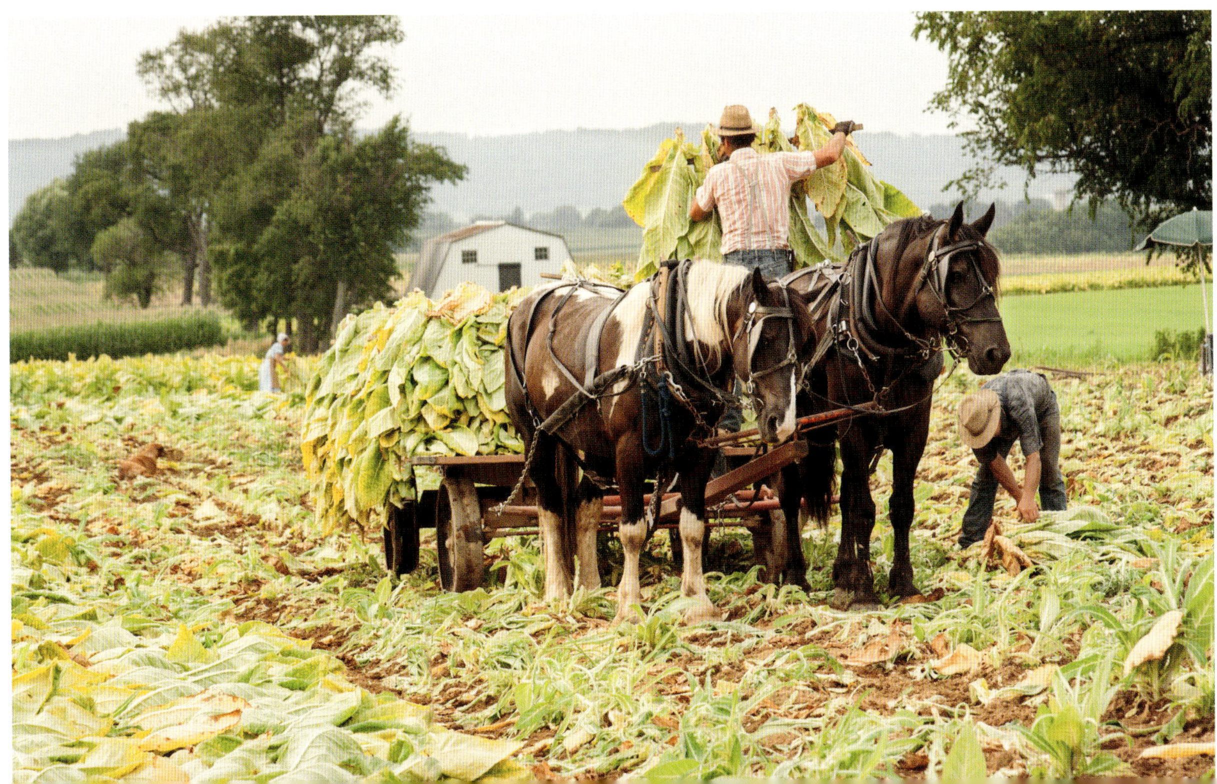

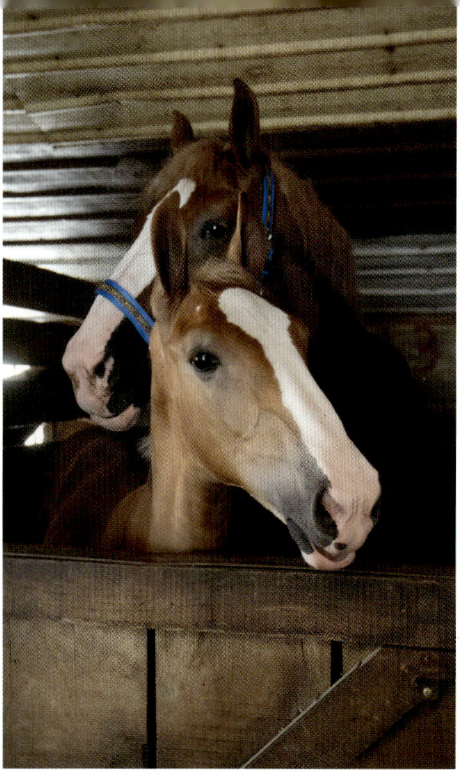

The number of horses employed on a farm is directly related to the size of the farm, method of cultivation, and number of livestock that needs to be fed. Unlike a tractor that operates the same each time it is put in gear, horses are individuals. The farmer views each as an employee, sussing out and encouraging strengths while working with personality quirks.

Teams are configured based on the kind of job to be done, and the equipment weight and width. Plowing may take eight horses to dig in and turn the earth while just six are needed to pull a no-till planter. A team of six abreast will pull a planter or baler; another team of six will be arranged in two rows of three to chop corn.

Farmers often have a go-to pair that is first in line for lighter jobs like tedding or raking hay, and a reliable quartet for a bit larger jobs like spreading manure.

Jonah's three Belgians, *right,* took the lead when picking corn, while his three Percheron-Dutch Harness crosses pulled in the second row. Percheron–Dutch Harness crosses are good, efficient workers ideally suited to jobs on small farms. Their size and temperament also make them good under saddle as hunters and jumpers.

After the corn is picked, Jonah will go back through the field and chop and bale the leftover dried stalks to use as bedding for his cows.

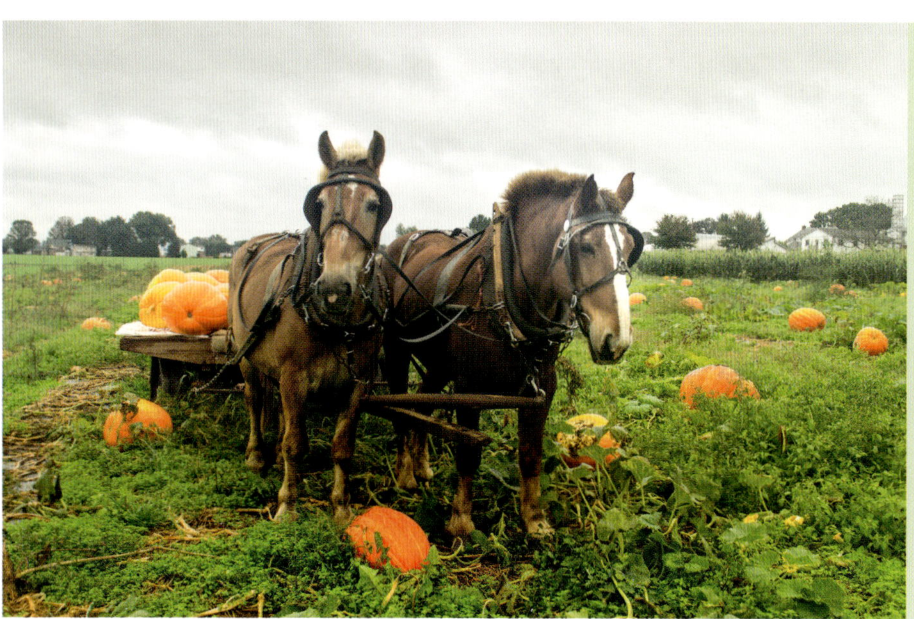

Pumpkin Harvest

Draft horses Chip and Matt pulled the wagon as Jacob and his son John picked pumpkins. Upward of twenty-five trips to the field in an eight-week period yielded 900 or more mammoth pumpkins, each weighing 75 to 170 pounds. An unusual amount of rain made the fields muddy and the pulling hard, but Chip and Matt continued willingly, stopping and starting on verbal command.

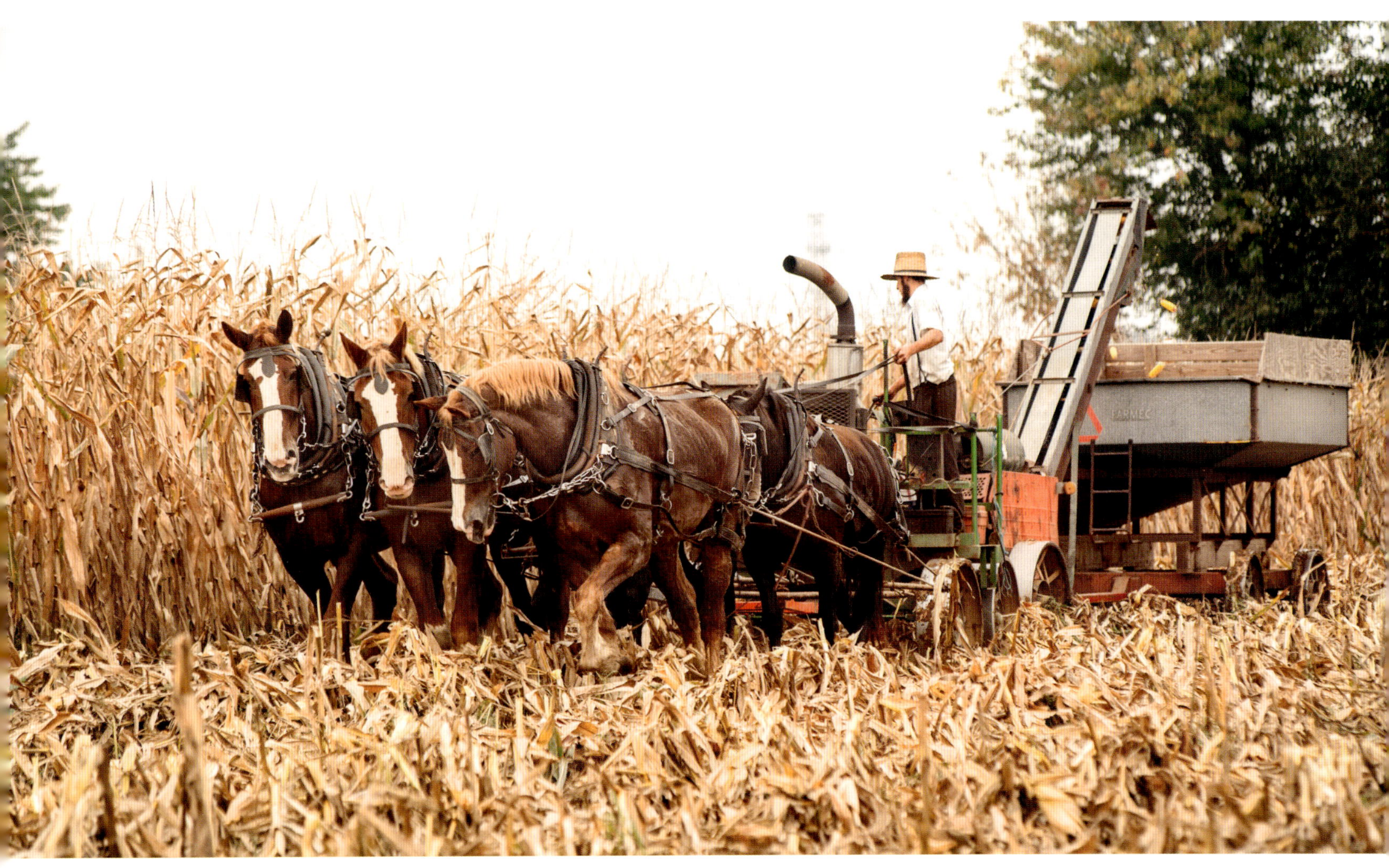

“The farmer views each horse as an employee, sussing out and encouraging strengths while working with personality quirks.”

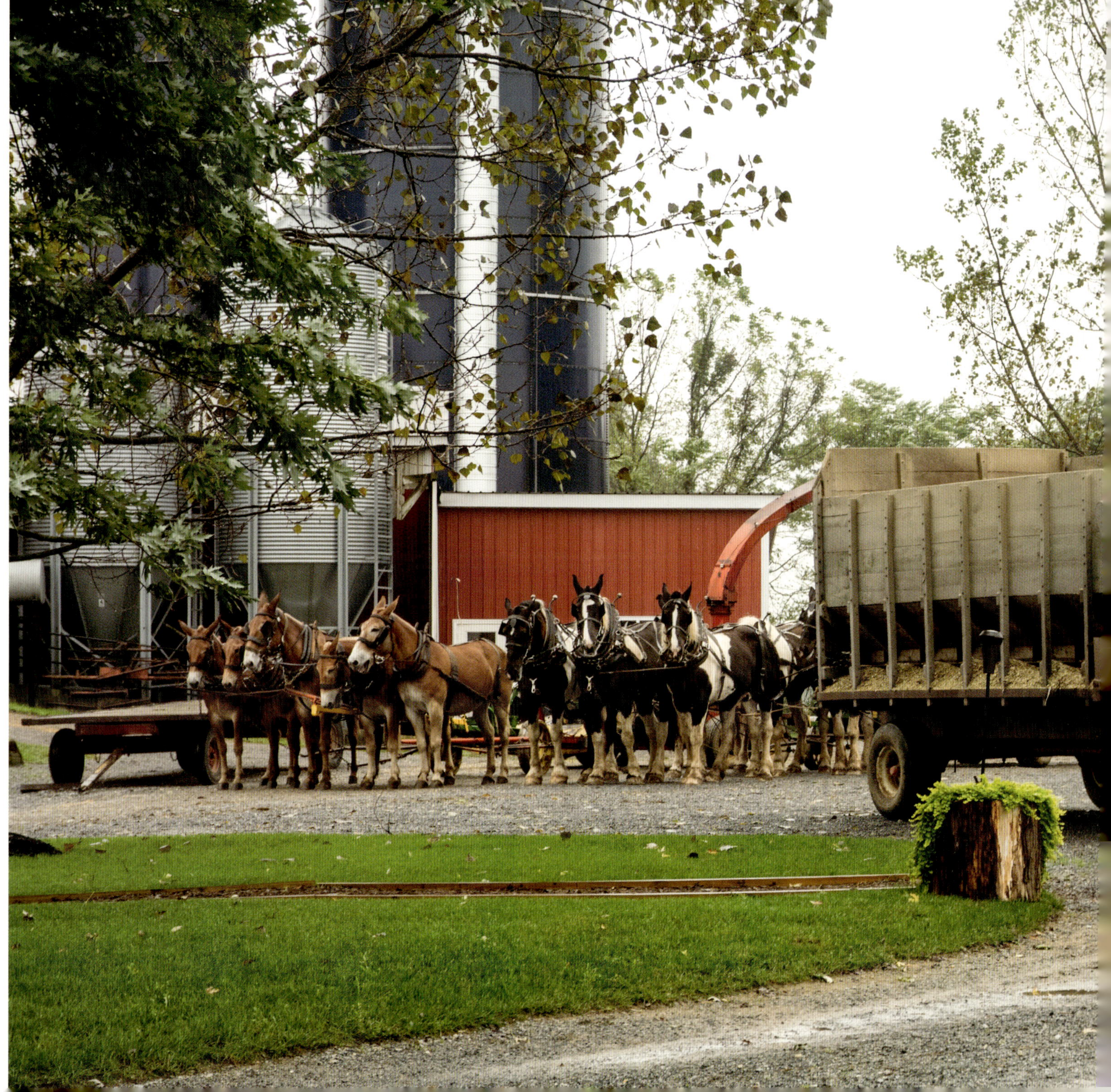

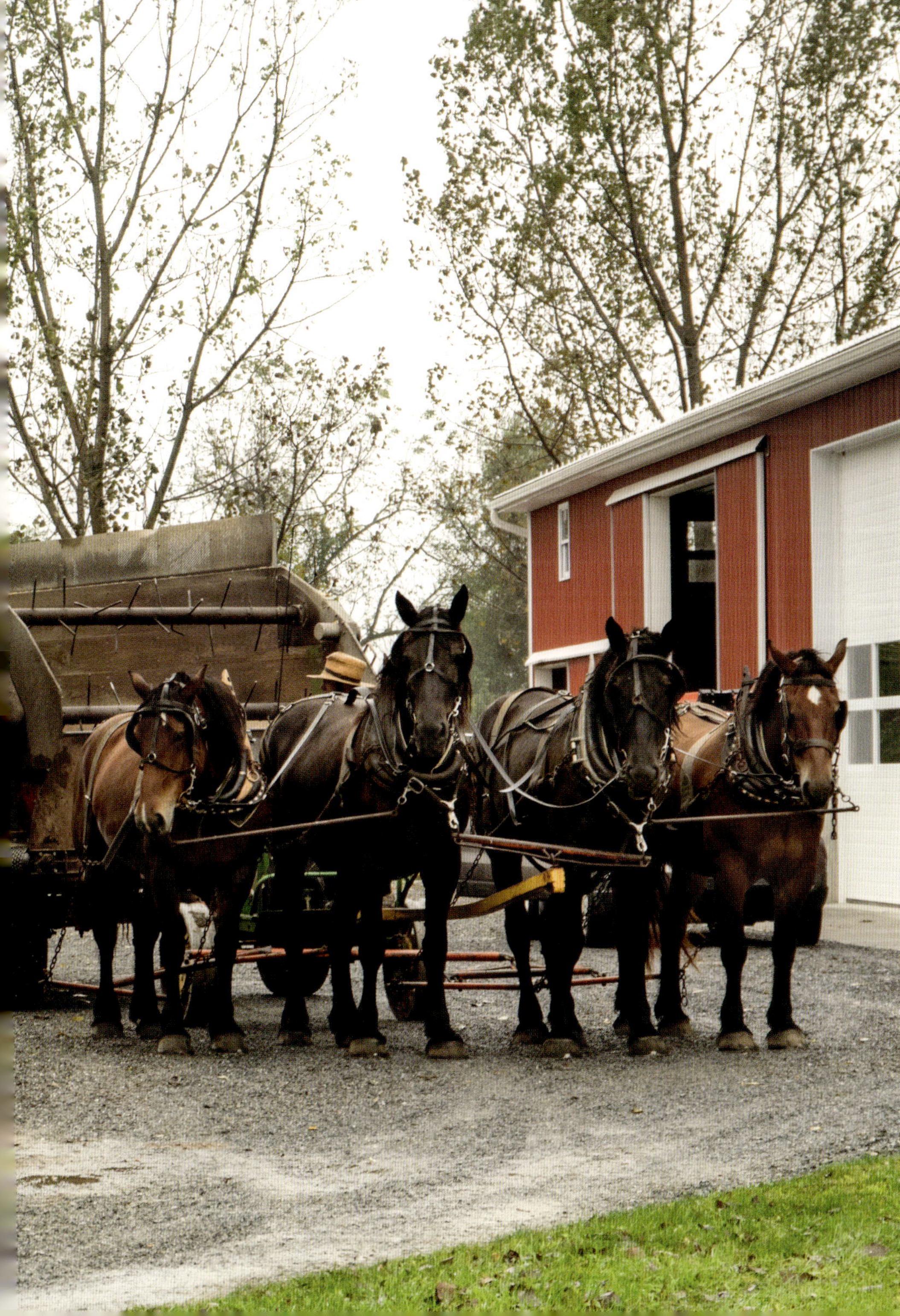

An unusually rainy spring pushed planting to late spring. The corn grew quickly over the summer, but rains continued into the fall and played havoc with harvesting plans. Despite the heavy mist, Levi's two neighbors met at his farm to help chop the ears and cornstalks and fill the silo.

Levi hitched his team of six Spotted Drafts to the corn chopper. The farmer to the east hitched his team of five mules to a forage wagon; Levi's nephew from several farms over hitched his Percheron and Percheron-Belgian crosses to a second wagon. The neighbors took turns driving the wagons beside the chopper to collect the corn. When a wagon was full, the driver would take it to the barn and transfer the chopped corn to the silo, and the second driver would move into place beside the chopper to collect the next round.

The fermented silage will provide nutrient-rich forage for his dairy cows through the winter. It took Levi several years to transition his fields to organic. His cows feed exclusively on organic hay, corn, and soybean meal to produce certified organic milk.

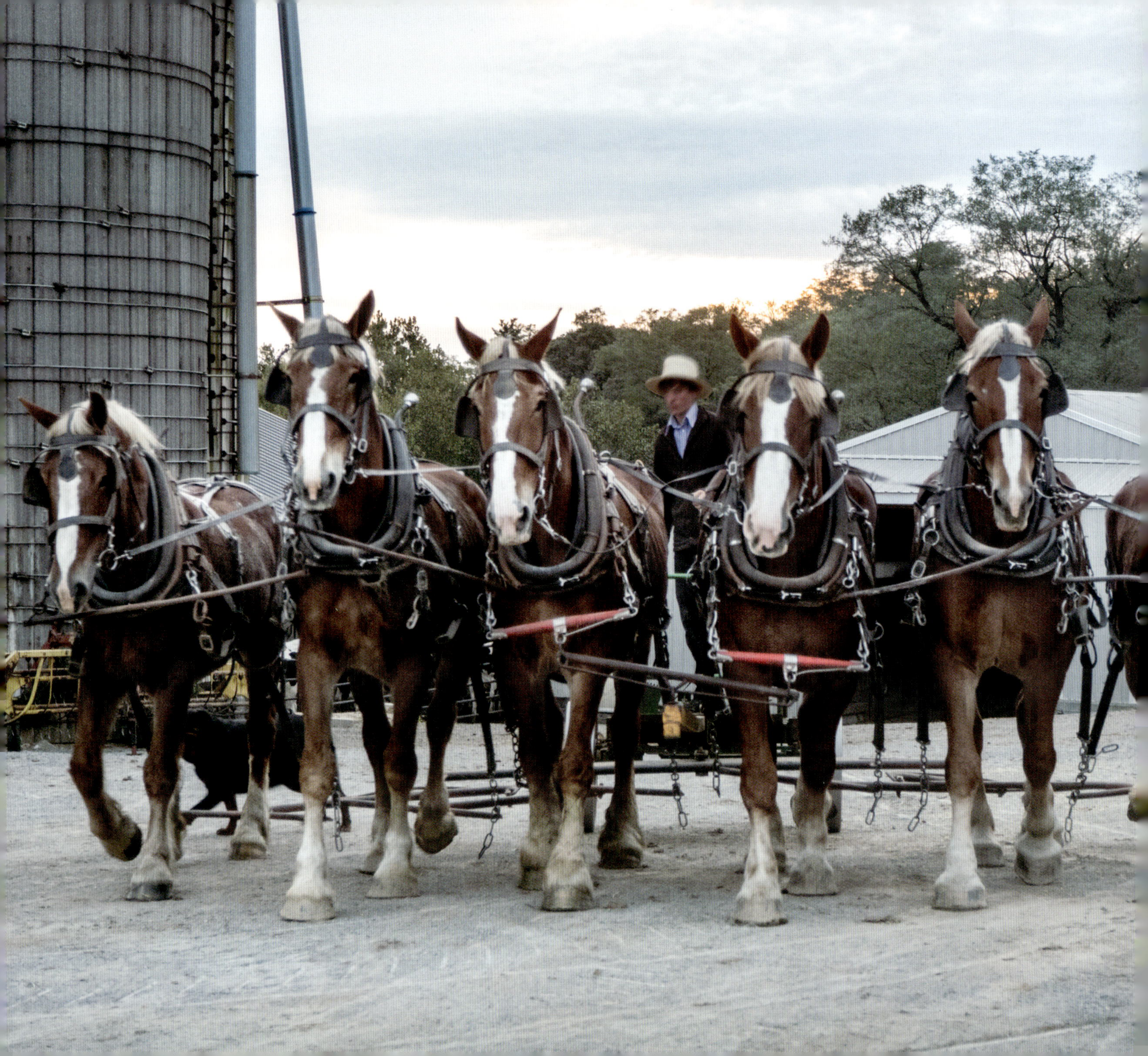

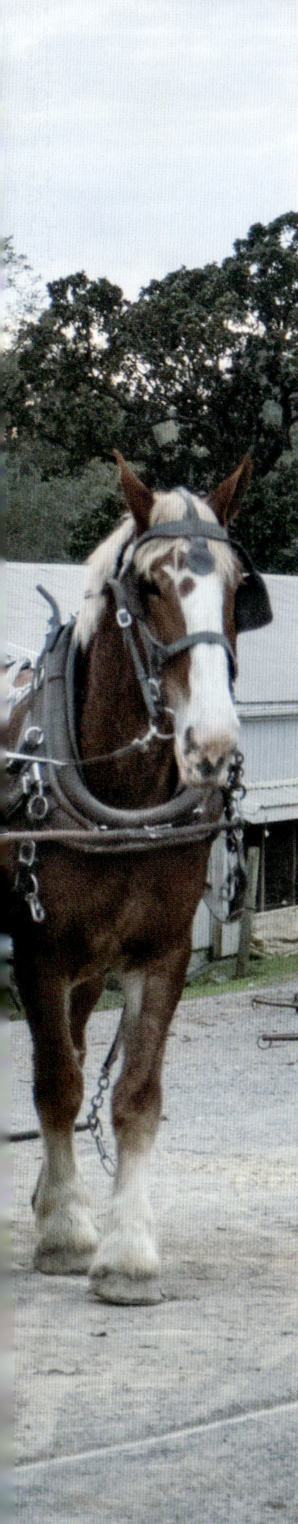

Belgian

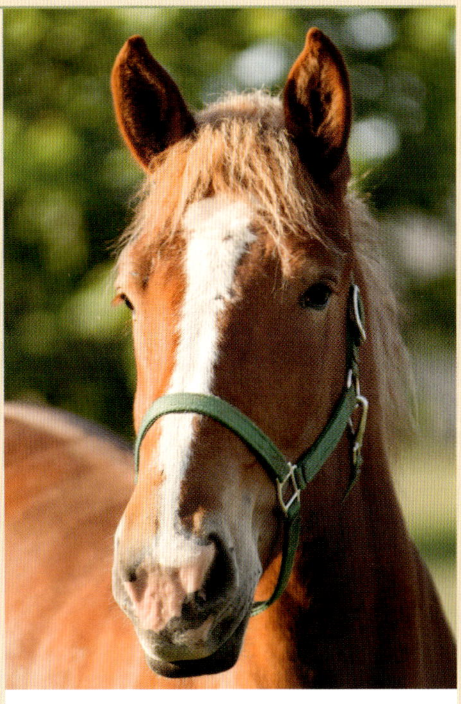

Origin: Brabant region of Belgium

Height: 16–18hh

Weight: 1,400–2,000 lbs, some stallions up to 2,400

Colors: chestnut with flaxen mane and tail, light-colored legs, often white stripe on nose

In late October. Lady, Janet, and Lill stood tethered with their more fancifully named teammates Glory, Crystal, and Paris. The six Belgian mares had been out raking hay that afternoon, came in for a break at suppertime, and were heading out again to bale after the evening milking. Junior's two older sons readied the team while three of his younger sons hustled through their tasks in the dairy barn.

Junior's oldest boy works off the farm in construction during the day and helps with chores in the evening. He likes farmwork and is glad for a chance to work with the horses.

The sun was quickly dropping toward the horizon as the horses hauled the baler and hay wagon out the lane to the far hayfield. After one circuit around the field, it was barely light. No illumination glowed from nearby roads or surrounding farms. Another time around and it was darker yet. But the boys were used to working outside hours after sunset; their eyes—and those of the horses—grew accustomed to the low light. Daylight was too precious to waste at harvest time.

"I fell in love with Belgians when I was young. They're in my blood."

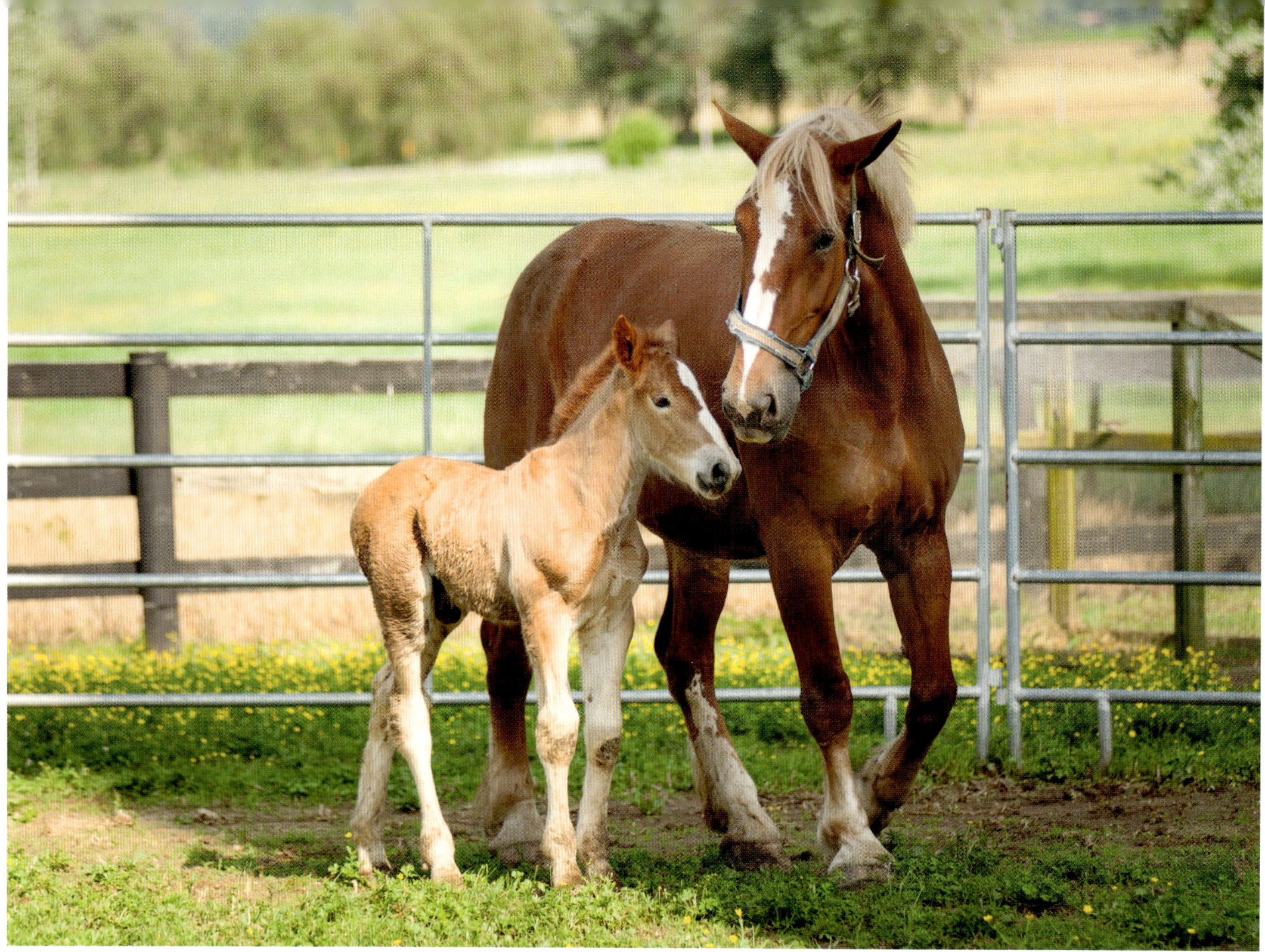

The Belgian is the most popular breed of draft horse in Lancaster County and the United States. Known to be easy keepers, hard workers, and mild mannered, Belgians are also appreciated for their versatility. They can pull a plow, strut in the show ring, or carry a rider.

In the first few years of this century, there were only four or five Belgian breeders in Lancaster County. Twenty years later there is double or triple that number. Belgian breeders need to strike a balance between producing a good, solid working horse and one that also has the athleticism to join a fancy hitch team. The hitch Belgian needs to demonstrate both the muscular build essential to a draft horse, and stylish animation.

Many local breeders employ their brood mares in the field pulling mowers, rakes, and balers to harvest the hay that feeds the mares over the winter.

Science and creativity inform a breeder's pairings. When choosing a stallion to service his mare, the mare's owner considers its features and bloodlines as well as the elusive something that will produce a special foal.

When the foals come along, the owners watch as they grow to determine their path. A filly may be kept to develop as a brood mare, while a stud colt may have a future as a breeding stallion or working gelding. A yearling may be a good possibility for the show ring and bring top dollar at the winter auction. Buyers for hitch teams look for a particular color, size, and leg action—and perhaps facial markings—to fit in with a matched team.

Very few draft horses meet the hitch team criteria; most go on to do fieldwork on a family farm.

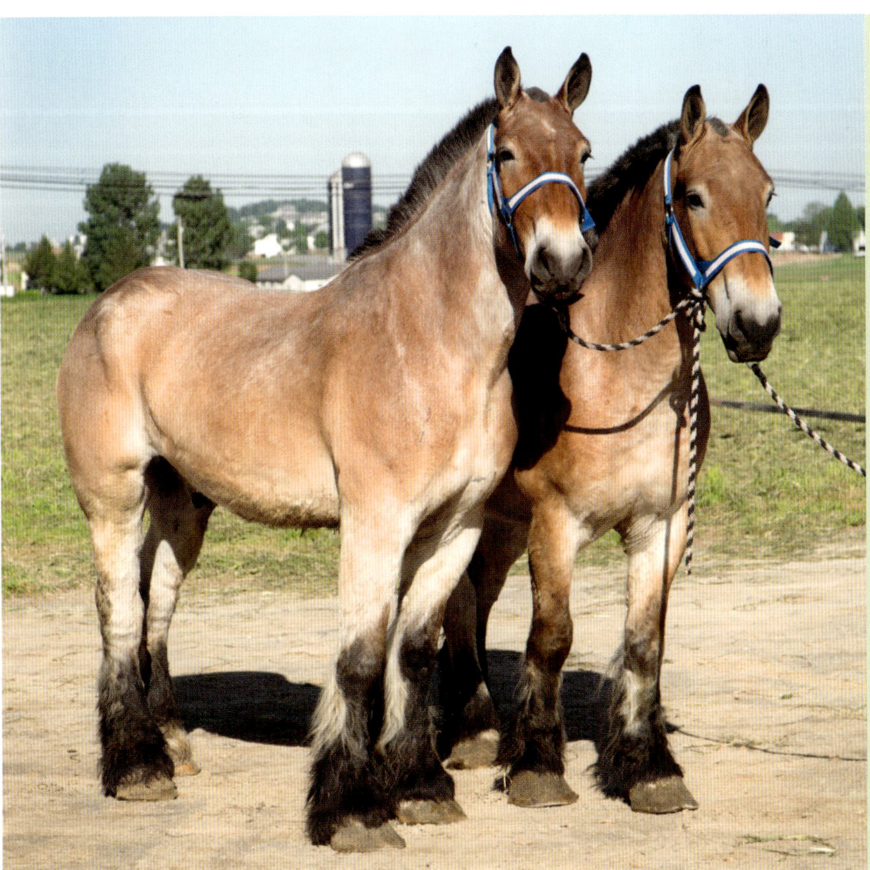

Brabant Belgians

The American Belgian is derived from the Belgian Brabant. Descended from the heavy horses of medieval times, this breed is thick-bodied with short, heavily feathered legs. Beginning in the mid-1940s, breeders in the United States began developing their Belgians to be taller, lighter, and clean legged.

While loyalists in Europe work to maintain the original breed, relatively few true Belgian Brabants exist in the US. The pair at left, crosses between American Belgian and Brabant, show the stocky build, roan coloring, black points, and dark feathered legs of their forebears.

Their uncommon good looks attract passengers when the team is hitched to a wagon headed out to the pumpkin patch or embarking on a haunted hayride.

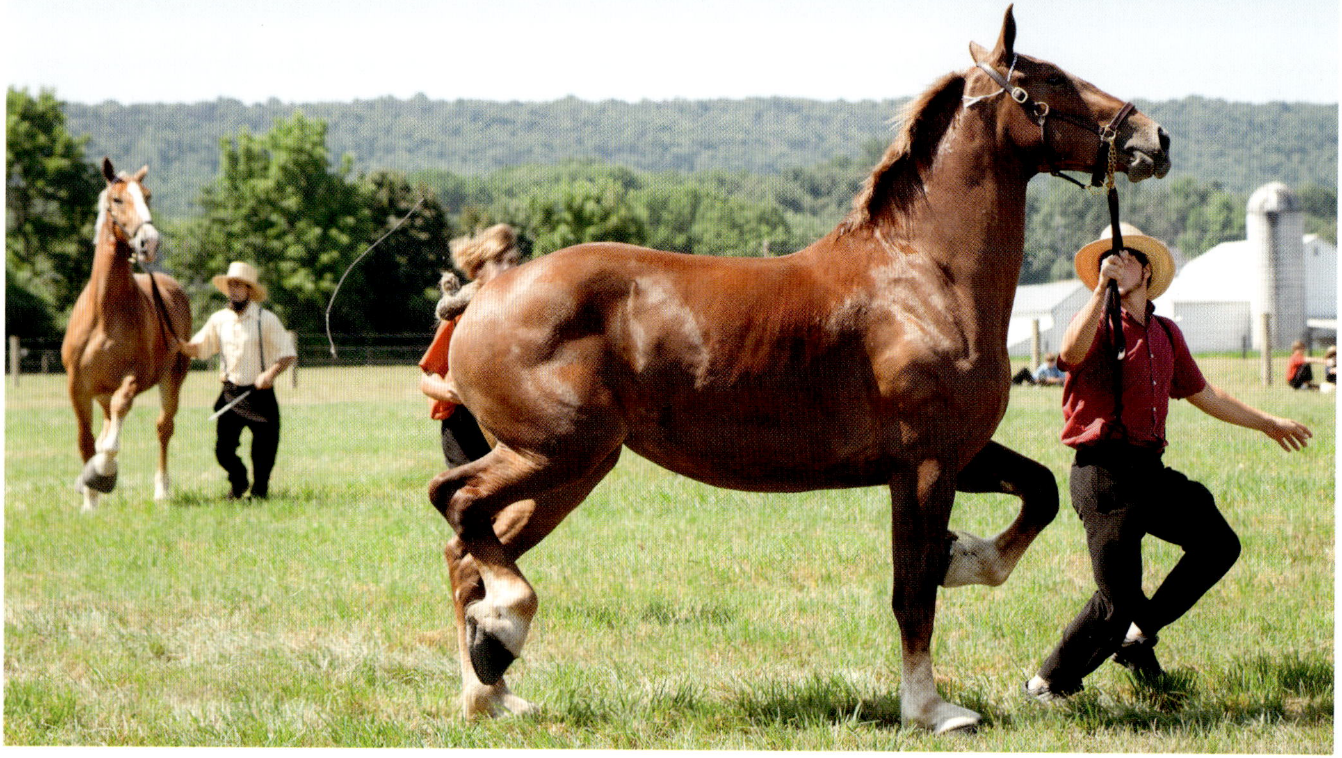

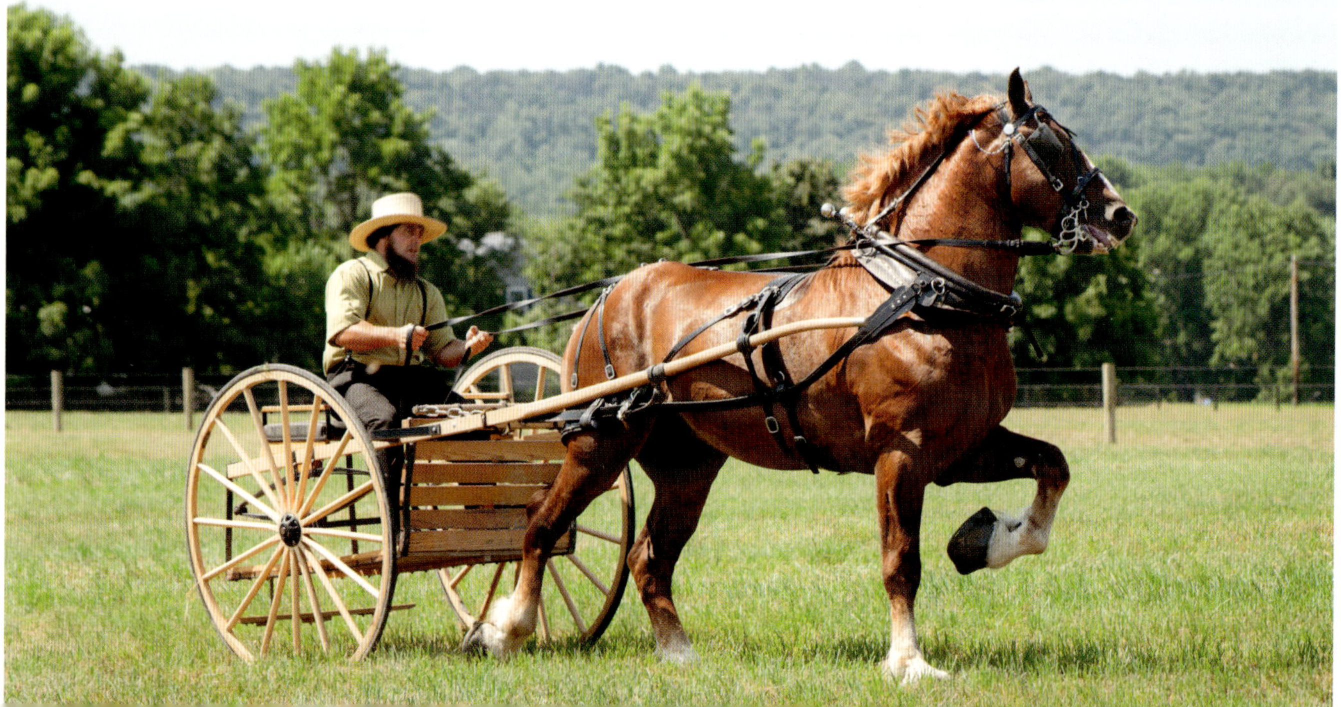

Owners welcome opportunities to present their stallions and mares at shows and expositions. Stallions by nature are not docile; exhibiting them at their best takes strength and strategy. Mares are a little more tractable but can still challenge their handlers.

Directed by the reins of a driver or a lead at the head and a whip snap at the rear, the Belgians, each weighing over a ton, show massive build and style, *left*. Onlookers take note, considering the best matches for their own horses or what might boost their bloodlines.

Stoltzfus's six-year-old Belgian Alex, *right*, will be presented for stud service in the coming season. At their farm, Stoltzfus hooked the side ties to Alex's halter. Then his sons went to work spiffing him up, one standing on an overturned bucket to comb his forelock, another applying a sheen to his coat, and another polishing his hooves. Two younger boys stood to the side, watching with keen interest.

Inside the house, in the corner of the kitchen, a toy barn filled with horses and cows awaited evening chores. The little boys in the household took good care of their livestock, modeling their work on what their older brothers and dad did each day in the barn.

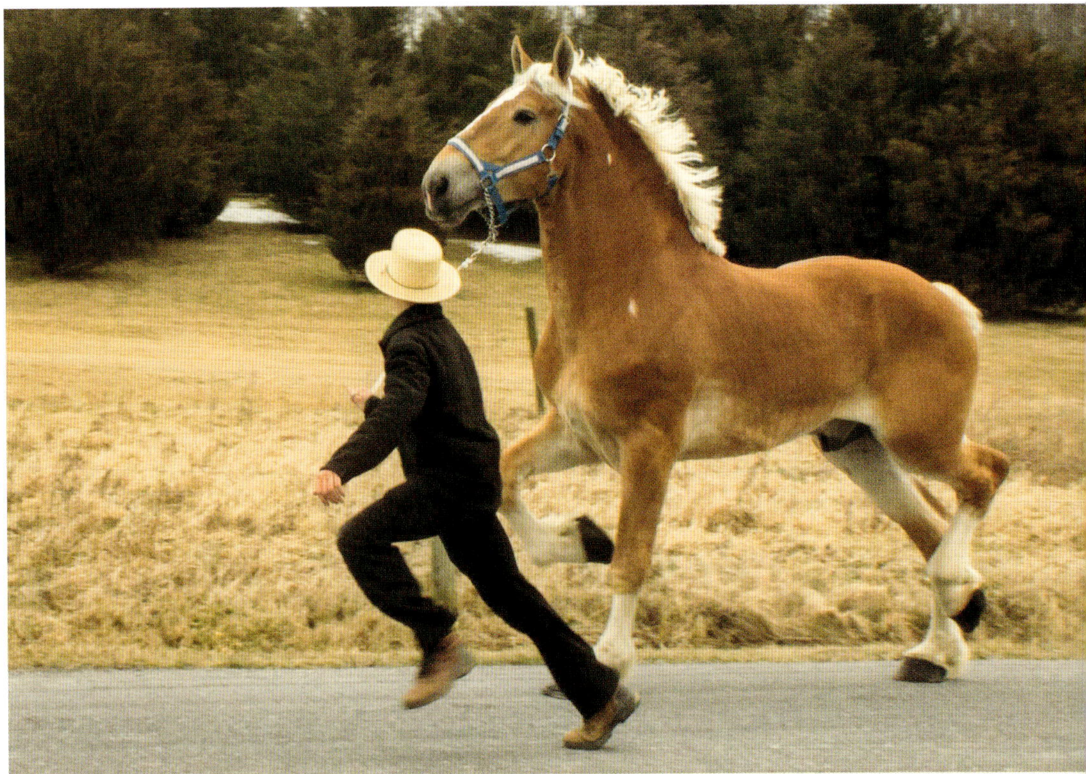

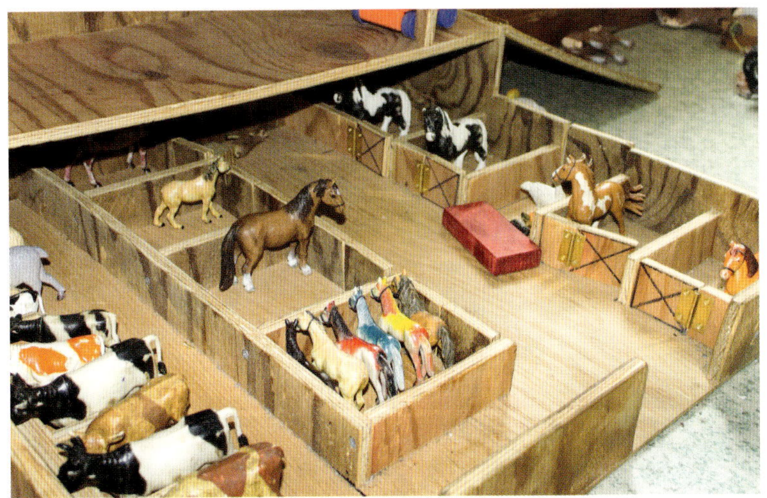

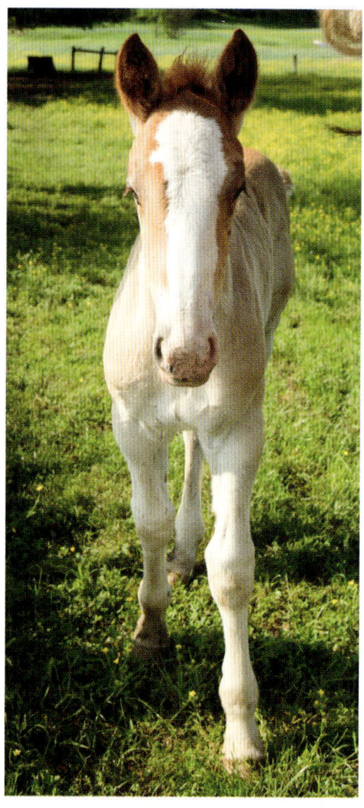

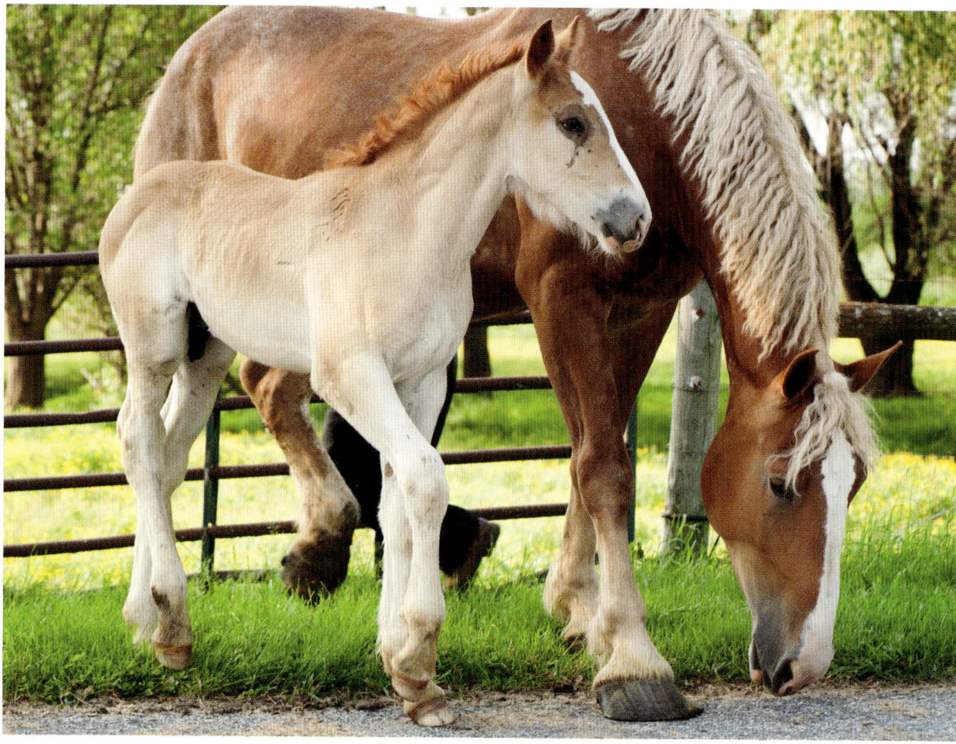

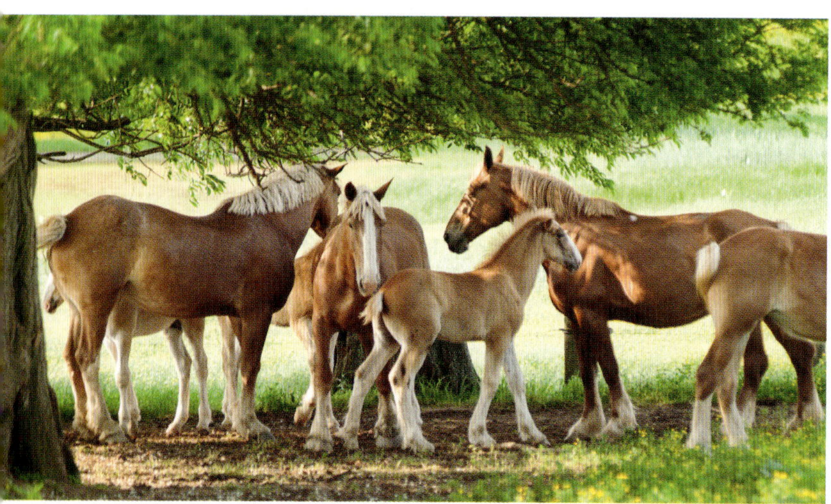

Owen's mother did not survive his birth. Because his owner's brother had a Belgian mare whose baby had just died, colt Owen and mare Lori were put together. With a little human nudging, the colt and his new mama bonded in just a day and Owen, *top left and above,* was feeding happily.

Doted on as a foal, Nadene, *right,* still considered herself a pet—however now she was a 1,500-pound yearling. It took some hands-on convincing to back her up when she made a pest of herself. She once crashed through a gate in her enthusiasm to join the others when she was left alone in a meadow.

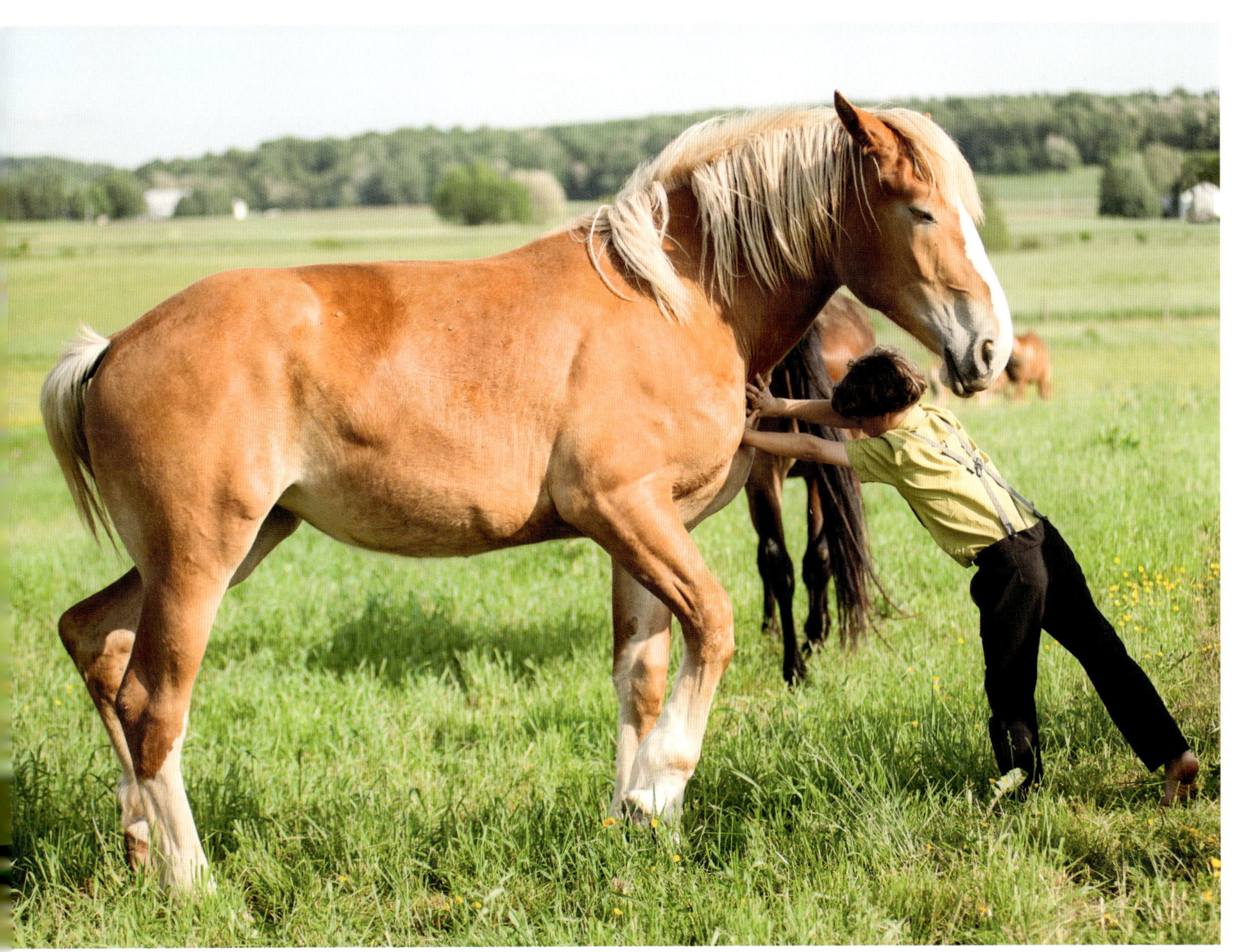

"You can make the home-raised just what you want."

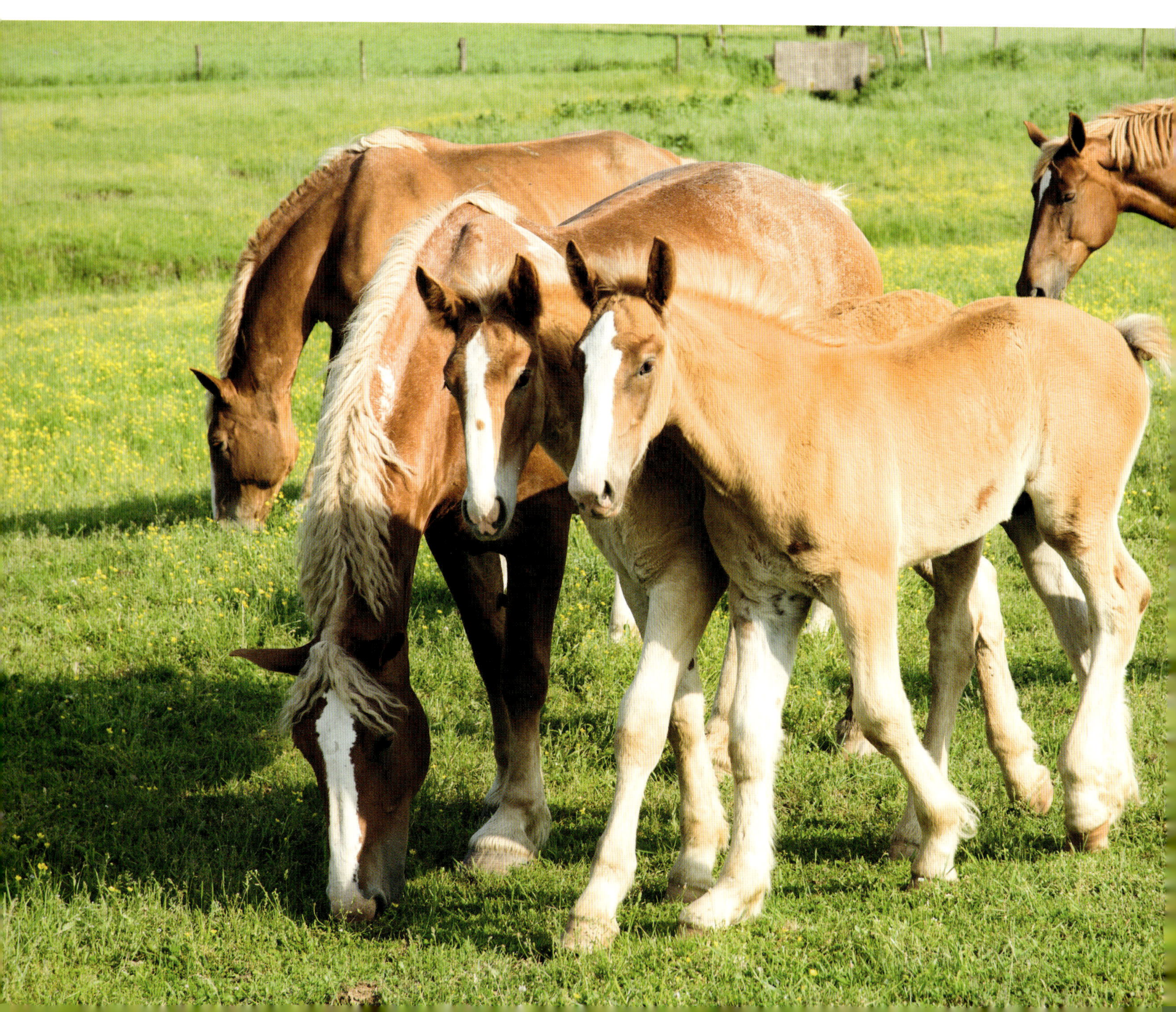

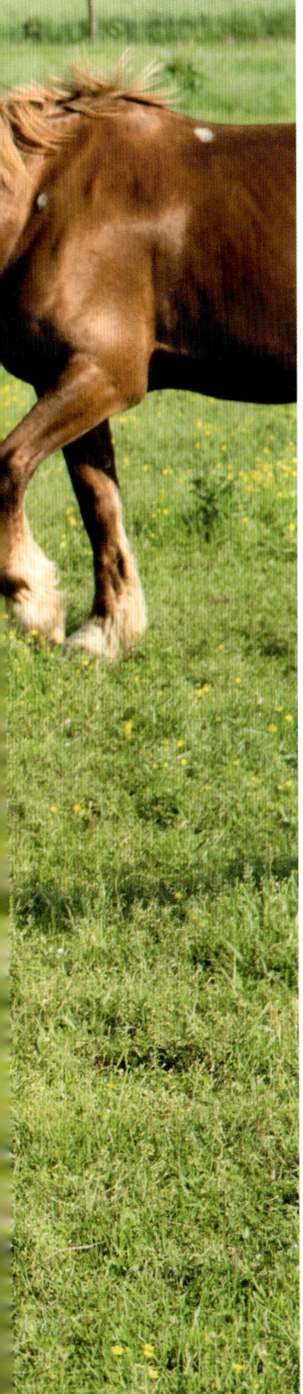

Three-month-old colts Oscar and Ozzie, *left,* were born within a few weeks of each other and have spent their lives together. In another month they'll be separated from their mothers and termed weanlings. All foals born on this farm in a calendar year are called names that begin with the same letter of the alphabet. Regardless of when foals are born, they are considered yearlings come January 1 and two-year-olds the next January 1.

At three months old, Oscar was nearly the size of a full-grown carriage horse. He started to lose his baby coat, and the darker shade on his nose and cheeks indicated the color he would be as an adult.

Eight months later, *right,* Oscar stood with other yearlings at a sale preview. He looked extremely grown up with his neatly trimmed mane and tail, and his polished hooves and new shoes.

When sold, he will serve as a stud or a gelding in a working draft team.

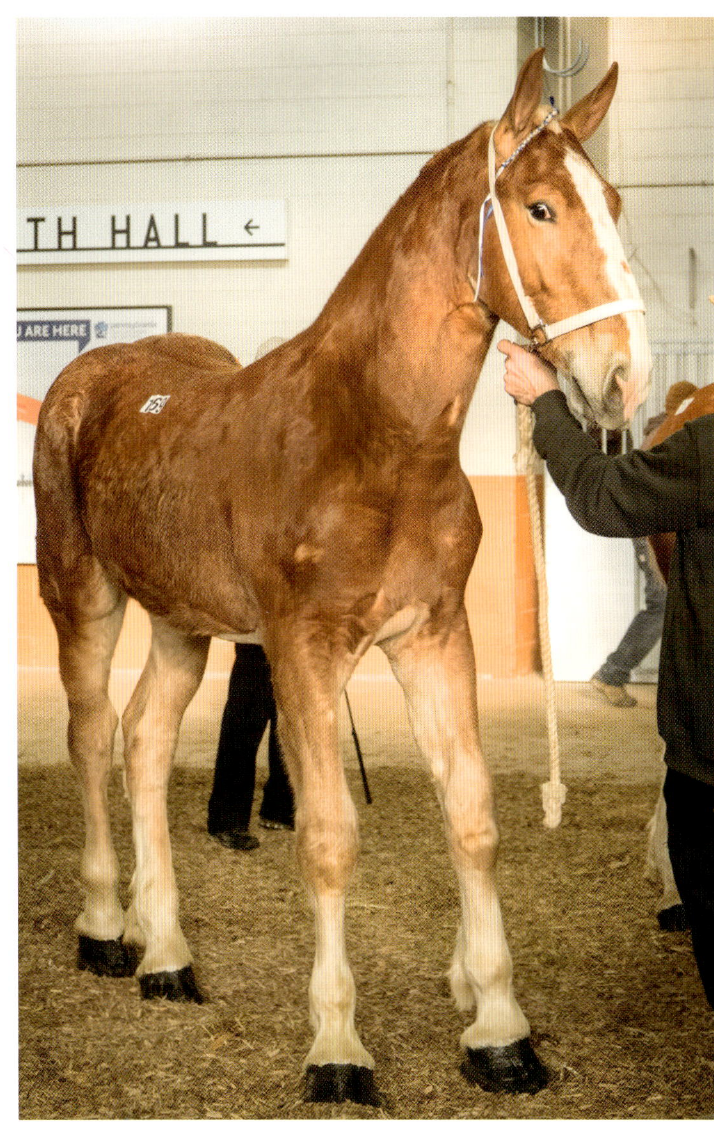

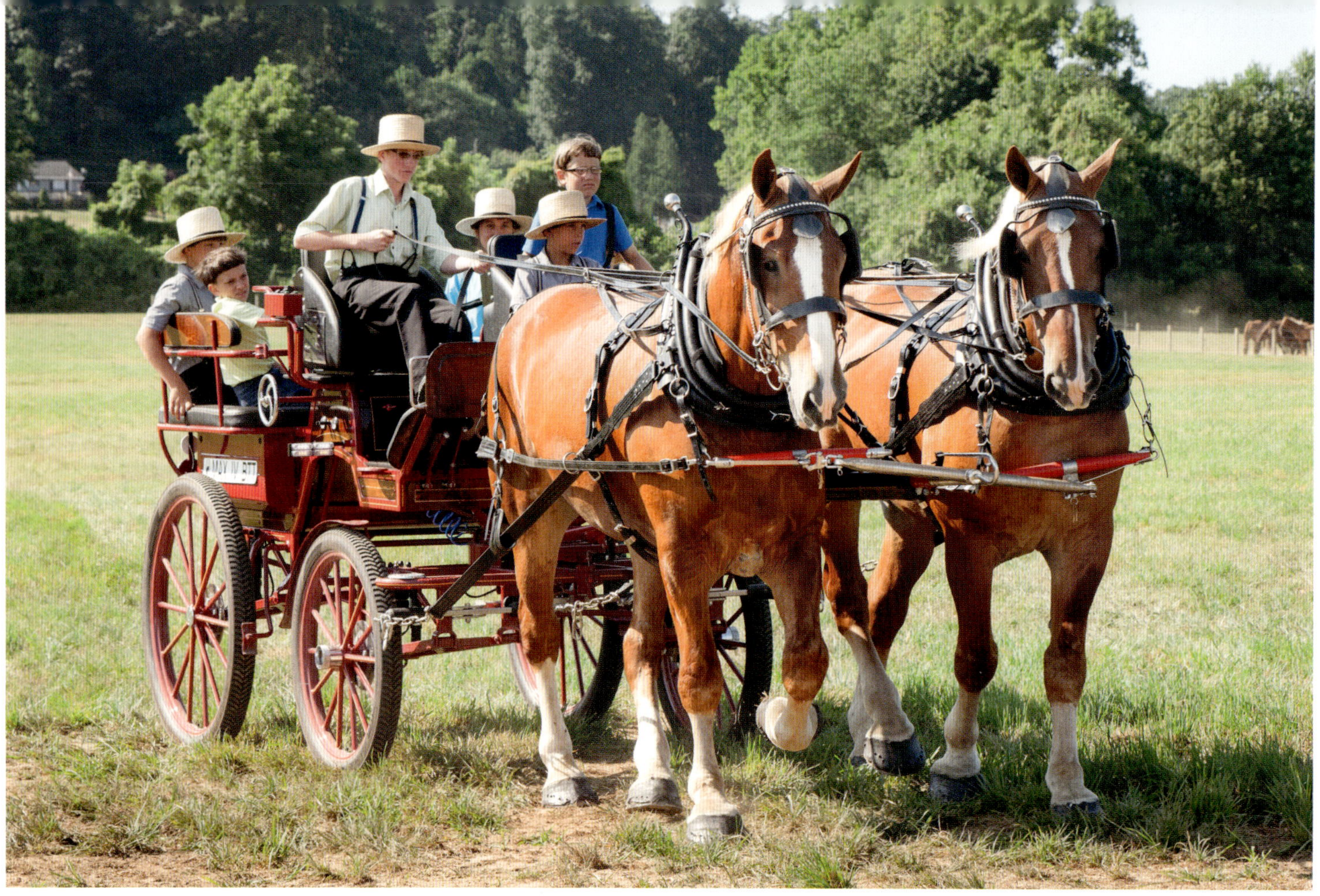

More than a thousand people gathered on a horse farm one hot, sunny day in July to celebrate at the Belgian Draft Horse Expo. Enthusiasts from Lancaster County and far beyond thrilled to six-horse hitches, stallion presentations, and breeders' parade. There were conformation, showmanship, and judging demonstrations.

A huge tent housed vendors' stalls with feed, supplements, and stable supplies while association representatives stood by.

Hundreds of people laid down ten dollars each to buy a chance to win a four-month-old blond Belgian filly. Aptly named, Winning Ticket had excellent bloodlines and a friendly demeanor. The young man who won her was thrilled to have such a great start to his breeding operation.

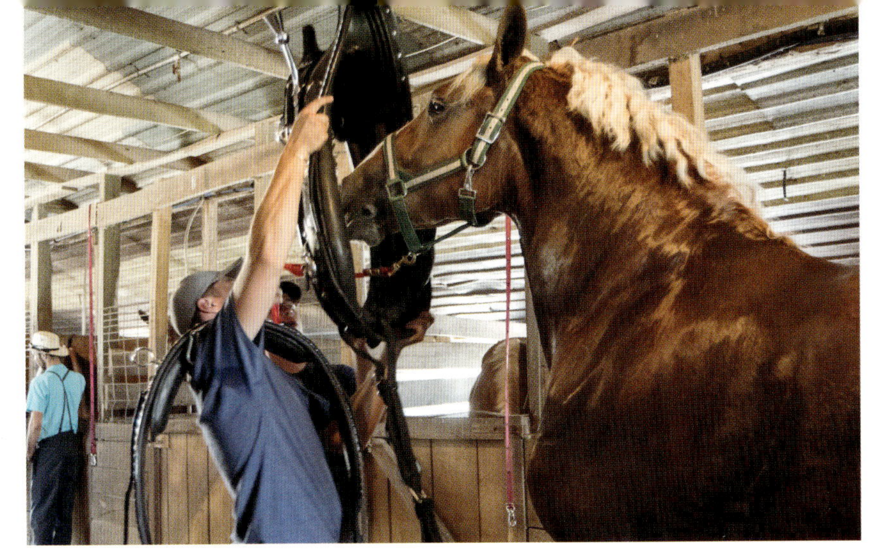

"The show judges look for 'fat and slick.'"

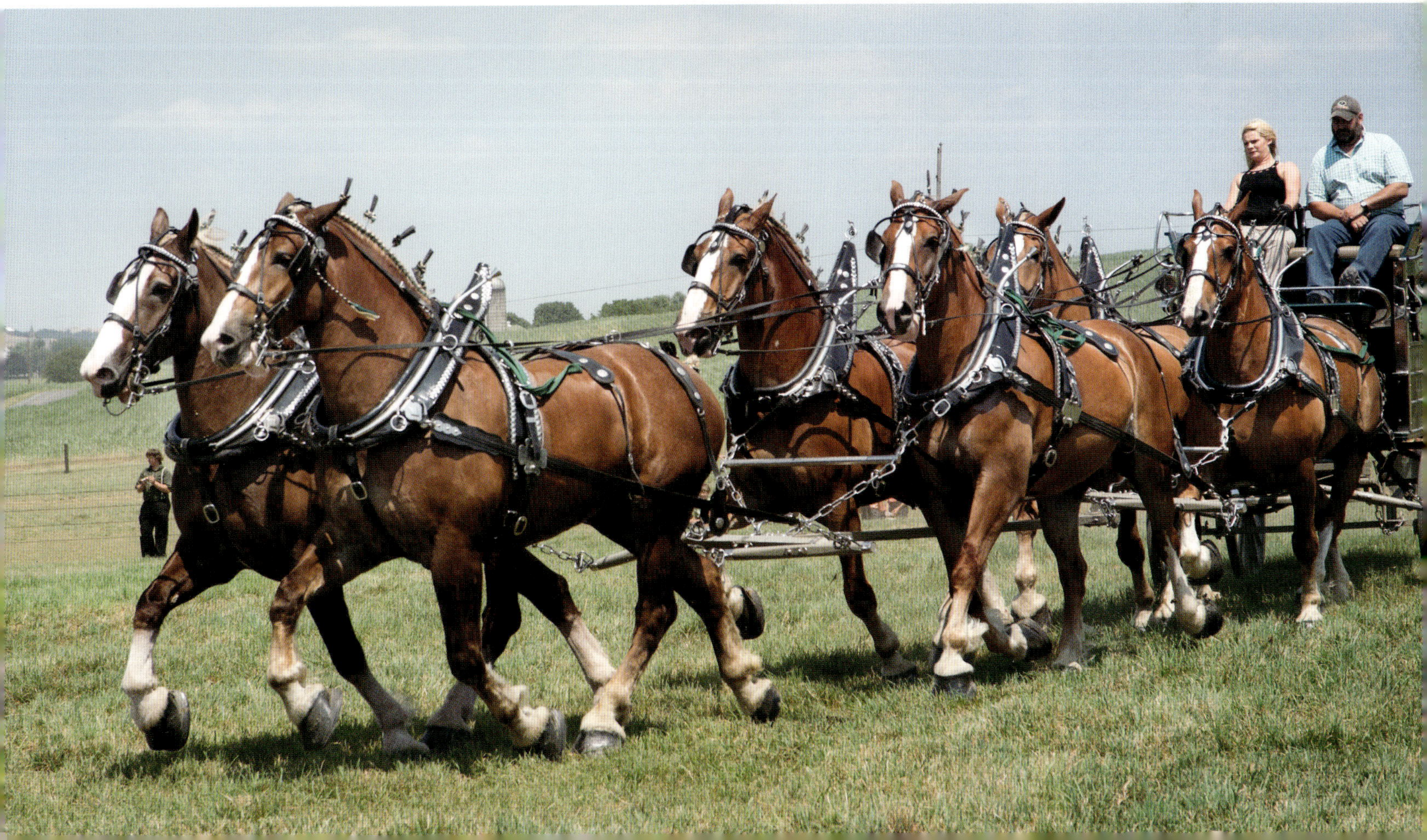

Young Aaron kept a firm hand on the rope when visitors came to see his dad's Belgians. He encouraged mare Beth to stand still, legs planted and head proud. Fortunately she was well trained and Aaron was experienced in handling horses, since his 80-pound frame would have been no match for her 1,800 pounds if she decided to head for the pasture.

When Aaron and his brothers and sisters get together with their cousins, they run all over the farm. In one of their games, they created a kid-powered six-horse hitch (three rows of two each) and harnessed the team with baler twine. The children took turns driving and pulling, demonstrating admirable conformation and action.

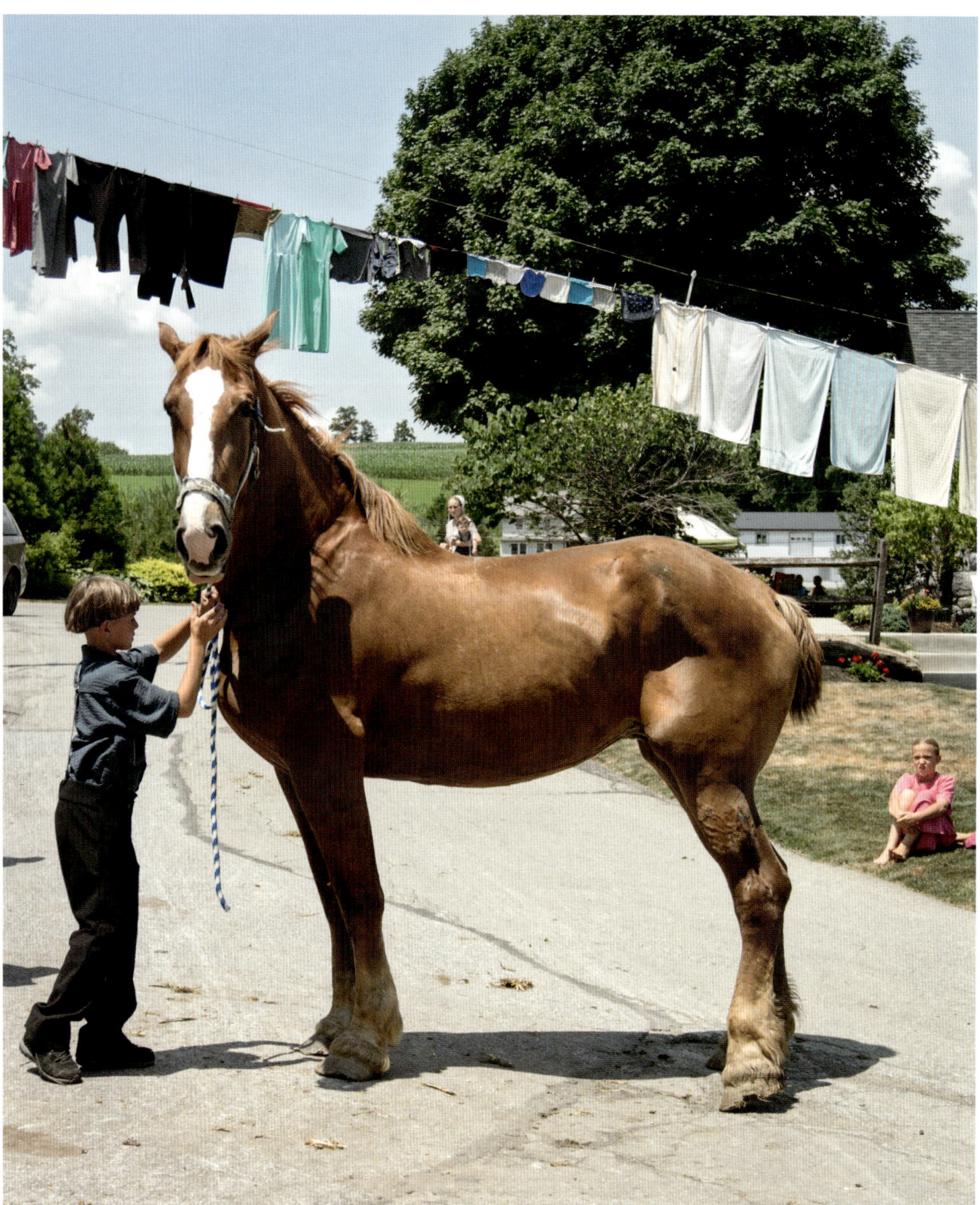

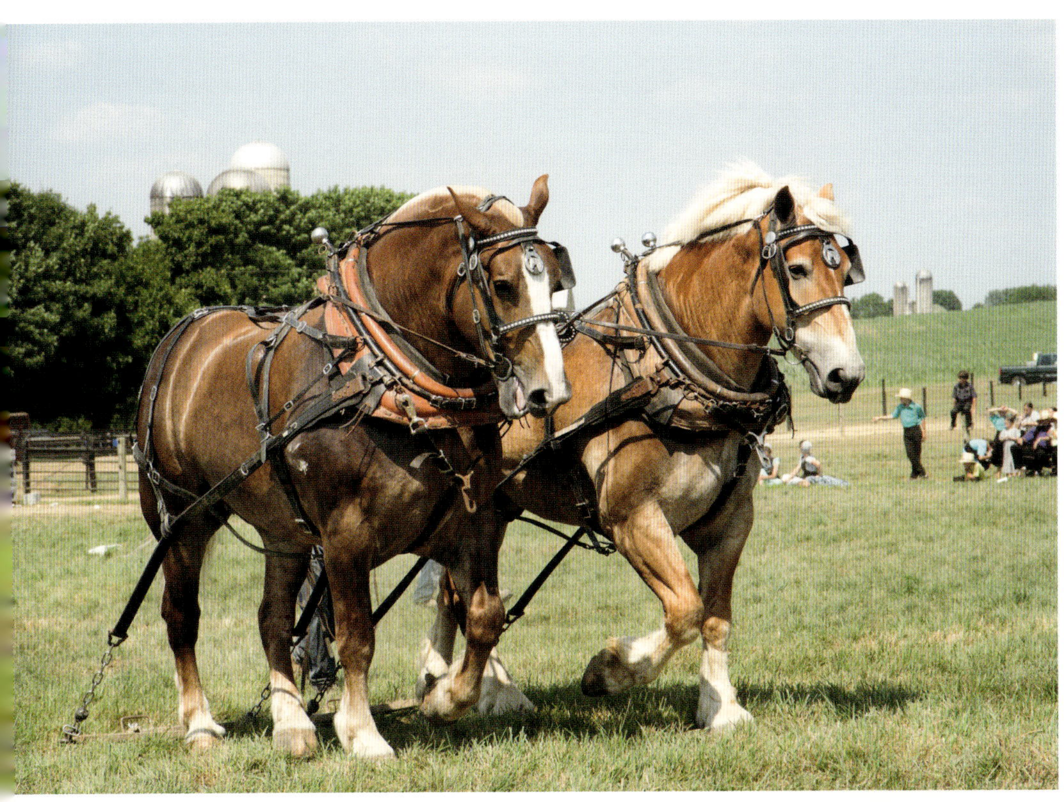

The Belgian breed is dominant in the sport of horse pulling, thanks to good bone density, strong muscles, and even temperament. A pair of pulling horses may weigh over 5,000 pounds and can pull double that.

Rather than looking for the showy steps and high head of a hitch Belgian, drivers of the pulling Belgian favor a horse with a compact, muscular body and good, solid feet on the ground.

The pulling horses wear specially constructed padded pulling collars and shoes fitted with caulk or studs to provide traction.

Competitive teams are not generally used for farmwork but are selected based on their musculature. They are fed well and carefully trained to pull safely.

When Belgians and other draft horses are spiffed up for show or sale, or driven in a hitch, they are fitted with Scotch Bottom shoes. The wide shoes distribute the horse's heft over a broader area, and are custom weighted and shaped to enhance the horse's gait and movement. The shoes are also antiskid and padded to cushion the feet as they hit the road.

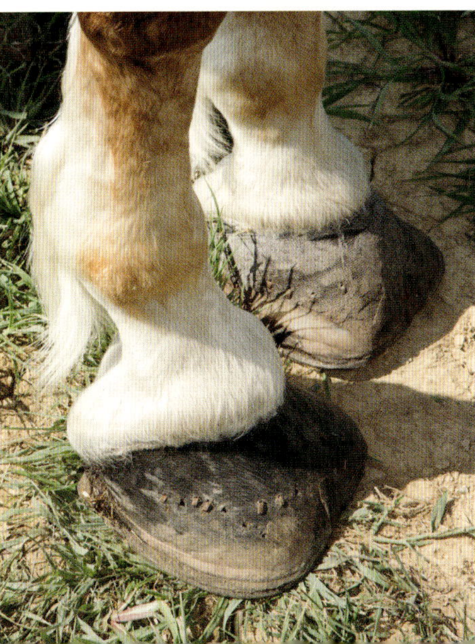

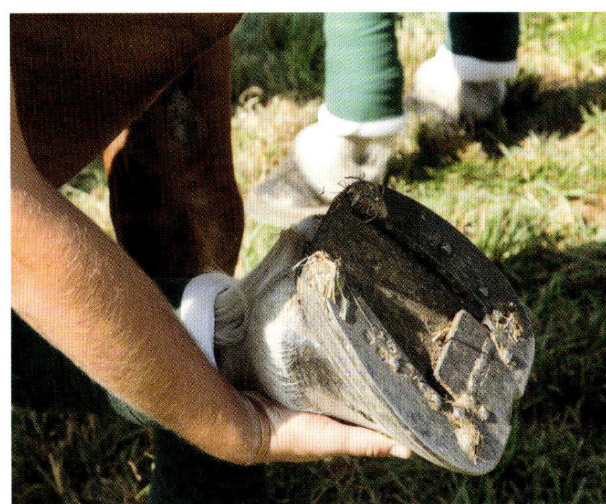

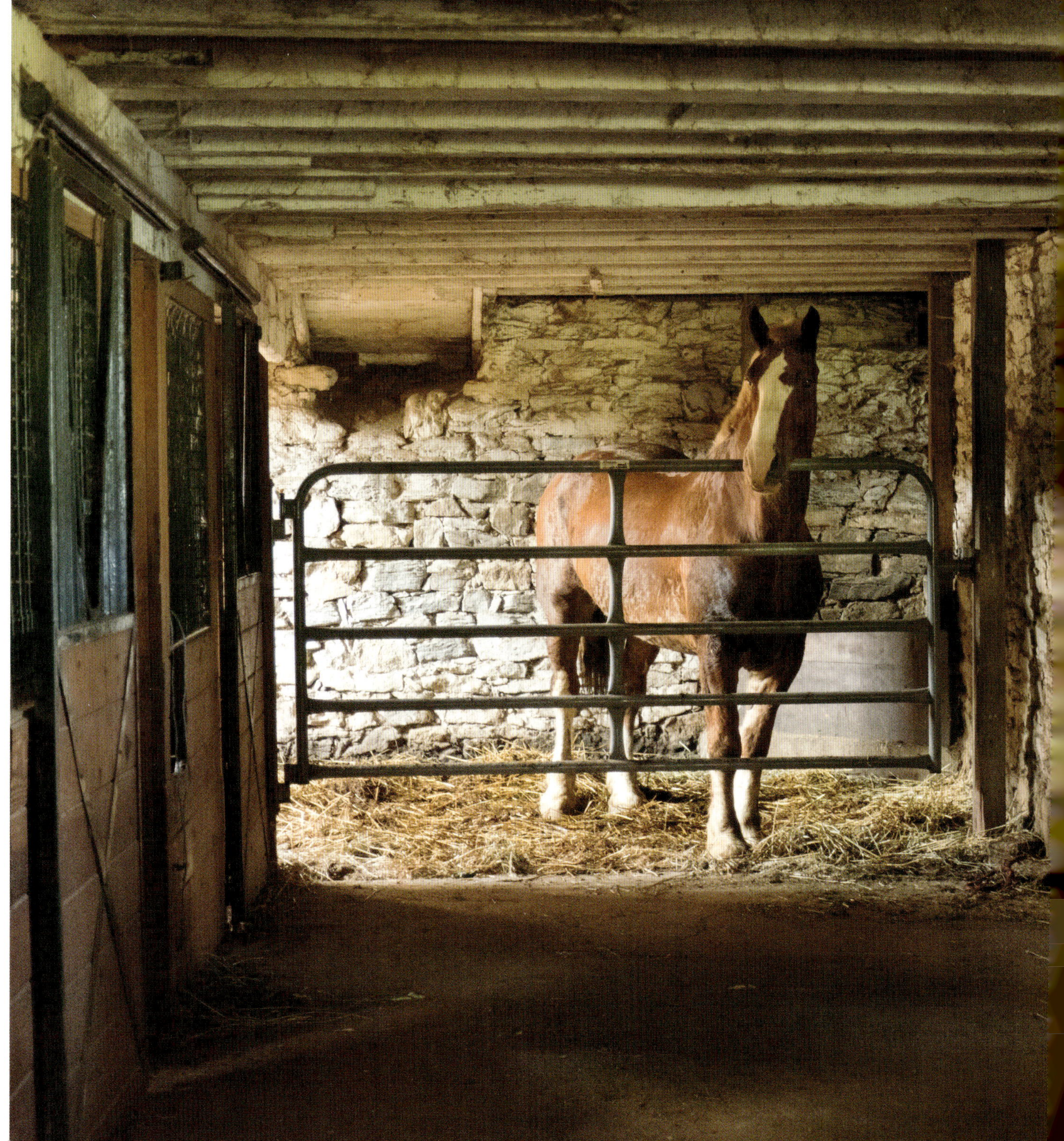

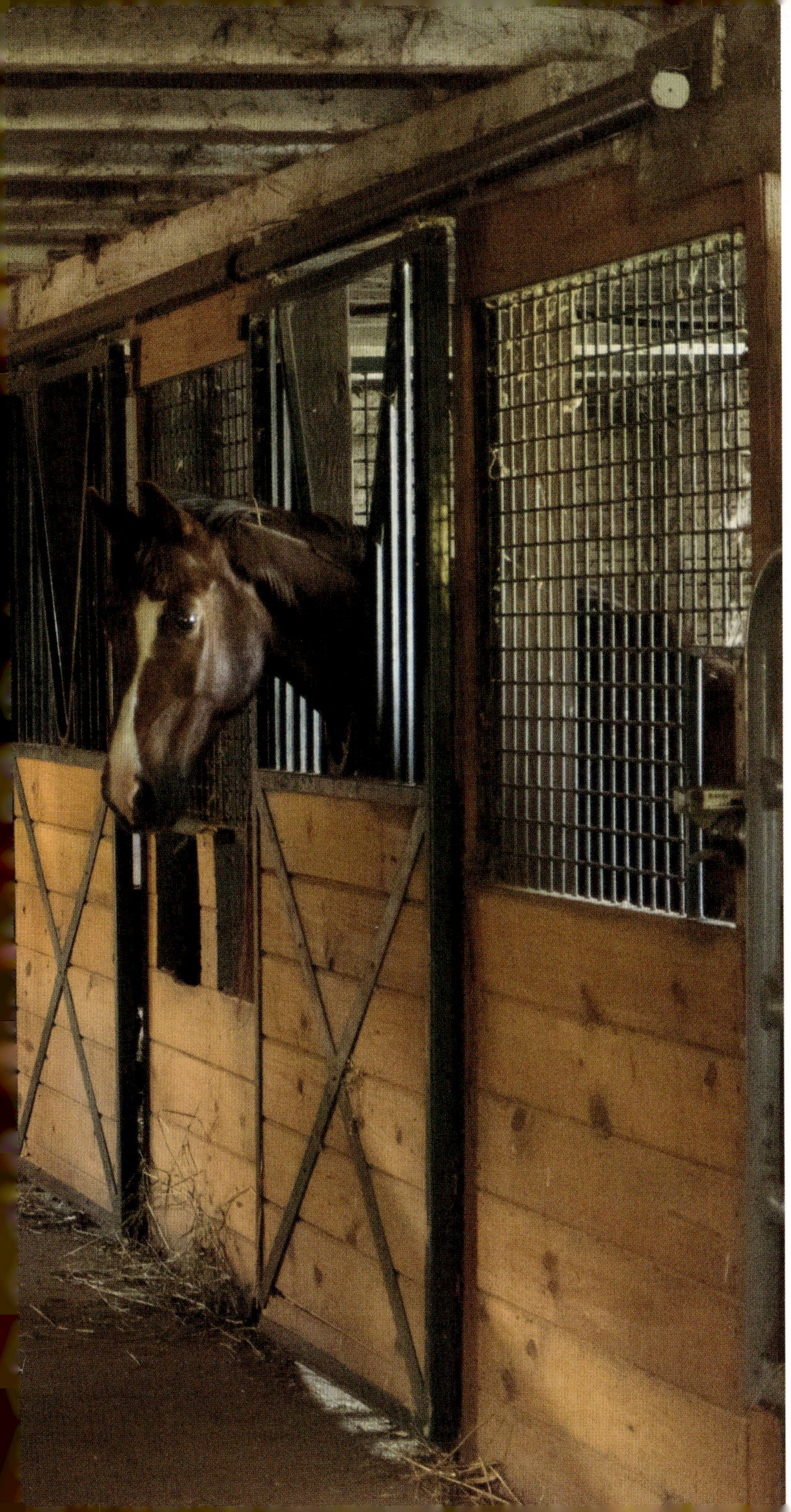

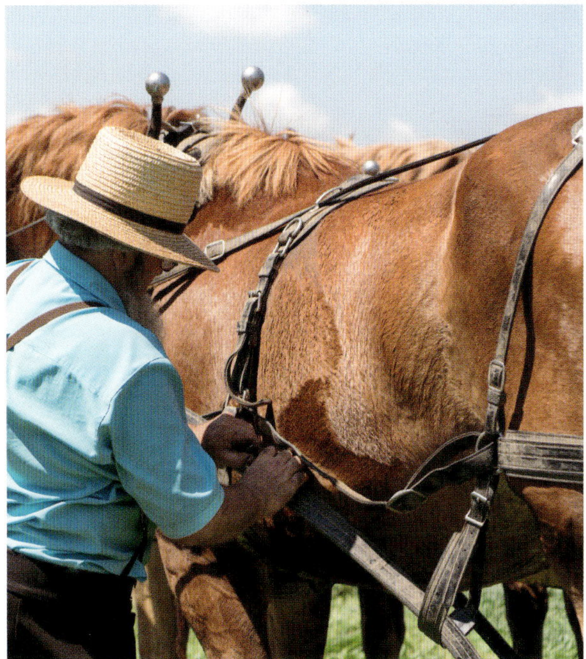

To use horse power is to literally harness energy. The horse engages the strength of its muscular chest, forelimbs, and hindquarters for pulling, turning, and stopping a load—maximized by its harness.

The harness is a network of straps, bands, buckles, loops, and rings. It is traditionally made of leather, although synthetic materials have been making inroads. Synthetic leather is lighter weight, easier to clean, and more flexible in cold weather—as well as less expensive. Well maintained, leather lasts the life of the horse. It feels and smells good, and there is less friction between the horse and the harness than with a synthetic material.

Even when the harness is leather, the lines are often made of synthetic material, which makes them lighter and easier to handle.

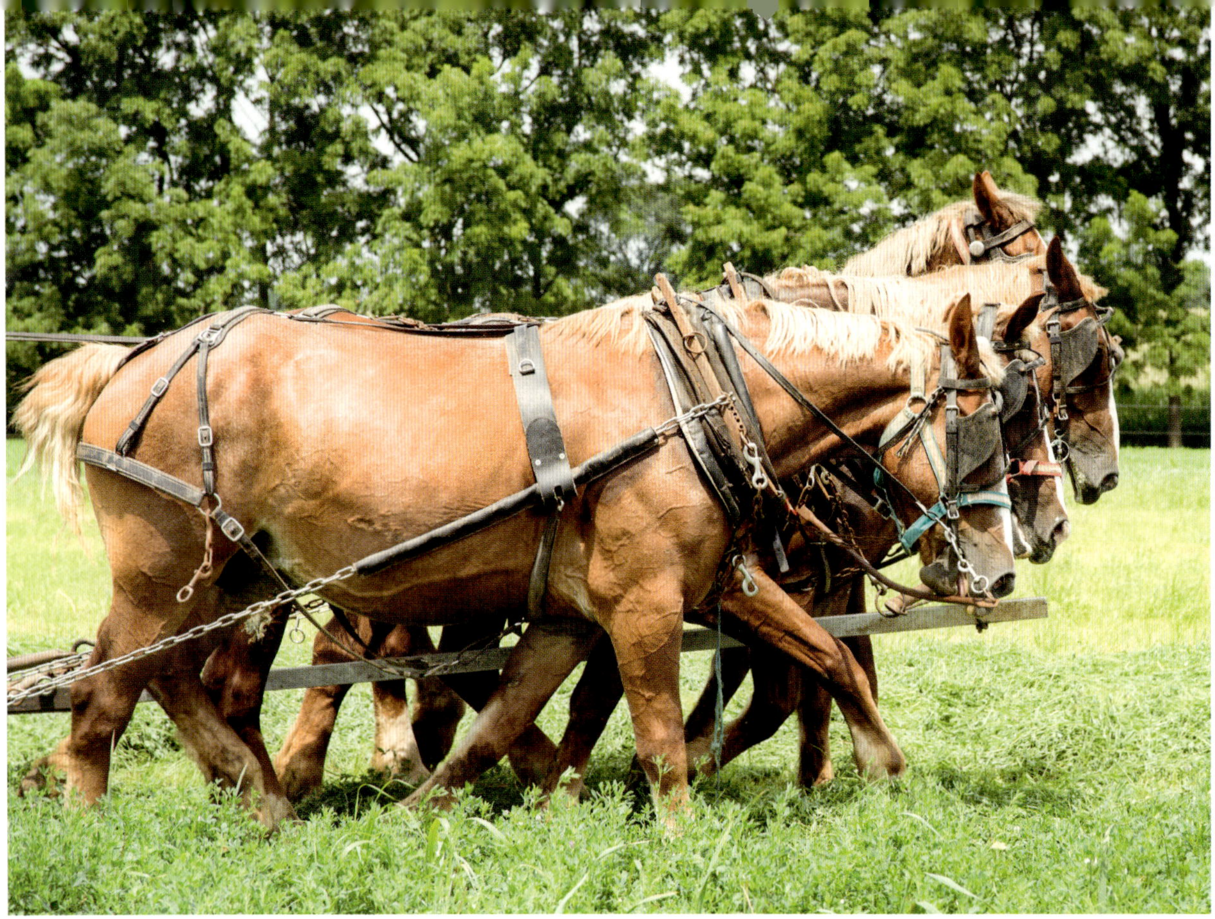

Seven days of sunshine, interrupted by a rash of thunderstorms, dictated Isaac's haying schedule in late July. He and his go-to team were out Saturday evening making as many trips around the field as they could before dark. He had doused the four mares with water before harnessing to keep them cool, and he would spray them with water again before returning them to their stalls.

After a day of rest on Sunday, they were out again on Monday morning as soon as the dew evaporated. Each step—cutting, tedding (fluffing), raking, and baling—required a half day or full day of drying before the next step.

The baler dropped the bales of hay at regular intervals in the field, *right*. Next, Isaac will drive the team pulling a stacker wagon that automatically picks up the bales and stacks them neatly on the wagon for the trip to the barn.

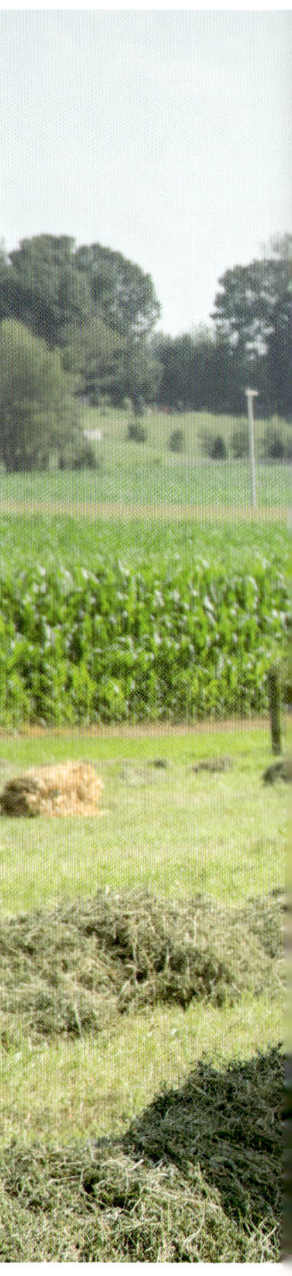

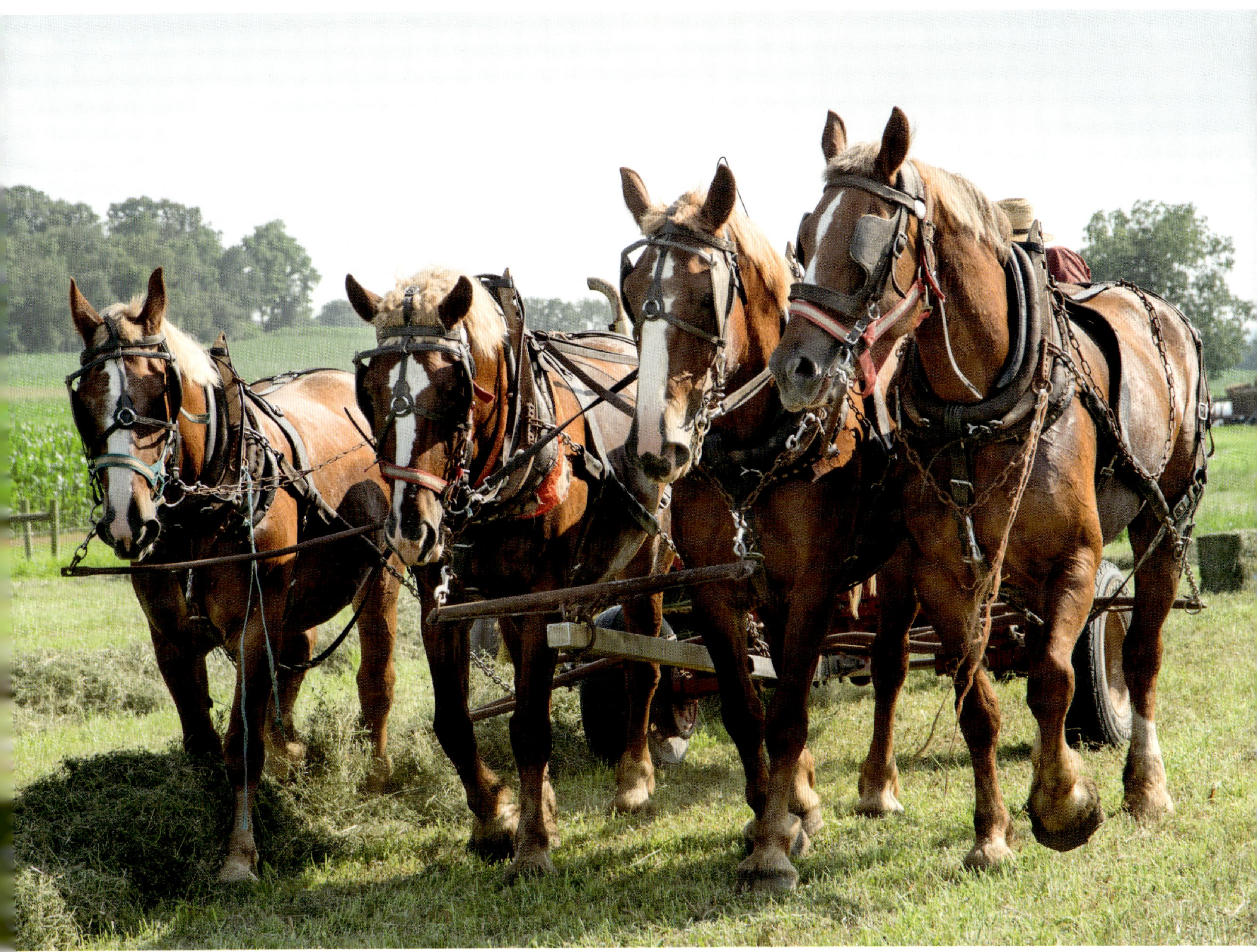

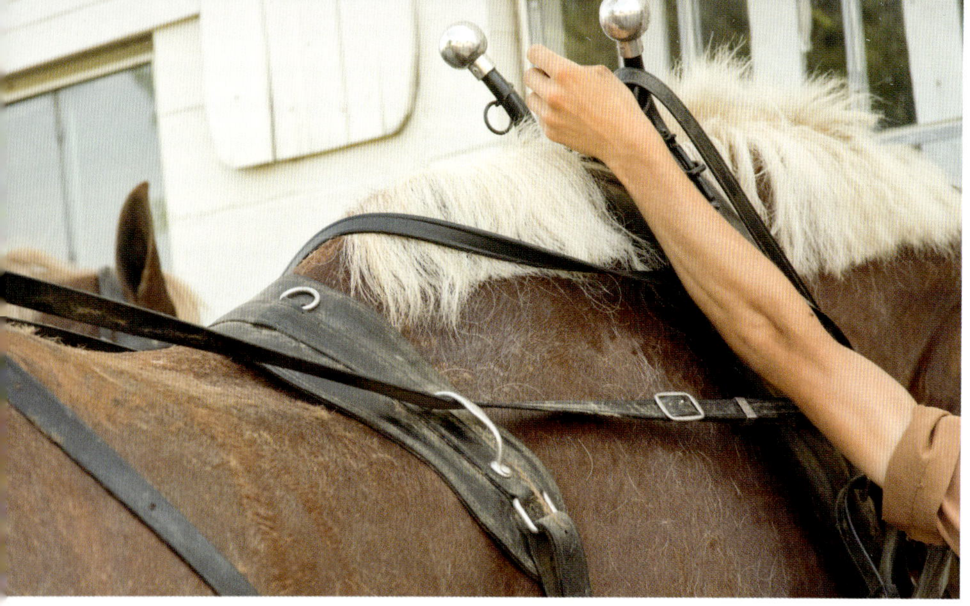

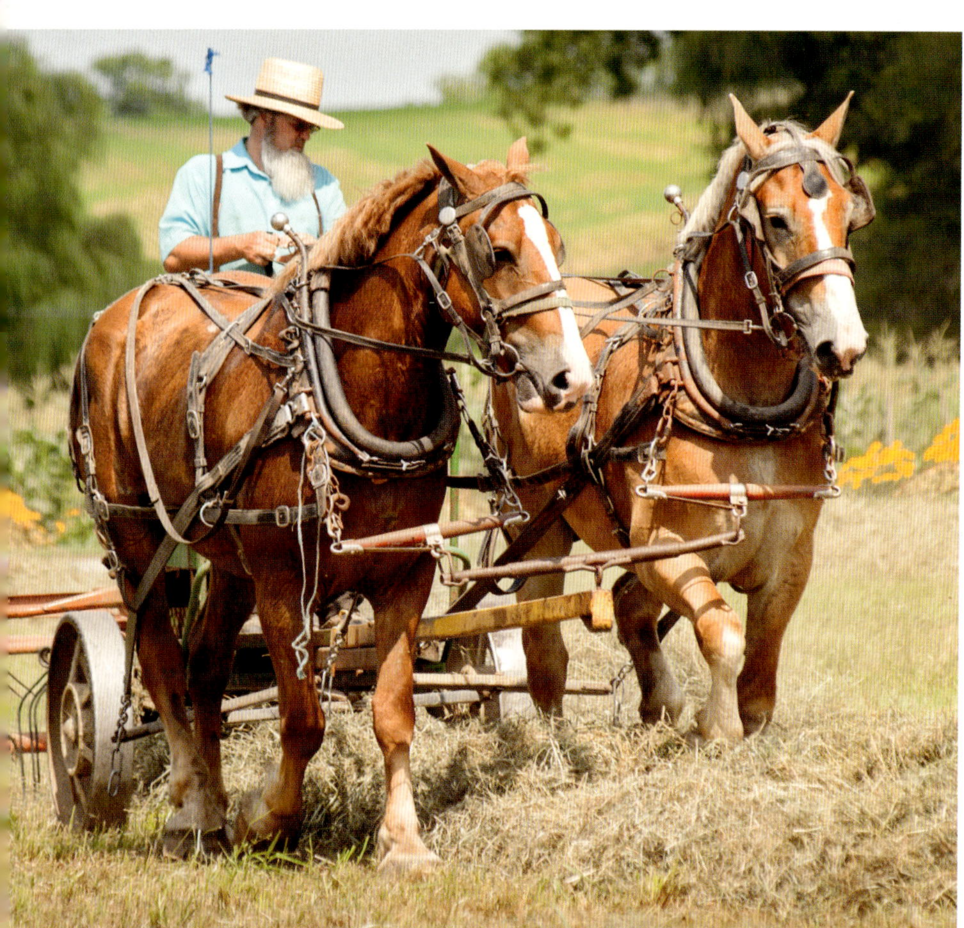

Many farmers train their own draft horses. Here is one farmer's training routine for his Belgians:

1. Start with a yearling and train it to halter.
2. When the horse is two and a half, put on a harness and have the horse wear it for a half day in the stall.
3. Work the horse when it's wearing a harness by walking behind it and holding the reins.
4. Give it voice commands to match what you're saying with the reins.
5. Hitch the green horse beside a lead horse that is pulling a light two-wheeled cart and get in the driver's seat.
6. Make sure you're in the middle of a field.
7. Hang on, because the green horse will run until he's tired and ready to trot. "That's an adventure!"
8. Hook up three or four times, then the green horse is ready to pull.
9. For starters, hitch the horse up to a cart or spreader, which is much easier to pull than a plow.

"Hang on! It's an adventure when the green horse is first hitched up to a cart."

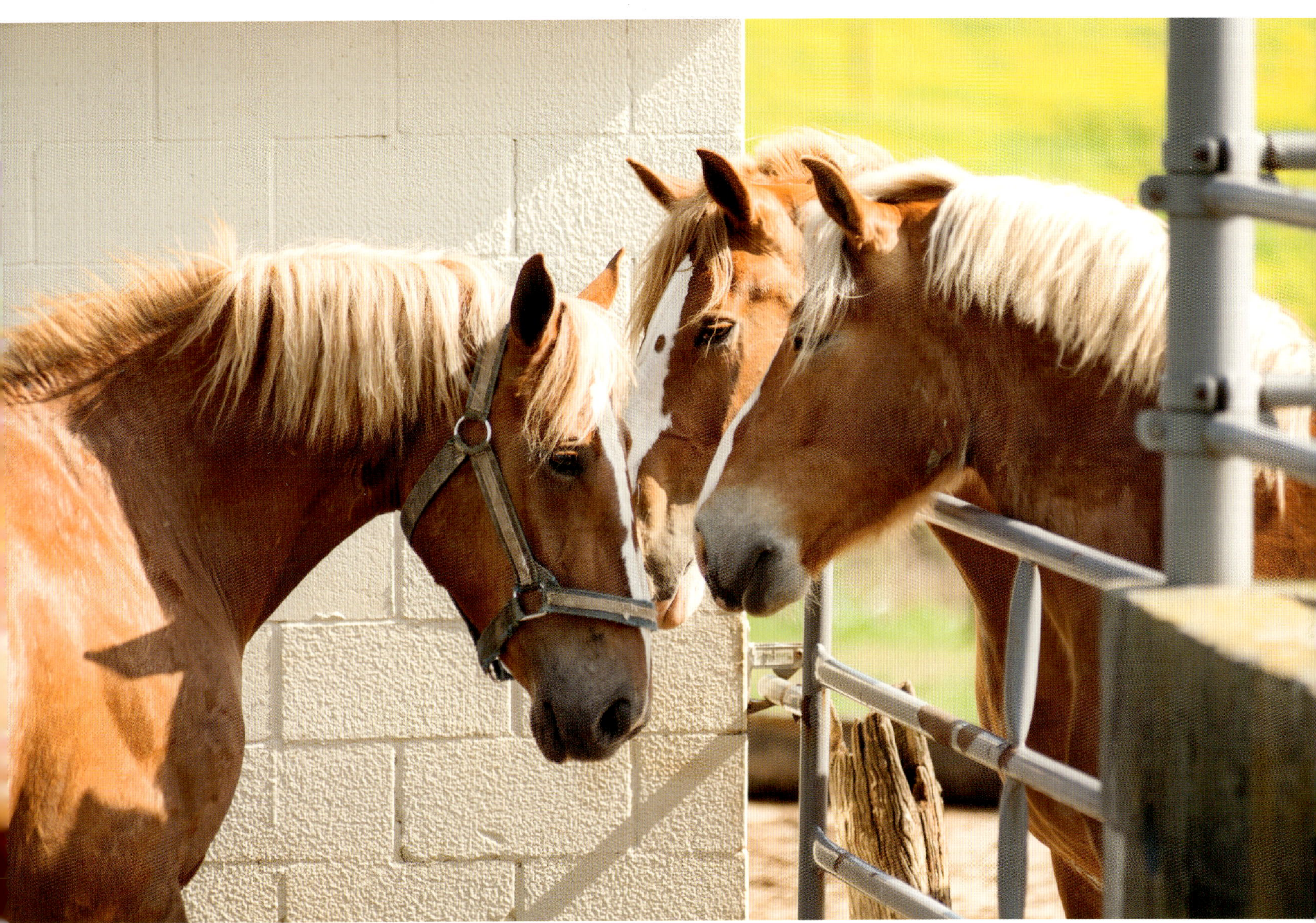

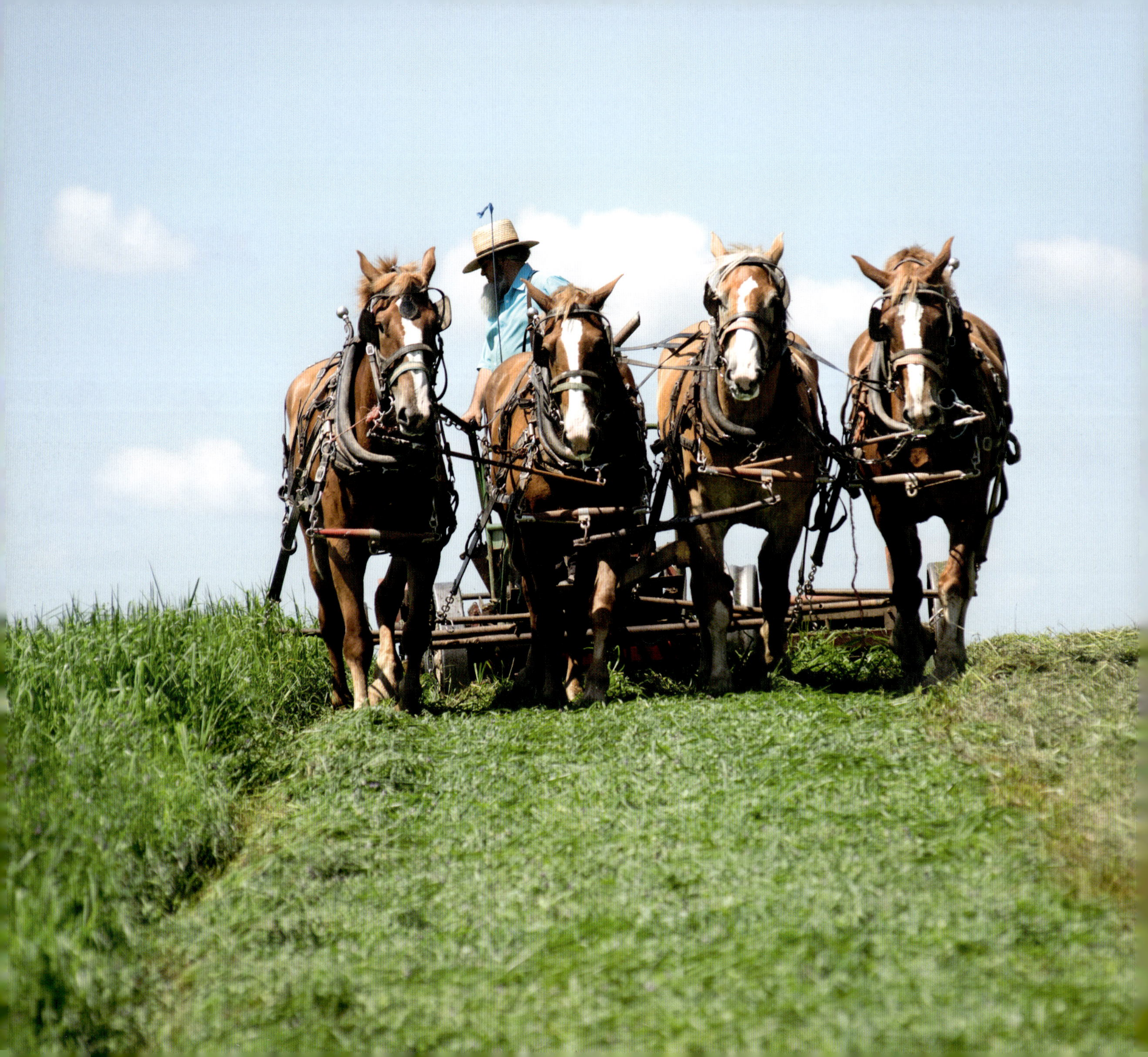

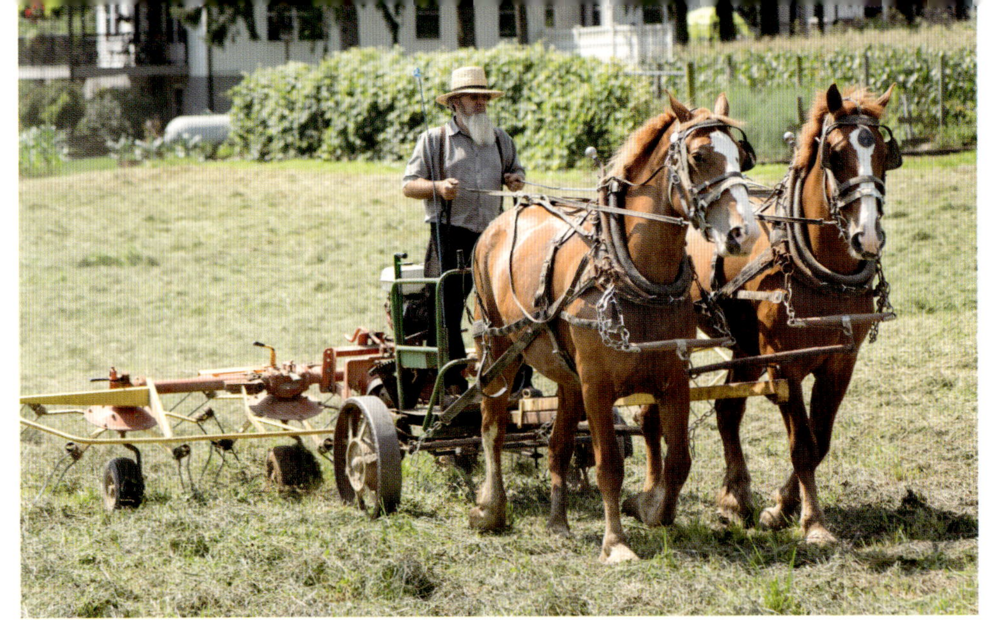

Jacob hitches up two, four, or six of his mares, depending on the job. The mower-crimper, *facing page,* is heavy, requiring four horses to pull it as it both cuts and conditions the hay.

Tedding, *left,* and raking are relatively light work, requiring just two horses. Six horses abreast, *below,* pull the baler and a hay wagon. When full, the wagon carries 110 bales that weigh roughly 45 pounds each.

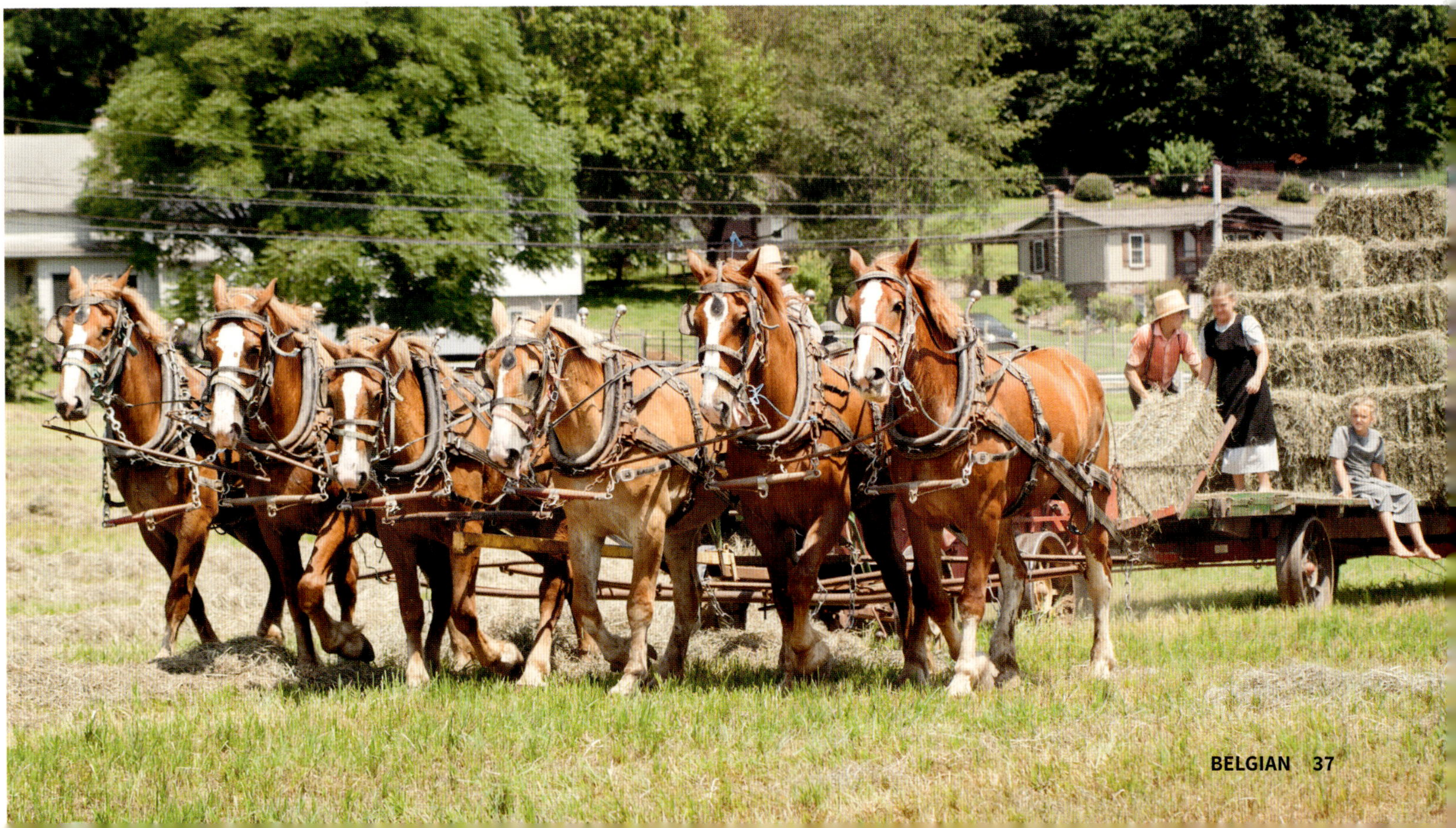

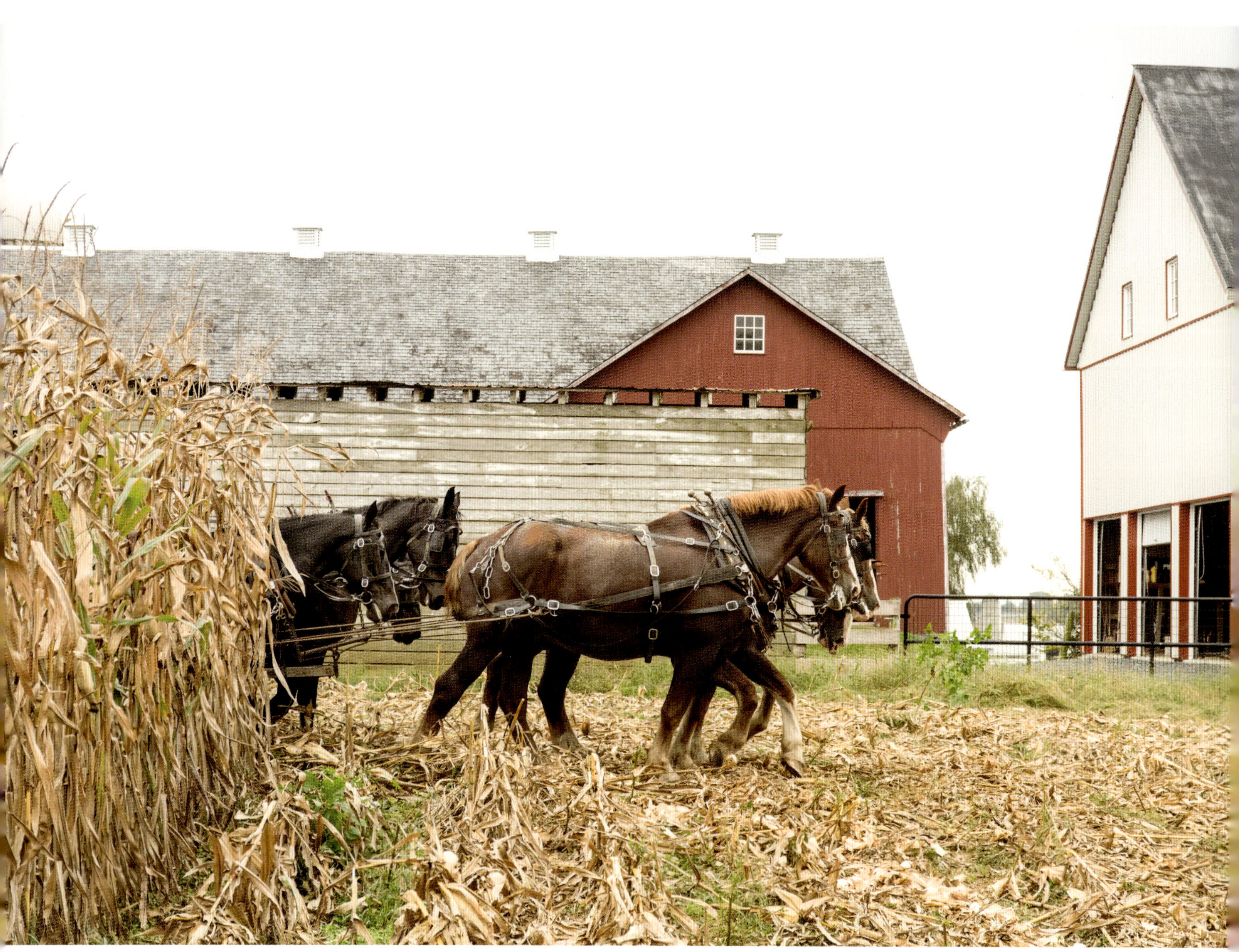

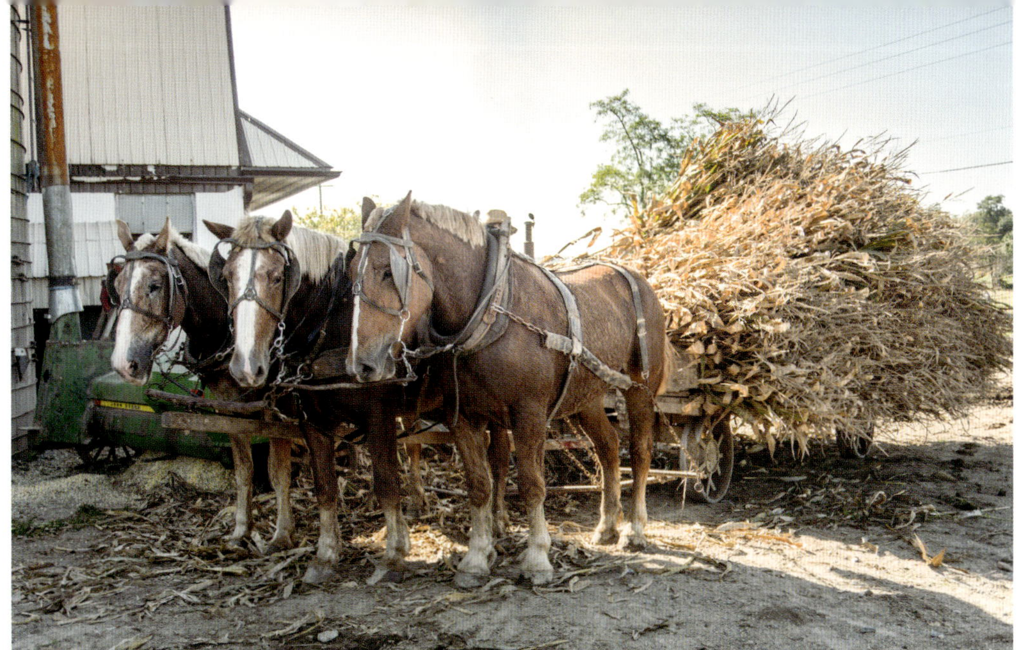

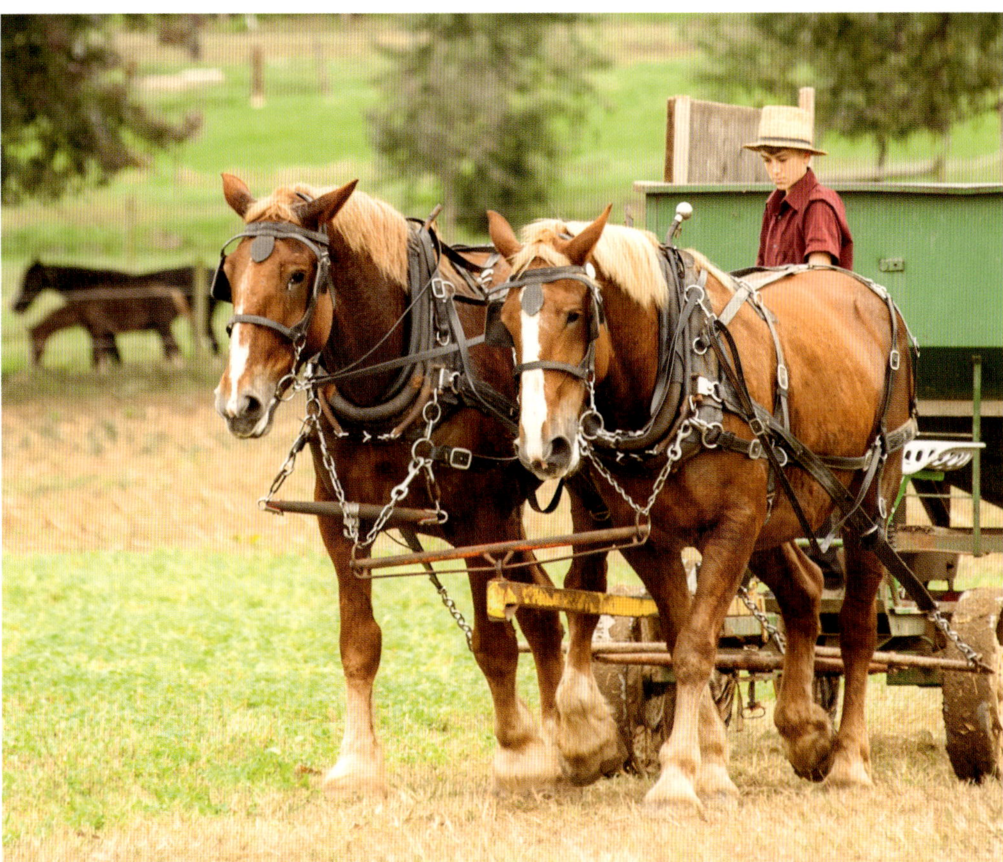

Three Belgians, *top,* ferried the corn to the barn as two other teams harvested the stalks and ears in the field. The horses are accustomed to waiting patiently between tasks, ready to move again upon a spoken command from the driver.

A pair of Belgians, *bottom,* at a neighboring farm transferred wagonloads of picked corn from the field to the barn.

Most farmers who grow corn in Lancaster county grow it for both seed and silage. Corn for silage—a high-energy forage for dairy cows—is harvested at a higher moisture content than seed corn. The entire stalk, including the ears, is chopped and placed in a silo for fermentation.

Late October saw a convergence of the first spring planting and the final fall harvest.

Two brothers, *below,* headed out to the field at sundown to bale hay. It was the fifth and final alfalfa crop of the season and would help feed their dairy cows over the next six months.

At another farm, King farms no-till because it is less labor intensive than traditional plowing and planting. It also maintains moisture and nutrients in the soil and helps prevent erosion.

He harnessed six mares and hitched them to a 10-foot drill planter, *right.* The seed drill sowed seeds in spaced rows, dropping them through tubes about an inch deep in the soil.

King planted a cover crop of rye soon after the corn was harvested, to avoid soil compaction and help build good quality. The rye will grow sporadically into the winter and spring, providing an early spring forage crop for his cows and heifers.

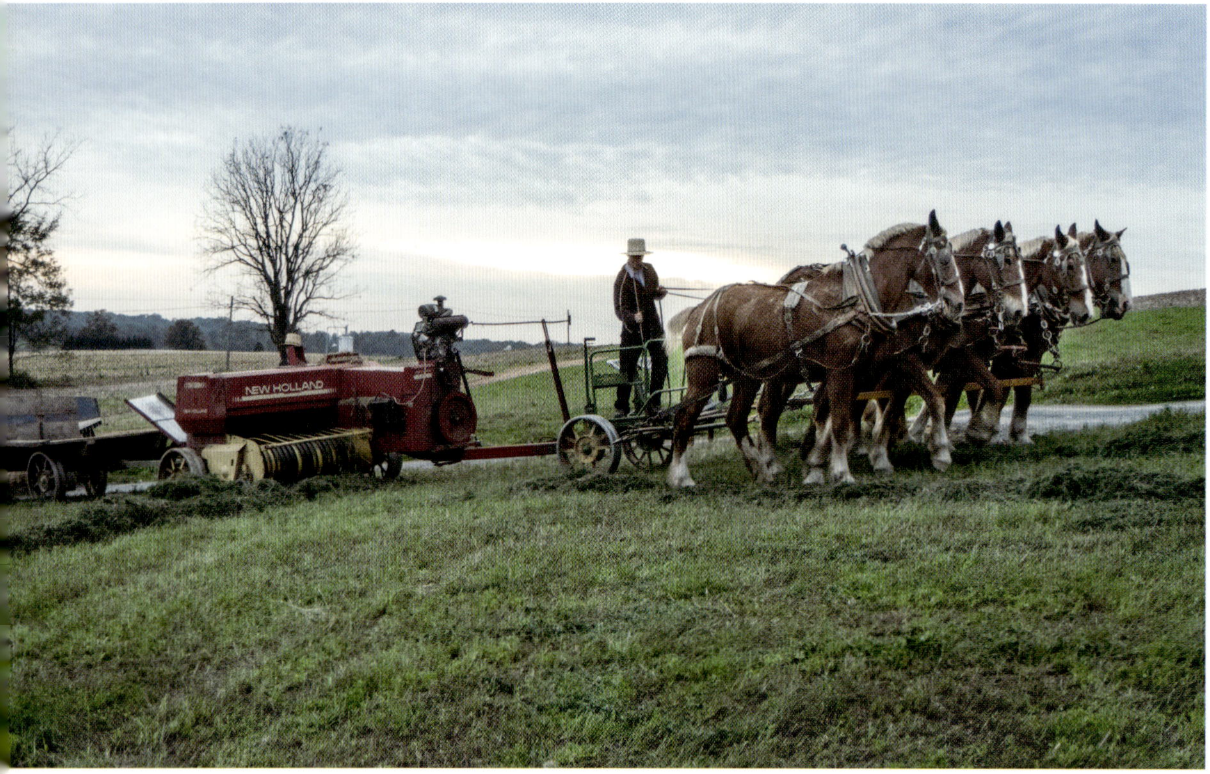

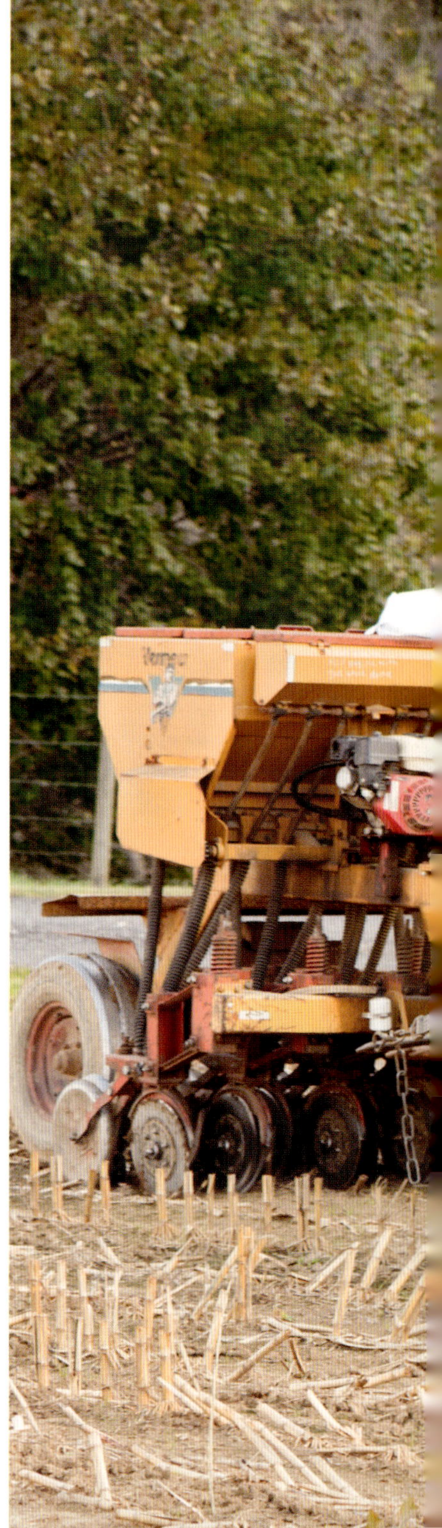

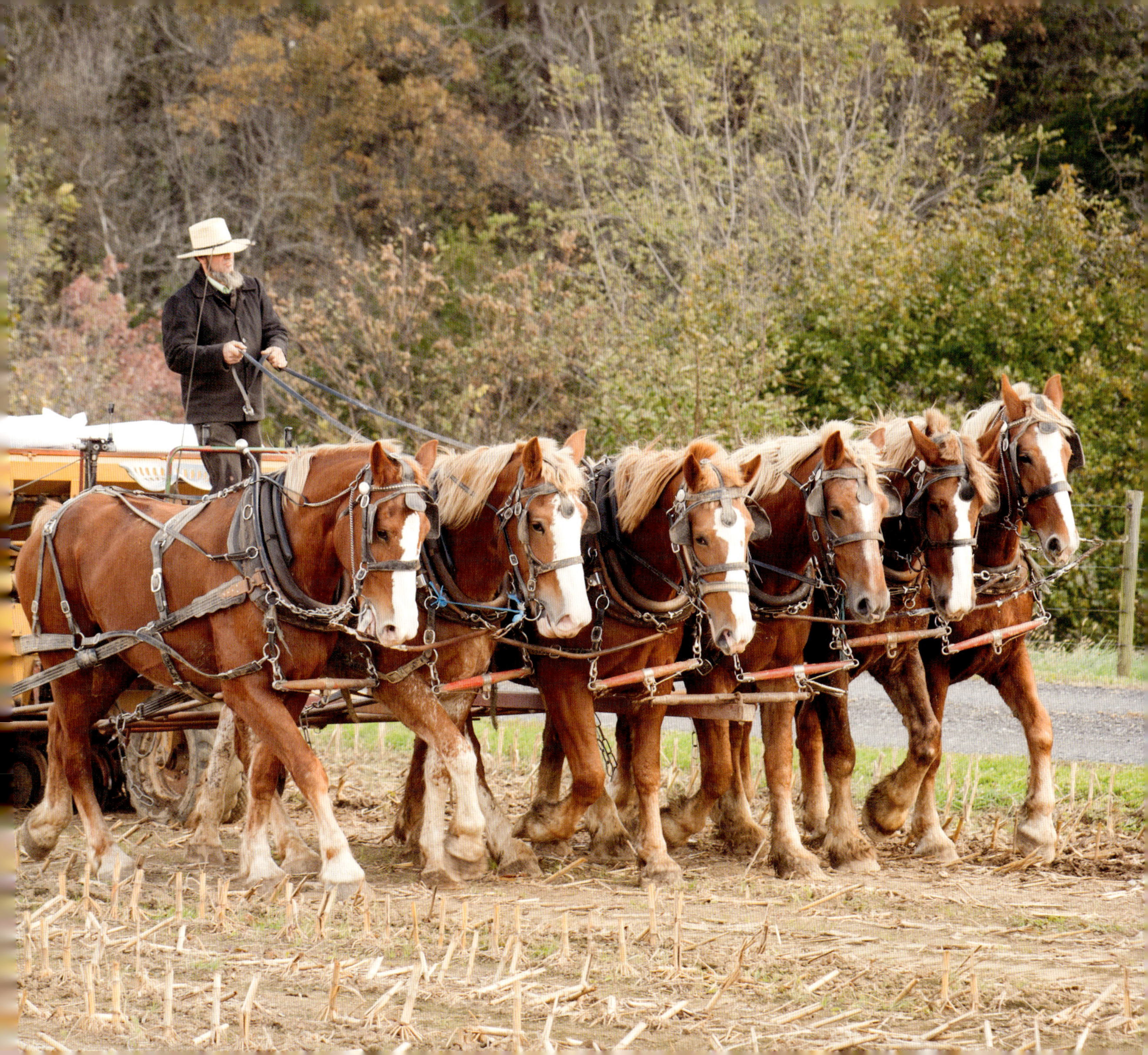

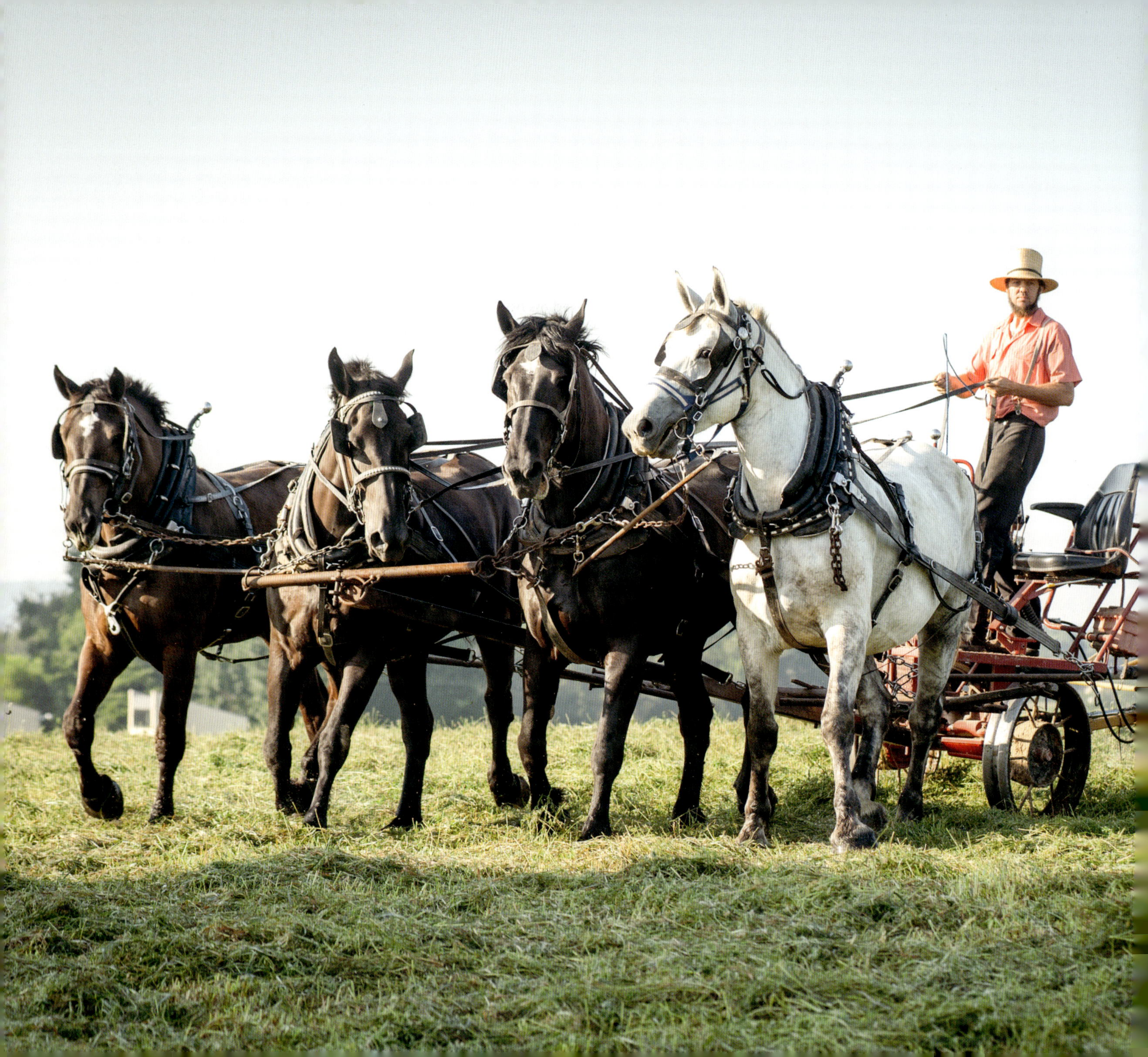

Percheron

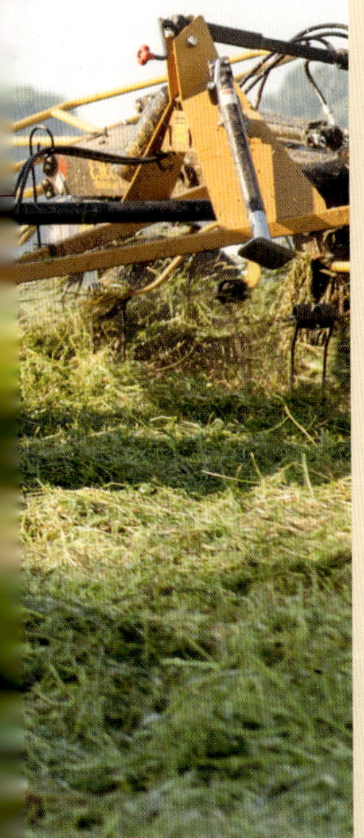

Emerging from the narrow lane, Amos urged his horses forward and released the lock to unfold the two 6-foot arms of the tedder. Molly, Gracie, Vanessa, and Mystery leaned into their collars. In short order the four Percheron mares were heading down the field, the four-star spinner tedder leaving a wake of fluffed hay. Since the tedder was a relatively light piece of farm equipment the horses broke into an occasional trot, Amos plying the reins from a standing position on the cart.

Tedding is the step in the hay harvest between cutting and raking. The hay is spun or tossed to ensure even drying. A particular moisture content must be met, depending on whether the hay will be fed to cows, horses, or sheep, and how it will be stored.

Not only a fan of black Percherons, Amos has black dogs, black pigs, black chickens, and a black spotted pony on his farm. The Percherons, however, are the stars.

Along with farming, Amos breeds and raises Percherons, championing the breed at sales and events.

> "When breeding a horse you have to look at both power and action."

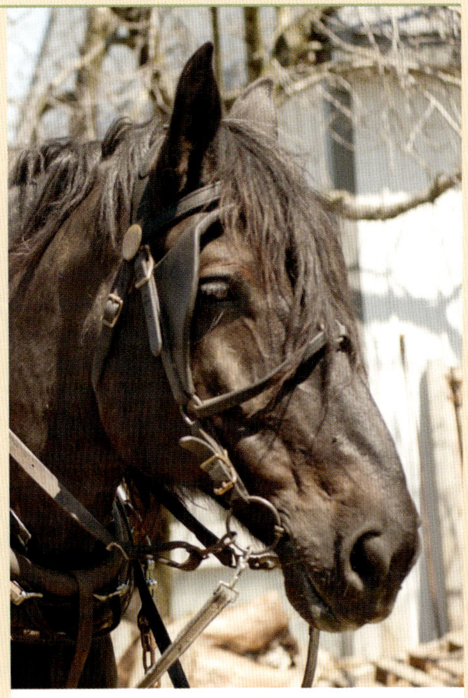

Origin: Le Perche (Normandy, France)

Height: 16–18hh, most between 16.2 and 17.3hh

Weight: average 1,500–2,000 lbs (up to 2,600)

Colors: black, gray, white

Though fewer Percherons than Belgians or mules work the fields in Lancaster County, their popularity is increasing.

Originally bred as war horses, Percherons are thought to be the only draft breed with Arab blood. They are sturdy and elegant, lively and graceful.

Often used in agricultural work, the versatile Percherons are also harnessed in attractive pairs to pull show carriages and exhibited in six-horse hitches. Riders who prefer a large horse often choose a Percheron for their power on the jump course or presence in the dressage ring.

Breeders look for good structure, size, and athleticism—described by one breeder as, "eighteen hands that can move." The ideal is a broad chest and high stepping action.

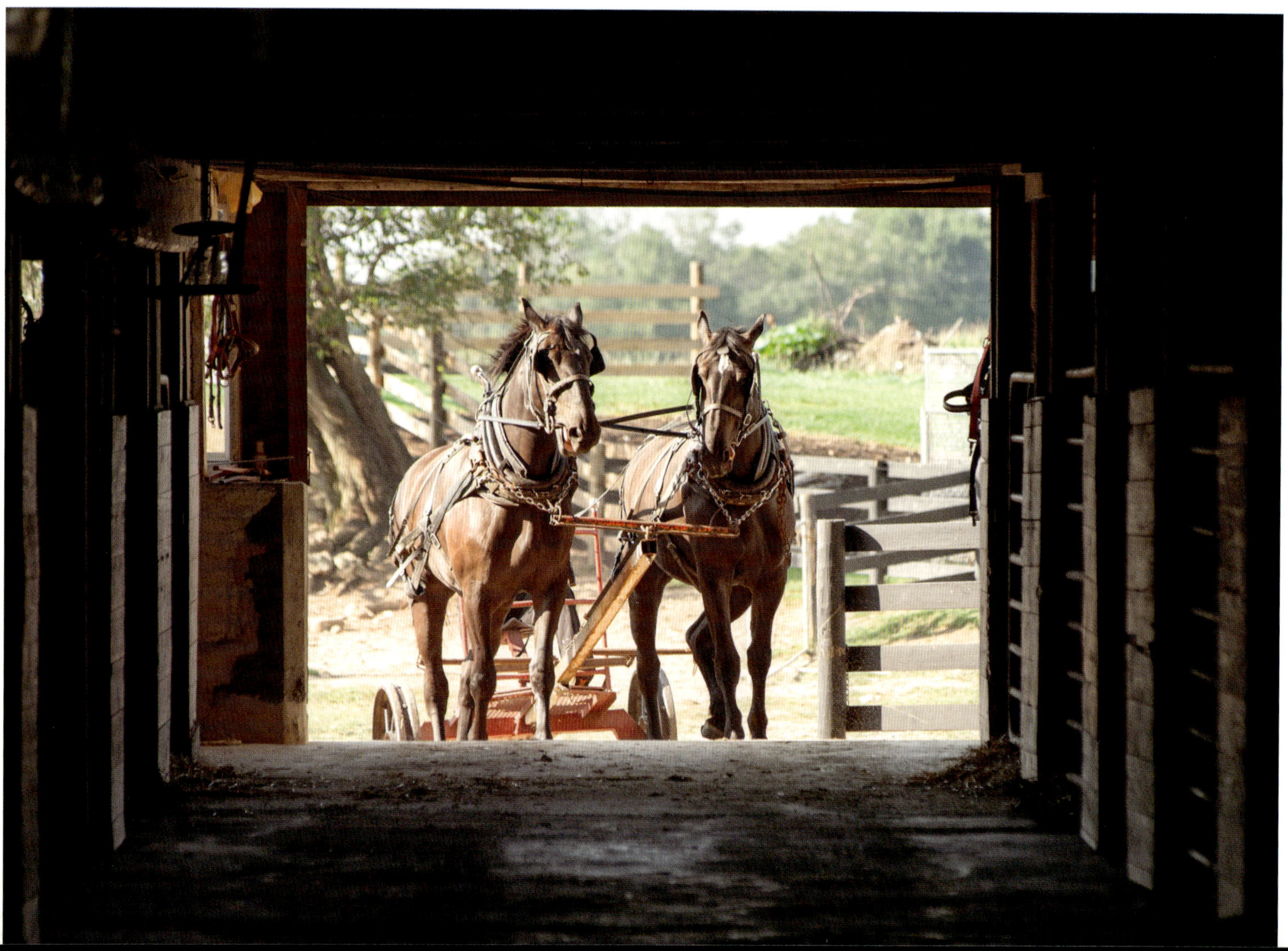

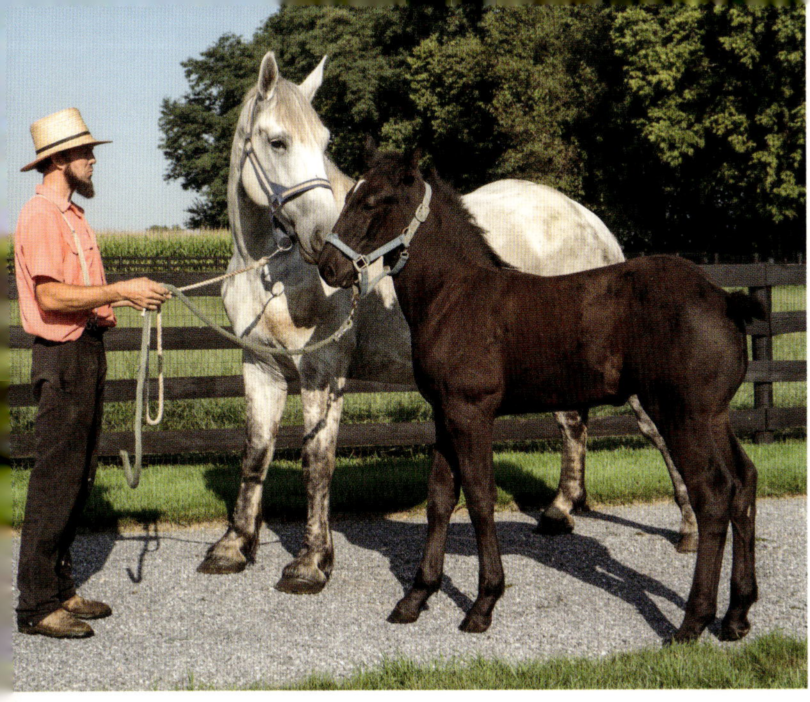

Most Percheron foals are born black or a very dark gray-brown. Depending on their parentage, some turn gray, then white as they age. Netan's owner expects that his seven-week-old colt, *left,* will be gray. The mare, Mystery, still has black legs; "they're the last to go."

Five months later as a yearling at auction, *bottom left,* Netan's coat was just starting to show a dusting of gray at his forehead and at the top of his neck.

Matching a pair of gray or white Percherons can be tricky because they may be at different stages in their color transition. The dealer who offered the pair below, ages seven and nine, said they would make good wedding horses.

"They would look pretty pulling a show carriage."

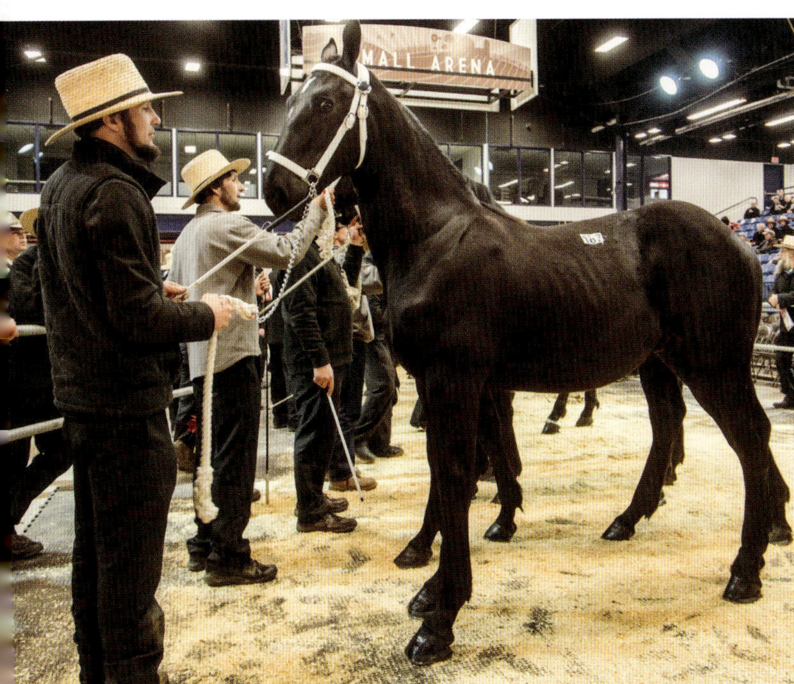

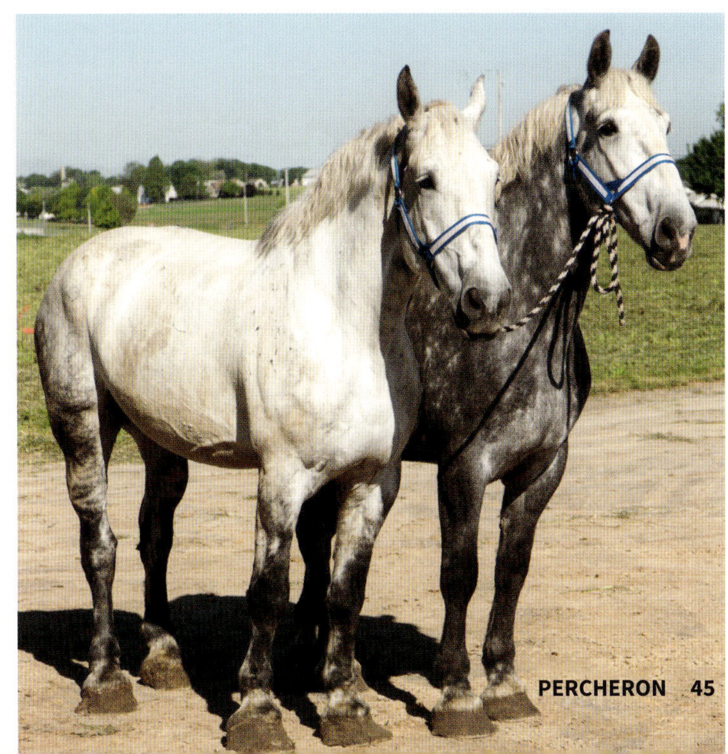

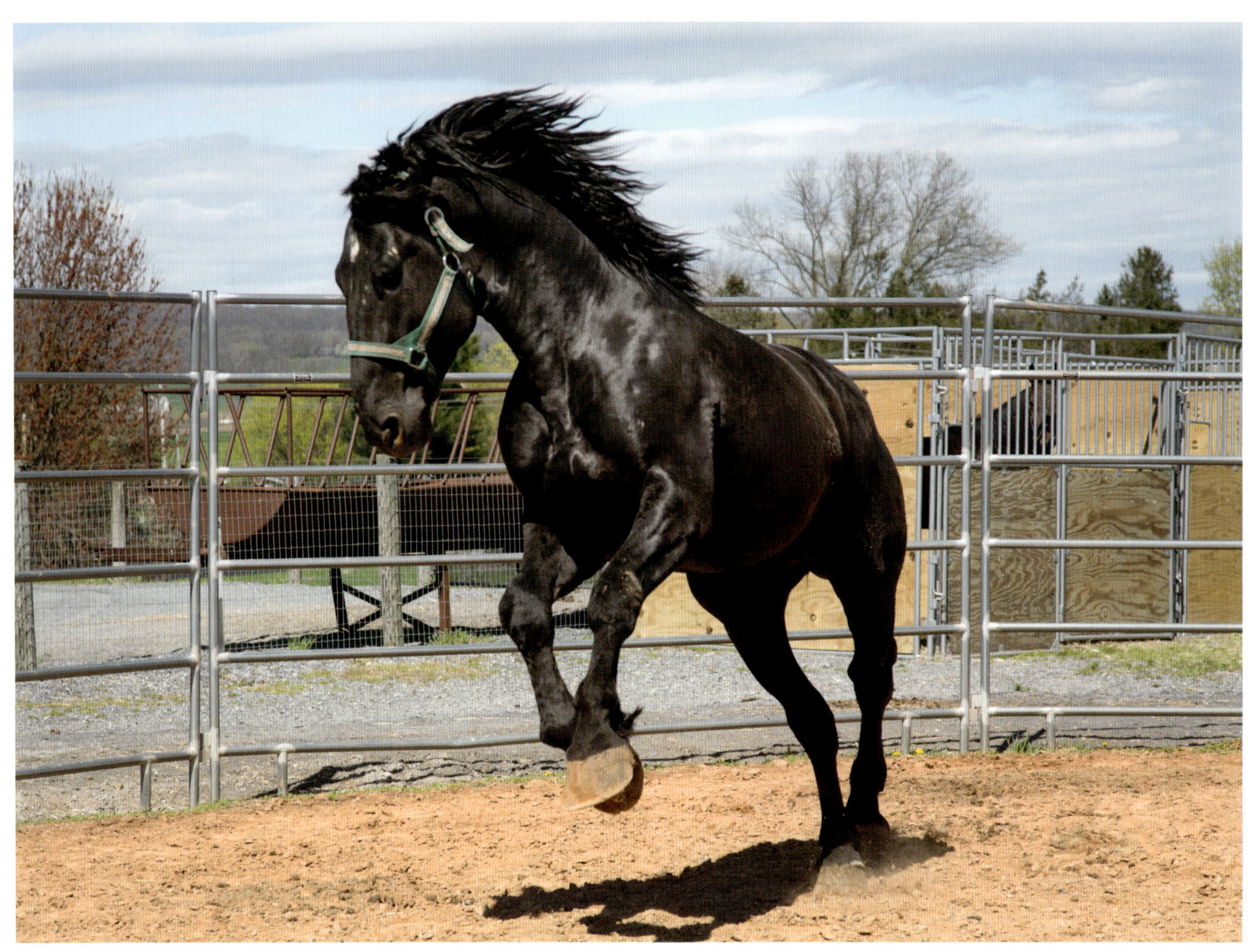

“Percherons have some fire and flash. But they’re also responsive and have a kind eye.”

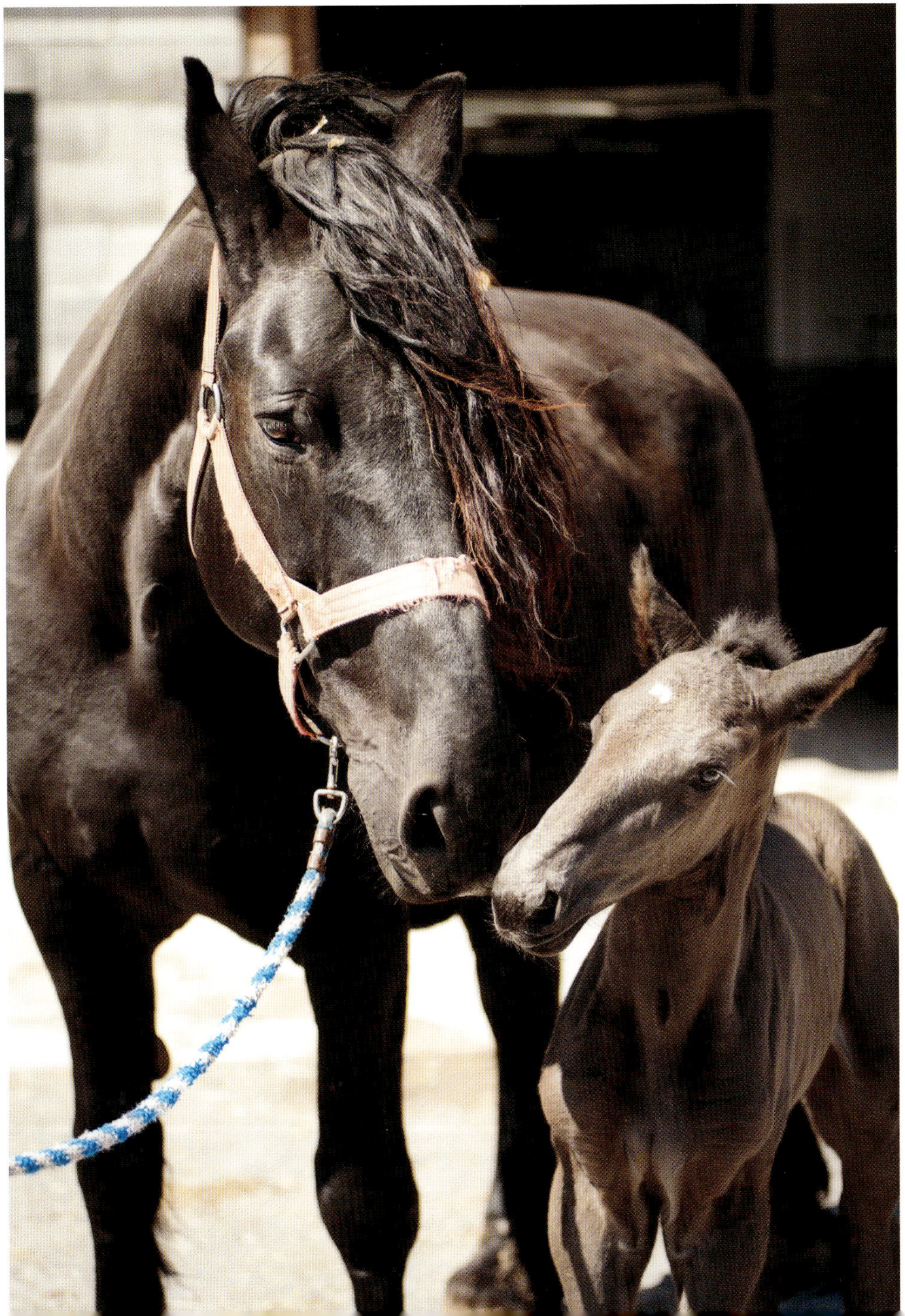

Even at birth, Percheron foals are big boned and muscular. While a carriage horse may weigh 100 to 120 pounds at birth, a draft horse weights 150 pounds or more, depending on the mare's weight.

The colt nuzzling his mother (*left*) is only a few days old, while the handsome fellow below is a sturdy two and a half weeks old.

Stallion Yankee, *facing page,* is 18.3 hands tall and weighs over a ton. At five, he's a popular stud with an excellent pedigree and plenty of energy.

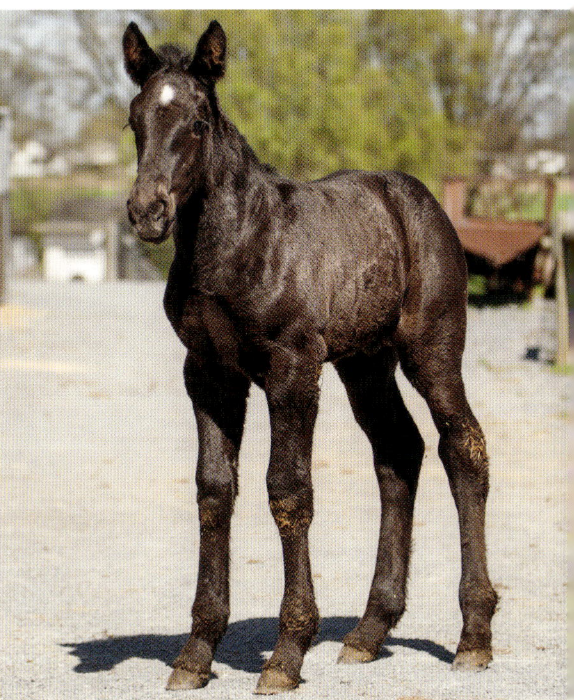

One farmer and Percheron breeder has what he calls a simple training routine when he is preparing a young horse for the harness.

He halter-trains his weanlings and yearlings, and handles them to worm them and clip their feet. Otherwise they are free to run in the meadow.

Harness training begins in the winter when the horse turns two years old. The training is the same whether a horse is destined for the show ring or the field.

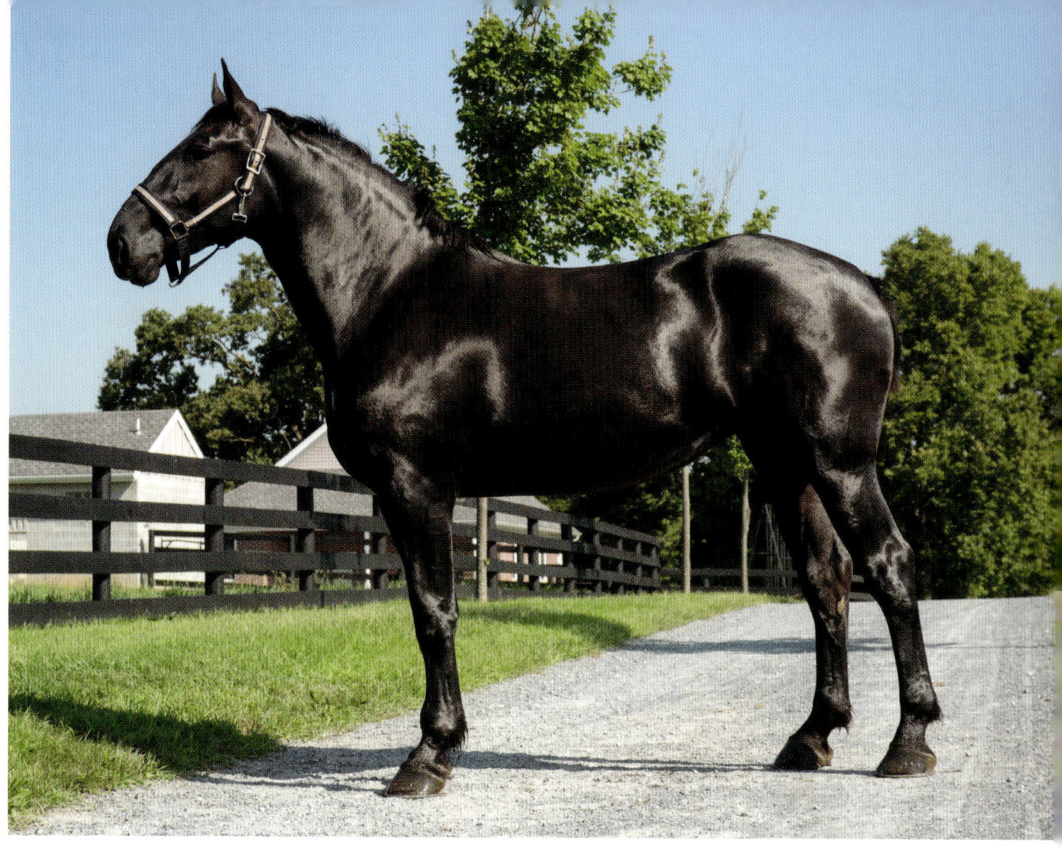

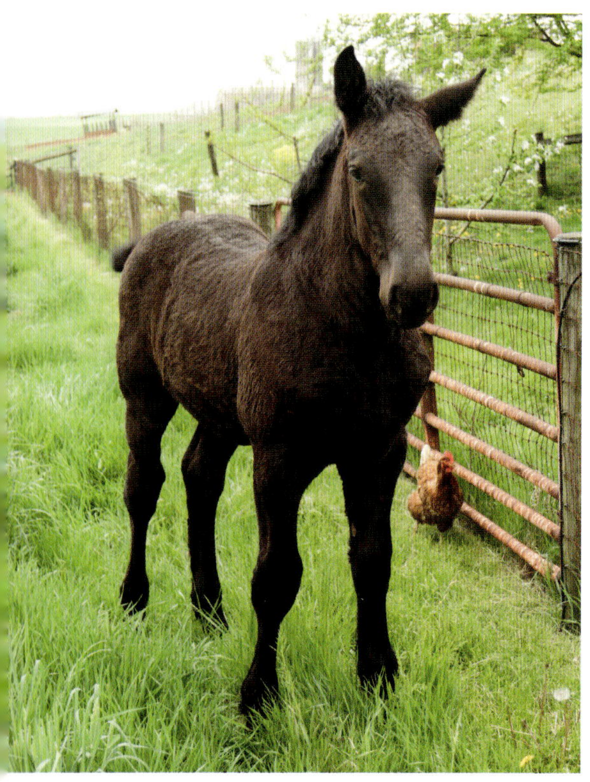

1. Work the horse so he is quiet and calm around people. He should be comfortable being brushed, being clipped into the crossties, and having its feet picked up and handled.
2. Put a surcingle harness (buckled strap with rings) around the horse's upper chest and allow him to get comfortable
3. Work slowly so the horse feels at ease with a bit in his mouth; leave the bit in for a period of time so horse doesn't fight it.
4. Attach a bungie cord at the one side of the bit and to the harness on the same side, with just enough tension so that the horse is comfortable only with its head tilted slightly to that side. This teaches them to yield and to not fight the bit, and it keeps the mouth soft (responsive). This may take a few hours.
5. Repeat on the other side.
6. Attach the lines to the bridle and walk behind; teach the horse to follow direction through reins and voice commands. (giddy up, whoa).

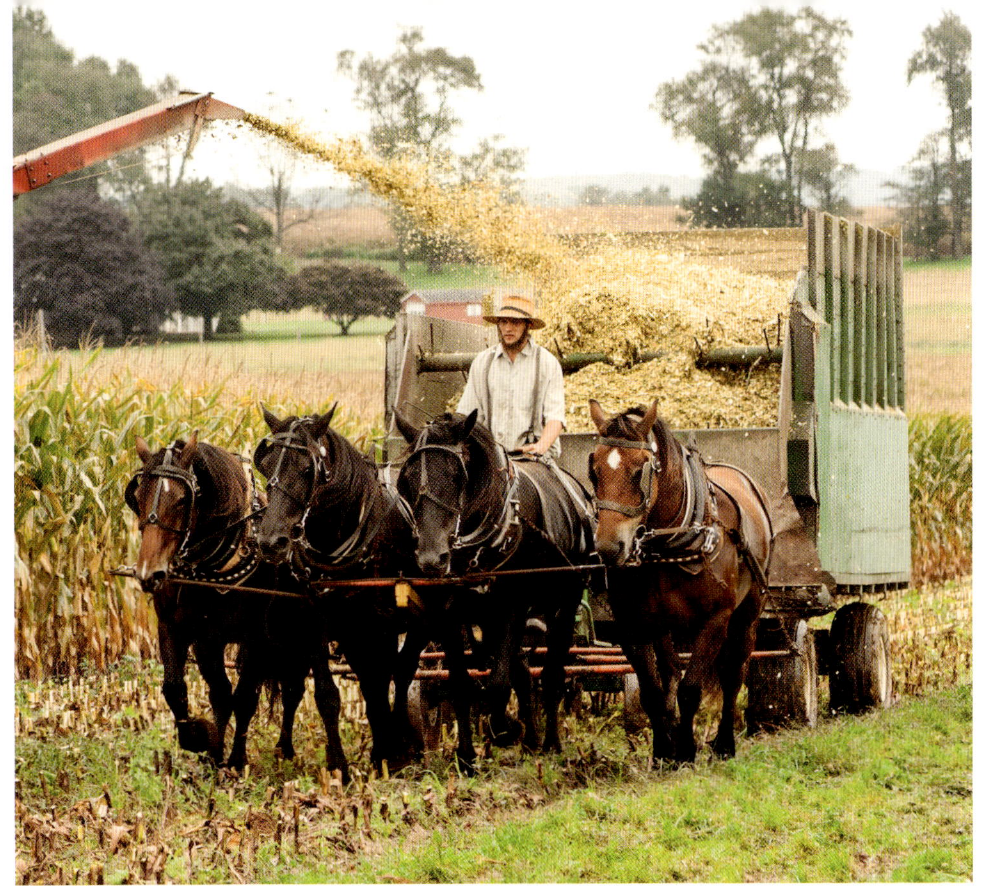

Jayson brought four of his horses—two Percherons and two Percheron-Belgian crosses—to help his neighbor harvest corn. His job was to collect the corn as it was chopped, then haul it from the field to the silo. When he had a full wagon, he guided the team toward the barn. The mud stuck to the horses' hooves, and the wet ground made the hauling hard—the four were unable to pull the load out of the field onto the lane. Jayson unhooked the wagon and headed to the barn to add a horse.

He came back with a Spotted Draft positioned on the outside, and with one of his leads switched out of the center. Some horses remember a failure and don't try very hard the next time they're asked to do the same thing. This mare was still willing to pull, but had lost her enthusiasm to lead.

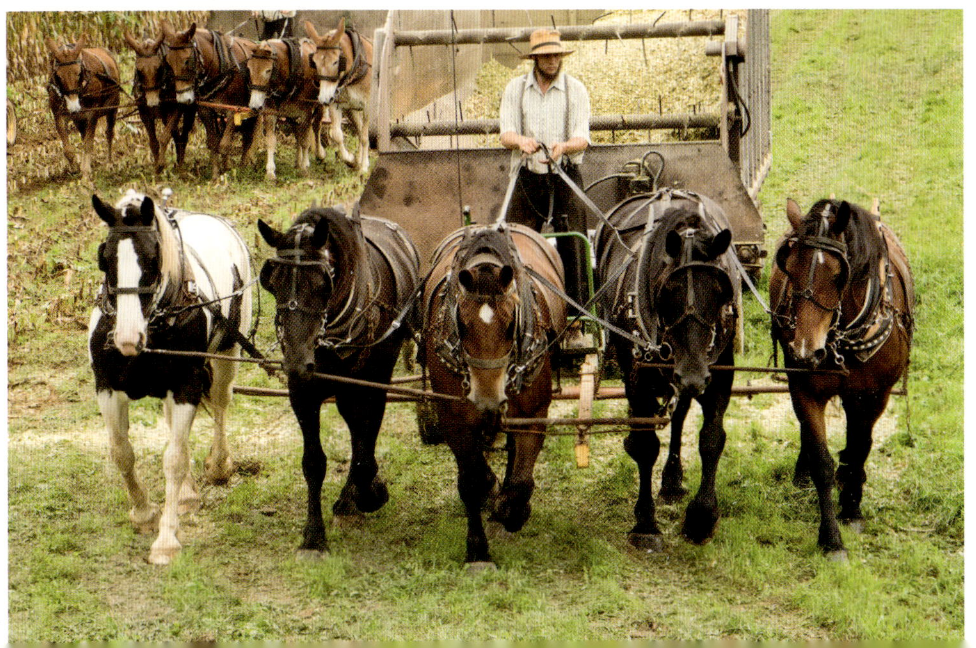

"If she could quit one time she'll think she can quit the next time."

Melissa and Reagan, spirited two-year-olds, *right,* were being trained to the harness in preparation to sell as three-year-olds. Amos worked them for short periods pulling light equipment, such as a hay rake.

The whole family helped when he took his yearlings and three-year-olds to a draft horse sale in Harrisburg in January. His sister-in-law brushed their coats, one daughter braided forelocks, and another daughter polished hooves. His father supervised.

When the hammer fell at the auction, Amos was pleased. He loves the idea that a young one he raised might be bought by a company that sponsors a Percheron six-horse hitch.

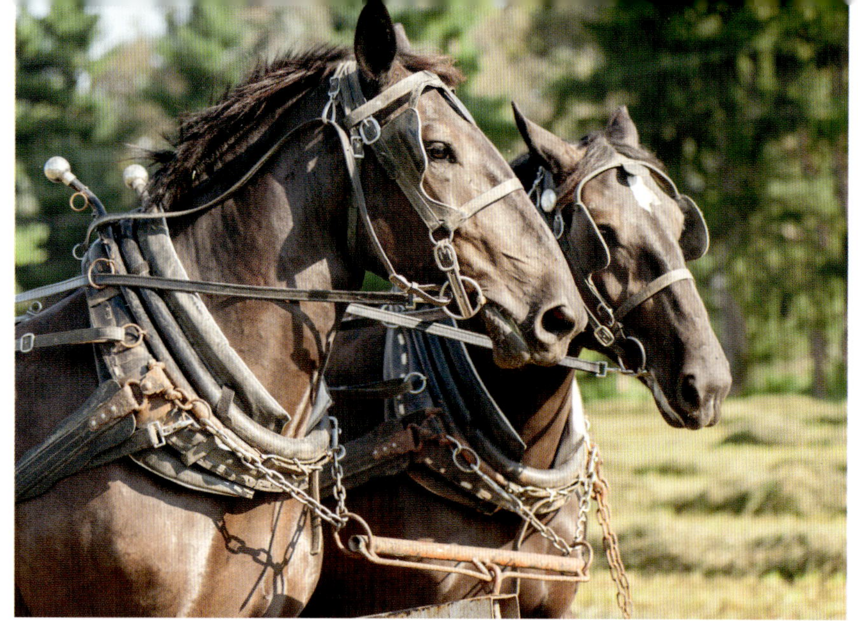

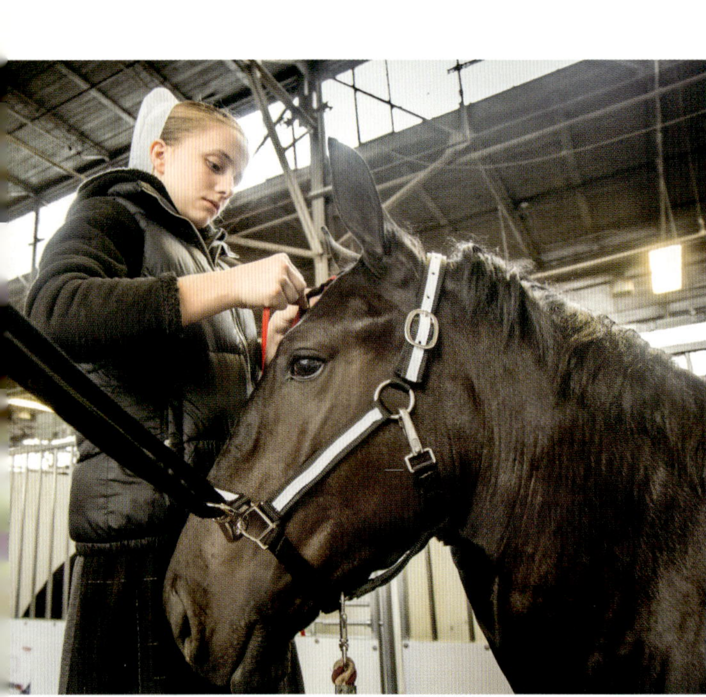

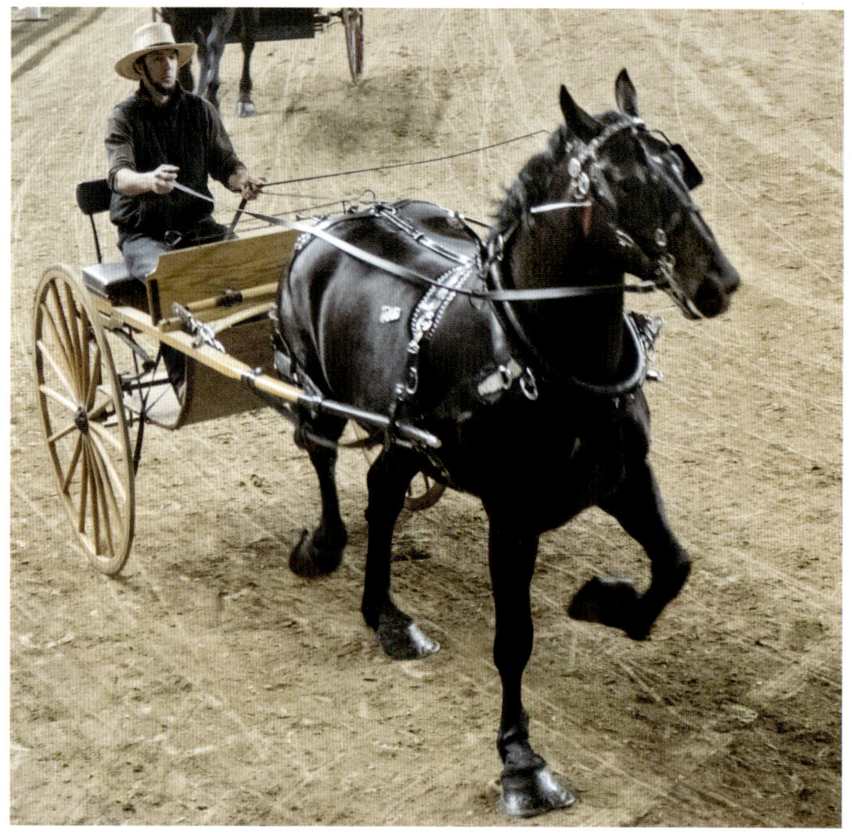

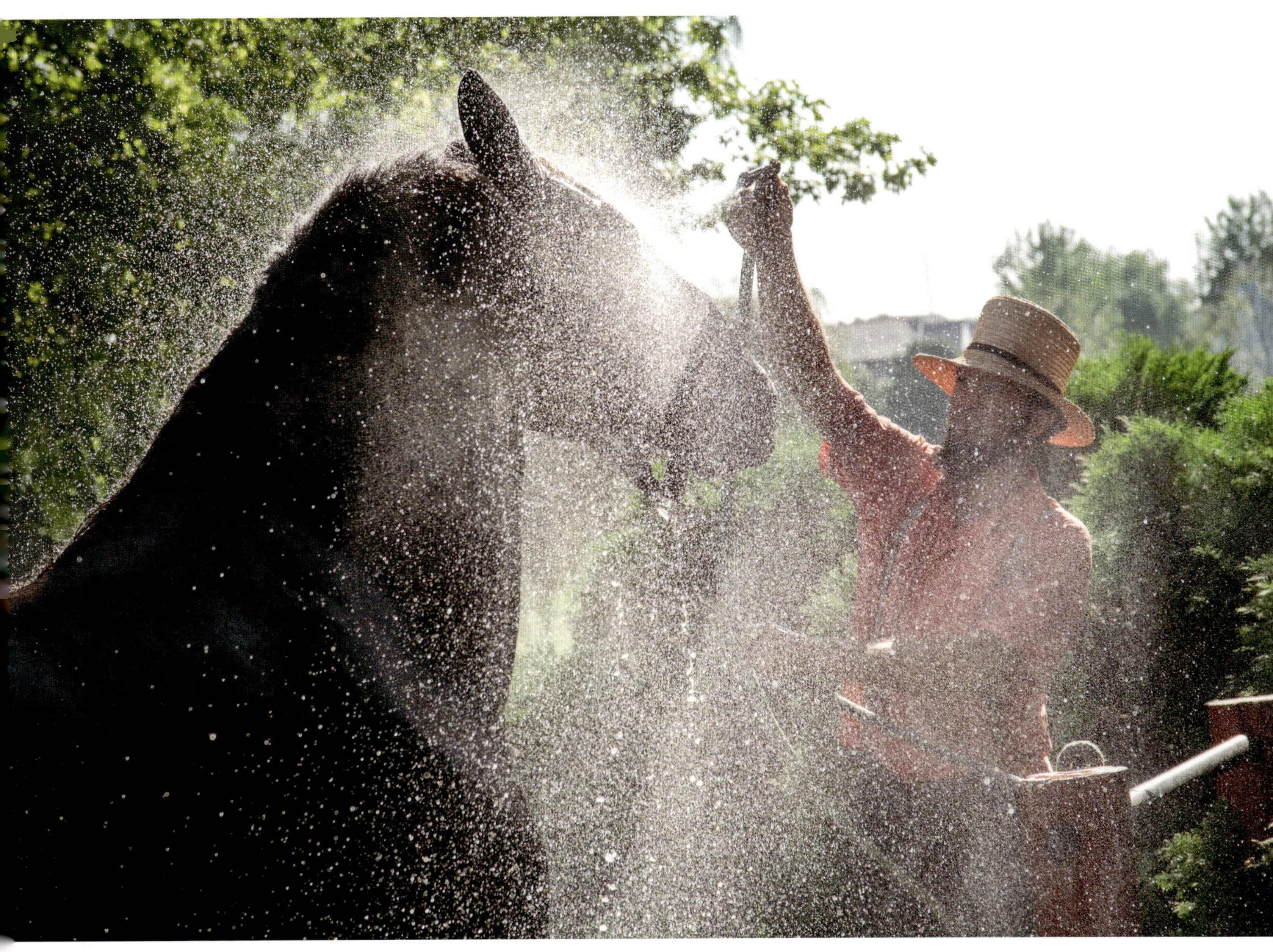

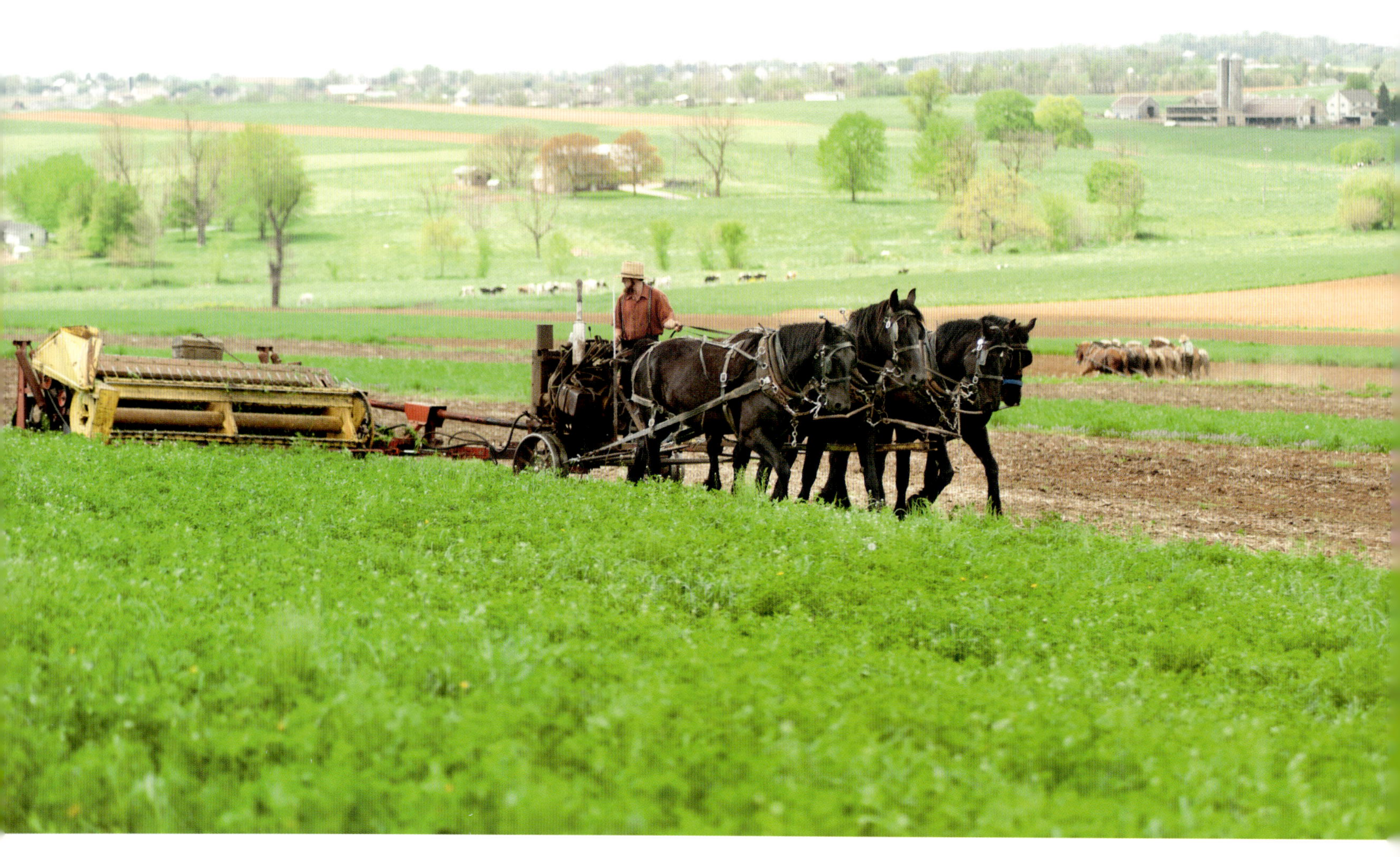

"At first it looks like a lot, but then you get going and get it done."

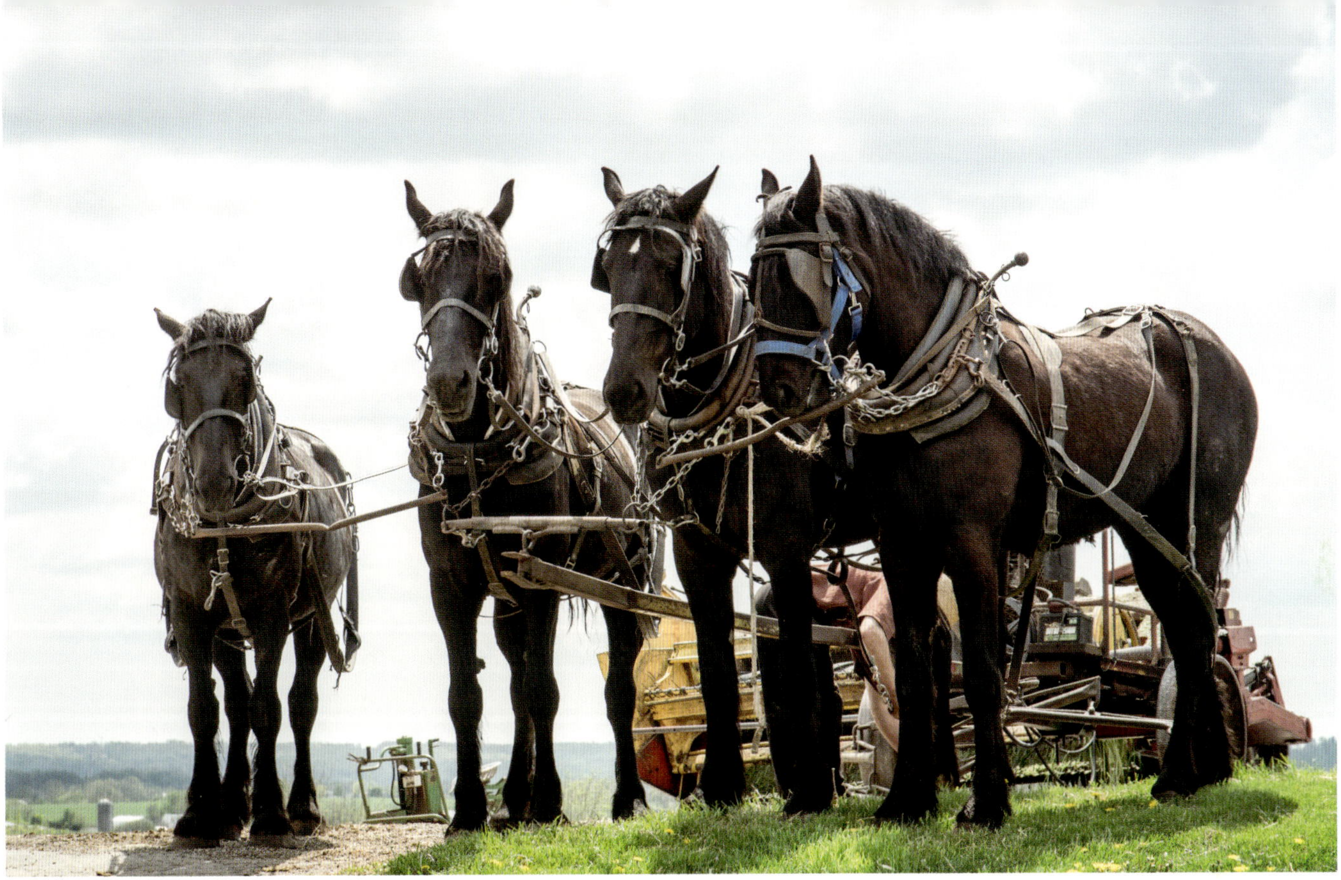

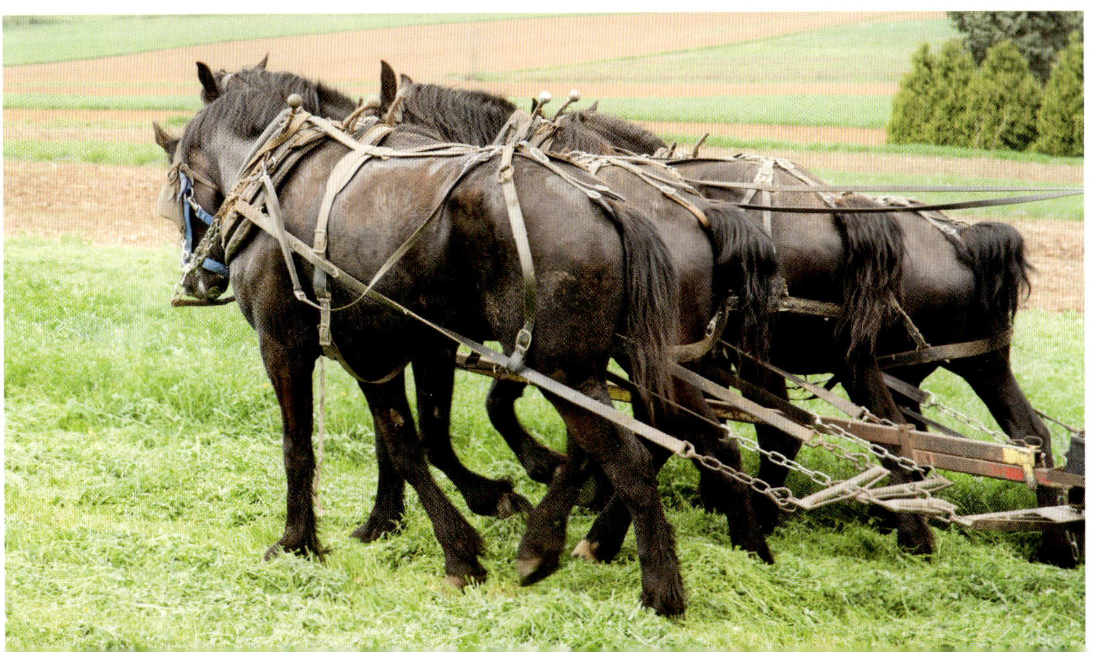

Esh hitched four of his mares, Tina, Angela, Mymy, and Angel to the cutter. On this May afternoon, they cut alfalfa prior to raking and baling it to feed to the cows. The horses are fed a less rich blend of alfalfa and grass. Alfalfa is planted every few years and is harvested four or five times each season.

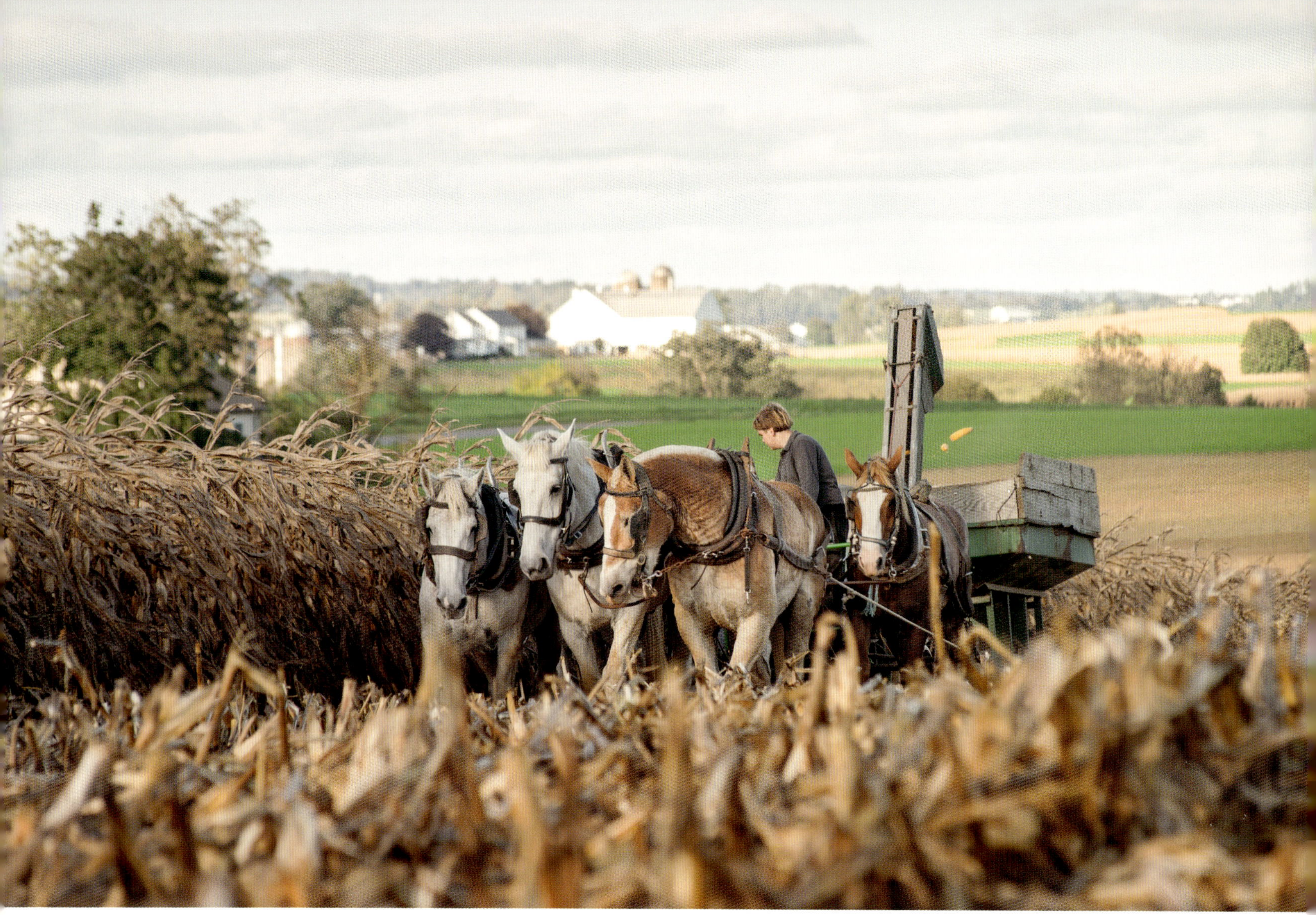

Joseph drove his dad's four white Percherons and two Belgians, *above,* as they pulled the corn picker and trailing wagon up and down the rows. When the wagon was filled, Joseph's next younger brother, *facing page*, guided the white Percherons, Bill and Bess, toward the barn. Two younger brothers were along for the ride. They unloaded the ears into the corn crib, then headed back to the field to exchange the empty wagon for a full one.

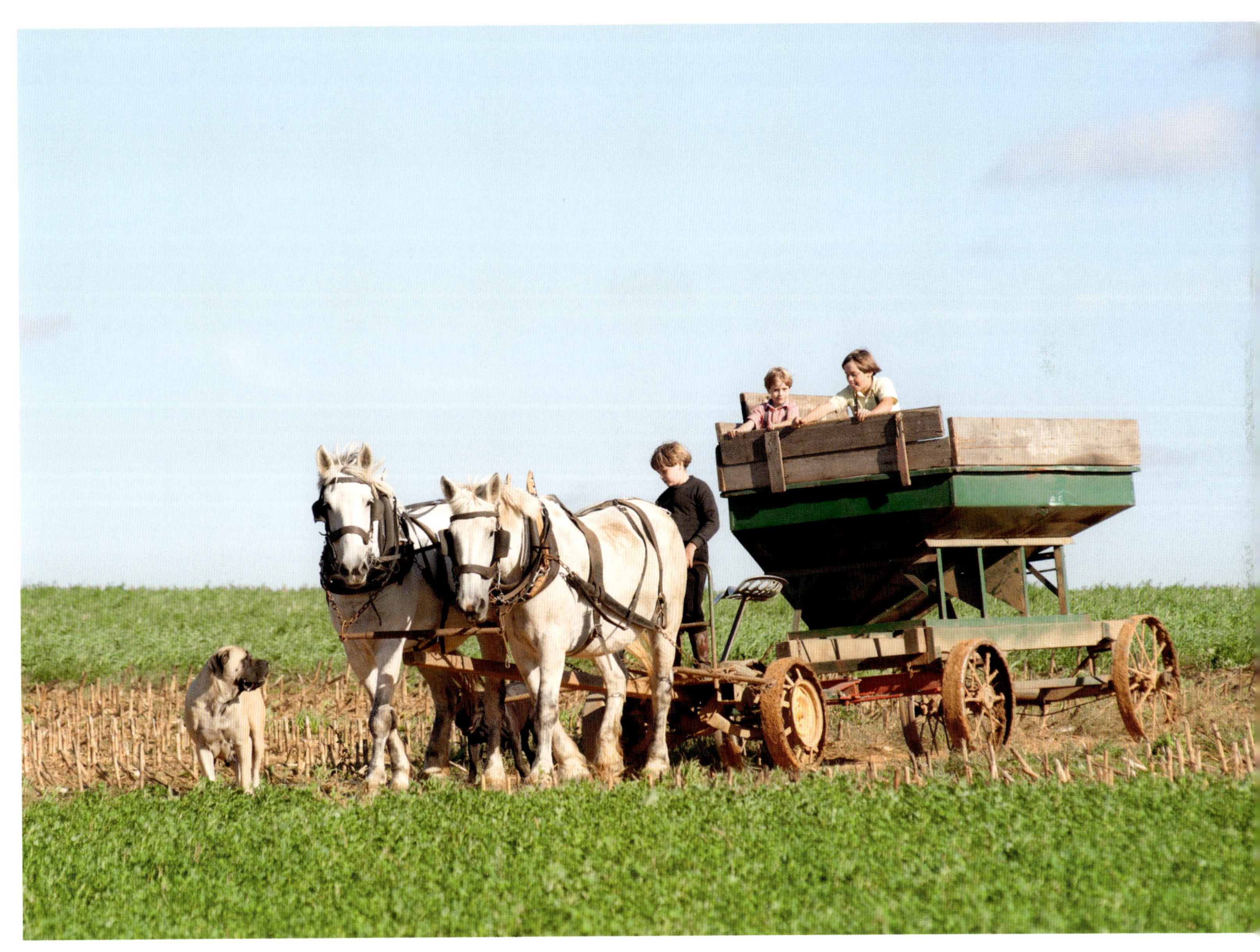

"The boys are good workers."

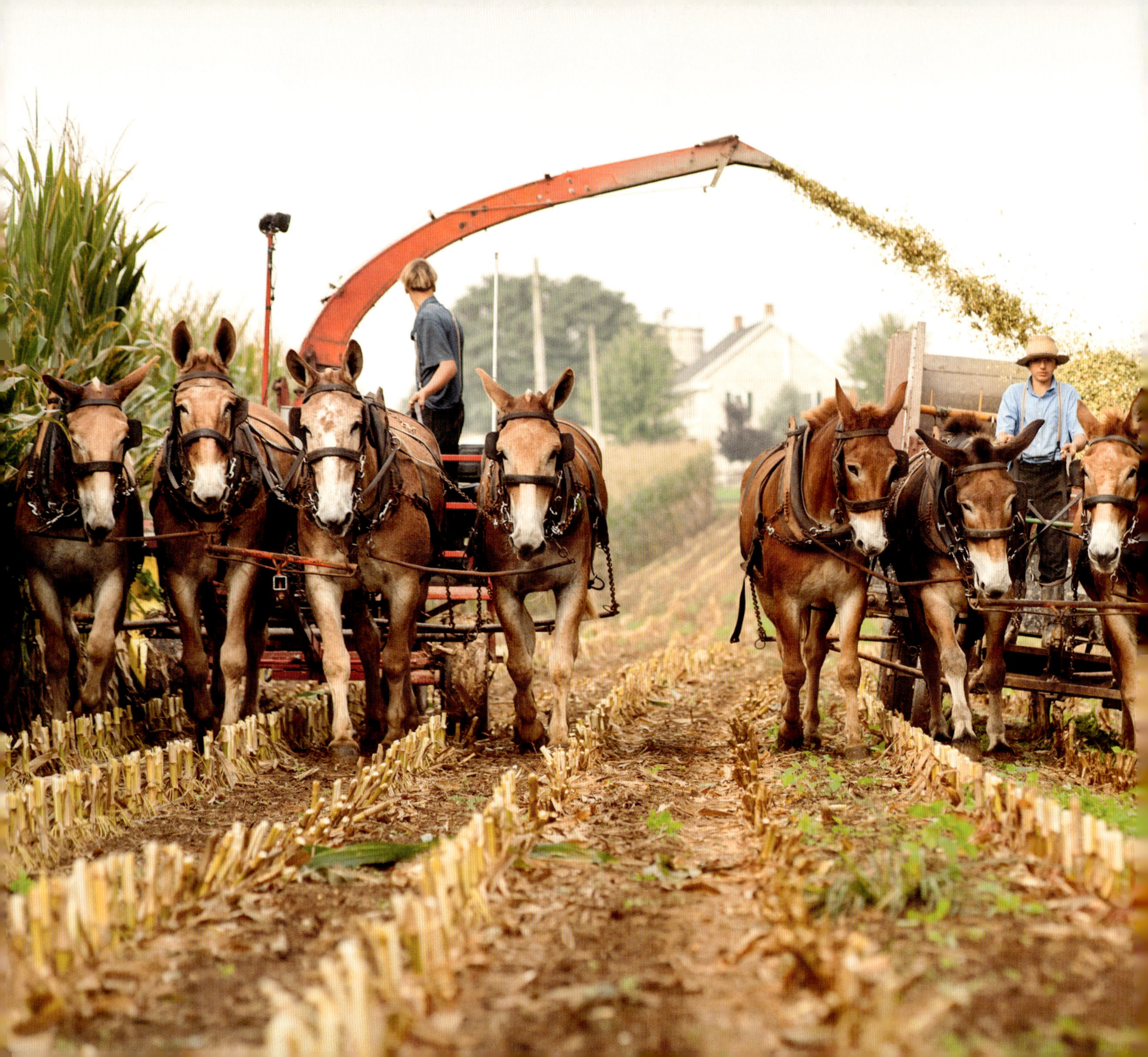

Mule

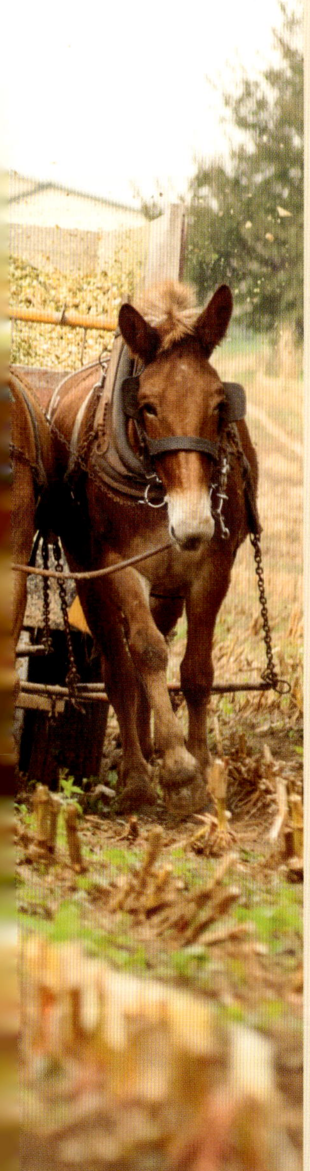

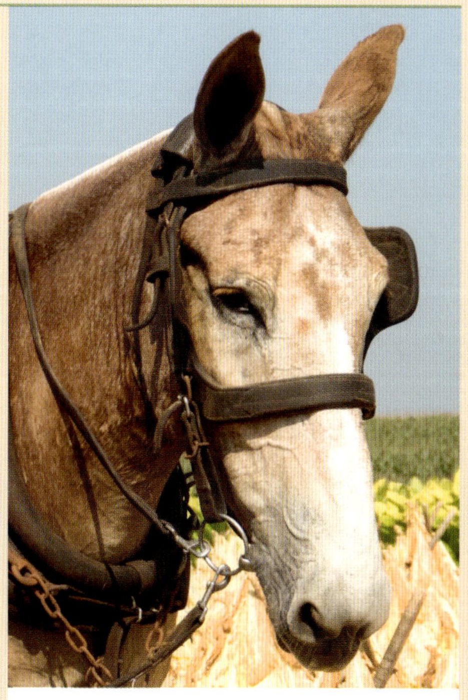

Junior's fields are across the road from those of his son and two brothers, one of whom works the family's home farm. His niece's family occupies the next farm over and a nephew's farm is just over the rise. This is mule country. Altogether the extended family owns more than three-dozen mules.

When it is time to harvest in the late fall, everyone pitches in, picking corn at each farm in turn. Cousins and siblings work side by side, guiding teams of mules in a practiced choreography. The mules pulling the picker and wagons step neatly within the 30 inches between rows of corn.

Mules have a reputation for stubbornness. Not true, says Junior. They learn quickly, follow commands, and work hard. He maintains that training is easy. "Mules learn on the job: tie a green mule to another mule rather than to the center shaft and he'll catch on pretty quickly how to pull."

"You stare at their rumps for hours. At least with mules you can see their ears."

Height: 15–17hh

Weight: 1,100–1,400 lbs

Colors: from both parents, light muzzle, brown or tan colored points

Both horses and mules are valued for their strength and skill as draft animals—though usually not by the same person. Farmers typically prefer one or the other and seldom mix mules and horses in a team. Mule fans and horse fans will quickly point out the value of their choice but are careful not to criticize their neighbors who have a different preference.

Working mules are a crossbreed between a Mammoth Jackstock jack donkey and a draft horse mare. A mule from a Belgian mare is generally sorrel or blond, while a mule from a Percheron mare is usually white, gray, or black. Most have light muzzles and may have a star or streak on their noses. They inherit many of the mare's characteristics such as structure, muscling, color, and height.

Compared to their dams, mules have more pronounced Roman noses, narrower necks, generally longer backs, tufted tails, less leg feathering, and much-smaller feet. A mule's ear length easily reaches 9 or 10 inches—shorter than its donkey sire's 12-inch ears and longer than the modest 7-inch ear length of its dam.

The mule combines the patience, sure-footedness and endurance of a donkey with the vigor and strength of the horse.

Horses originated in the Asian steppes and have an ingrained tendency to run from danger. In contrast, mules, which came from North Africa via their donkey roots, are more likely to stand their ground.

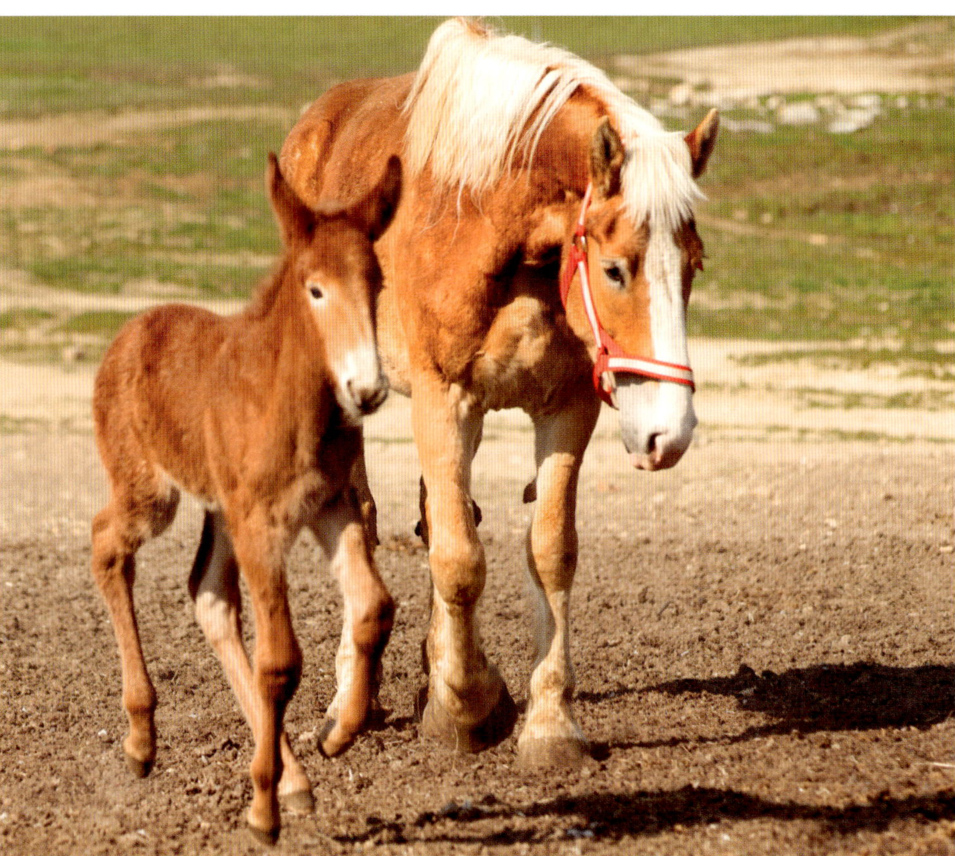

Hence mules may appear obstinate, when in reality they are demonstrating their intelligence and common sense. They will strongly resist or simply not do something that they perceive as nonsense.

Like horses, mules may begin training at age two or three but mature more slowly than horses and are not fully grown until age four or five. A mule trainer must work slowly and deliberately, taking the time to break things into logical, sequential, doable steps. A mule will quickly establish and rigidly adhere to patterns.

A mule has high expectations for excellence from its leader; horses are intelligent, too, but are more accepting and willing to forgive grievances.

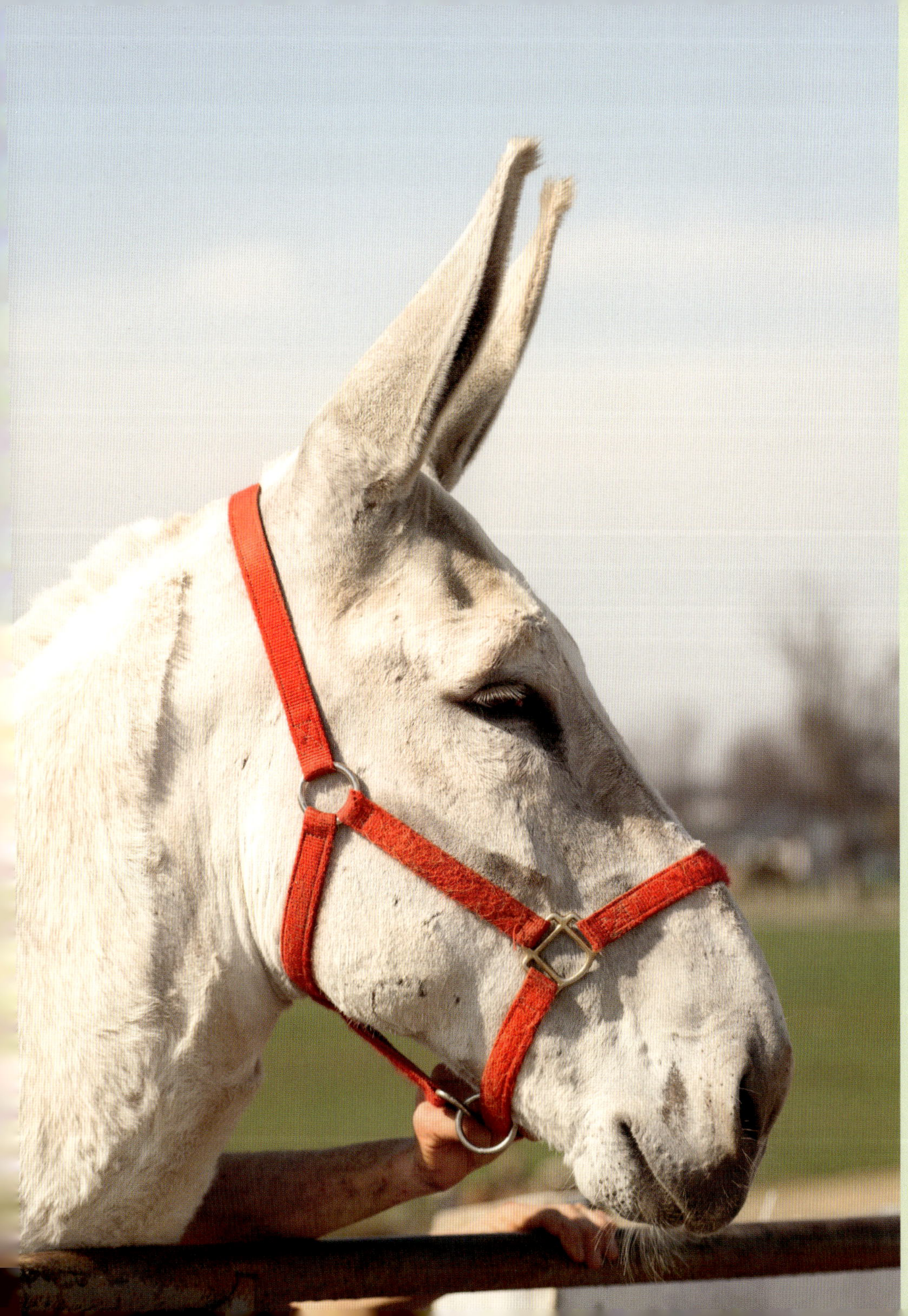

Mammoth Jackstock Donkey

The largest breed of donkey, a Mammoth Jackstock stands 14.2 hands or taller and weighs from 900 to 1,400 pounds.

Jackstock jacks (male donkeys) are used largely to produce mules. Since they are relatively rare, they're usually not gelded. The heavier jacks are crossed with draft horses to produce draft mules, while the lighter jacks are bred to light mares to produce saddle mules.

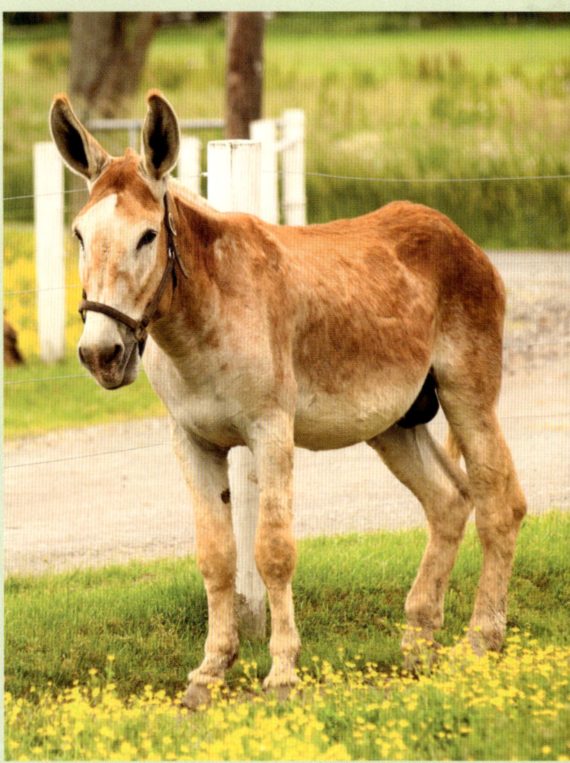

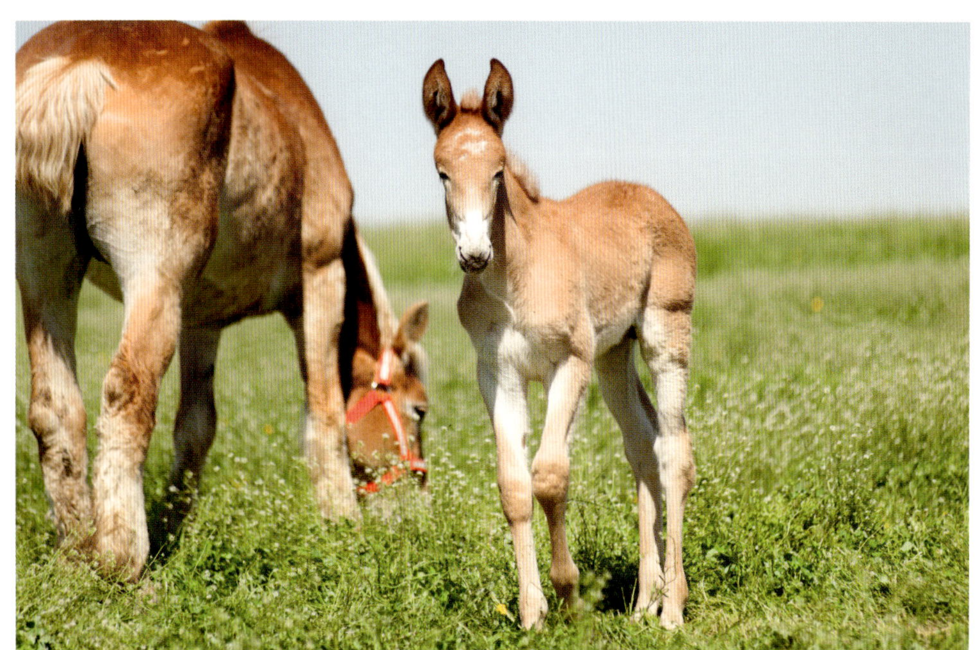

Farmers who work with mules are well acquainted with their hardiness and strength. Mules are more sure footed than horses, work better under difficult conditions, and thrive when challenged.

As demonstrated by strings of mules that carry riders over rough, scenic terrain in places such as national parks, mules don't mind heights. They can take the heat too, and their strong sense of self-preservation keeps them from overworking or overeating.

When mules are treated with respect and gentleness, they are hardworking and loyal to their owners.

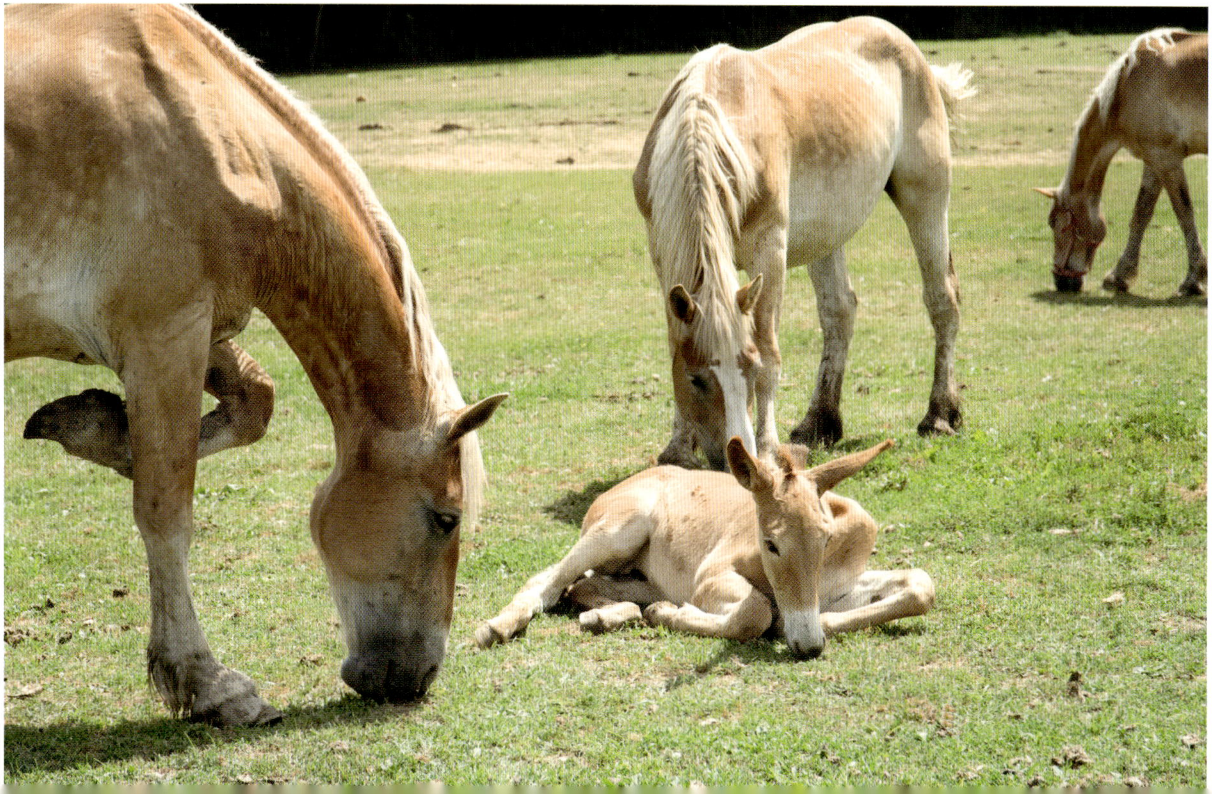

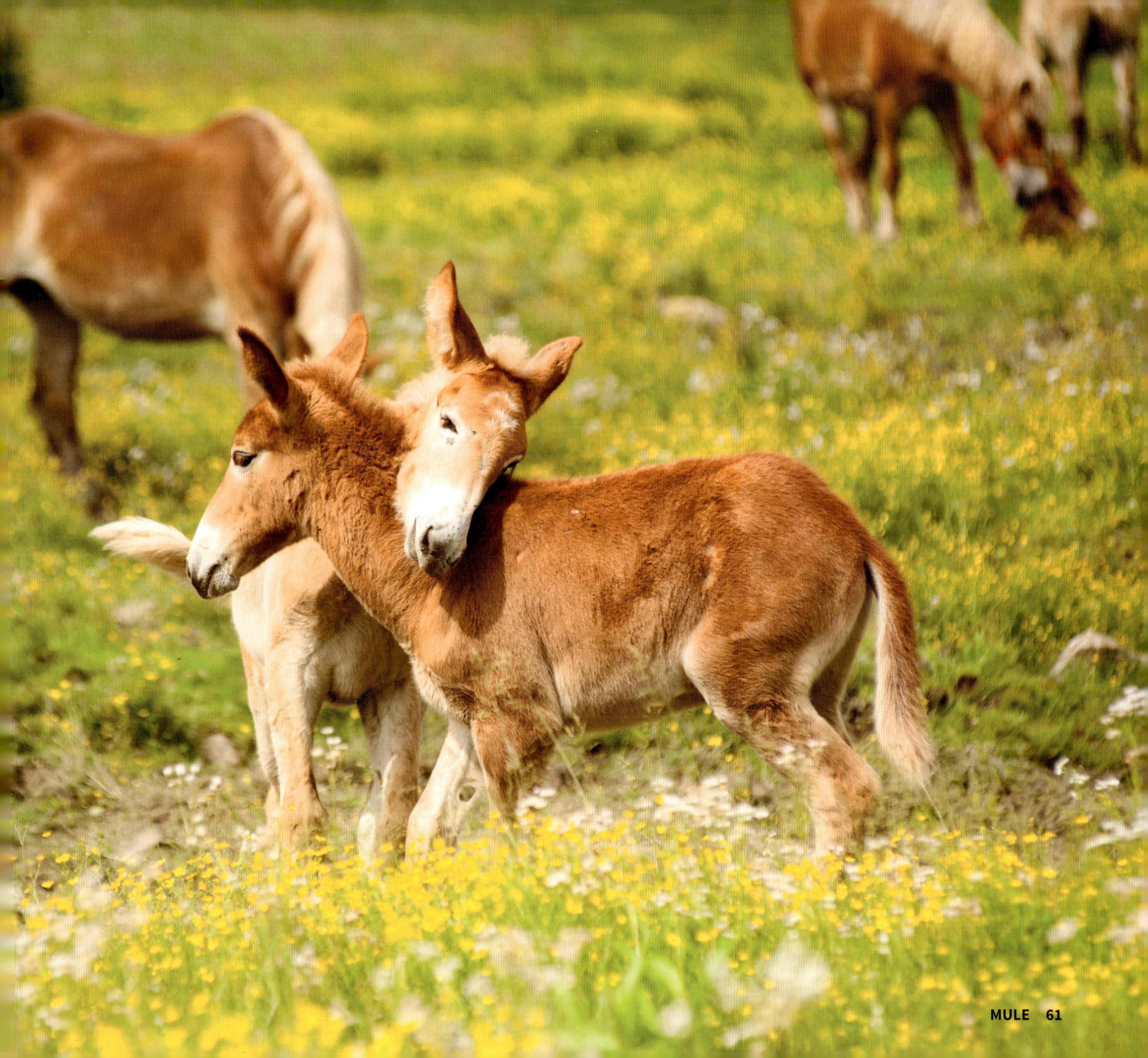

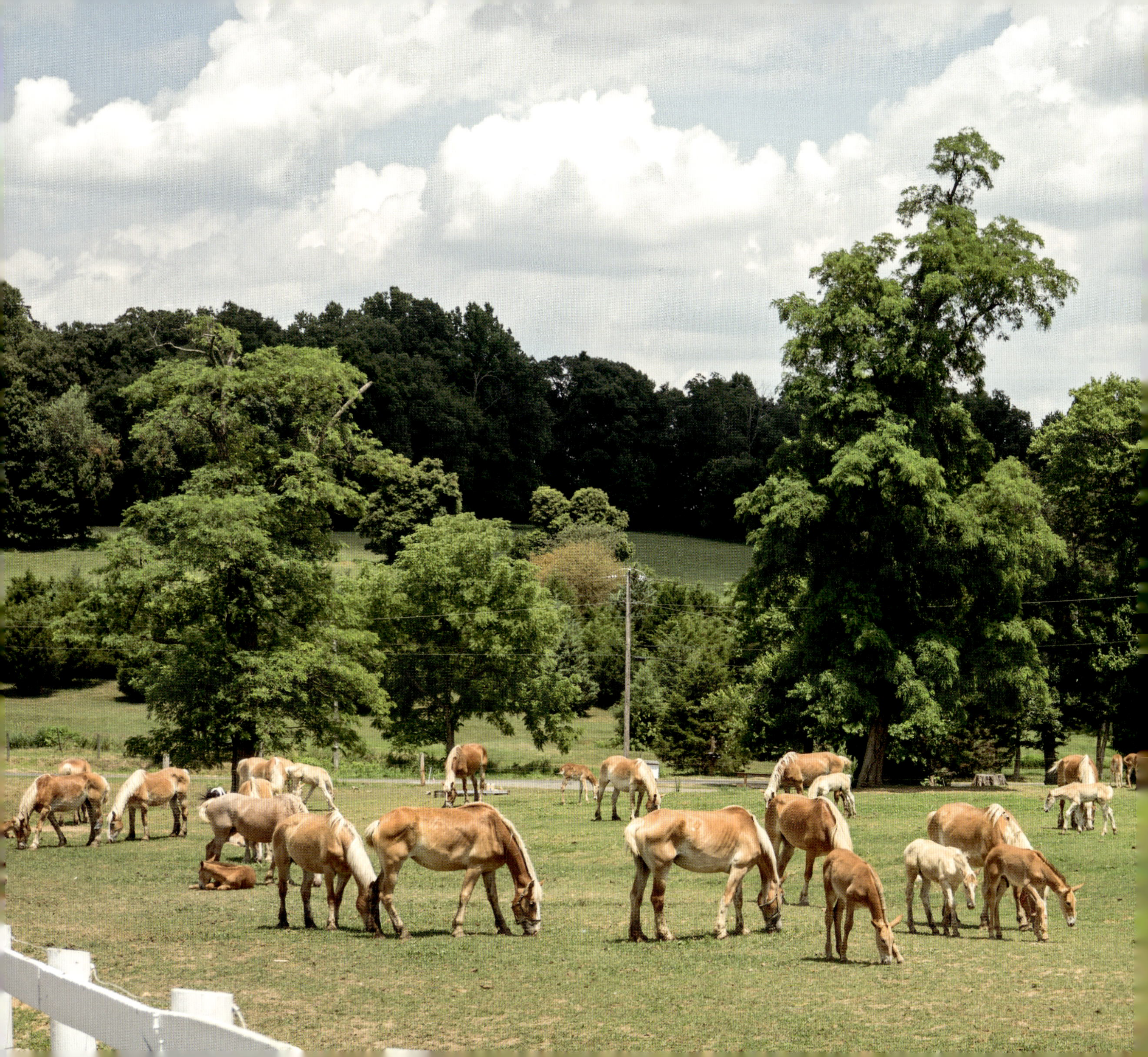

“Two of my mares wouldn’t settle with a donkey, but did settle with a horse. I can’t blame them.”

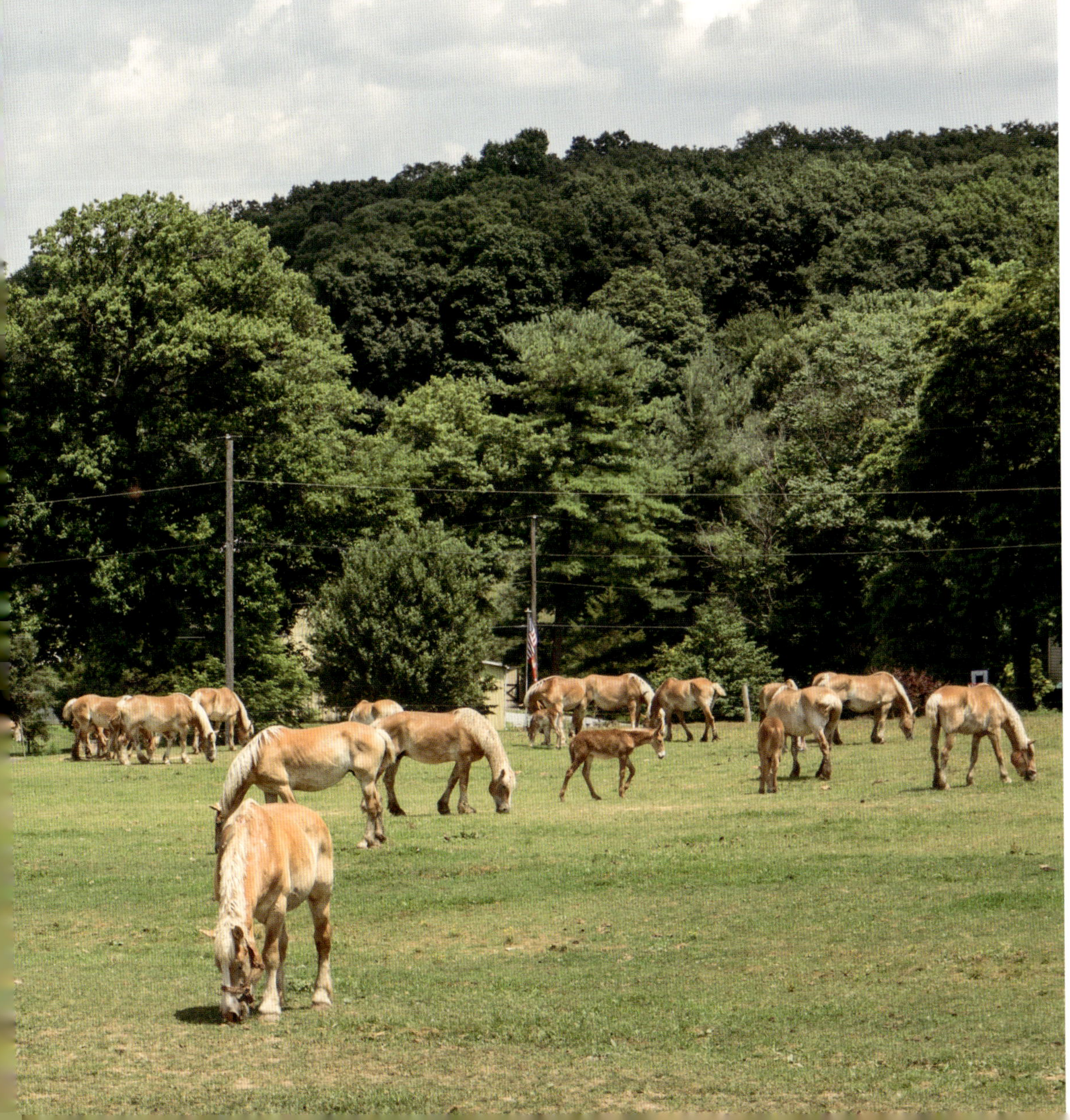

Stoltzfus found great satisfaction in looking out over his herd of Belgian brood mares and their offspring—most of them mules. Since mules rarely reproduce, few farmers breed their own. Stoltzfus specializes in breeding mules for sale, both to work in the field and for the show market. Thirty of his mares gave birth between March and July this year. He expects to sell the foals as weanlings in the fall, many to out-of-state buyers who return them to Lancaster County in a few years nearly grown and ready to be trained.

An estimated 50 percent of draft animals working in Lancaster County are mules. Mules are so woven into the cultural fabric that the Southern Lancaster County School District sports teams are called the Golden Mules.

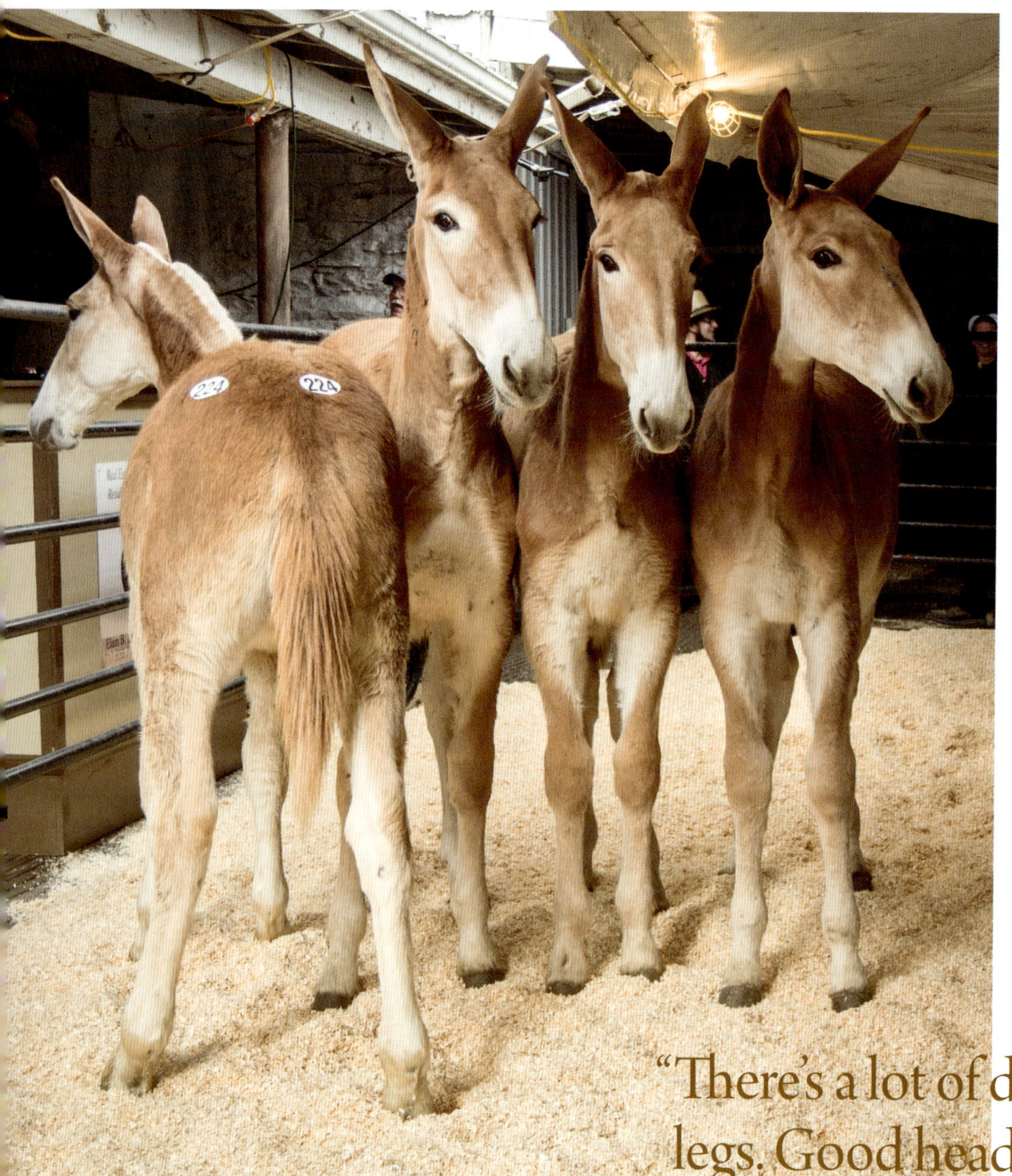

At sale time, Stoltzfus's oldest son directed the young mules into the small arena, four at a time. Thirty-three weanlings, brushed and trimmed to show their best features, were on offer from Stoltzfus and another Lancaster County breeder. They had been given haircuts the week before to "cheer them up." Potential bidders lined the railing, looking at the handwritten sale program. Among the buyers were farmers and dealers from Tennessee, Kentucky, and the Carolinas.

Some of the weanlings bought here will be shown in competitions at ages one to three. Depending on their degree of success, the mules may be back in the county in a few years and sold to work in the field.

One bidder from Tennessee who trains mules for pleasure riding and harness work outlined what he looks for when he buys a mule. The ears should be long and narrow with a hook on the end. The mane, belly, and tail should be blond, though they may get lighter as the mule matures. He also wants to see a broad chest and broad butt—"them is pulling mules."

When the bidding started, the auctioneer highlighted features buyers would appreciate.

"There's a lot of daylight under them legs. Good heads, good necks."

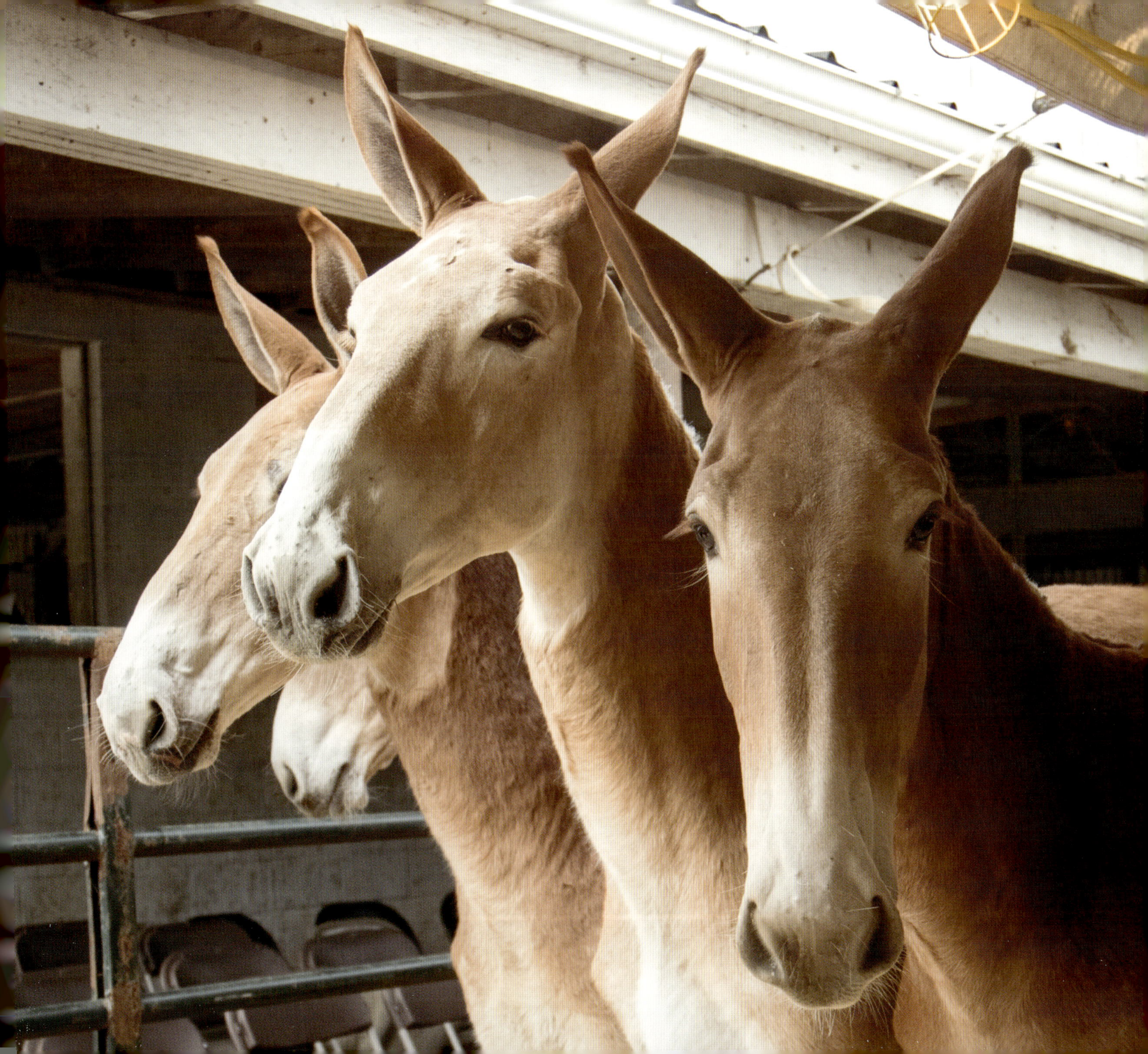

Forty-five minutes after Jacob began harnessing his eight mules, he had them hitched—in two rows of four—to the cart and plow and headed out the drive to the field. His lead mule was at center left. Plowing is the most demanding job he gives his mules each season, and he'd borrowed a mule from his brother to make up the eight.

Most mules in Lancaster County are sorrel-colored offspring of Belgian mares, as is half of Jacob's team. But Jacob is partial to the white and dappled gray coloring of a mule born to a Percheron mare and he hopes to build an all-white team.

Last year he grew corn in this field, followed by winter rye. After plowing and disking this year, he will again plant corn. Next year, it will be alfalfa. Crop rotation keeps the soil's nutrients from being depleted.

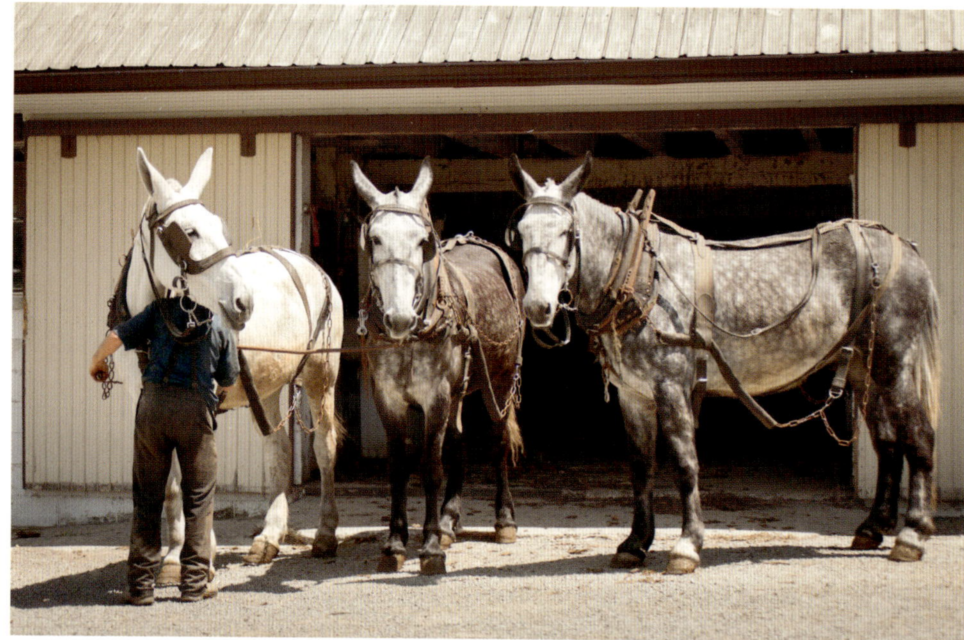

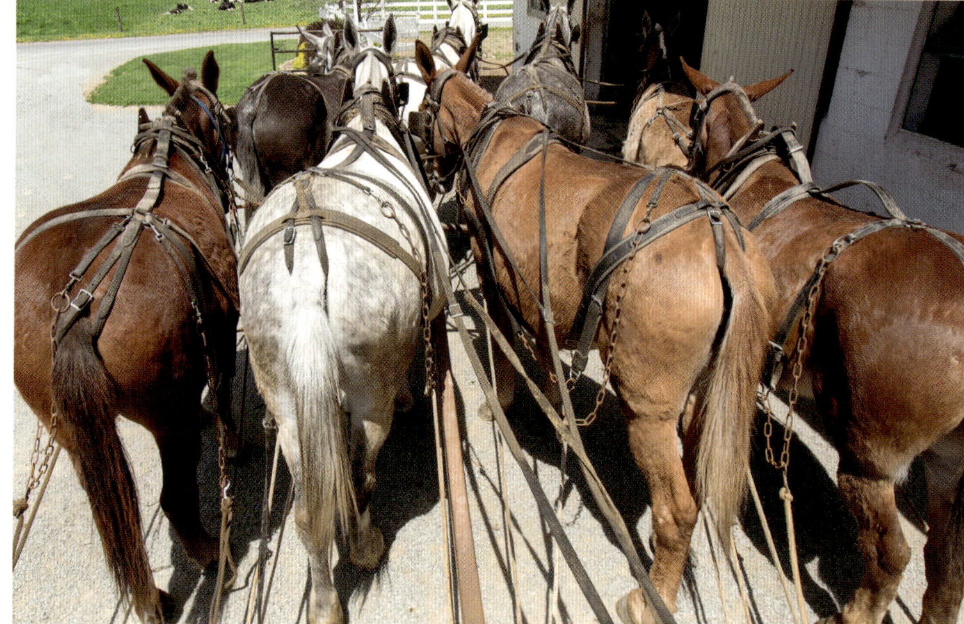

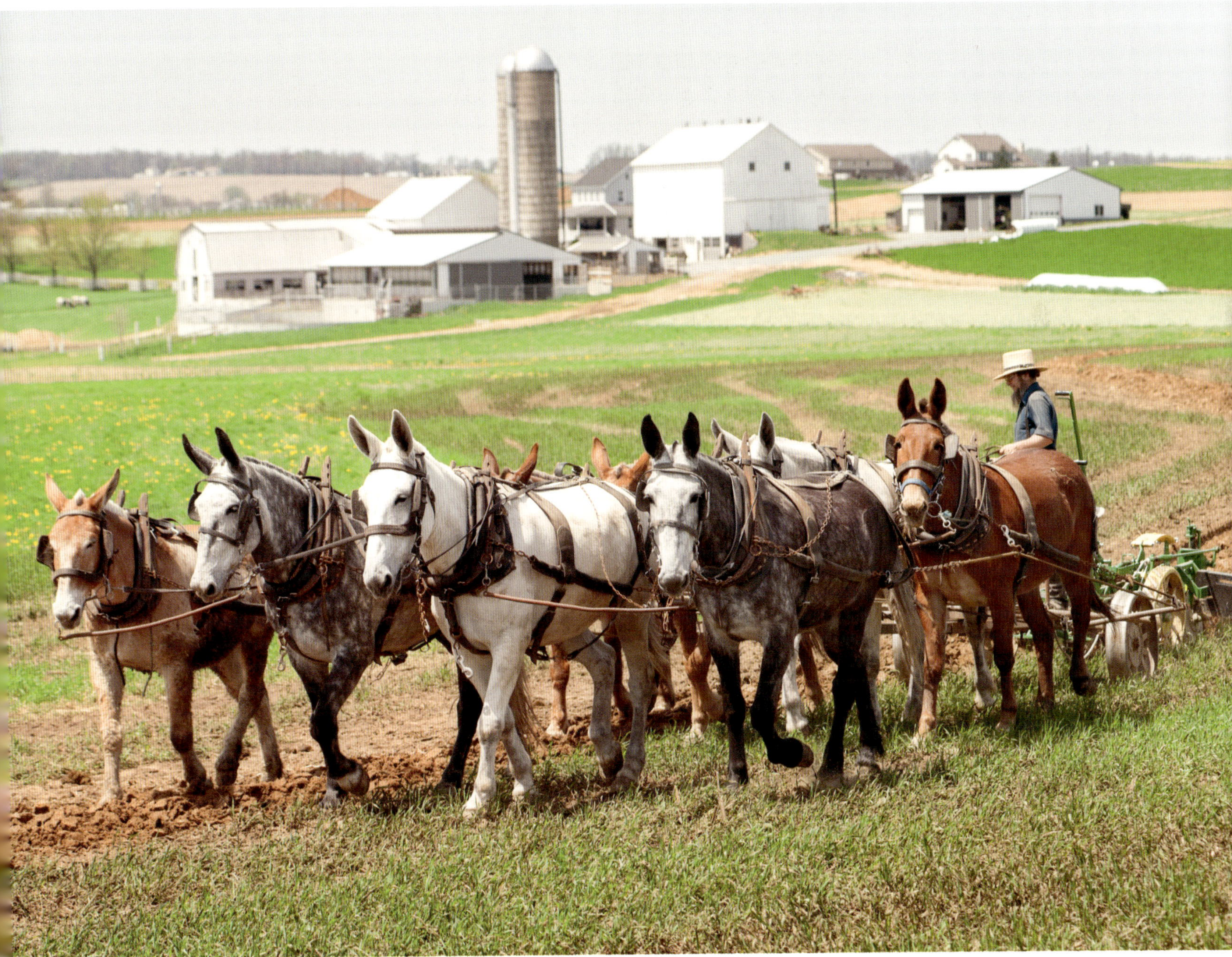

Whenever a flock of young chickens leaves the chicken house and before a new flock comes in, the house must be cleaned and disinfected. The litter, a combination of bedding and manure, must be disposed of. Some farmers contract with an outside buyer to pick it up.

Others spread it on their fields to enrich the coming crop. The nitrogen-rich chicken litter is especially beneficial for fields where corn will be planted.

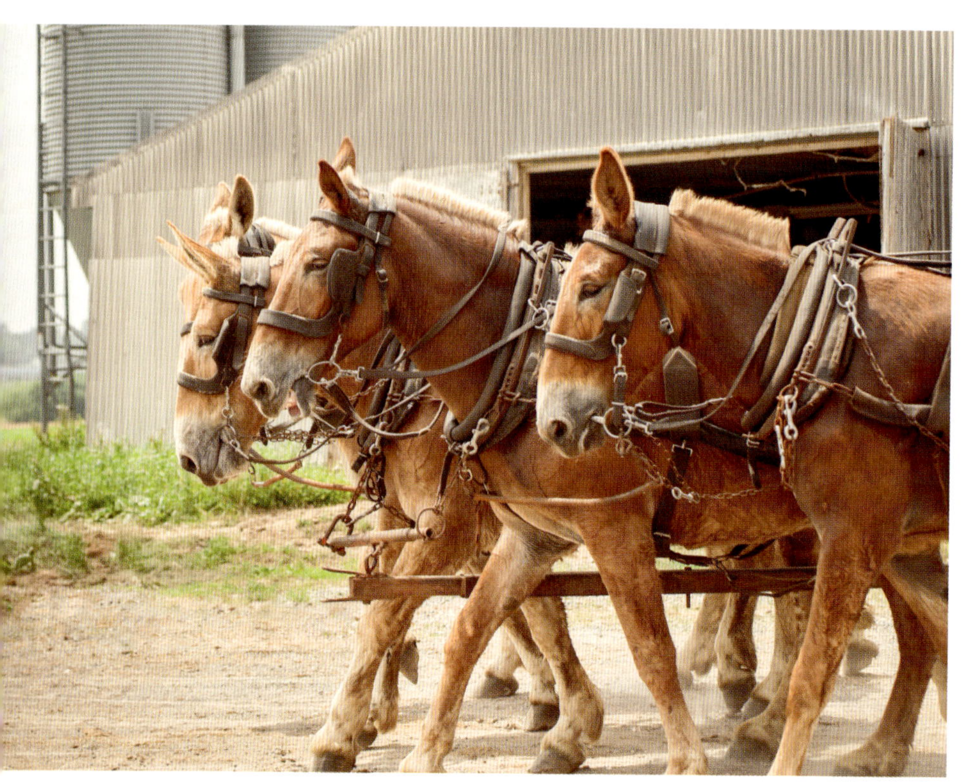

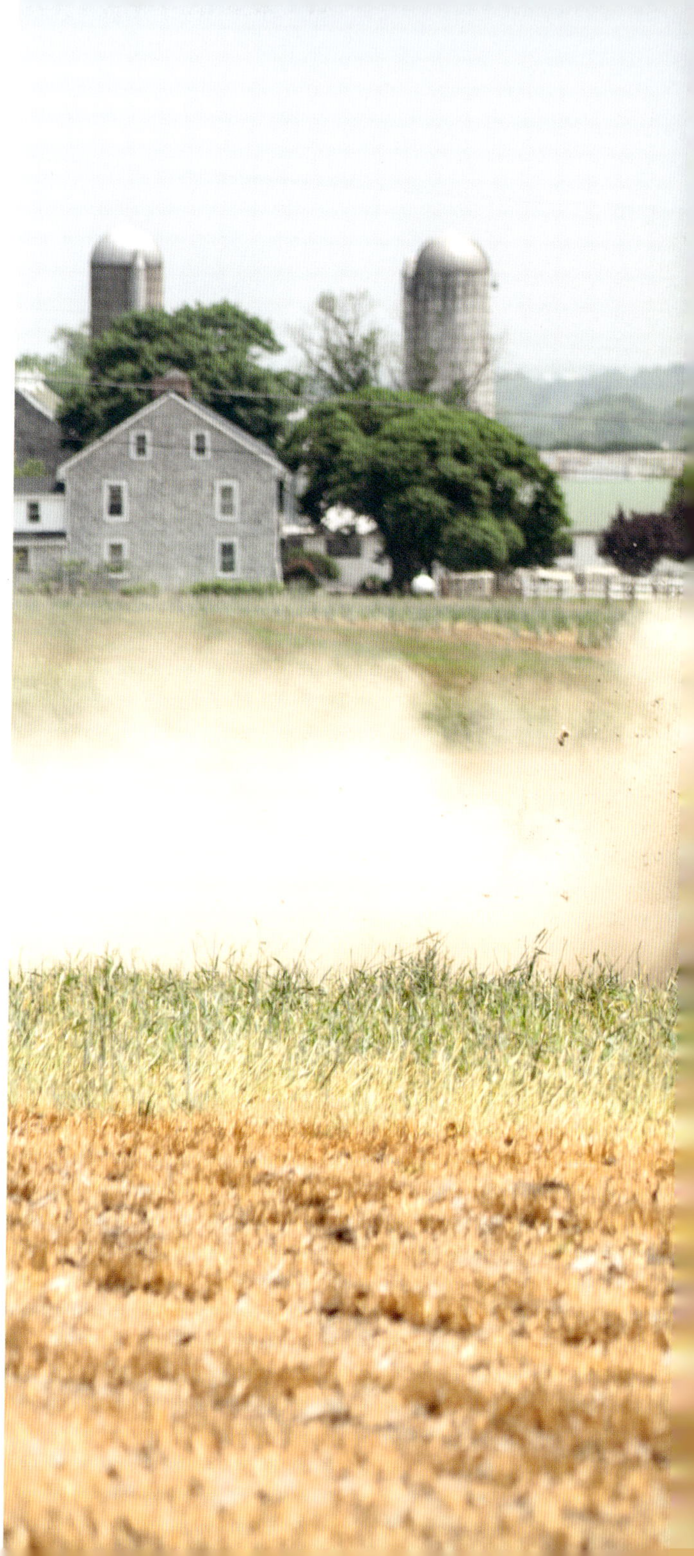

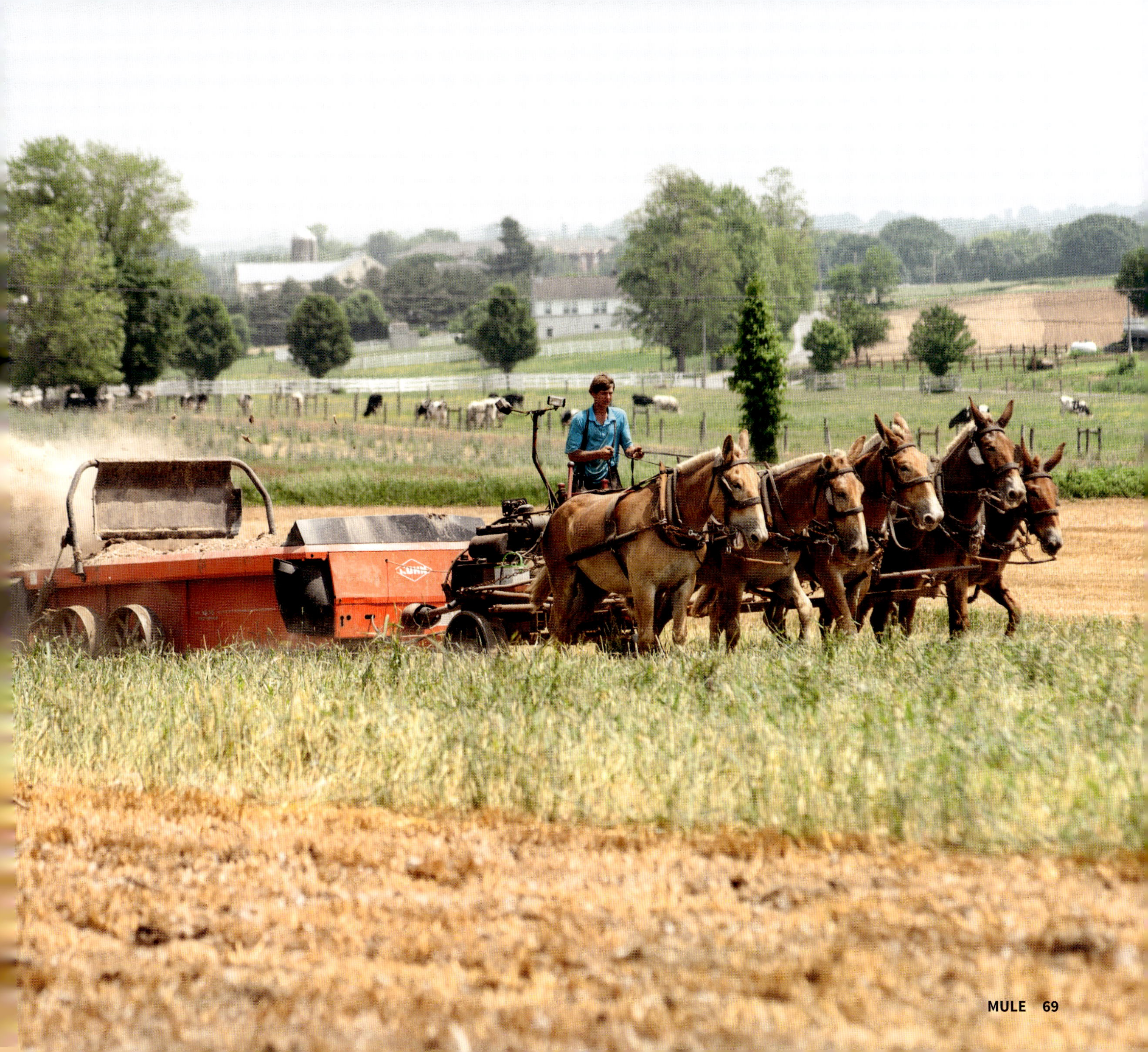

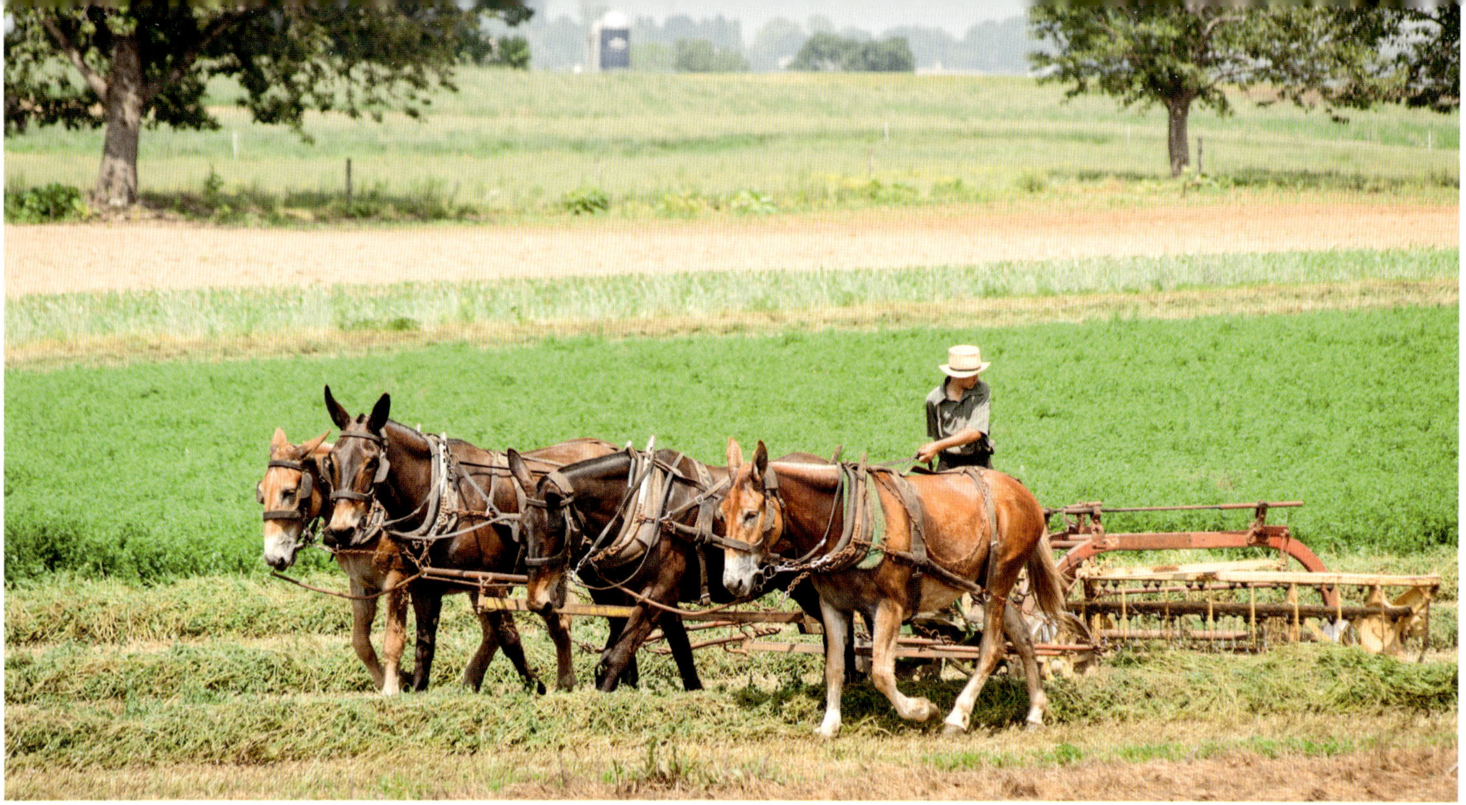

While Jake drove a team of six mules planting corn, *right and facing page,* his thirteen-year-old son raked hay in an adjoining field, *above,* using the family's four other mules. Jake favors planting corn no-till because it eliminates the need to plow and disk prior to planting, and the cover crop residue keeps the weeds down.

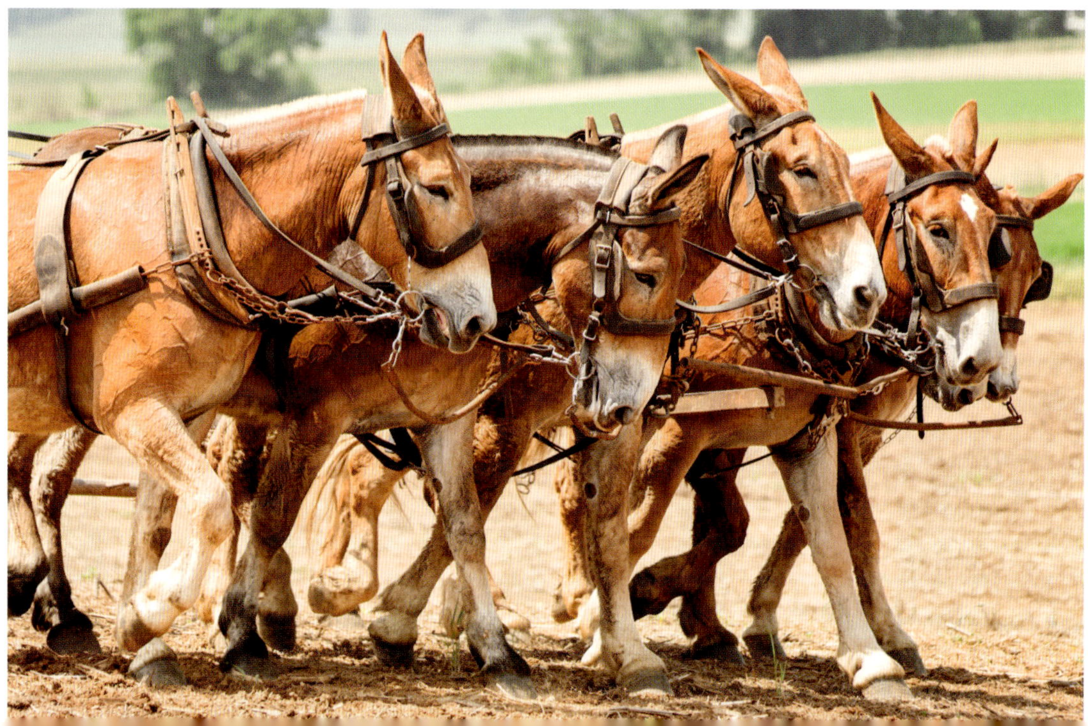

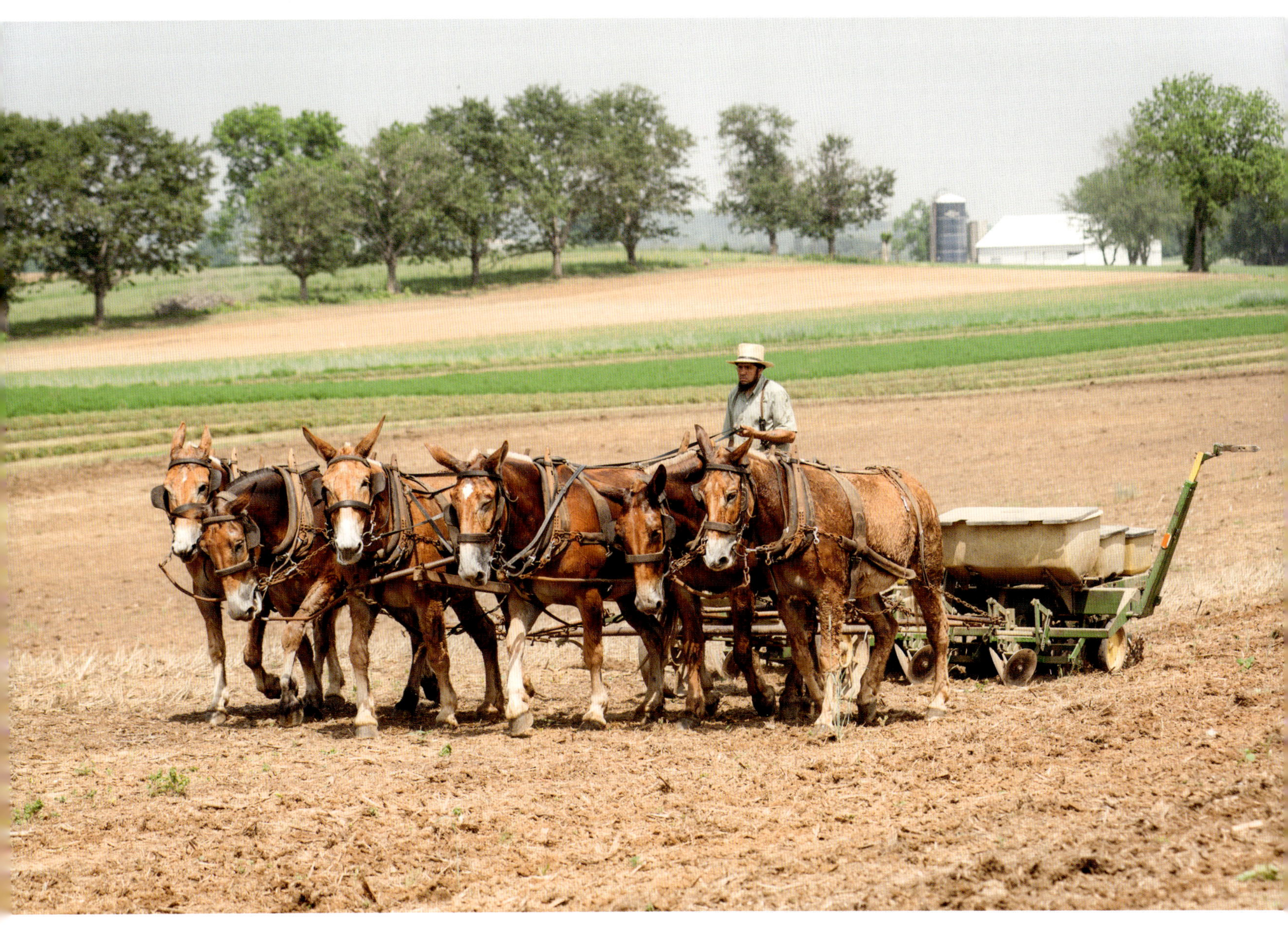

"You've got to be a mule to drive a mule."

Growing tobacco is labor intensive, requiring all available hands. Matt, twenty-one, has been helping in the tobacco field with his dad since he was small. Now they are partners. They farm 6 acres of Burley; each acre yields an average of 2,800 pounds of dried tobacco leaves.

A good tobacco harvest relies on timing and precipitation. Matt's sisters, twelve and fifteen, helped their dad cut and spear the tobacco stalks onto laths several days earlier. They propped the loaded laths from two rows together for efficient pickup.

Sunny weather dried the tobacco, making it lighter and easier to handle. Fortunately, rain, which invites rot and could kick up soil that dirties the leaves, held off until after the harvest.

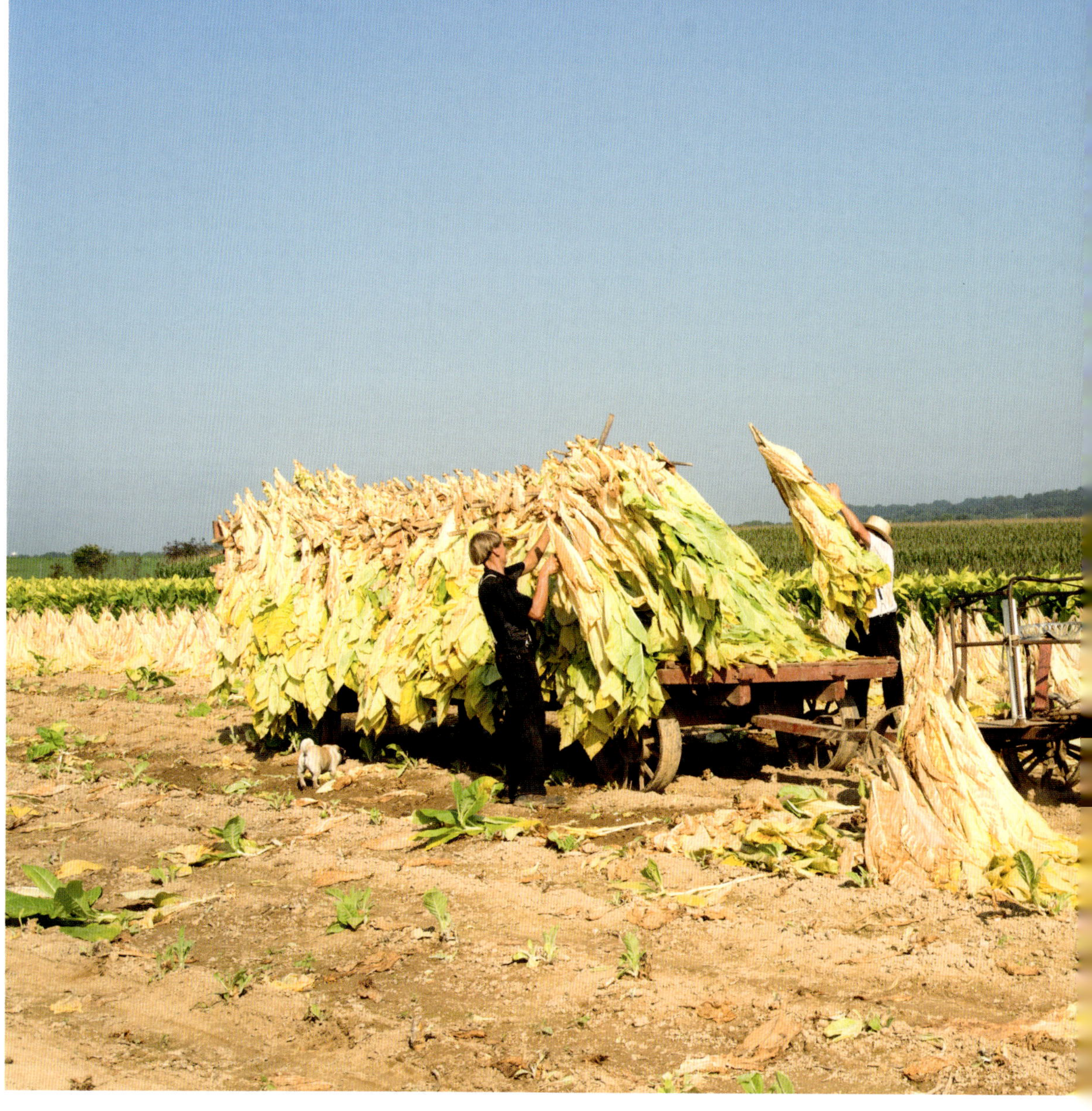

"The mules have loaded tobacco hundreds of times. When I come out here, they just know what we're doing."

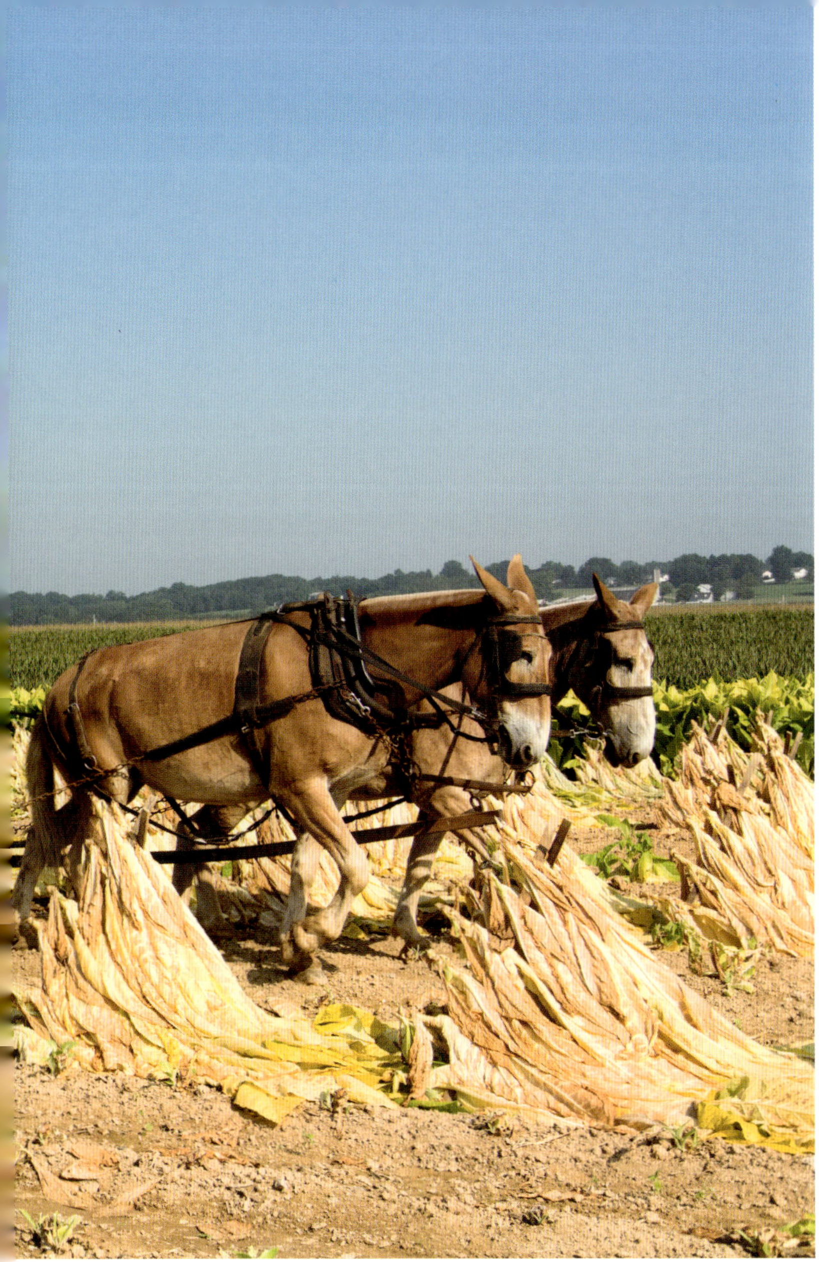

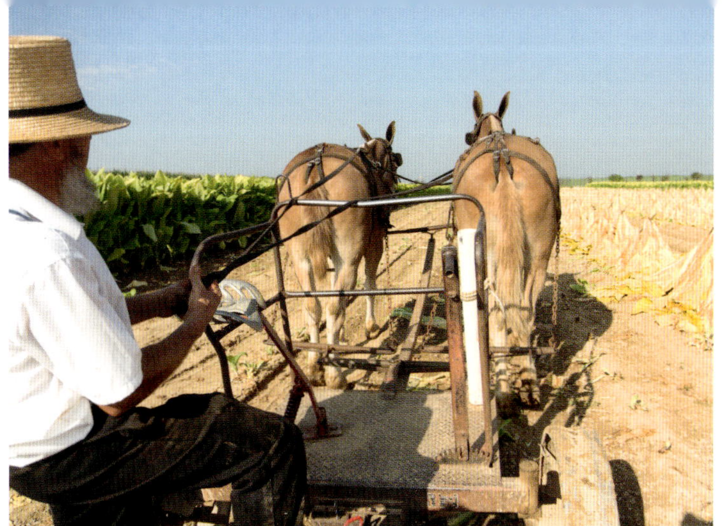

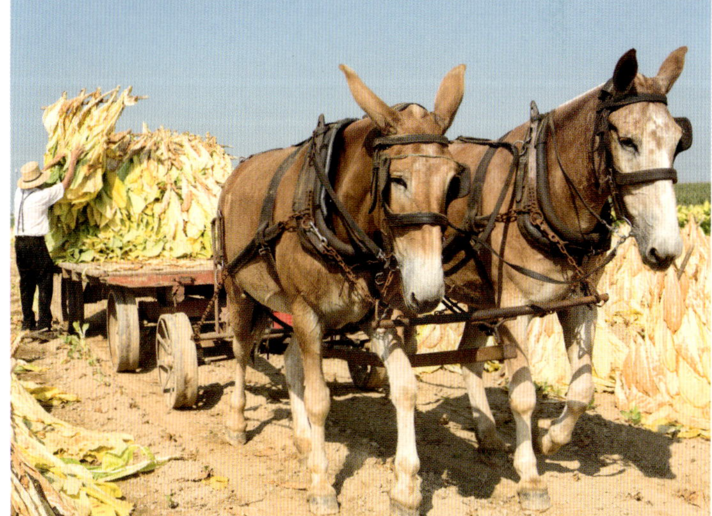

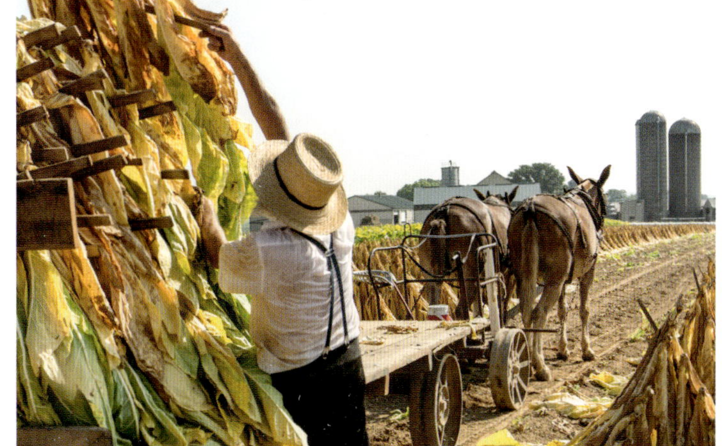

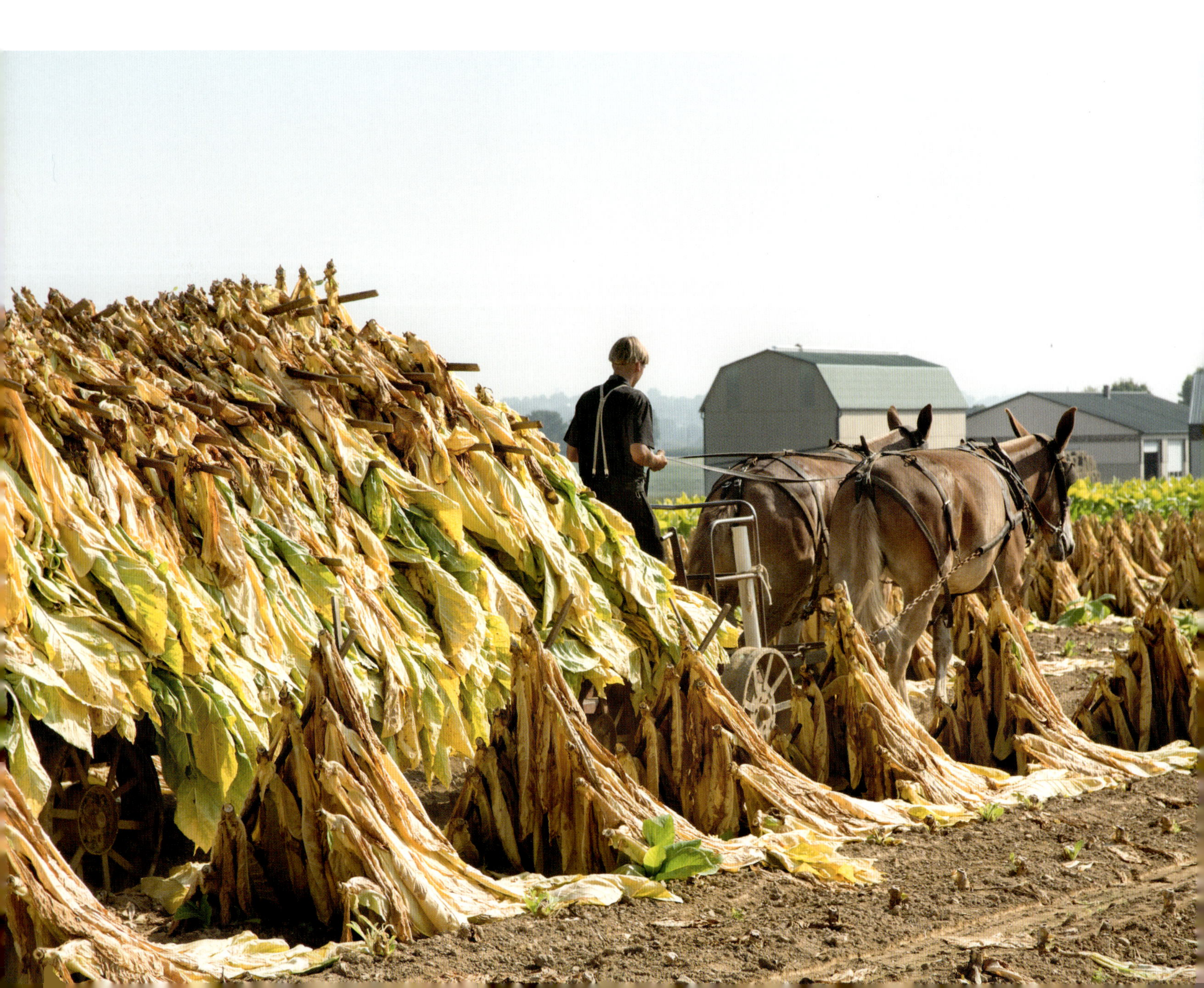

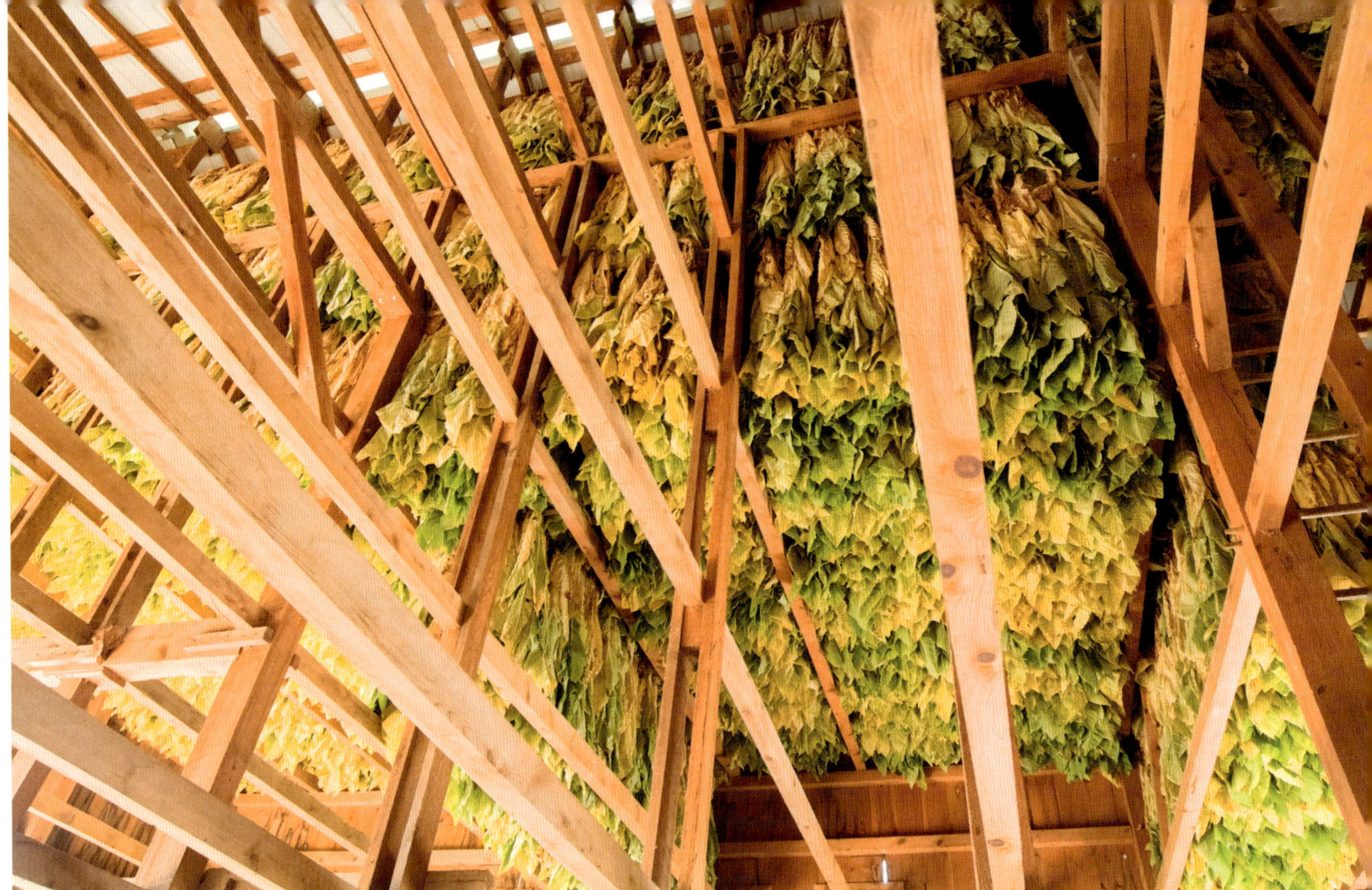

Matt and his dad, on opposite sides of the wagon, worked steadily loading laths of tobacco. Jason and Jen, their trusty pair of mules, stood patiently waiting for the "giddy up" command or walked slowly, stopping easily at "whoa." When the wagon was filled, Matt hopped onto the cart and drove back to the barn to unload.

A tobacco barn is a model of efficiency. Three-by-four beams create a grid on which the loaded laths are hung. The distance between beams allows 2 or 3 inches of space for the ends of each lath to rest. With just enough height to pull the wagon in below, six levels of cross beams reach up to the rafters.

Matt stood on the bed of the wagon and handed a lath up to his uncle standing on the first level, who handed the lath to his hired boy at the next level, and so on, hanging the tobacco in rows from the top down.

After roughly three months of drying, the tobacco was moved to the stripping room. Over the next several months, the whole family stripped the leaves from the stalks and graded them, then packaged the leaves into bales for sale.

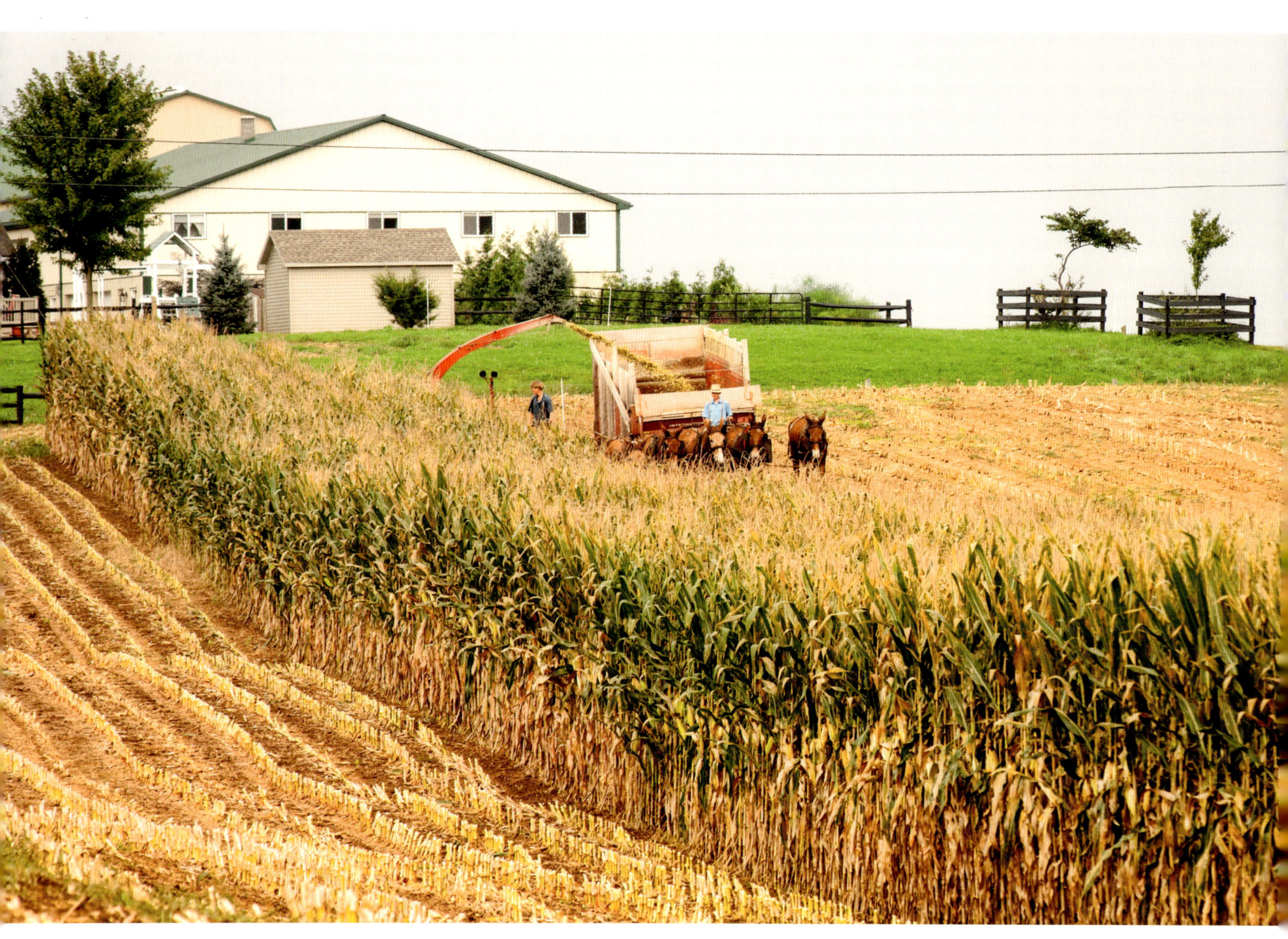

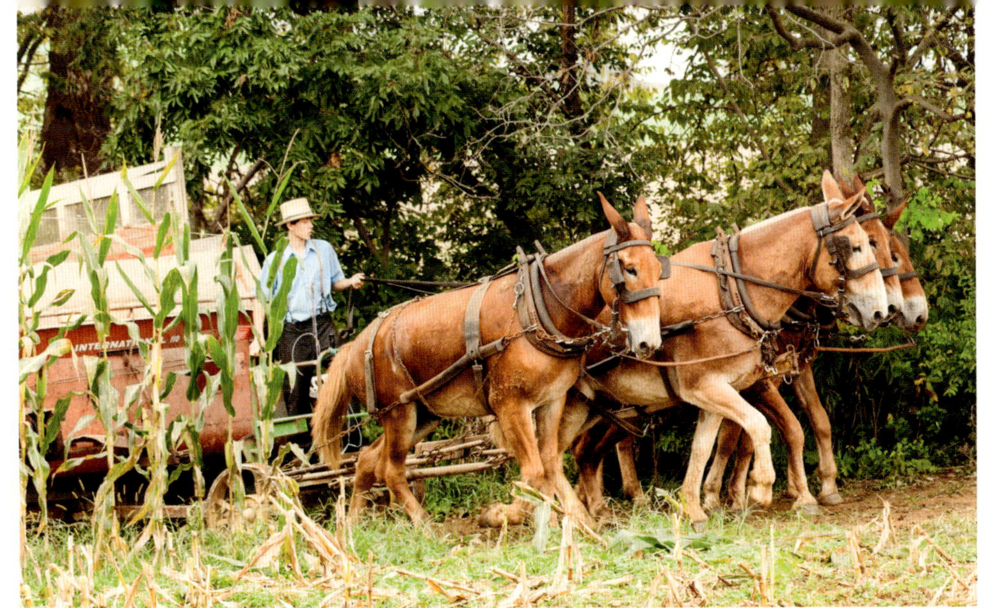

Lancaster County's terrain includes flatland and gently rolling hills. Even small rises require draft animals to lean into their collars.

Though mules and draft horses are employed in the field, tractors may be used for power back at the barn. Here, chopped corn is transferred into a blower that shoots it up a pipe into the silo. The blower is powered by the engine of a parked tractor that is used only for its power.

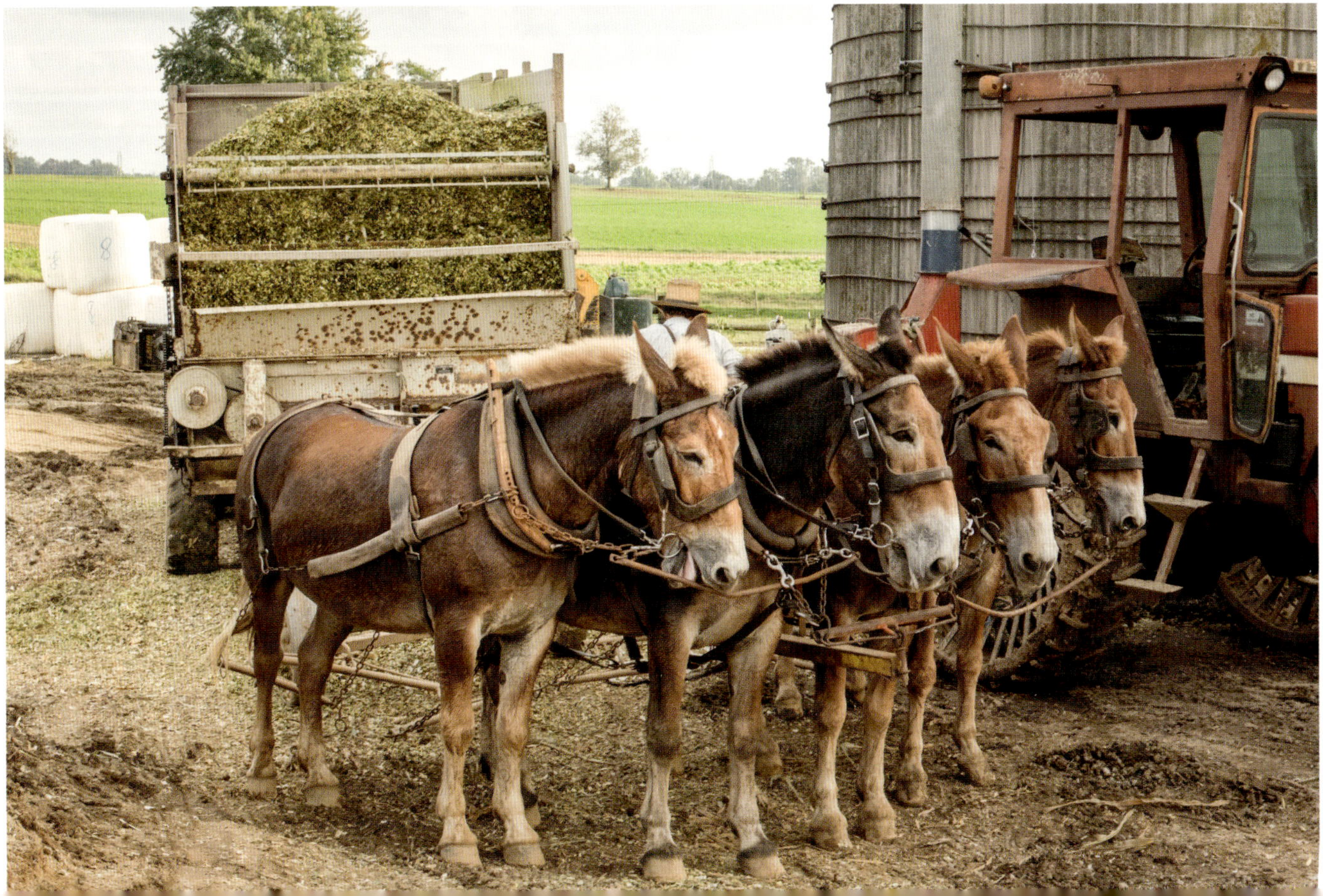

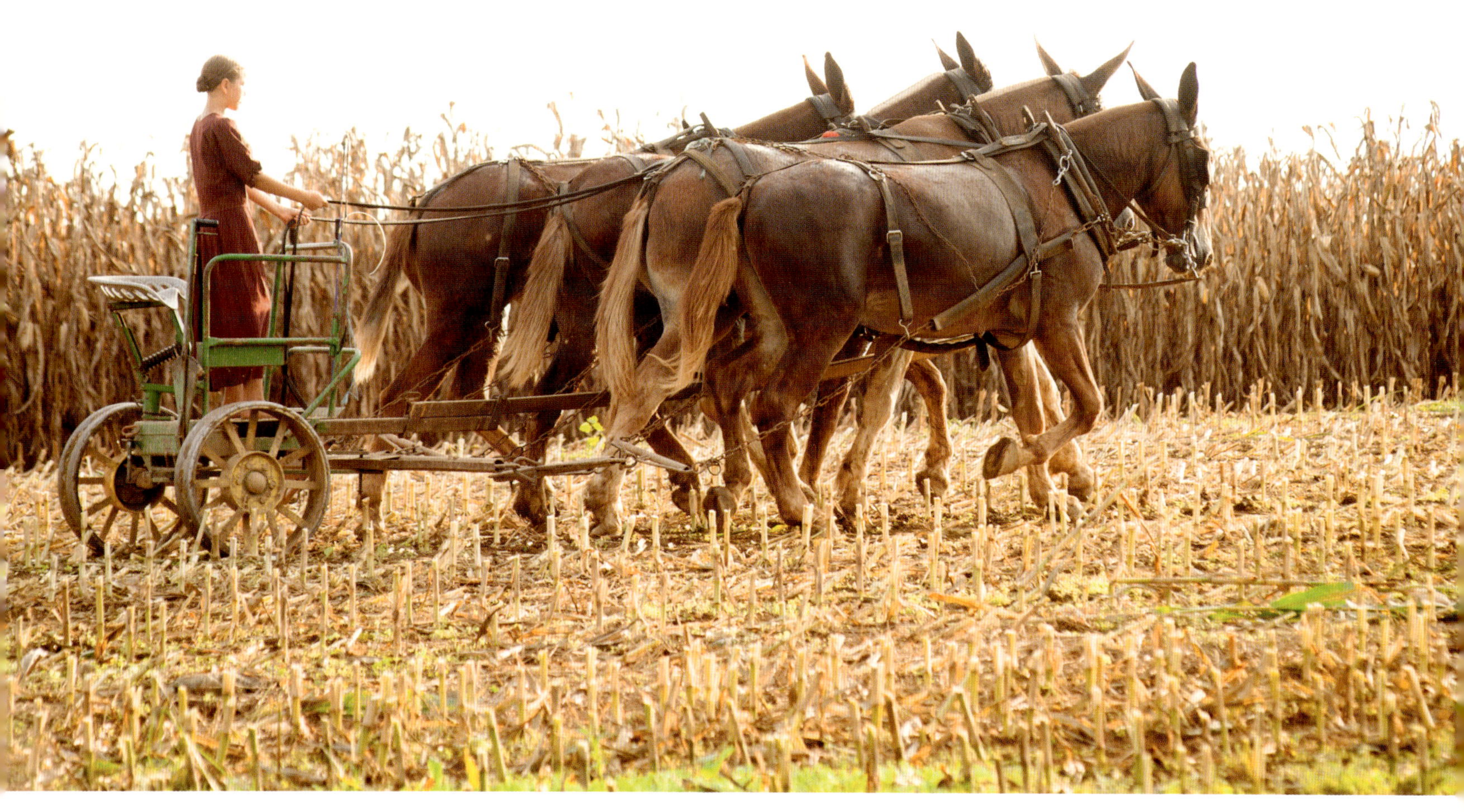

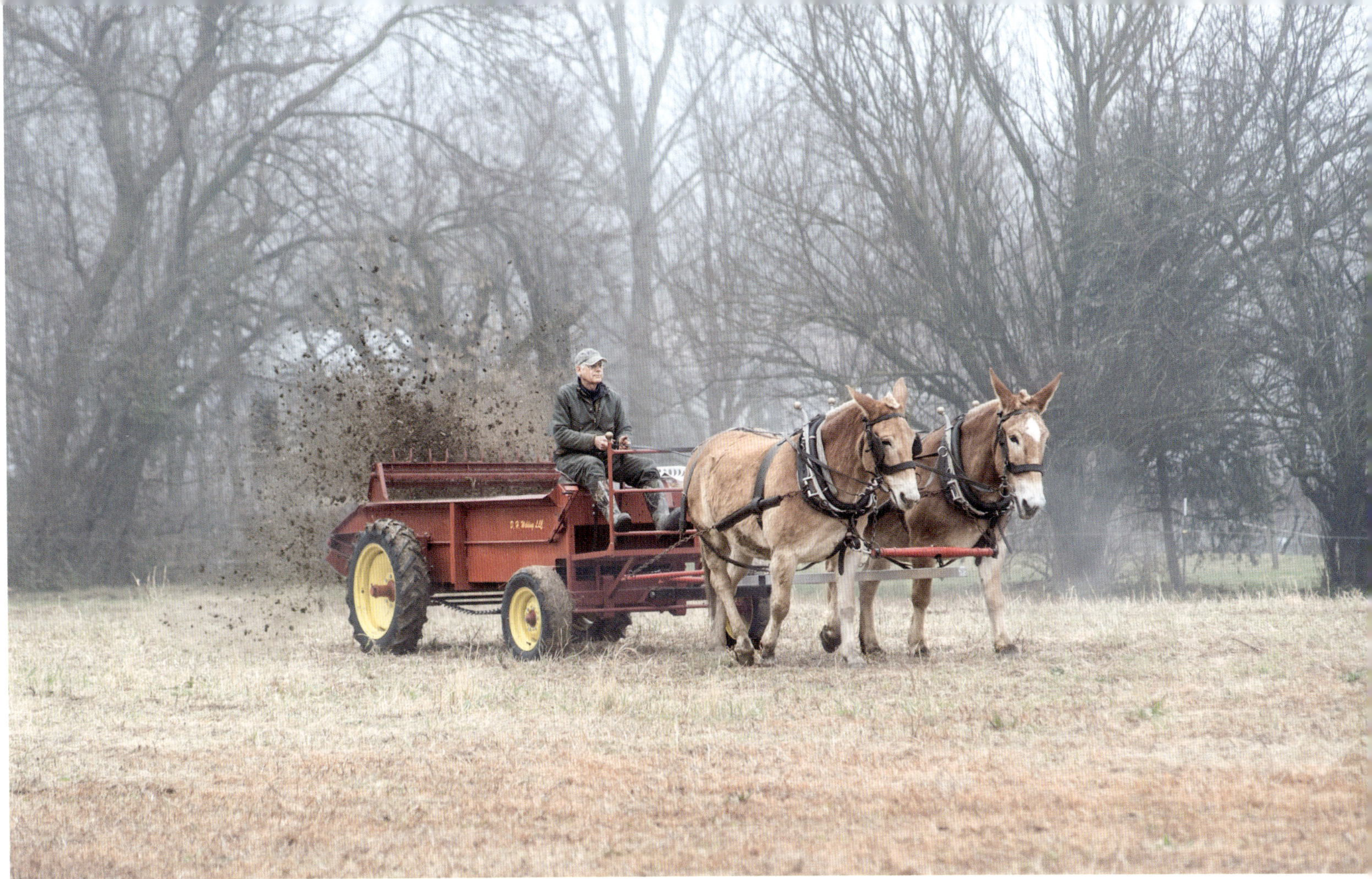

Jake's girl Emma, nearly twelve, took the mules home, *left*, after a day of harvesting corn. She likes being outside and active, especially working with the animals.

As a girl, her primary job is housework—gardening, cooking, cleaning—but there is some latitude since she has two older sisters at home. She helps prepare the family's sixty cows for their twice-daily milking and works in the field beside her brothers when she is needed to help with the planting or harvest.

Though he doesn't rely on farming to make a living, Frank Abel is a draft horse and mule enthusiast. A retired small-animal veterinarian, Frank works his garden and 26-acre farm with pair of well-fed mules, Ben and Kate, *above*. Belgian horses are generally more placid than Percheron horses, thus Frank describes his mules, offspring of Belgian mares, as calmer than mules from Percheron mares would be. He finds molly (female) mules hold their weight better then jacks (males) and are easygoing around the barn.

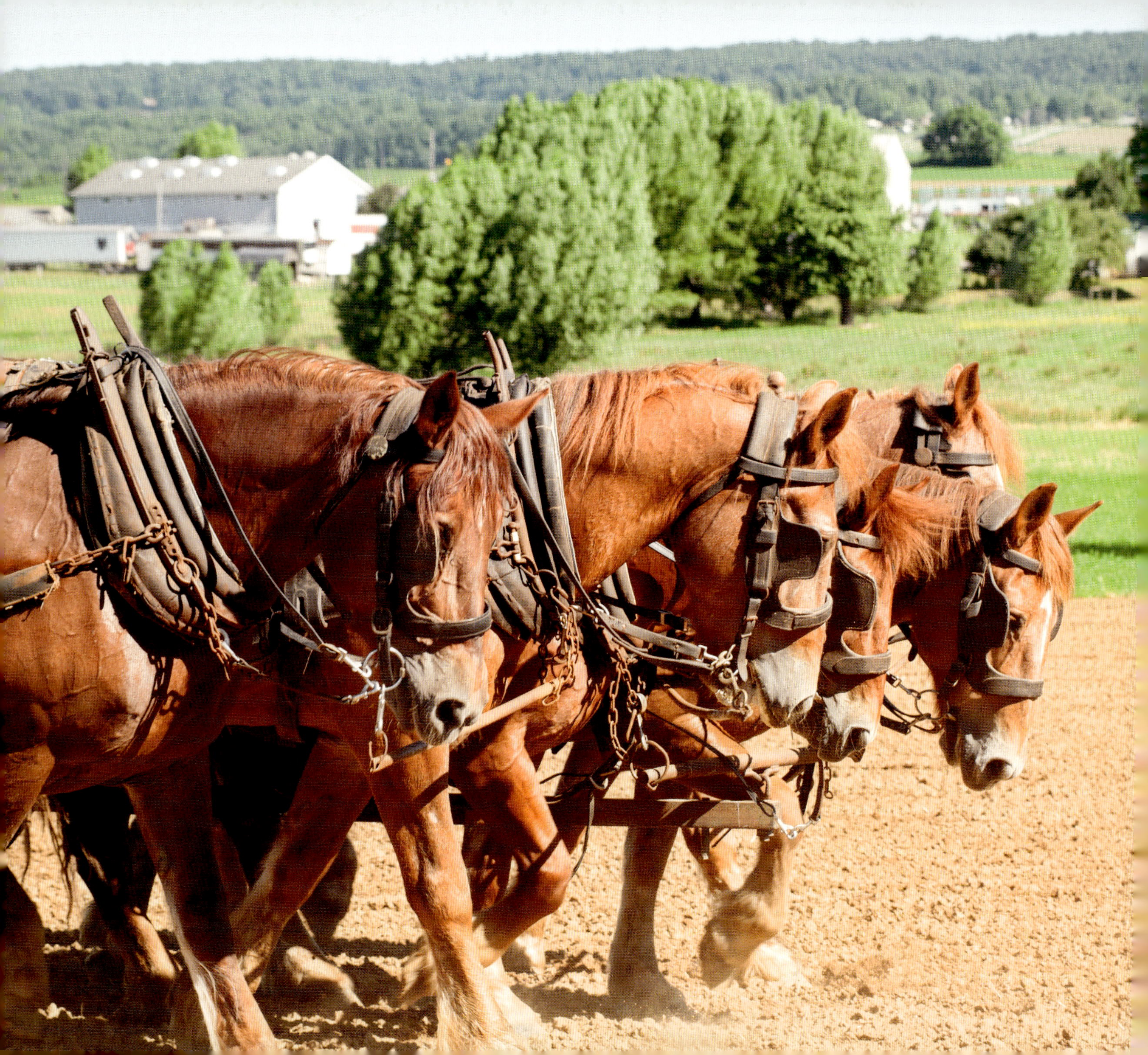

Suffolk

Arie has the most farm experience in the family and loves working outside. She takes the lead when she and her husband hitch up the horses. When all five had harnesses and bridles in place and were hitched to the job cart, she walked along in front of the row to check their readiness.

At a glance, she confirmed that the welter of lines, chains, hooks, and rods was correctly arranged to connect the team. The reins from the right side of the two line horse's bridles were threaded through a series of rings and buckled together into a single rein to be held in her right hand, and vice versa.

Arie took her position on the cart behind the team, picked up the reins, gave them a snap to get the team started.

The Suffolks that she and her husband use for farming are not common in Lancaster County. One of the oldest breeds in England, Suffolks were originally developed for farmwork in East Anglia, where the soil has a high concentration of clay. The Suffolks' relatively short legs and heavily muscled bodies gave them the robust power needed to break up the dense ground.

"Working outside with horses is what I love."

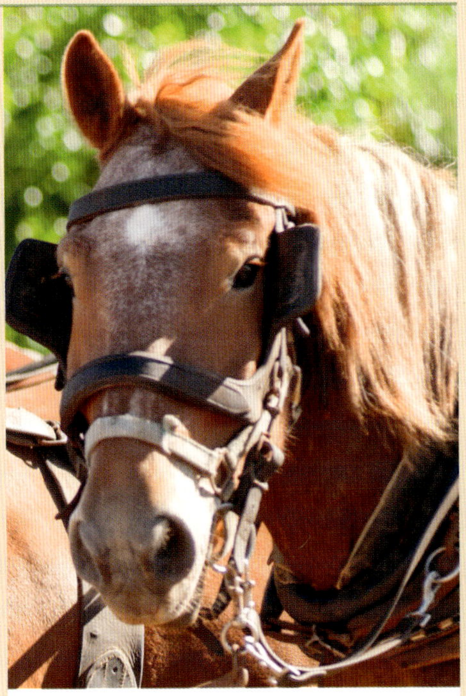

Origin: Suffolk in East Anglia, England

Height: 16.1–17hh

Weight: 1,500–2,000 lbs

Color: chestnut (seven shades of chestnut are recognized when registering), may have small white star

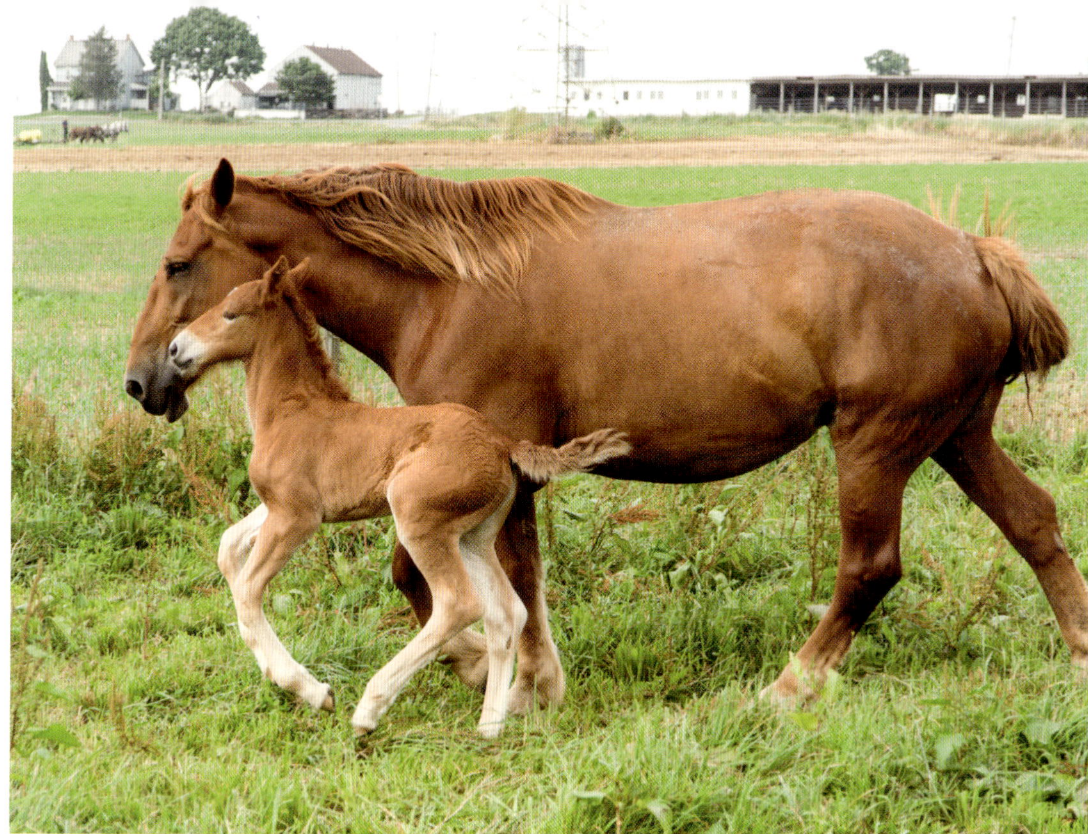

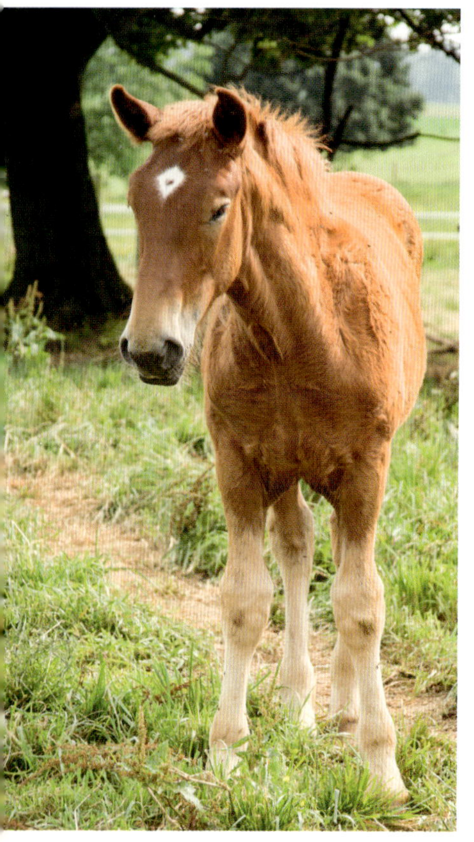

Suffolks are showstoppers, with coats that glow a beautiful, burnished red brown. A few farmers and breeders in Lancaster County appreciate the Suffolk's combination of concentrated power, stamina, and docility. Not as high strung as other draft breeds, Suffolks expend less energy turning food into fuel.

Four-month-old Ginger, *left,* displayed a small circle within a perfect diamond shape on her forehead. Four-day-old Gypsy, *above,* frolicked in the meadow beside her mother, Star. At 16.3 hands, Star is relatively short for a draft horse but is right in line with other members of her compact breed. In a few years, fillies Ginger and Gypsy will become brood mares for their owners' growing Suffolk-breeding operation.

The comparatively small number of Suffolks in the United States has helped maintain the breed's purity; the short, muscular build shows a direct line to its origins. They are known for their "heart"—willingness to work hard—as well as their great pulling power.

Christ and Arie grow orchard grass rather than alfalfa. Unless it is harvested very young, alfalfa is too rich to feed their horses and sheep.

After the hay had been cut and allowed to dry for two days, Christ hitched Star and Dot to the cart and attached the tedder. Arie stepped up to drive. The fluffer tedder, resembling a rake and with tines like pitchfork ends, aerated and spread the hay. Tedded hay dries more quickly than hay that is raked into rows.

The hot sun did its work, and Arie came back several hours later and raked the dried hay into rows. With rain on the horizon, Christ and Arie moved quickly to bale the hay and haul it into the barn. Then the rain hit.

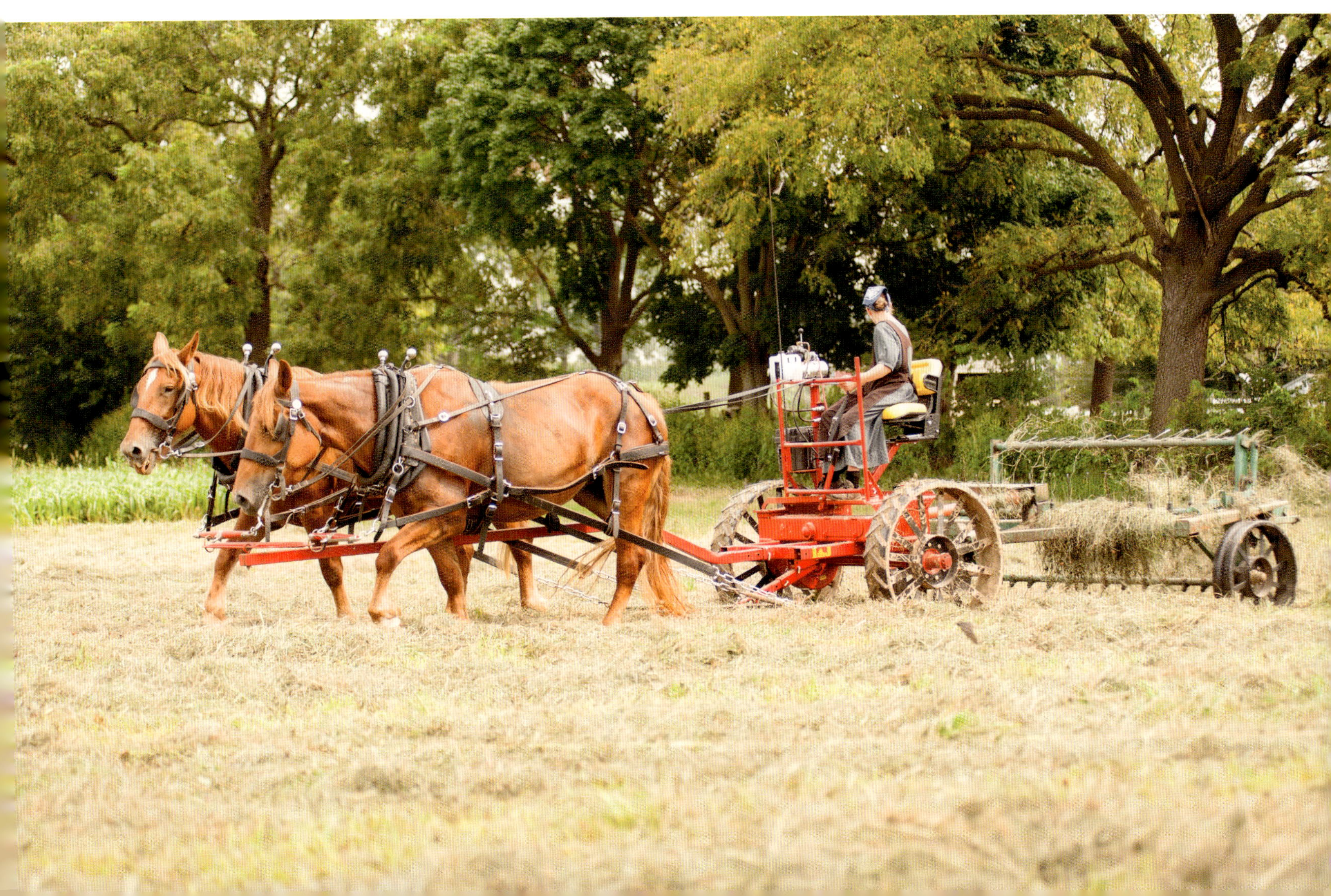

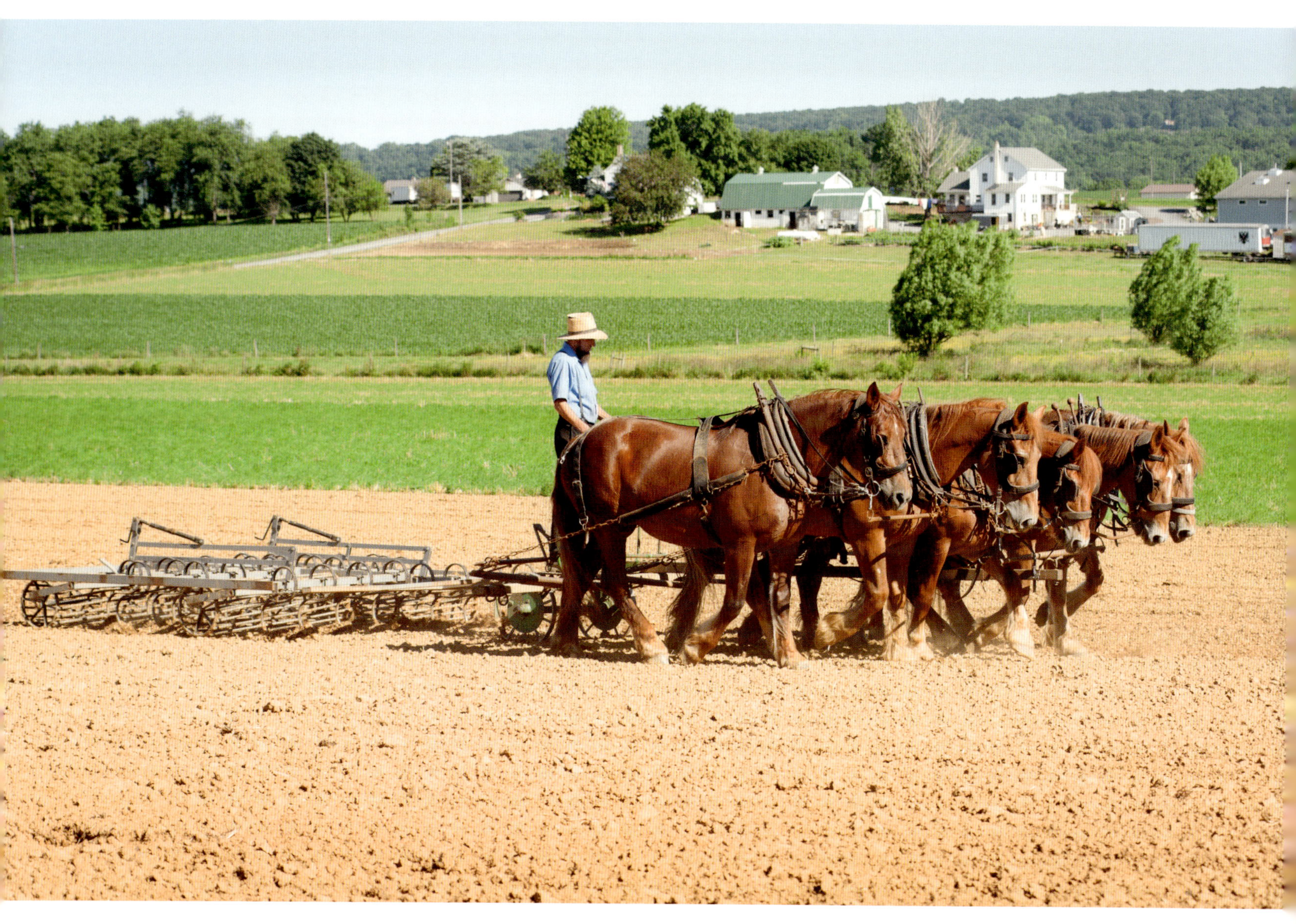

“Goldy is my favorite Suffolk—she has a nice head set.”

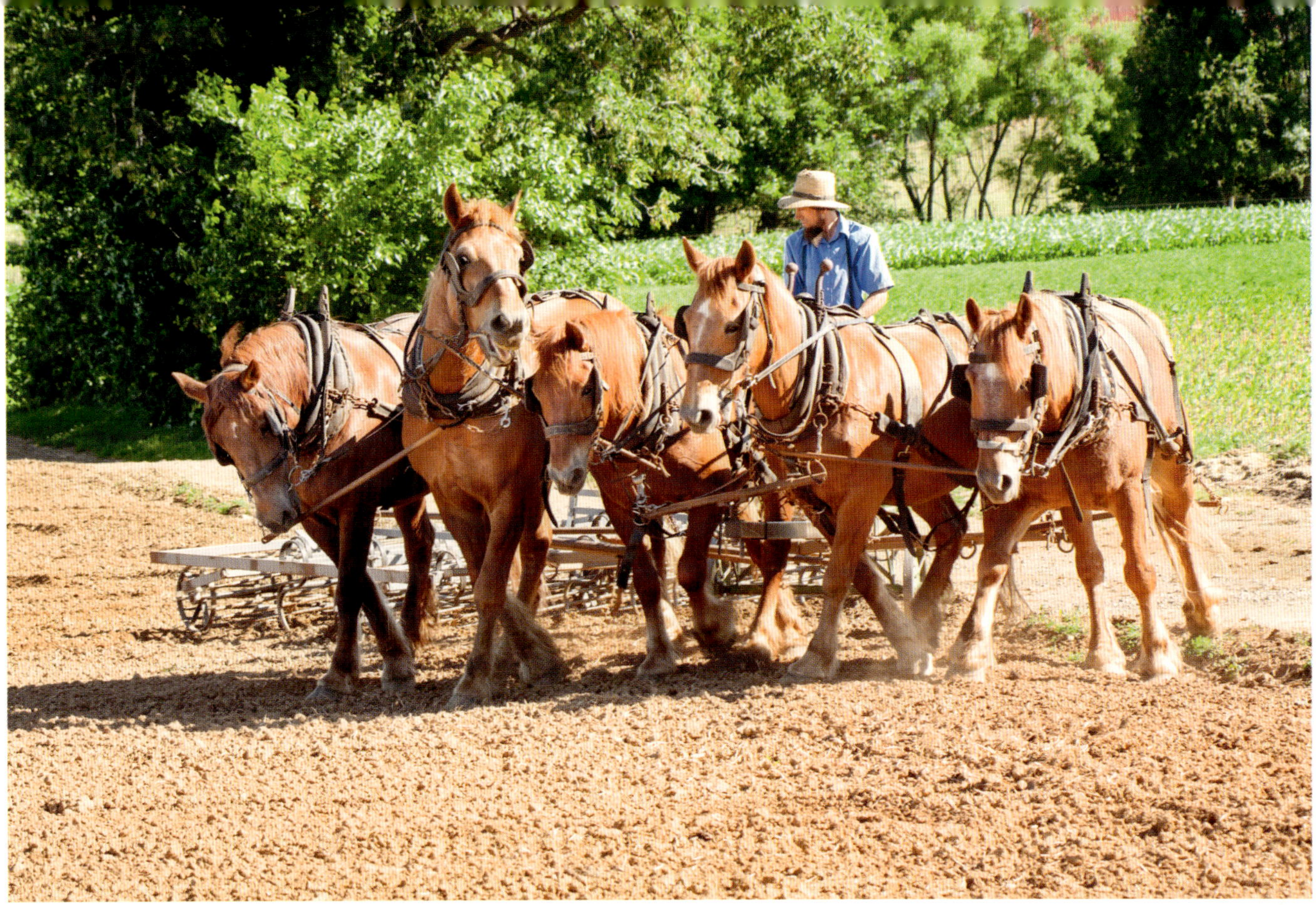

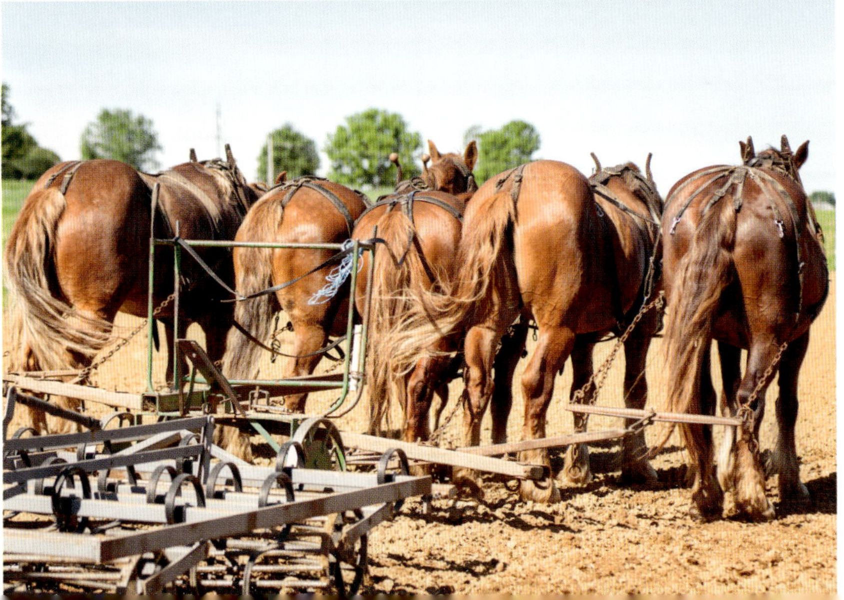

Stoltzfus's father farmed with Belgians, but when Stoltzfus was a boy he read about Suffolks and liked the idea that they were bred specifically for farming. When he got his own farm he invested in a team of Suffolks.

After plowing, Stoltzfus drove five of his Suffolks abreast to harrow the ground, breaking up clods and smoothing the soil before planting corn. The team worked in unison. At the end of each row, they executed a 180-degree turn with aplomb. Directed by Stoltzfus, Goldy, on the inside, took very small steps while Jimmy, on the outside, took giant steps. The team neatly turned the harrow and headed down the field again.

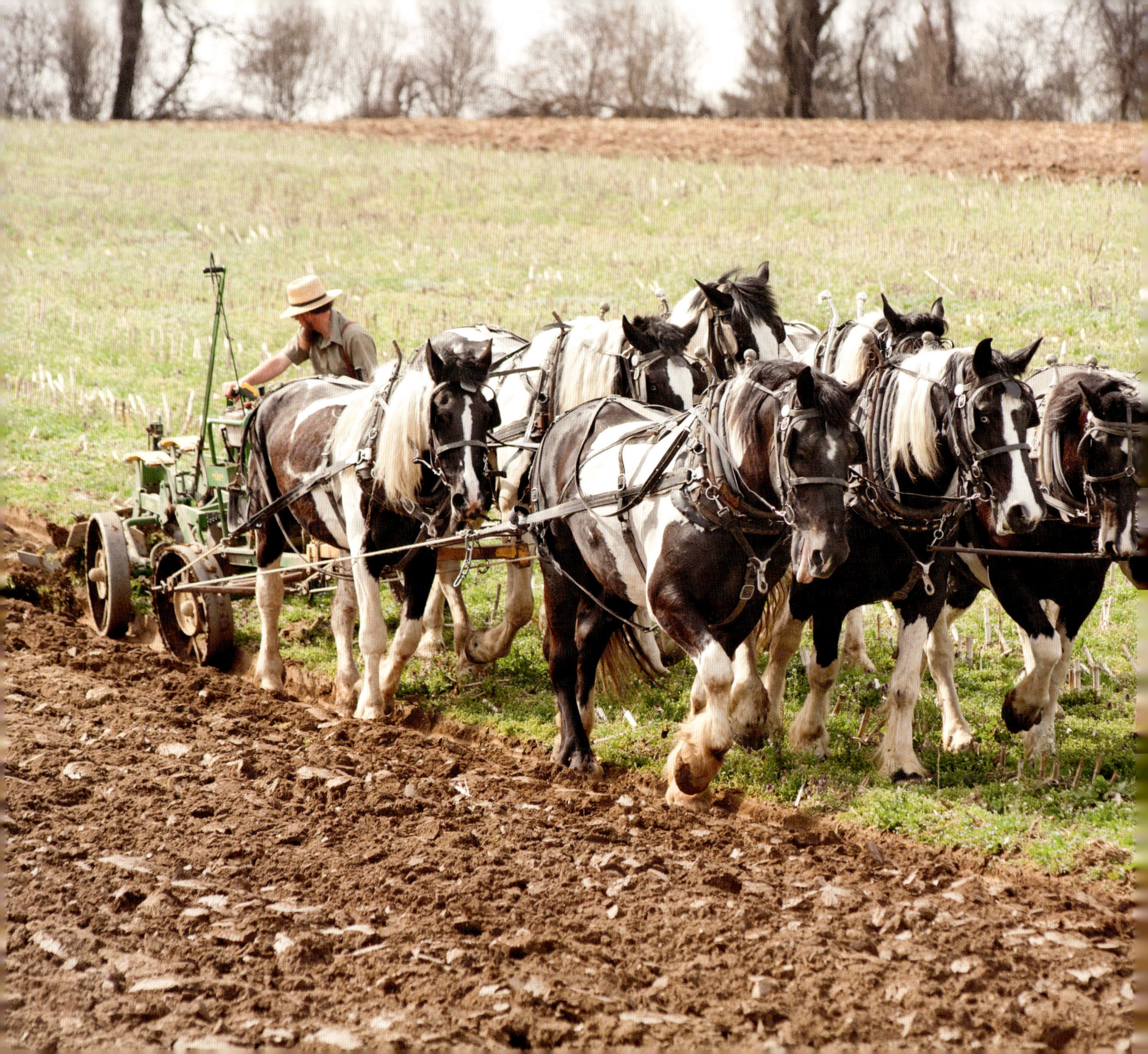

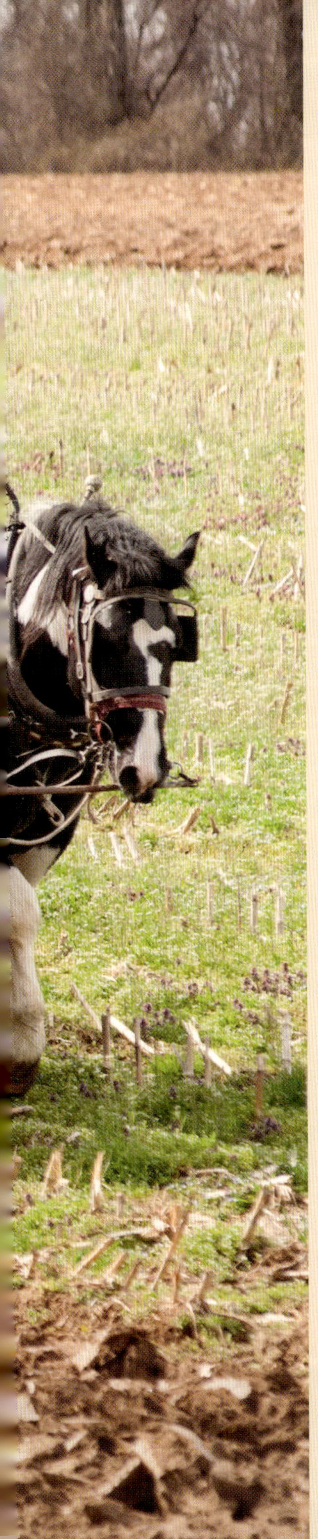

Spotted Draft

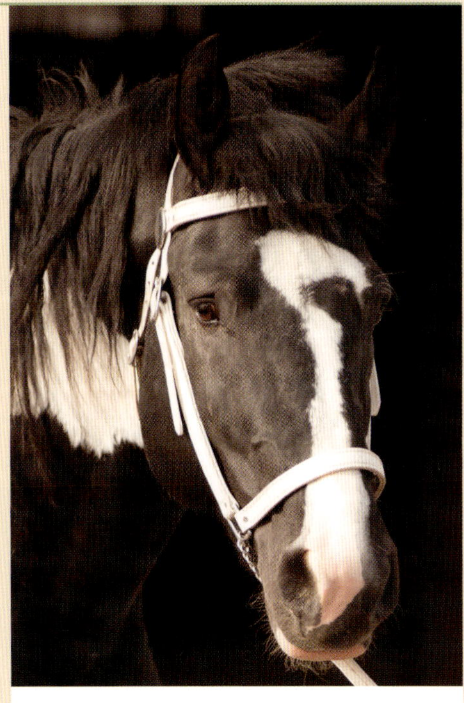

Pleased when his daughter made plans to marry a farmer, Levi did what he could to help the young couple. Since his future son-in-law was just getting started in farming, Levi took the opportunity to set him up with a team of Spotted Draft horses.

When Levi's dad began farming in the early 1970s, there happened to be two Spotteds among the five horses he bought. He was so pleased with the looks, strength, and work ethic of the huge pintos that he began breeding his own. His children and grandchildren carry on the Spotted tradition.

Recognized as a breed in 1995, the Spotted Draft is in the minority of draft horses working in Lancaster County. Spotted Drafts are identified more by their spotted coloring than any draft type they resemble. While smaller than some draft horses, they compensate with power and athleticism.

"I like the sound of the horse's chains and the sweet smell of the freshly turned earth."

Origin: United States

Height: 16–17hh or more

Weight: 1,200–2,000 lbs

Colors: pinto; most-common base coat colors are black, bay, and brown

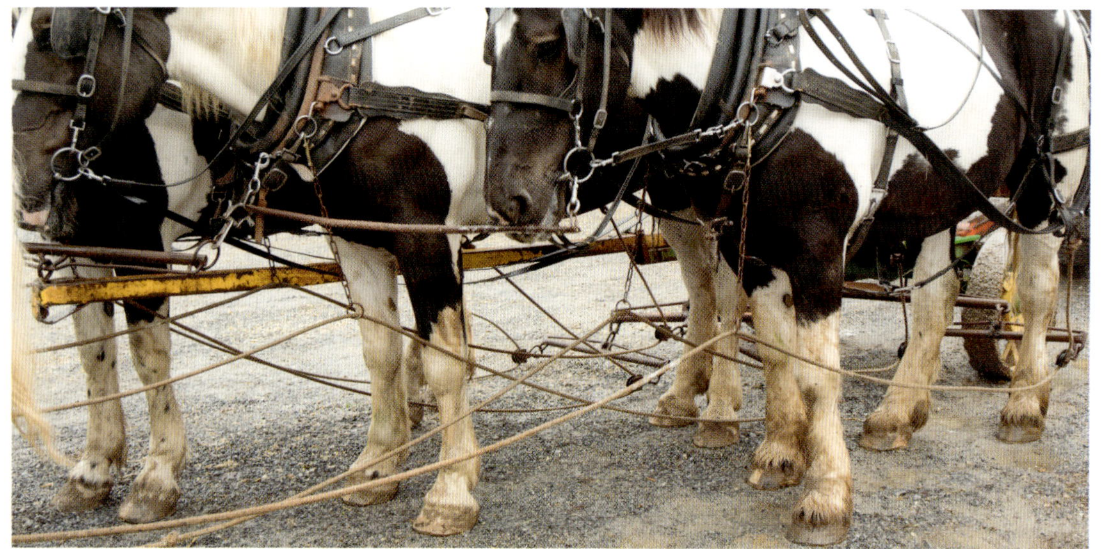

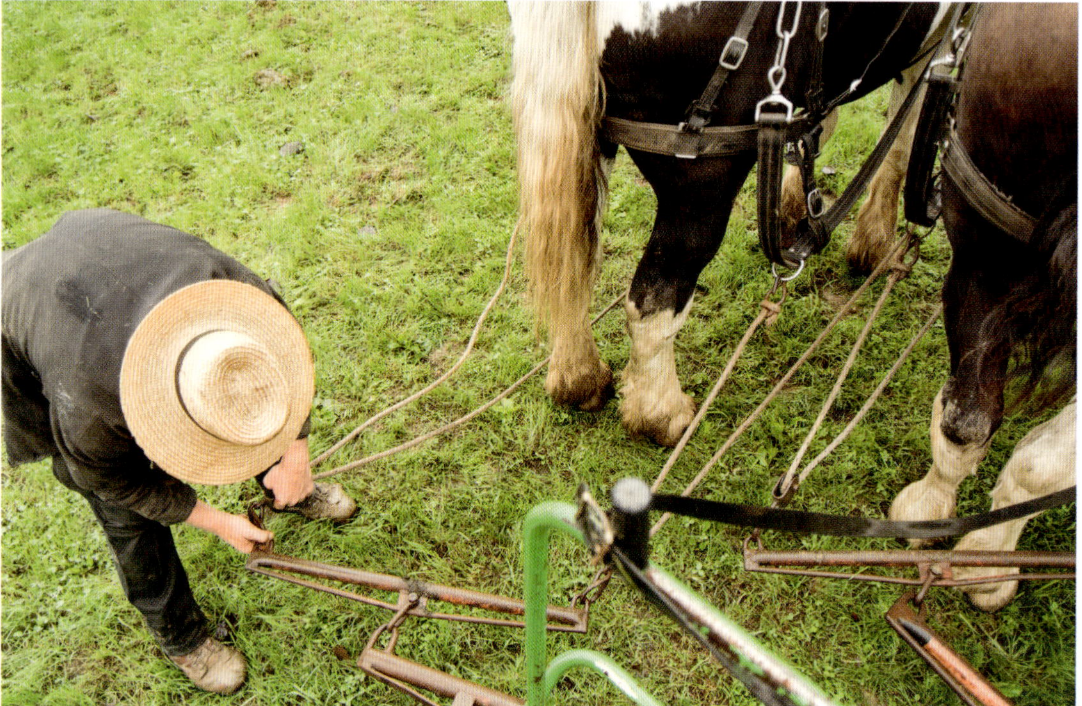

In preparation for hitching his horses to the cart, Levi laid out the lines on the ground. Then he led each harnessed horse out and they delicately stepped into place. A series of chains, clips, and snaps connected the horses to each other and the cart.

He coaxed stallion Turbo into place at the front left. Turbo hadn't been worked for nearly six months and wasn't too pleased to be there, kicking out with his back legs in a bit of a tantrum. Levi's two sons stepped in to help; one held Turbo's head while the other provided calming pats on Turbo's rump.

To complicate things, this was only the third time the gelding behind Turbo was driven in a work team, and he was nervous. Levi quickly finished hitching and guided the team out to the field. A few hours of plowing would settle everyone down.

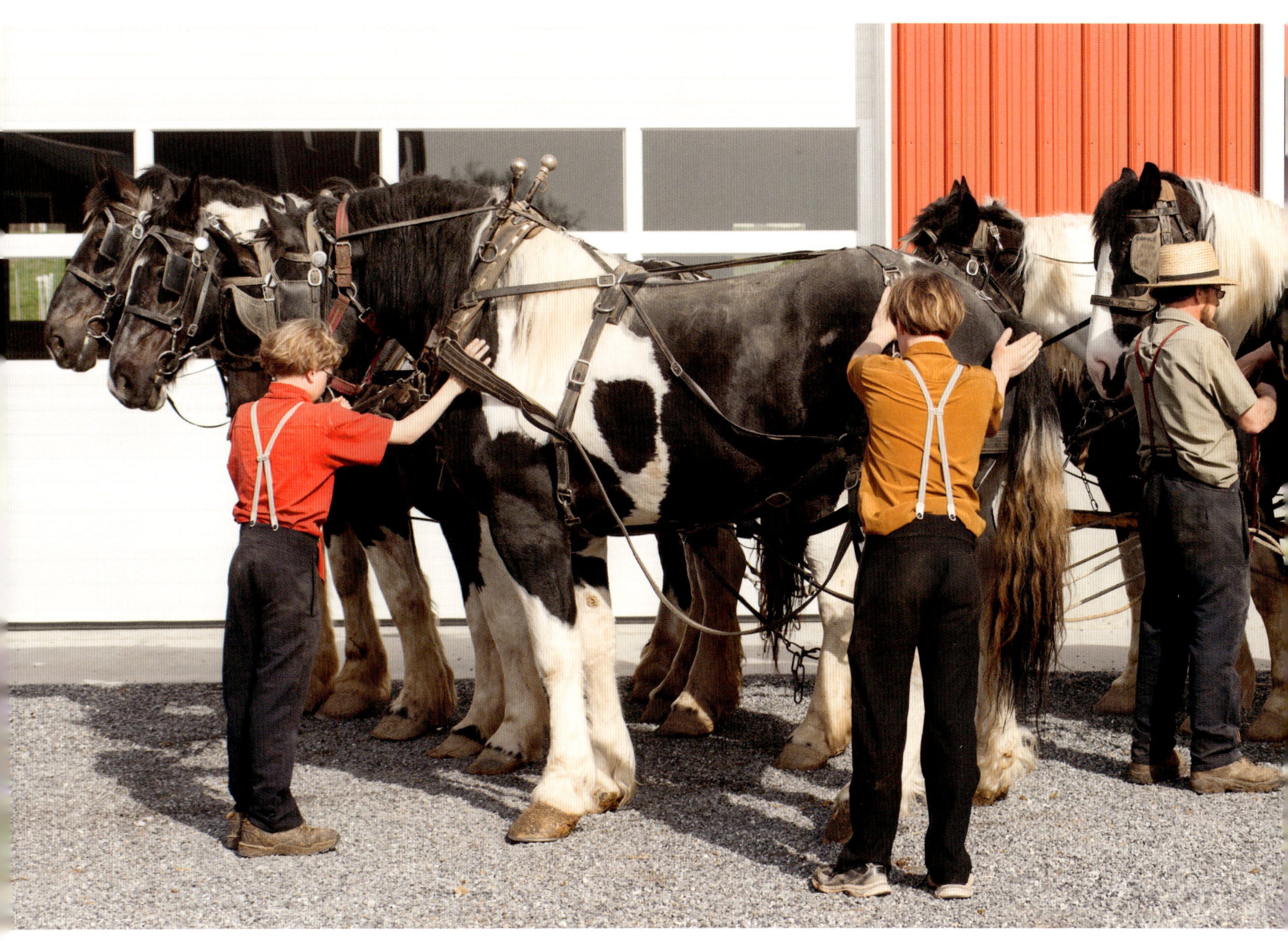

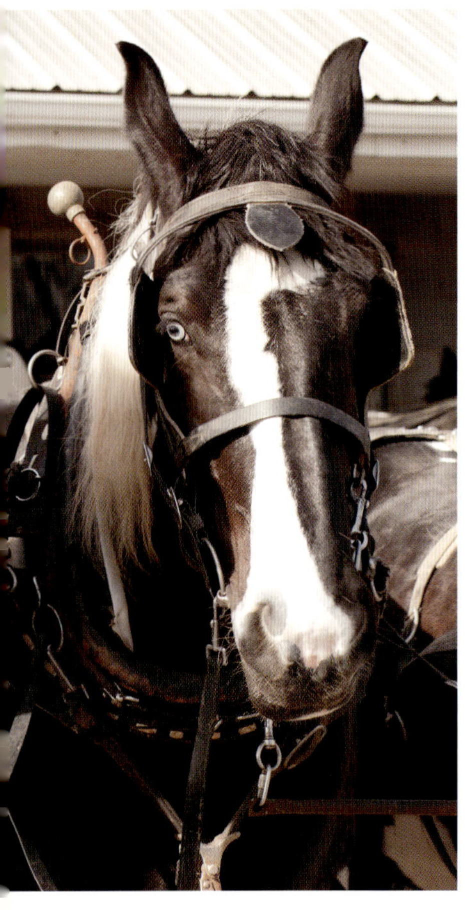

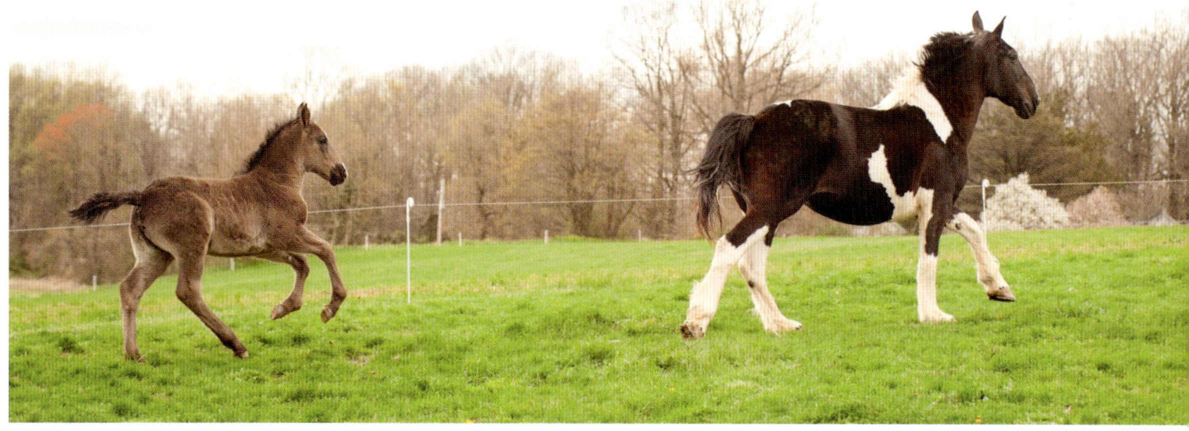

Spotted Drafts are typically the result of a flashy pinto crossed with a solid-colored draft horse. Percherons are usually chosen since they are known to throw colored foals more often than do other draft horses.

One of the pleasures of breeding Spotted Drafts is seeing what pattern of spots a foal will carry. Every once in a while an unexpected pattern appears—just a splash of white on the foal's face, for example.

Blue eyes show up occasionally, *left,* especially in horses with white spotting. Some owners view blue eyes as a negative feature; for others it indicates wisdom. Levi says it's a sign that the horse is smart—but then, *all* of his horses are smart.

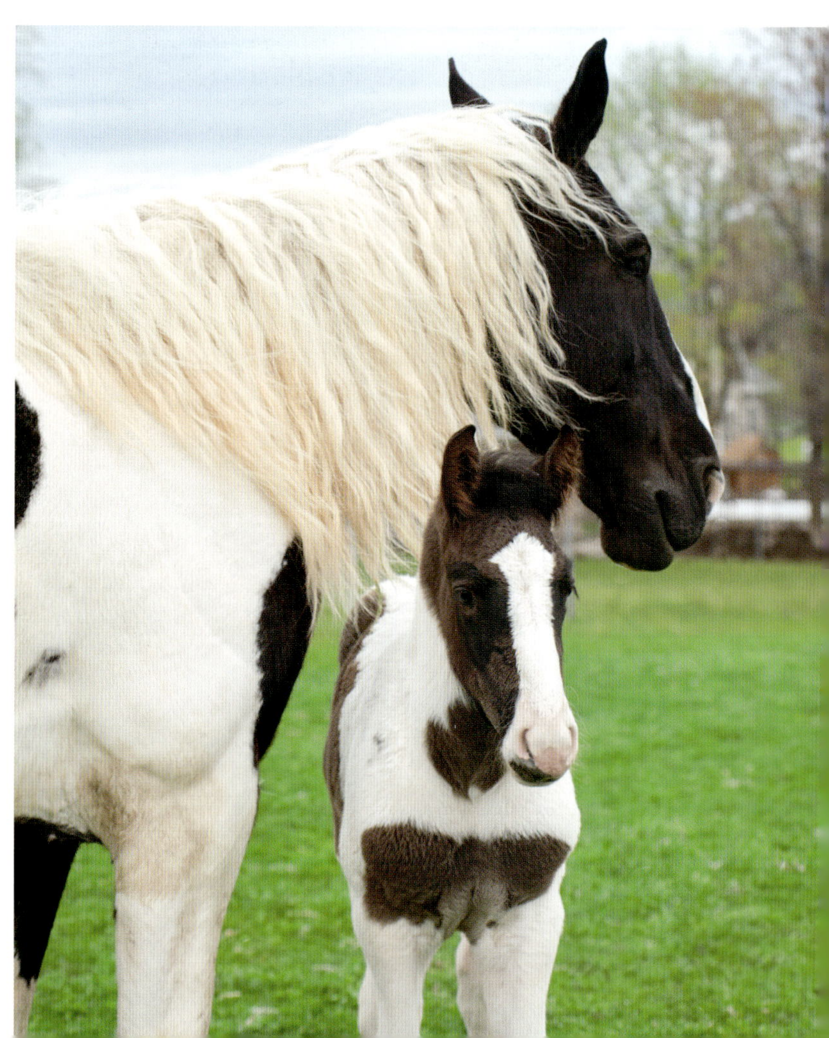

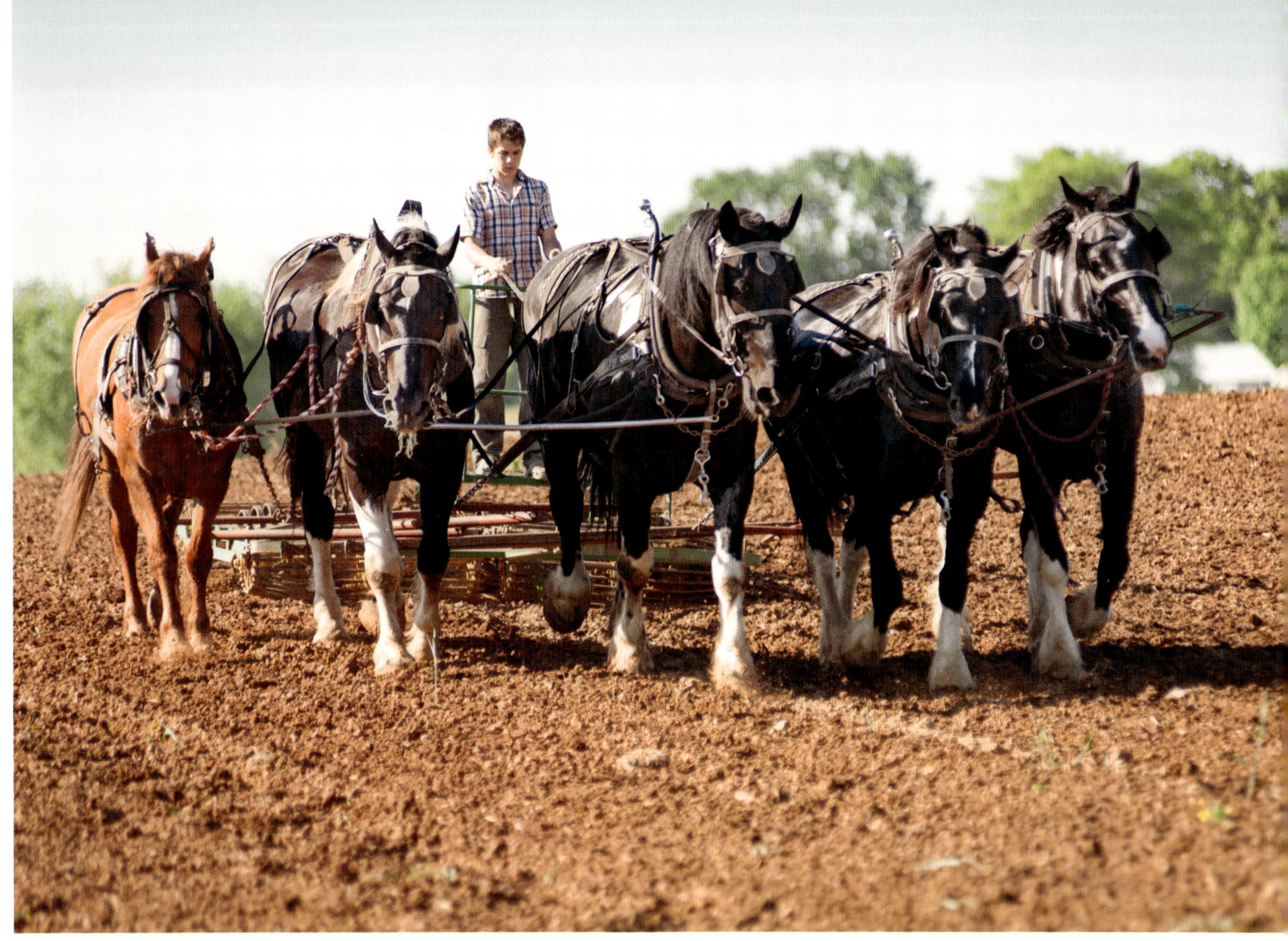

Charlie, a Morgan-Belgian crossbreed at the driver's far right, joined his heavier Spotted stablemates to harrow the ground. This was one of his last days of field work before taking a job in the big city—pulling carriages in New York's Central Park.

Peanut, at the center of the team, is destined to stay on the farm. A friendly disagreement about weight led to him being coaxed onto a truck scales at a neighboring business. Peanut, clearly named for his delicate build, weighed over 2,200 pounds.

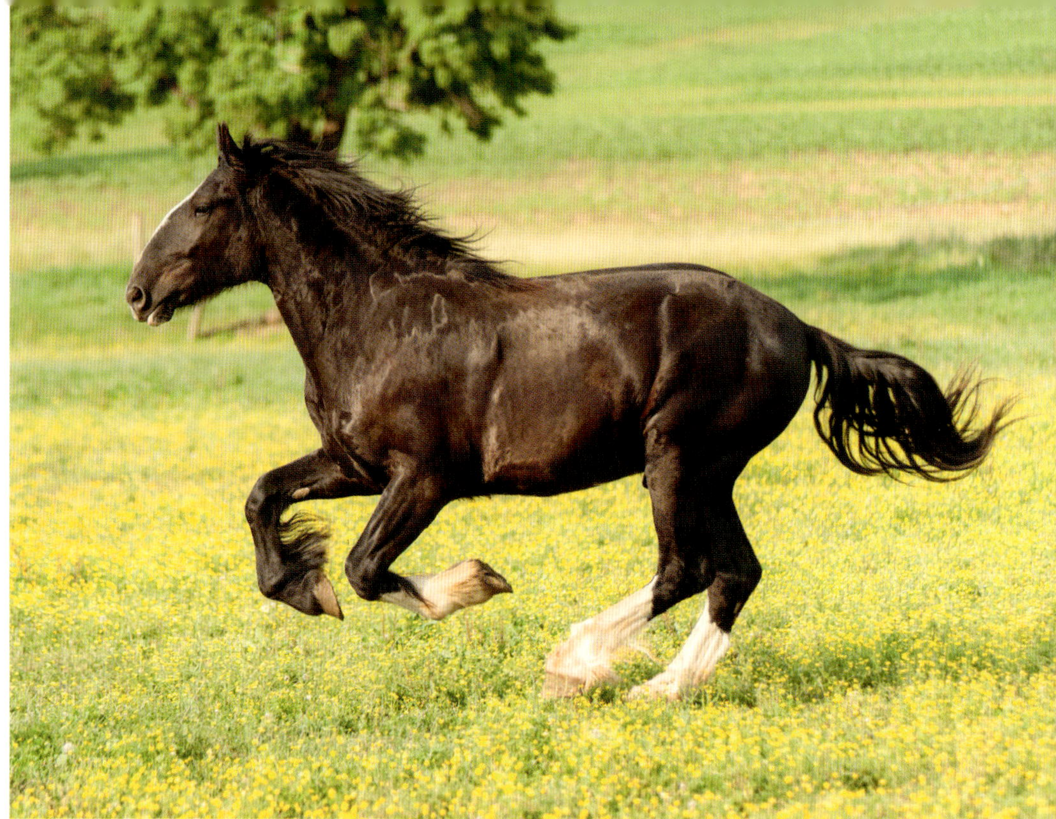

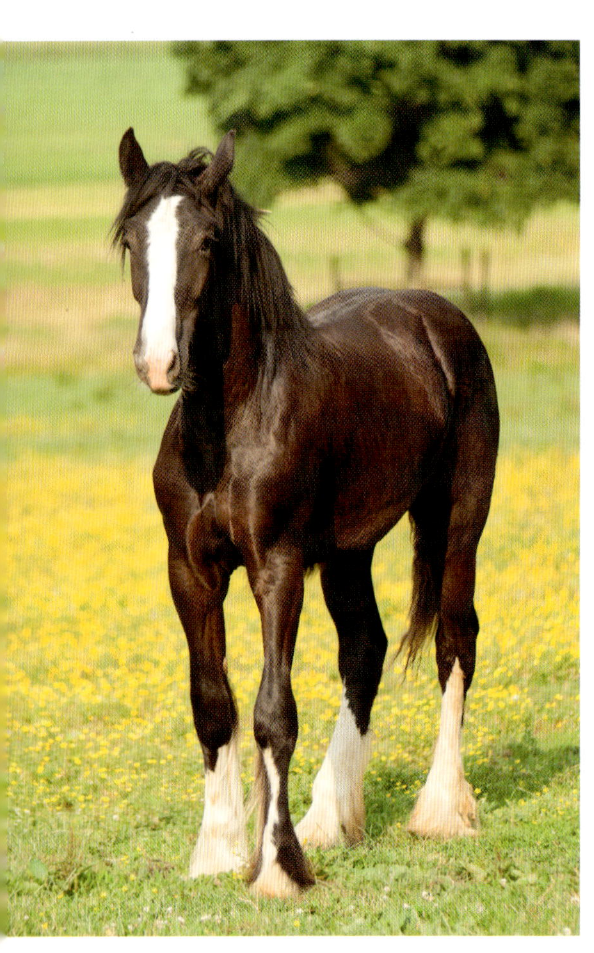

Shire

Origin: England

Height: 16.2–19hh

Weight: 1,600–2,200 lbs

Colors: black, chestnut, gray, bay

Elam watched with quiet satisfaction as yearling Crystal, *left,* and two-year-old Jasper, *above,* galloped in the meadow. Elam had farmed with Shires up until a few years ago but continued his Shire breeding program when he got out of farming.

With an eye toward selling them, Elam has started to train Jasper, a gelding, for driving and will begin training Crystal in another year. Since some Shires are ridden in dressage and other competitions, he'll introduce the saddle as well.

Gentle Giants

Though admired and appreciated, few Shire or Clydesdale horses are called into service for fieldwork in Lancaster County. They are more often seen in company-sponsored hitch teams or in show rings, where their size, grace, and elegance inspire awe. Similar in looks and bloodlines, both breeds have long, distinctive strands of hair, known as feathers, below their knees. They are bred to have high hocks and long legs—which results in the high stepping action favored by buyers. Feathers on the lower legs, however attractive, are a challenge for farmers to keep clean and healthy.

Clydesdale

Origin: Clyde Valley, Scotland
Height: 16.2–18.2hh
Weight: 1,700–2,200 lbs
Colors: black, gray, bay, roan, pinto

Visitors to the Landis Valley Village & Farm Museum are delighted by Hank and Hunter, a handsome pair of black Clydesdales on loan from a museum volunteer. The enormous geldings, each weighing roughly a ton, are hitched up regularly to take groups of school children and other visitors on wagon rides around the grounds. Hank and Hunter are also used to seasonally demonstrate historical farming techniques.

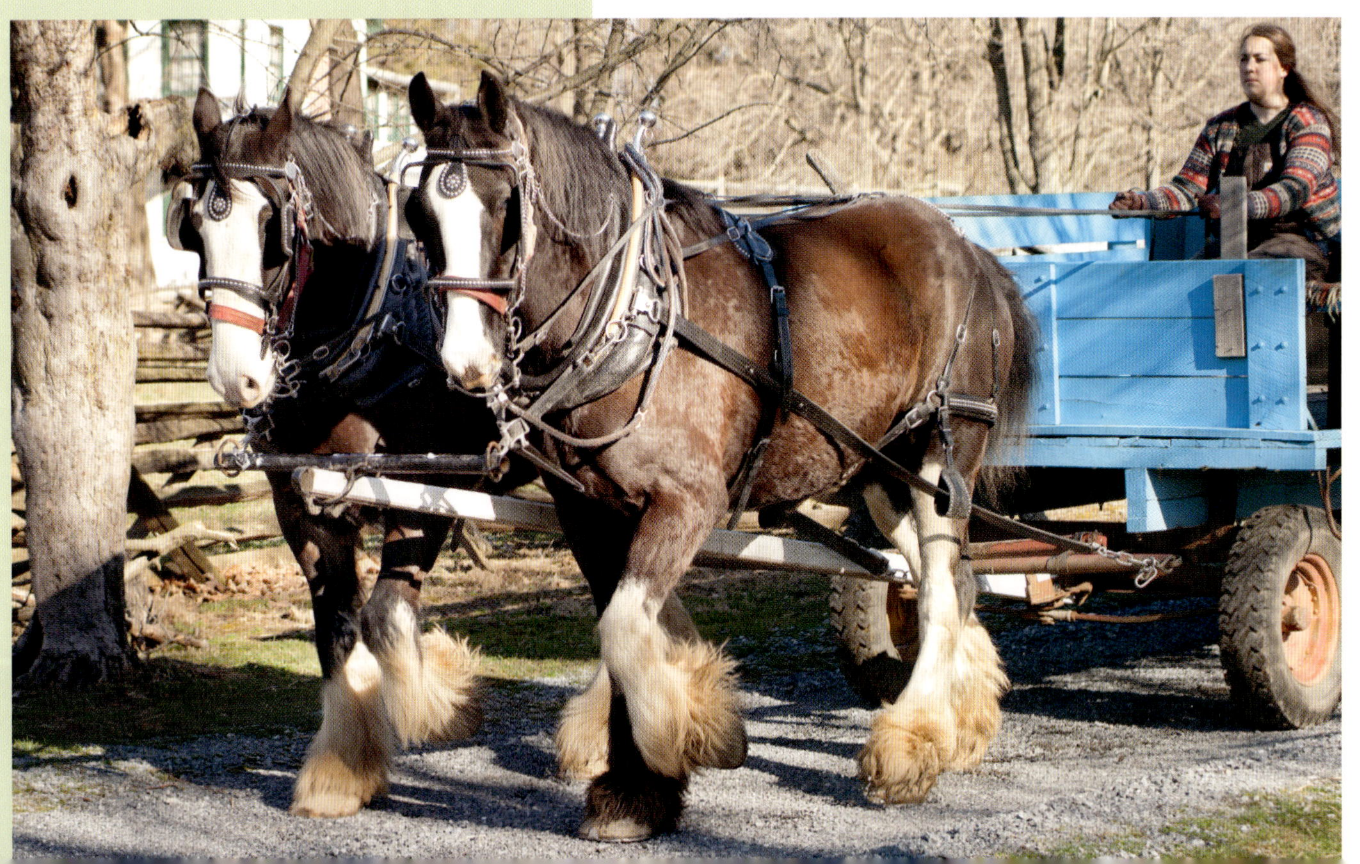

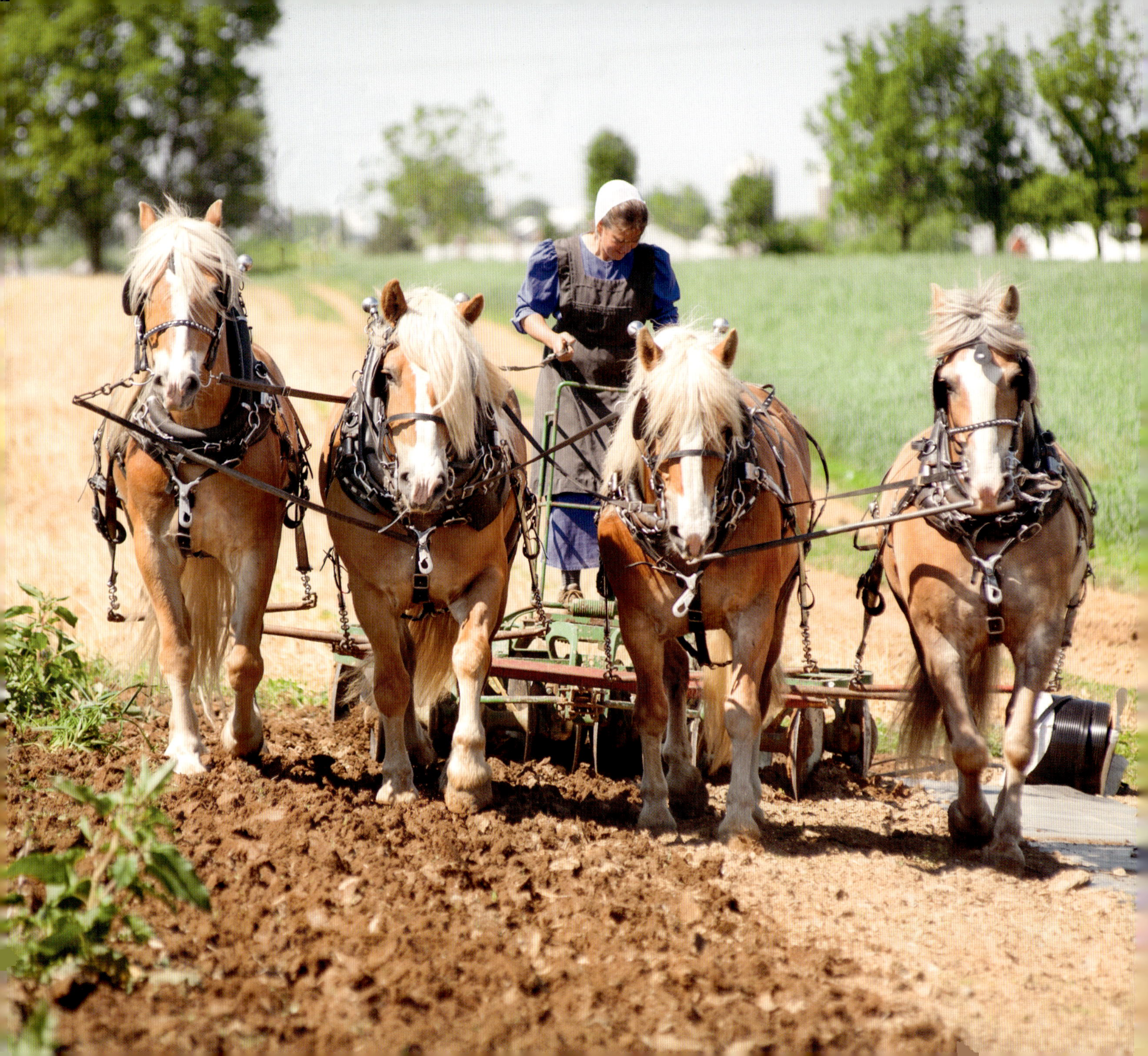

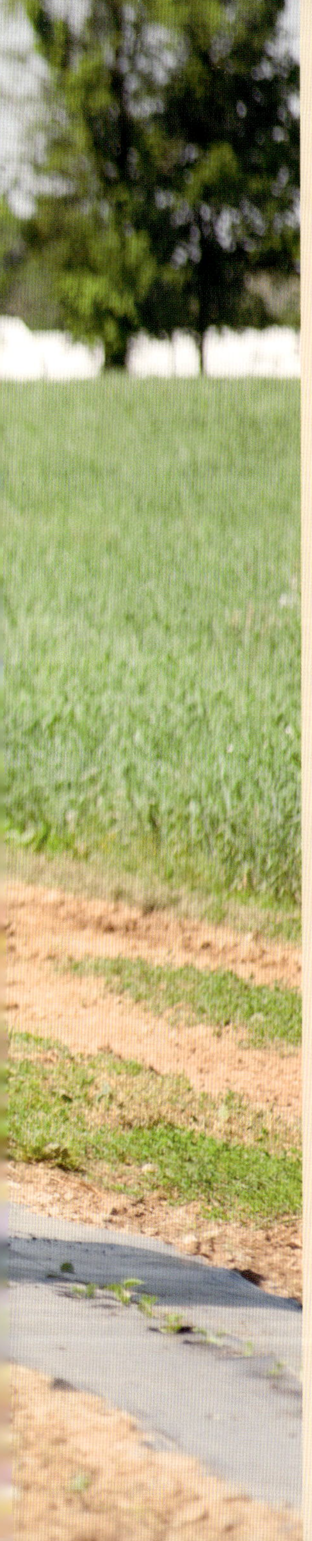

Haflinger

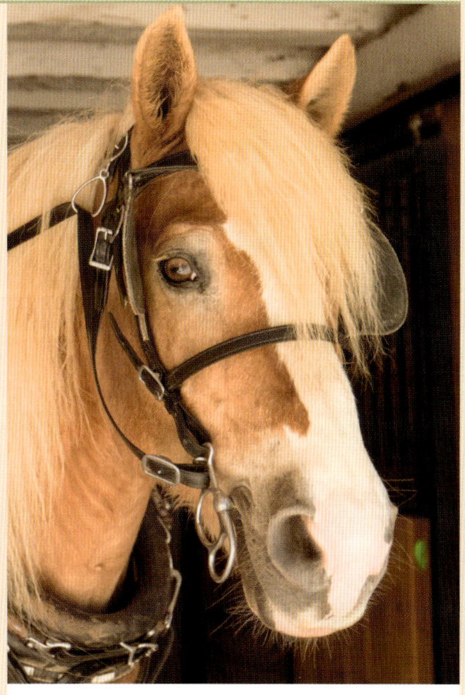

Anna is a great fan of Haflingers—for their good looks, sweet personalities, and hardworking natures. She first bought a Haflinger thirteen years ago and was so impressed she bought another from Holland. She may hitch one up to cultivate the garden, two to mow the meadow or cut hay, or four to disk a field.

At a soft word from Anna and a flip of the reins, Cloud, Junior, Jeff and Jasper leaned into their collars. They pulled the disk through the rich earth, preparing the ground to plant vegetables.

Anna and her parents and sisters grow tobacco, alfalfa, and pumpkins, and tend a huge vegetable garden. Anna also creates oil paintings of horses, makes picture frames and birdhouses from reclaimed wood, and breeds horses. She trains horses in a recently built indoor ring connected to the stable, which also has space to hang hundreds of laths of tobacco to dry in its upper reaches.

"Haflingers are classy, with white manes and feet—and they're really strong for their size."

Origin: village of Hafling, Tyrolean mountains in Austria (now part of Italy)

Height: 13–15hh

Weight: 700–1,200 lbs

Colors: chestnut with flaxen mane and tail

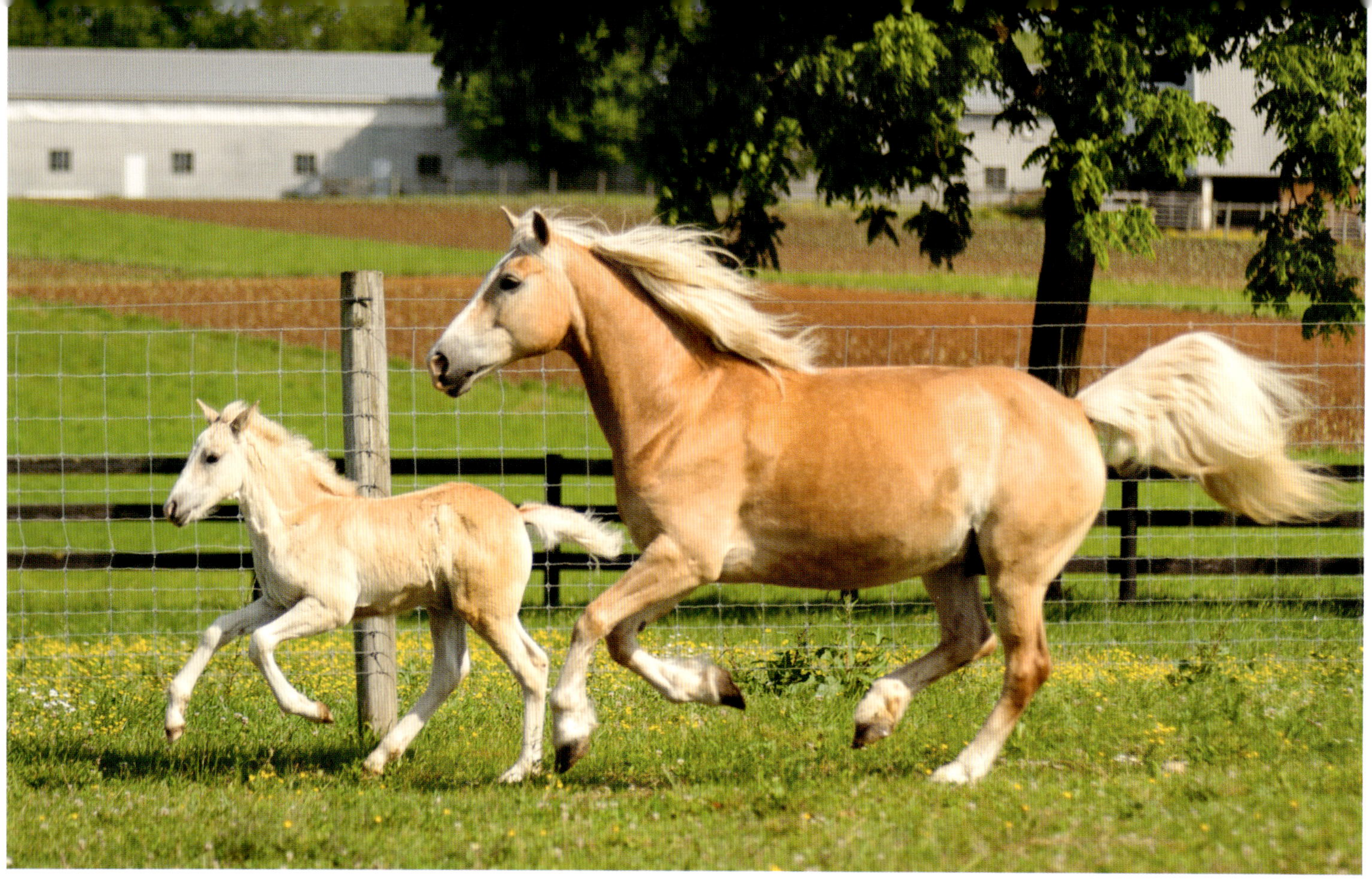

The Haflinger is the crossover vehicle of the horse world. Officially categorized as ponies because of their compact size, Haflingers are versatile enough to do fieldwork, pull a buggy, or carry a rider. They have a clean build, a pleasant temperament, and are well muscled.

Haflingers quickly gained favor when first imported to Lancaster County from Austria in the early 1990s. Their light coats and golden manes and tails captured imaginations, especially when working in matched teams. Soon it was not unusual to see an Amish or Old Order Mennonite buggy pulled by a Haflinger. A few years of boom were followed by a bust when breeders oversaturated the market, and prices dropped. When the population dwindled again, prices evened out.

Their popularity is again growing, and the number of Haflingers in Lancaster County is increasing. More economical to feed and care for than a big draft horse, they're a good fit for tasks on a small property, and they also make fine carriage horses.

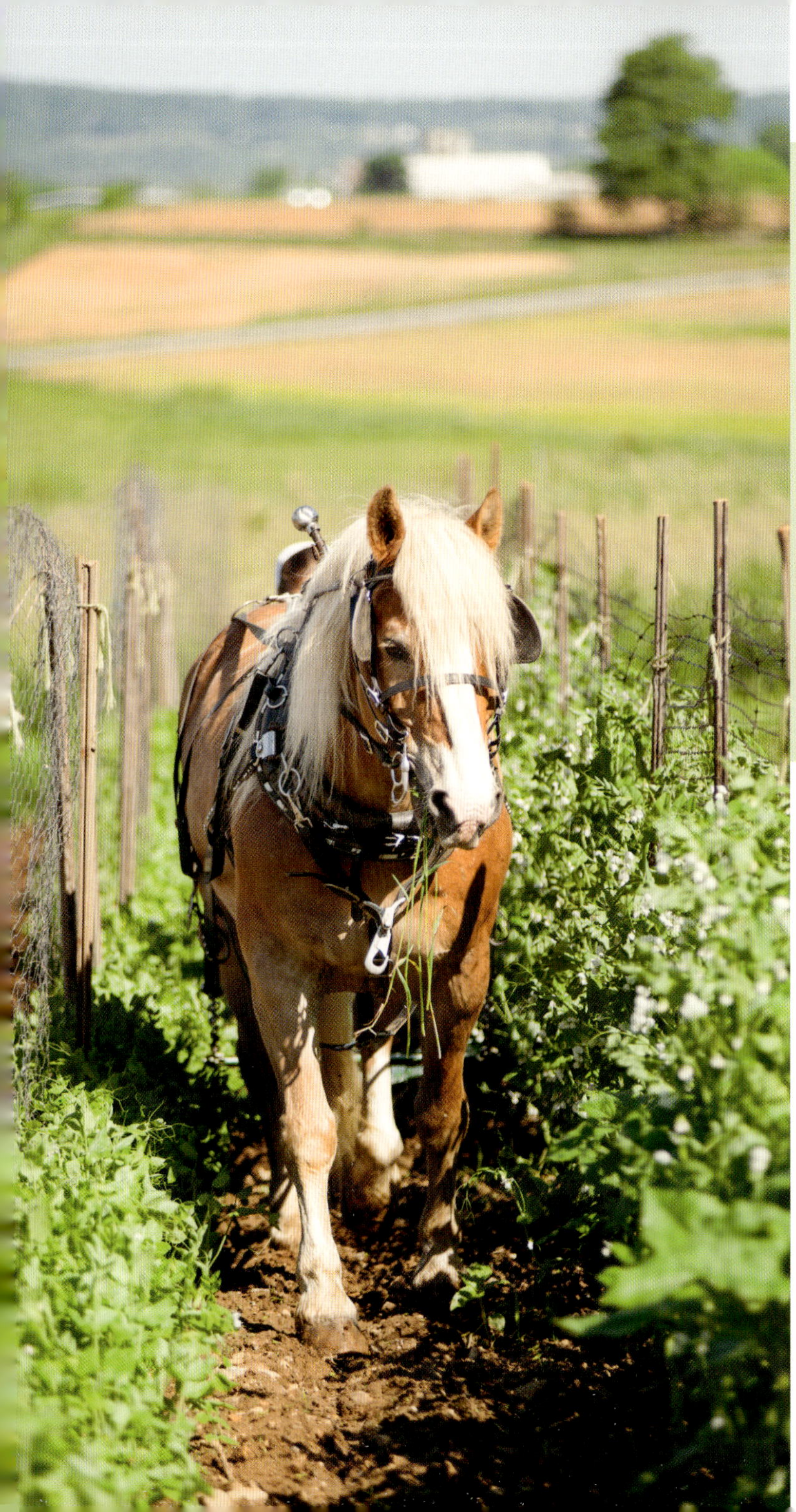

Jeff and Mrs. Wyeth

Phyllis Wyeth visited a local farm a few years ago looking to buy pair of Haflingers. Mrs. Wyeth, wife of artist Jamie Wyeth, walked with canes because of a long-ago car accident. She wanted a team of smaller horses that would be easy to handle. When shown what the family had for sale, she speculated that perhaps they kept their best horses hidden.

Pressed, they brought out their favorite, Jeff, paired with Josie. Mrs. Wyeth talked them into parting with the pair, however after some weeks it was clear that Jeff was a little too feisty for his new owner.

When the two were returned to the farm, the family declared that Jeff was never leaving again. His short mane and forelock took months to grow back in; otherwise he fit right back in with his old team.

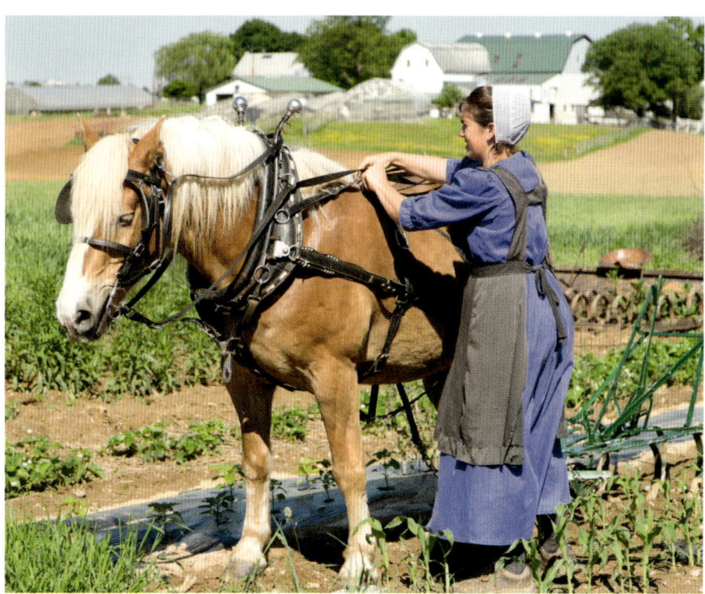

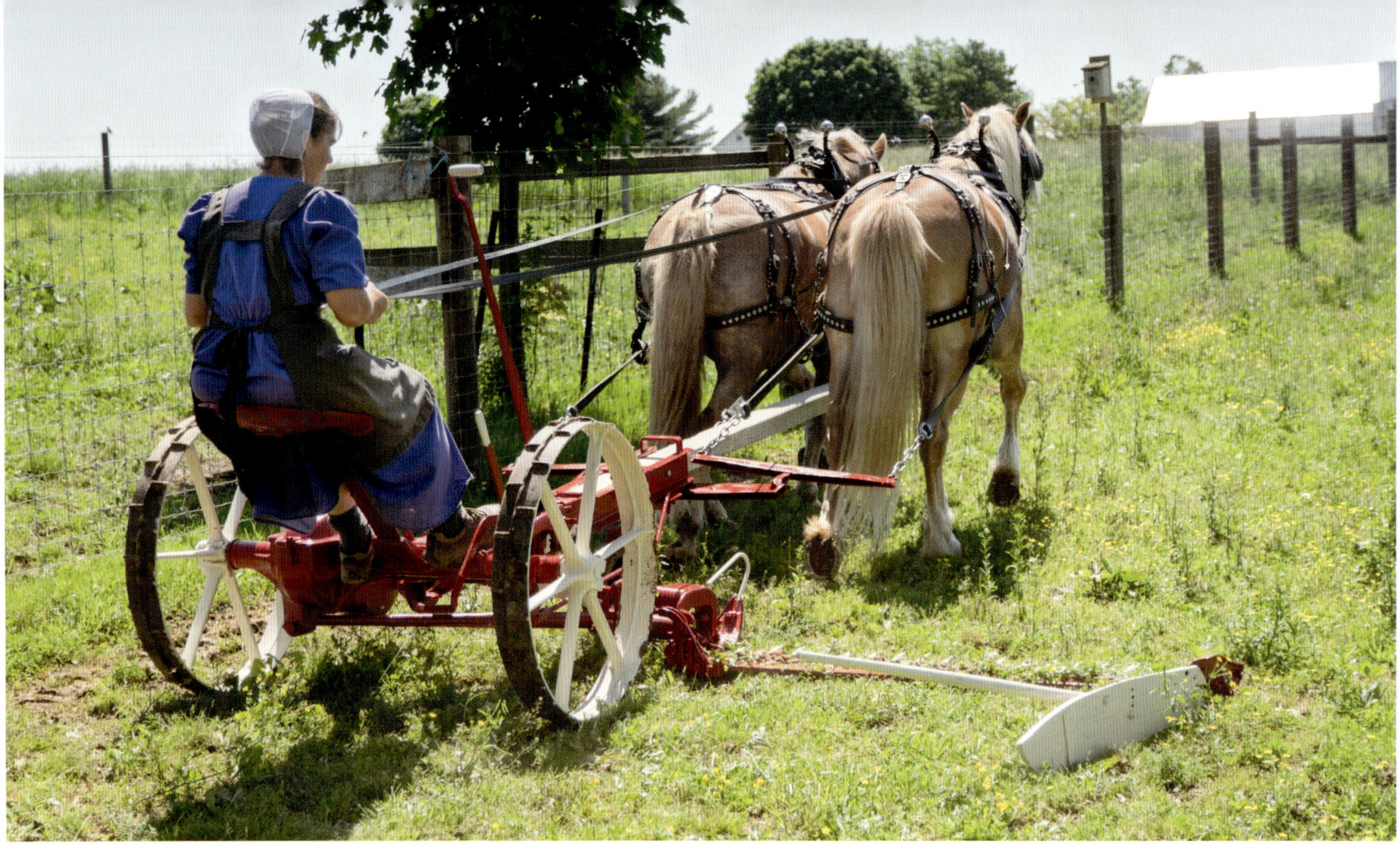

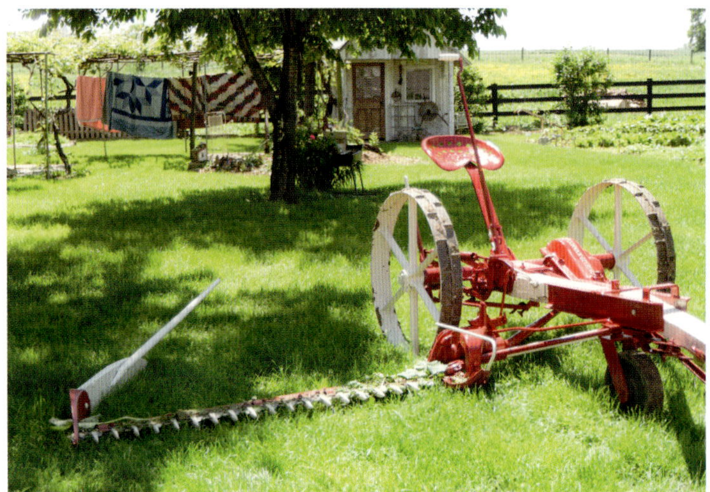

Anna drove Jasper and Cloud when she mowed the meadow. The McCormick-Deering No. 7 sickle bar mower that her dad bought when it was first manufactured in 1929 has been in regular use on the farm for over ninety years. Though they have no intention of retiring it, the mower, repainted in its original colors, looks as lovely parked as it does at work.

"It's pretty enough to sit on the lawn."

Jason grew up in a family of horse enthusiasts. Since his father owned a construction business and there was no farmwork to occupy the eight children, they took up training horses.

The hackney ponies the older boys trained for driving and riding were beautiful and elegant, but the market for them was too small. And zonkeys (a zebra-donkey cross) were only a passing fancy.

They switched to training miniature horses, which were popular and sold quickly. The children prepared fifty to seventy-five minis to sell at auction each year. Even though each child had their own pony, it wasn't easy to part with the other ponies they'd put so much time and love into raising. Jason remembers his sister sobbing at sale time.

Now Jason trains and sells Haflingers in addition to working in construction with his father. Jason's girlfriend, Kirsten, could comfortably harness and drive a buggy horse, but had no particular affinity for horses. That changed when she met Jason. Now they enjoy working with Haflingers together. She helps harness and groom them at sale time and Jason drives them for the previews.

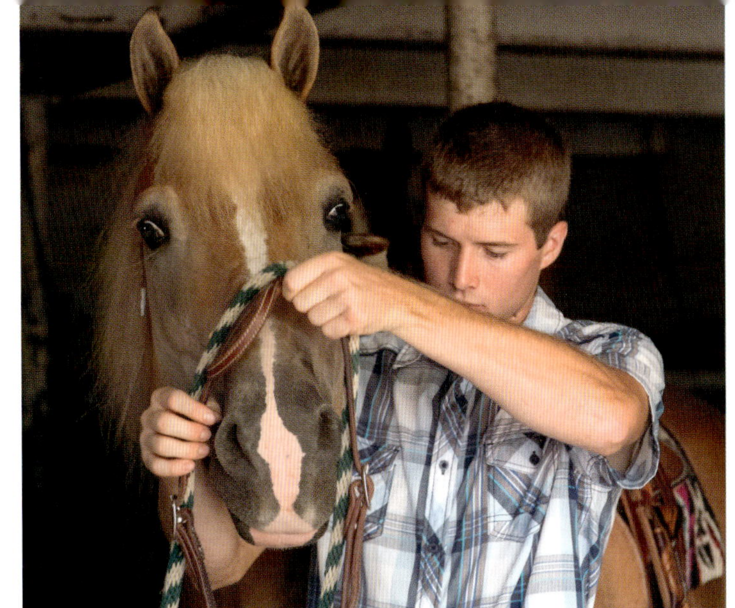

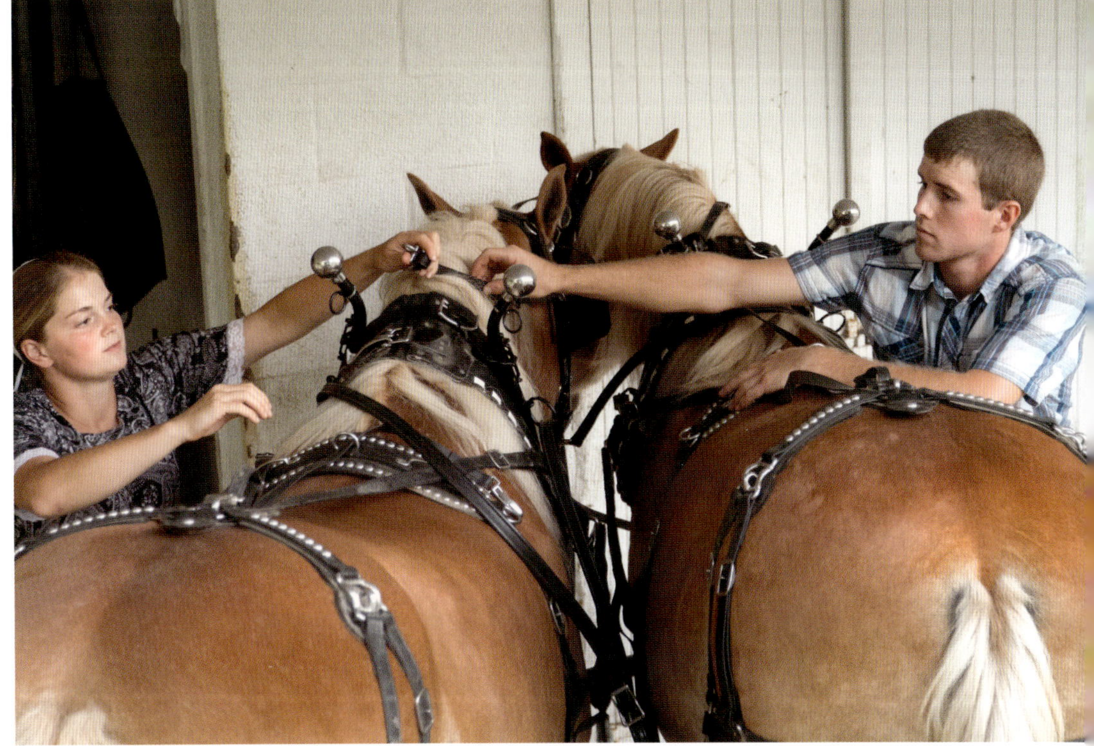

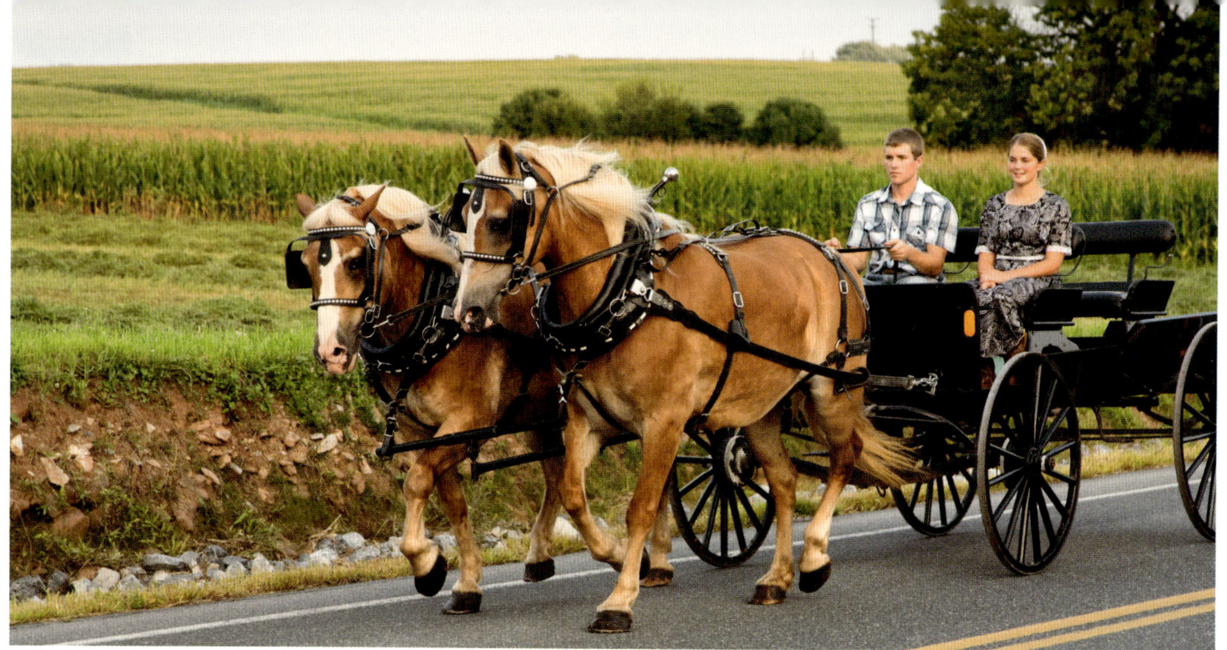

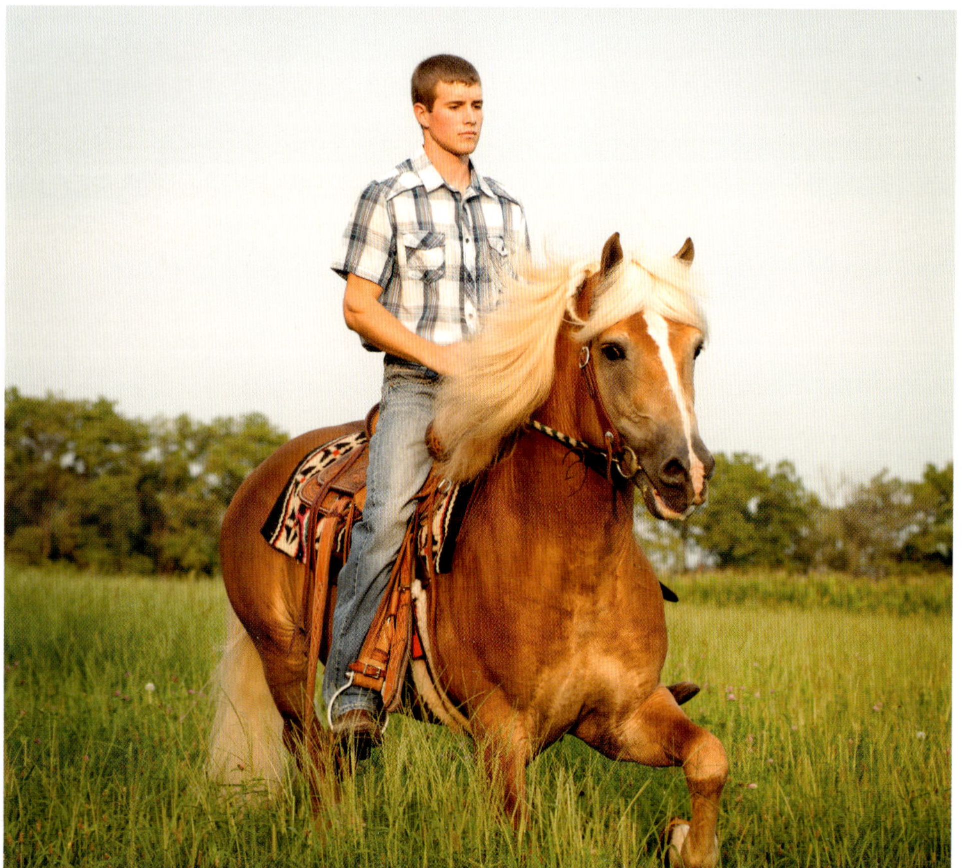

At the end of the summer, Jason took ten Haflingers to the local pony auction. He was especially pleased with his matched pair, Buster and Beauty, *above*. He'd worked with them for months and described them in the sale recommendation as "broke single and double, traffic safe and sound, kid broke."

He presented Captain, *left*, a registered Haflinger stud, standing 14.3 hands and weighing around 1,000 pounds.

Jane, a lovely eleven-year-old Haflinger-Belgian mare, *facing page*, and her harness mate were sold to work on the bidder's small farm in New York State.

Jason sold all ten Haflingers and within a few weeks was buying more horses to polish for the spring sale.

"Buster and Beauty don't pull too hard or too soft—it's just the right amount of rein tension."

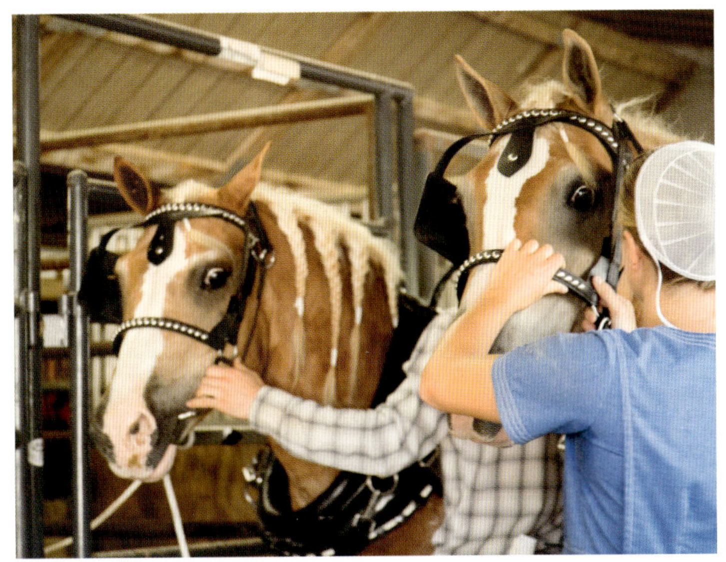

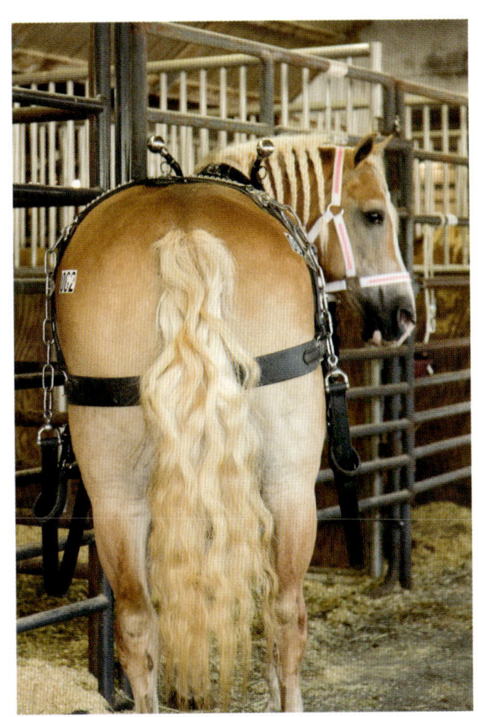

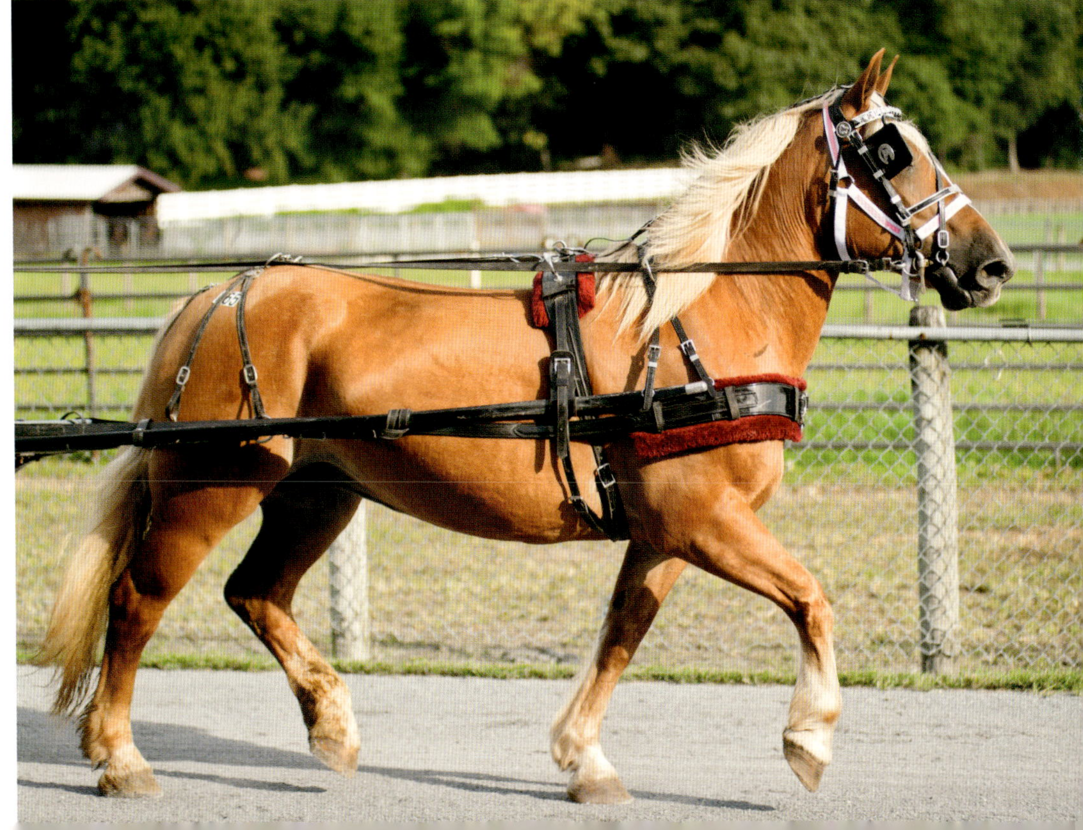

Snowball, a bichon frise, snuggled on the buggy seat while Ada harnessed her favorite pair of Haflingers, brother and sister Pearl and Casey, right.

Ada and Elam have nine horses and a variety of horse-drawn conveyances. There is a closed four-wheel carriage, a four-wheeled open buggy, a four-wheeled spring wagon, and a one-horse open sleigh with slick runners that curve up at the front. The sleigh doesn't get much use since snowy roads are quickly salted these days.

Raring to go on a crisp winter day, the Haflinger team stepped out smartly, perfectly matched in size, coloring, and stride.

Pearl, fourteen, surprised Ada with her first foal in the spring. Last year two neighbor boys had cut across the pasture to go fishing and hadn't latched the gate securely, and a Morgan stallion went visiting. Ada is raising the young one to be a buggy horse and already has her lined up for training when she is a yearling.

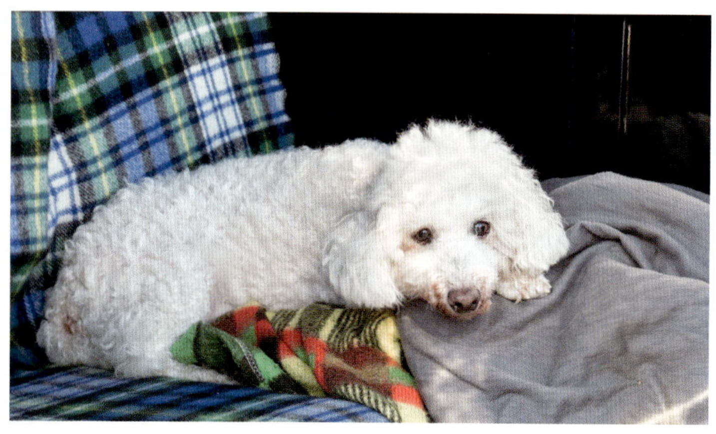

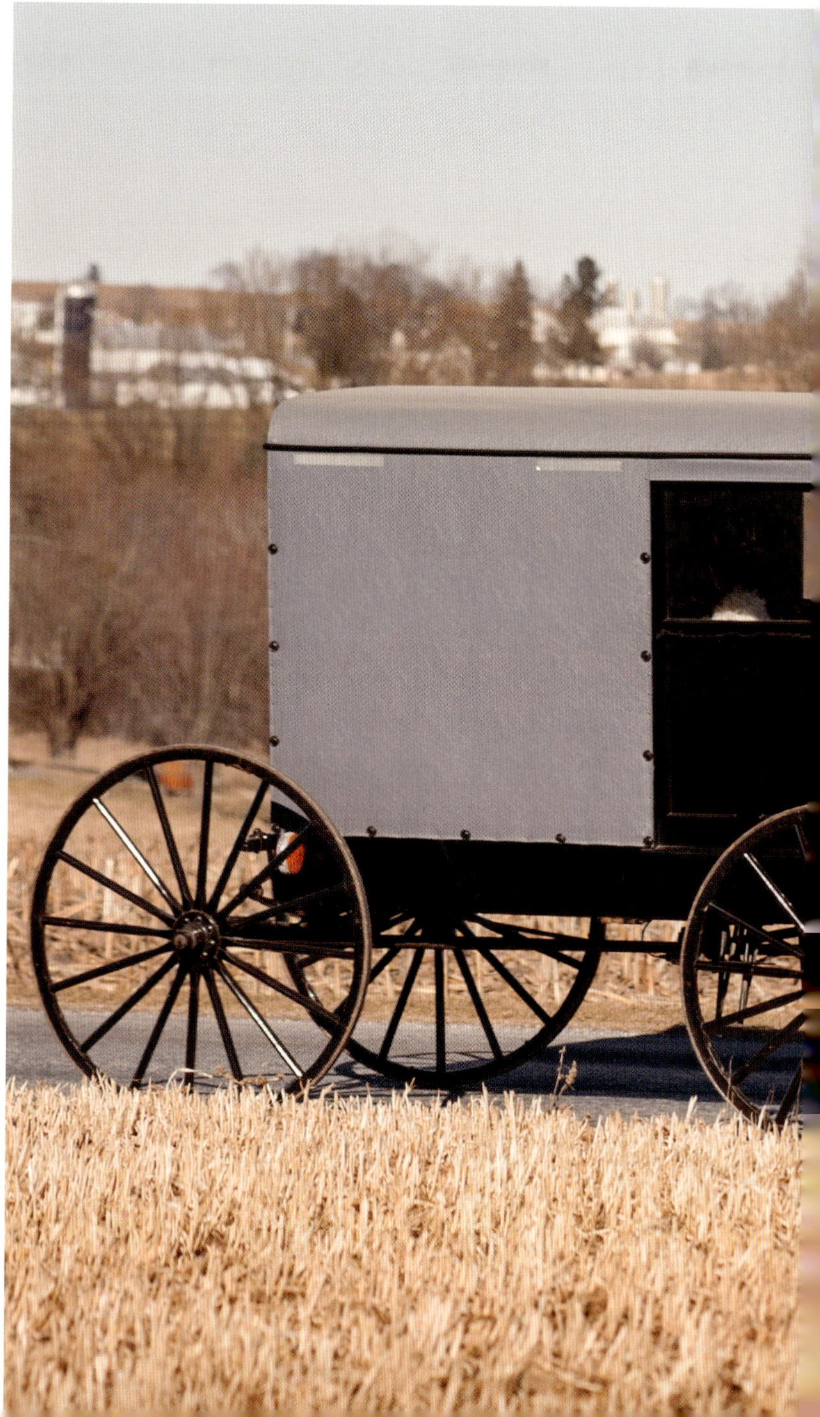

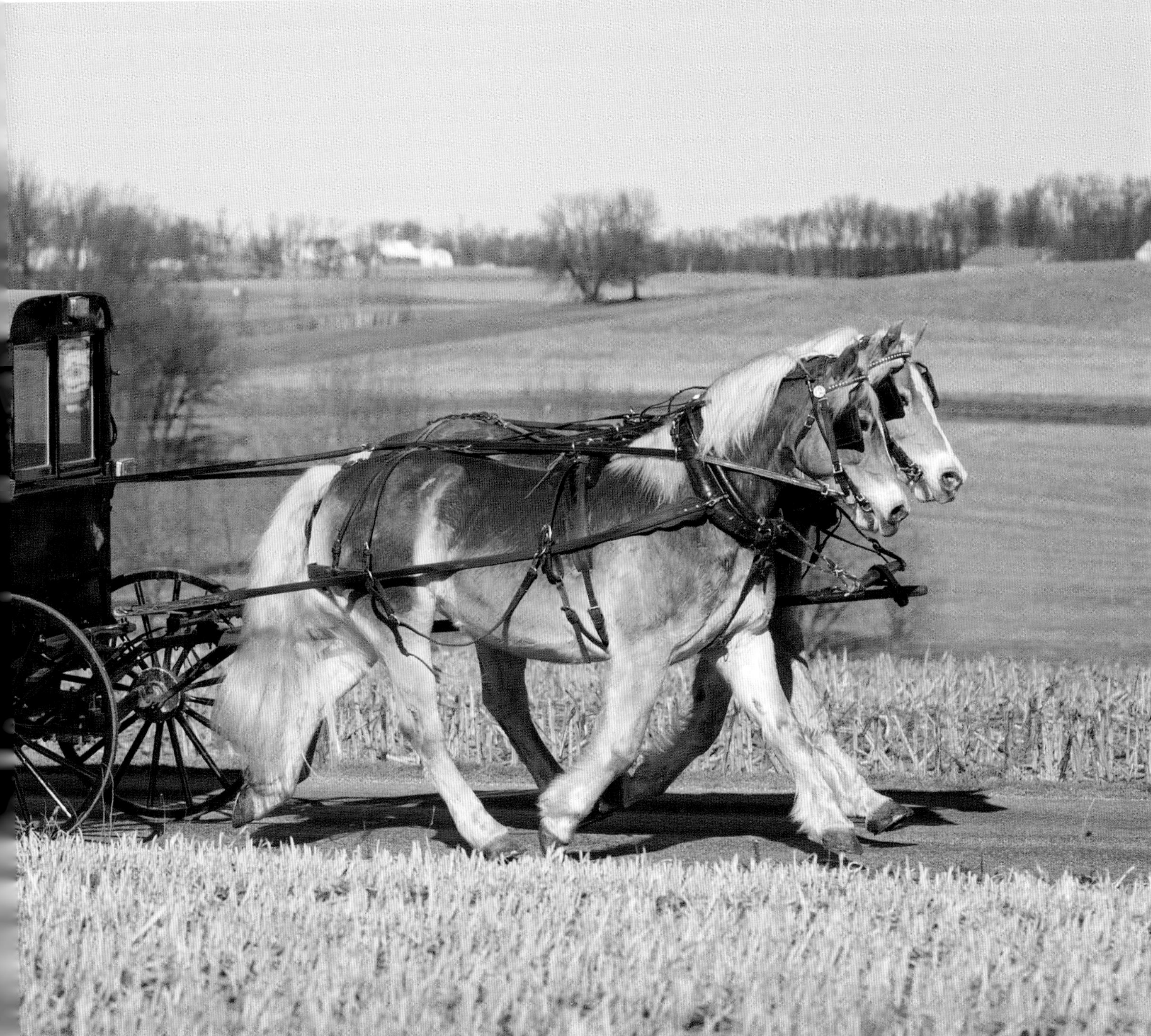

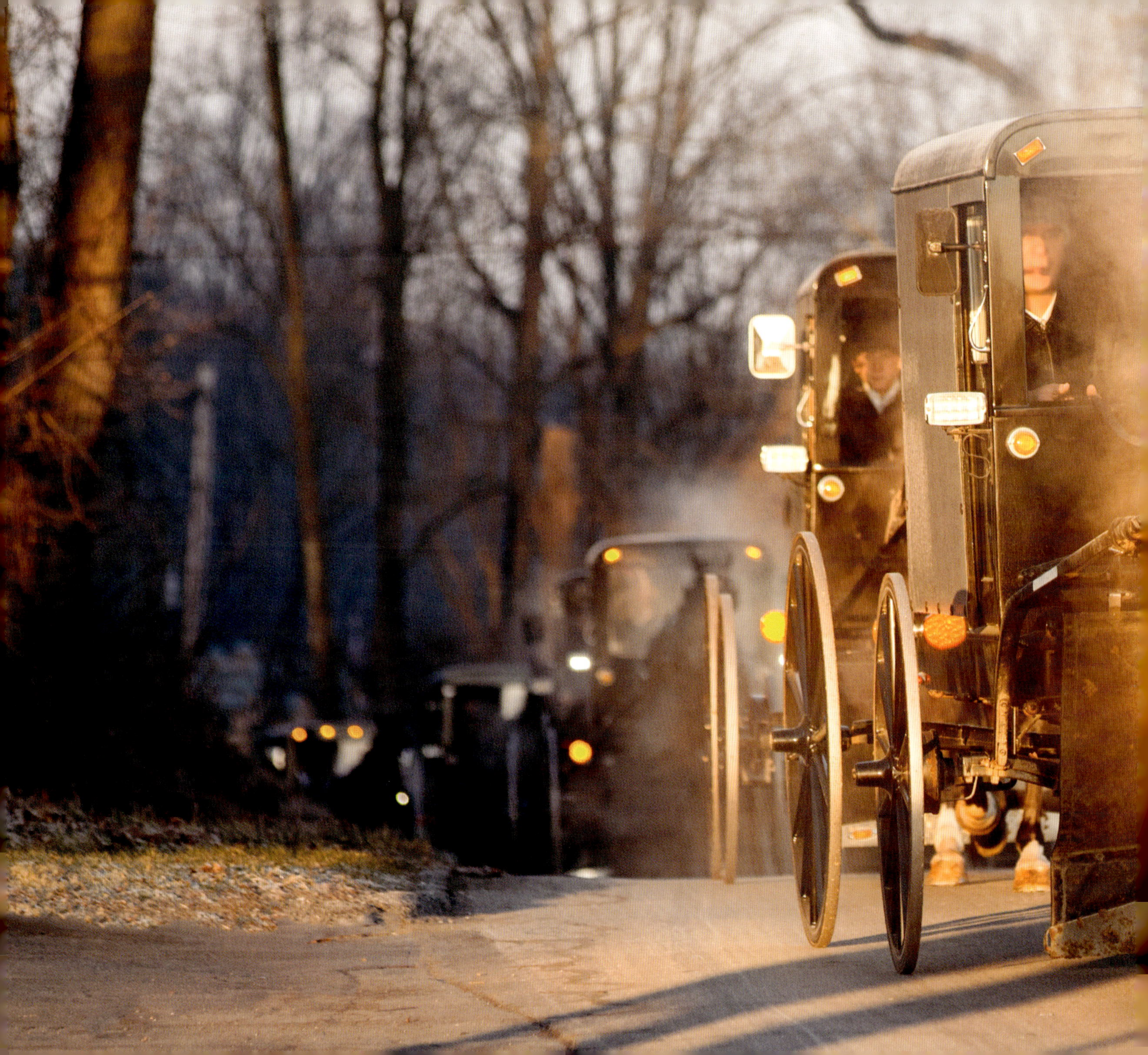

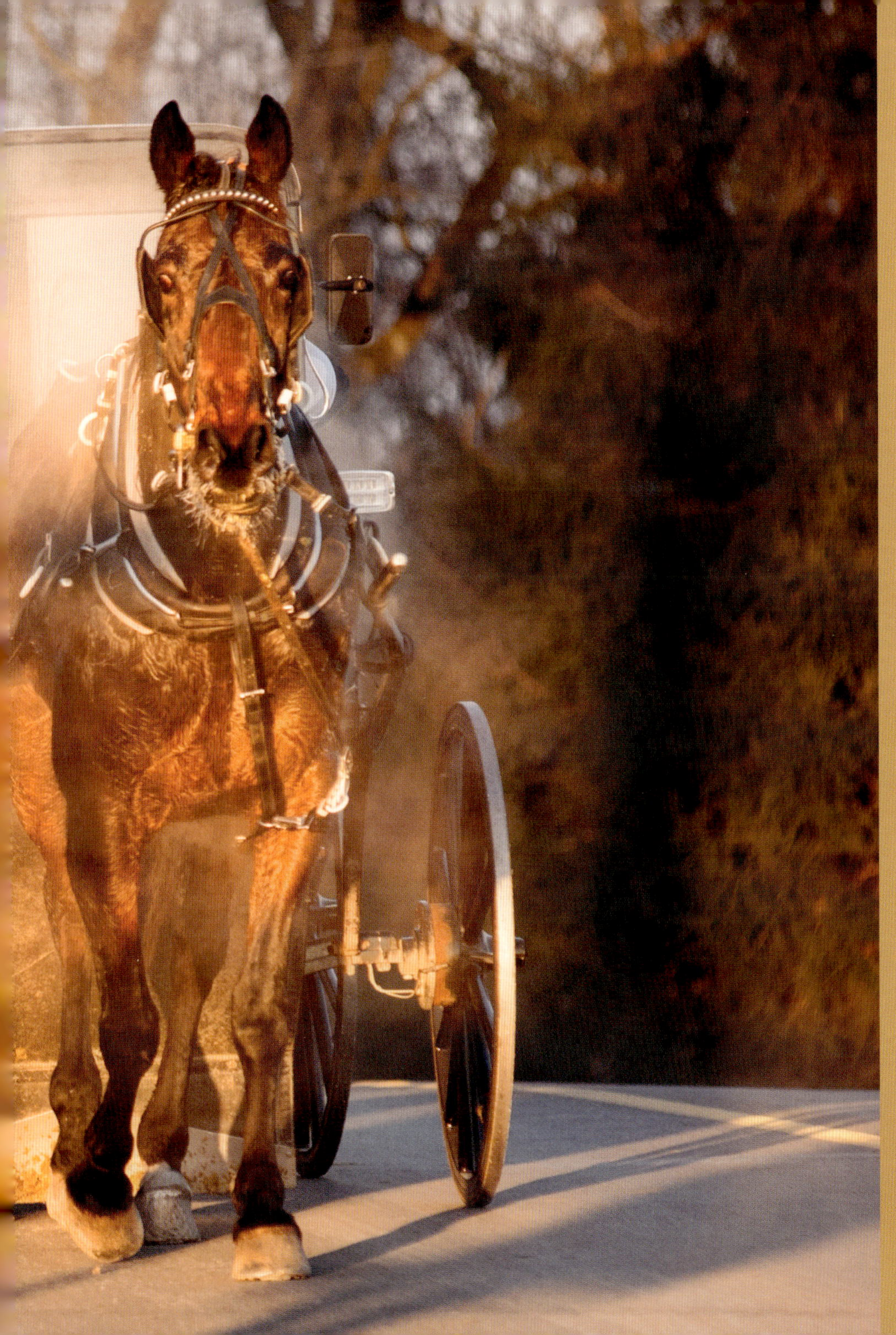

Carriage Horses *of* Lancaster County

Standardbred

Morgan

American Saddlebred

Dutch Harness

Friesian

Matt, sixteen, had been thinking about the ideal horse. Most of his family and teenaged church friends drove Standardbreds, so that was a natural choice. But he wanted something a little special.

Many influences come into play when a young man chooses a buggy horse. As with other major decisions, he looks to his community for guidance. There may be a breed loyalty going back generations. Friends or older brothers may advise. Since his dad will help finance the purchase, the two will look at the possibilities together.

Young women typically use the family buggy horse when needed rather than buying their own.

Matt's dad maintained that he simply wanted an easy-to-handle horse for Matt that would get him from here to there safely. He leaned toward a gelding rather than a mare. Matt's mom reminded them of the importance of good looks and spirit. They certainly didn't want a horse that "looks like a cow going down the road," head down and plodding.

They planned to buy at an auction, and Dad read the catalog ahead of time to review the horses' bloodlines, ages, and whether they were traffic safe. The auctioneer gave a description, known as a "recommendation," when he introduced each horse. Bidders studied the horses as runners led them one at a time at a fast trot around the ring to show how they moved. Matt and his dad wanted a horse with good looks, not the showiest, but one that carried itself nicely and had potential.

As Dad reminded Matt, the final decision, really, is the amount you have in your purse.

They were pleased to bring home a nearly black six-year-old gelding. Strike had excellent bloodlines and was bred for harness racing but didn't quite make the grade. Matt loved the name Strike and felt as if he had struck gold with such a good horse that had plenty of spunk. Dad decided to drive Strike for a couple of weeks to make sure he handled well before passing him on to Matt.

Matt enjoys driving Strike, but he's not sure how long he'll have him. Some young men keep their first horses well into their married years, while others make a change to accommodate their young families.

When Matt's older brother was courting his girlfriend, he had an agreeable horse that he drove 10 miles twice each weekend to visit her. After they got married, the horse wasn't used as much and got too feisty for his wife to drive. The couple bought a calmer horse that they could both drive and that would be reliable when children came along.

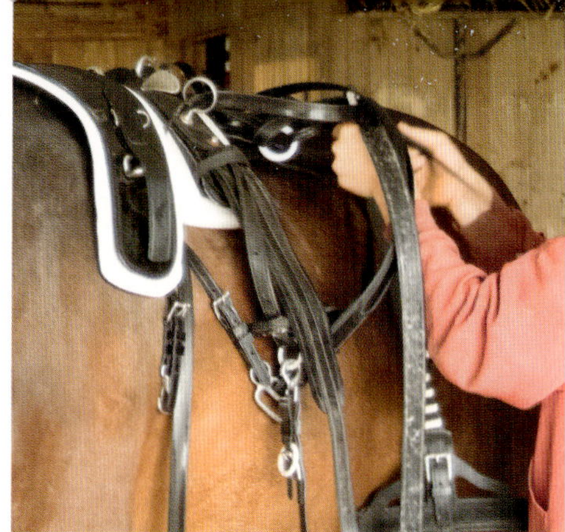

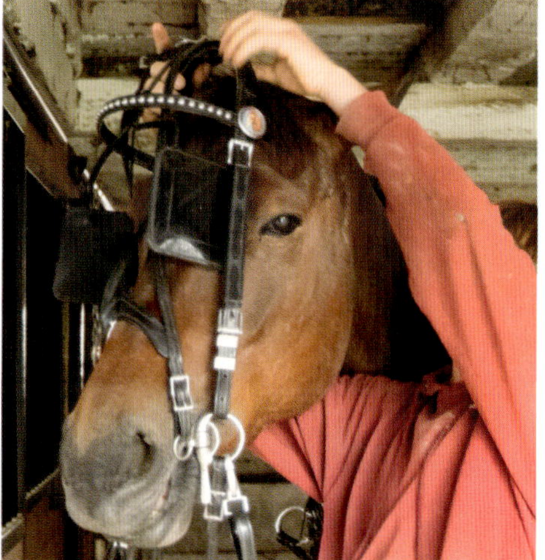

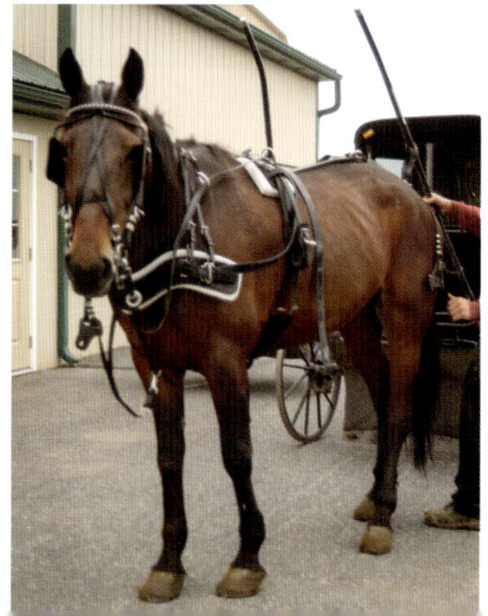

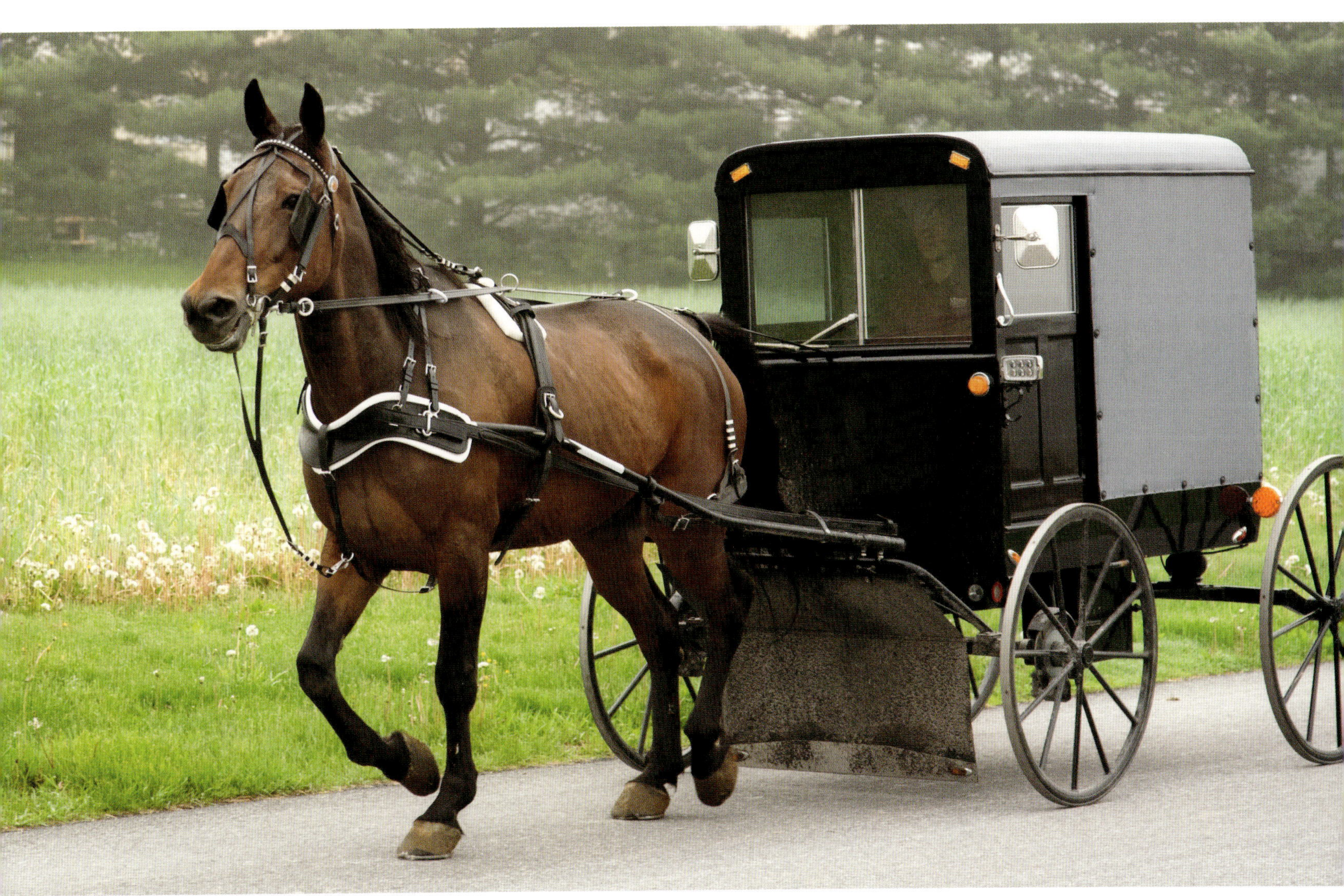

"We wanted to buy a horse that had hidden promise. Then the price wouldn't be too high."

Horses that pull Amish and Mennonite carriages in Lancaster County generally stand 15 to 16 hands tall and weigh around 1,000 lbs. The most common breed is Standardbred, followed by American Saddlebred and Morgan. Employed less often and usually crossed with Standardbred or Saddlebred are Dutch Harness and Friesian.

When horse-and-buggy people gather for large events such as weddings, funerals, family gatherings, or church services, there are dozens of horses to manage. Drivers park their buggies or carts in rows and put their horses in the barn.

If it is a public event or the number of horses exceeds the space in the barn, flatbed wagons are parked and filled with hay. Horses are tied around the perimeter, as shown at the right.

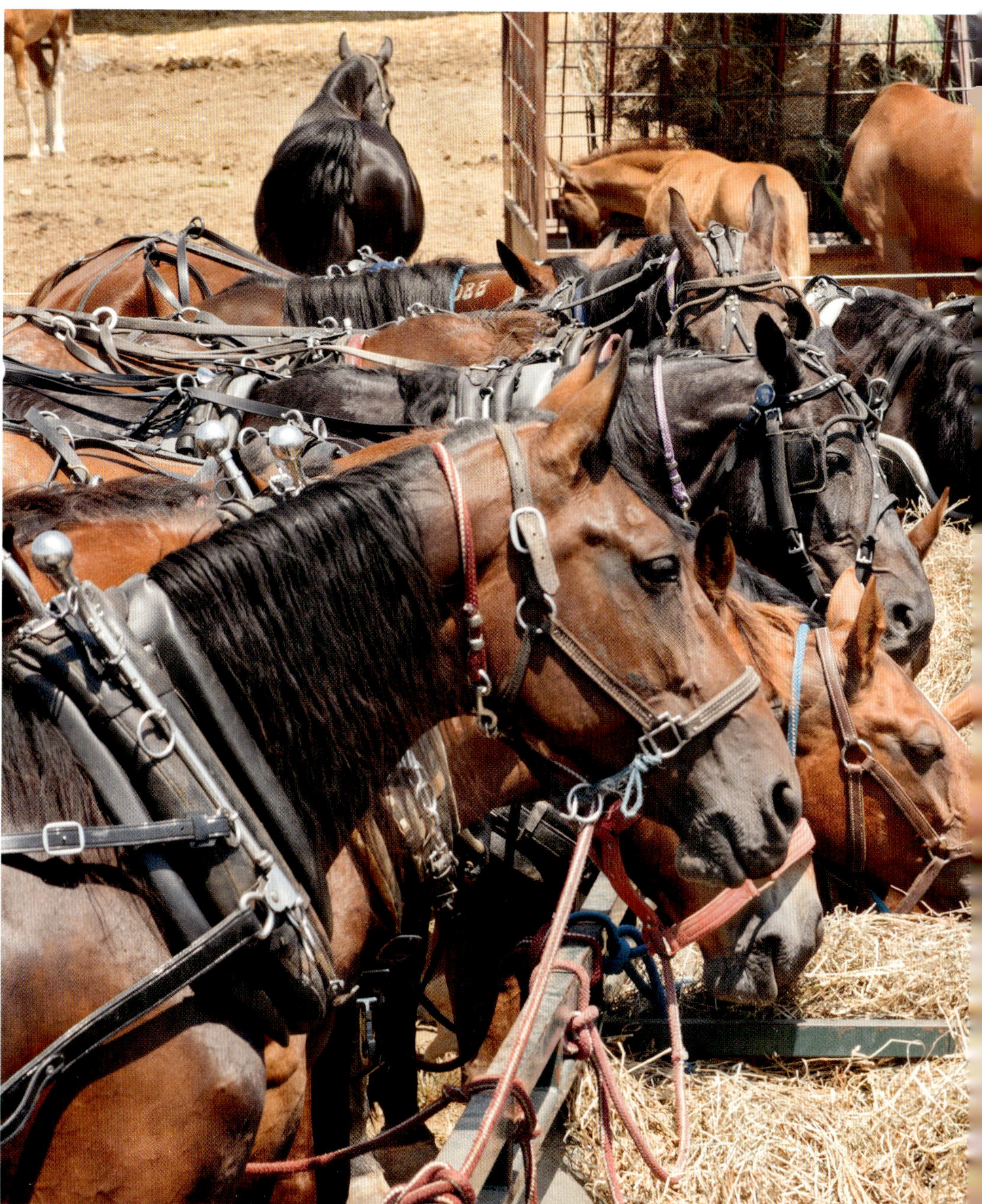

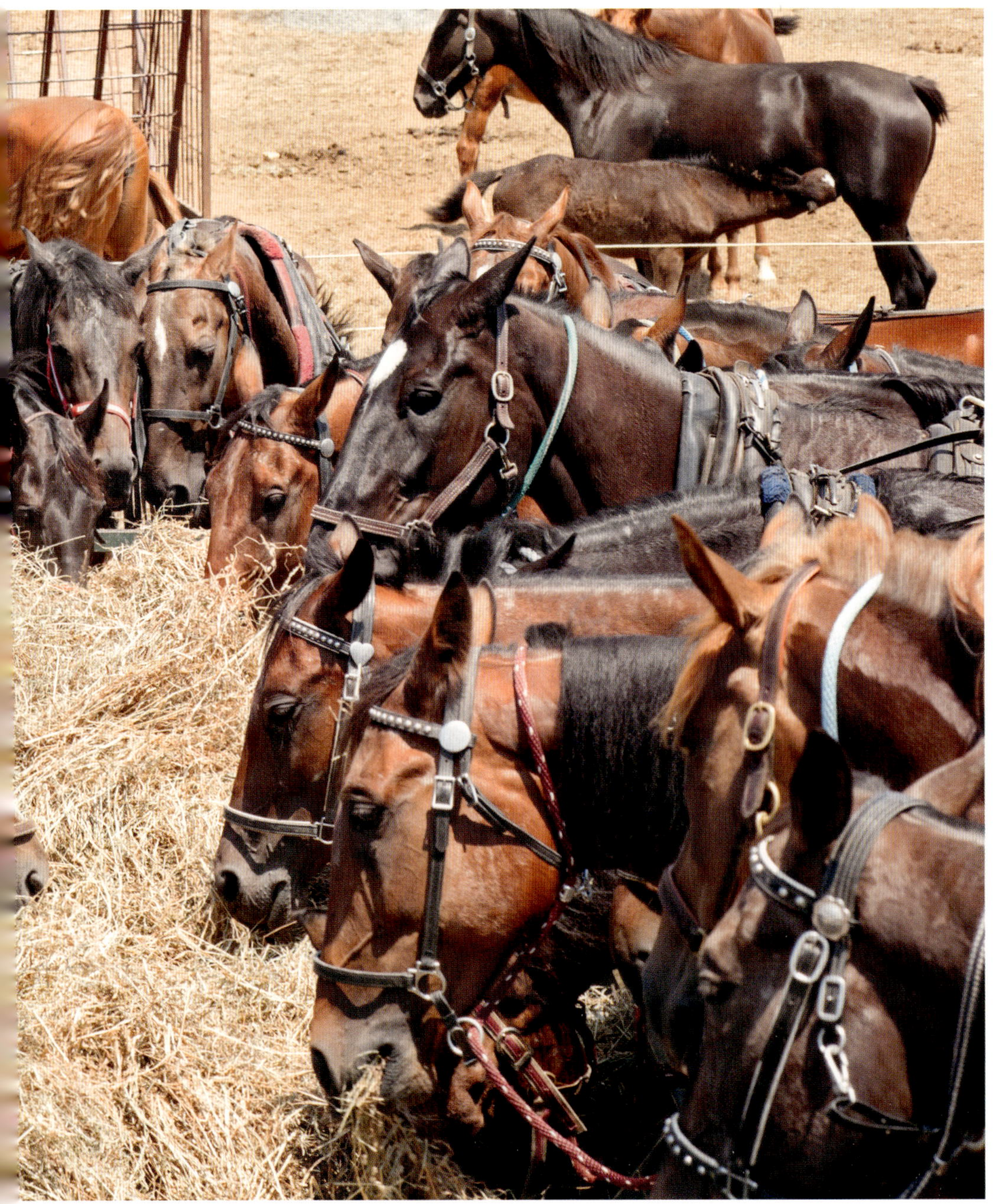

A carriage horse is generally trained at age two and will work until eighteen or twenty or older. Each age has its merits. Buy at age:

- three or four and you will need to finish to the horse's training;
- five or six and your horse will be ready to drive—this age is the most expensive;
- eight to ten to know what you're getting—it's a good time to buy since any weaknesses will be evident;
- eighteen to twenty and your horse may be slowing down, depending on its health and breed.

Horses, like people, go through phases from young and lively to mature and sedate. If the timing is right, a horse coming up on eighteen or so will be matched with a driver who is also slowing down. An older horse is often called a "pappy horse." That means the horse is appropriate for an older man to drive and won't give him any trouble. Just like with Grandpa and his car, families sometimes have to have a conversation with Pappy about which horse he should be driving, or if he should even drive at all.

An untrained horse is initially turned into a round pen, *right,* and guided to trot around the perimeter through body language and verbal commands. When the horse demonstrates an understanding of the basics by maintaining a consistent pace and changing directions as instructed, training advances to the long lead, *far right.* The horse is introduced to a bridle and is guided by lines threaded through rings on a narrow training harness.

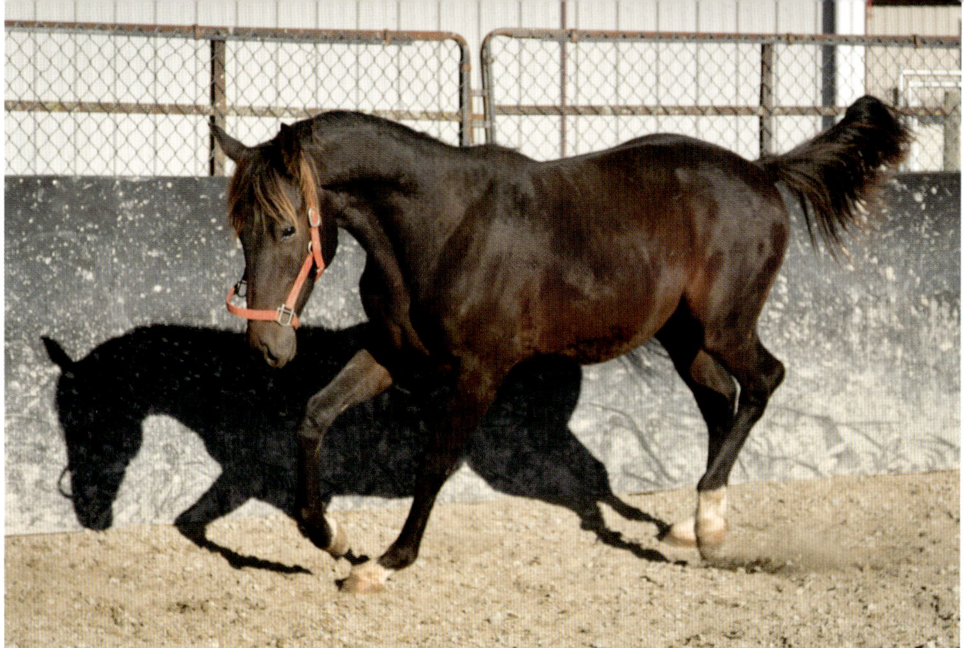

Some horses are more sensitive than others. It is essential that a trainer or driver working with an inexperienced or highly responsive horse proceed logically with extra gentleness and understanding.

One example: If a sensitive horse is asked to pull a carriage on gravel and has to pull a little harder to get the buggy moving, it may simply give up. The horse needs to be encouraged and supported so that failure is averted. Just a bit of progress each day may be all that is needed to reassure such a horse.

Good care also means protecting them from the elements and making accommodations in extreme weather. Horse owners are cautious about taking them on the road when it is especially hot or cold, or when rain is heavy or winds strong.

When fall arrives and the temperature drops, horses' coats grow longer and thicker. Horses can fluff their hair out, which increases their natural insulation and provides more warmth than a heavy blanket. The winter coat is also naturally greasy, which helps it repel snow, ice, and sleet.

Since horses acclimate well to winter conditions, when given a choice they often prefer spending time outside to being inside.

To prevent the horse from catching a chill after a cold-weather drive, owners blanket their horses upon arrival. Horses driven in a few inches of snow sometimes have dressing applied to their hooves to keep snow from sticking and turning into ice.

When traveling in hot weather, drivers give their horses frequent breaks and plenty of water; when horses sweat, it helps cool them. If it's especially hot and the sweat dries quickly, some owners carry a gallon of water to pour over their horses midtrip. Horses are tied in the shade at their destination; when they return home, they are hosed off.

Fly spray and soft mesh face masks are sometimes used to protect eyes and ears from gnats and flies in the meadow.

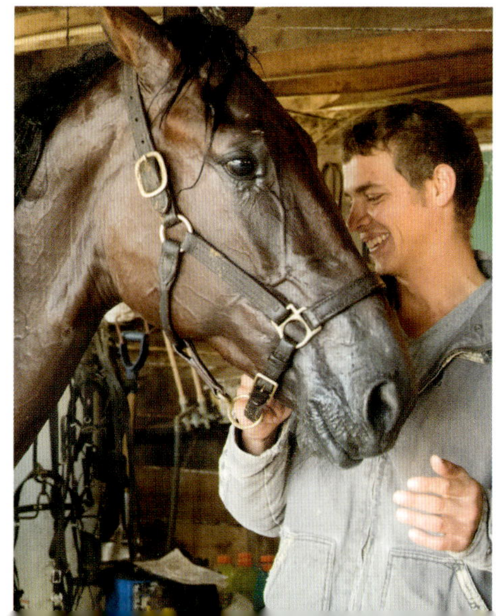

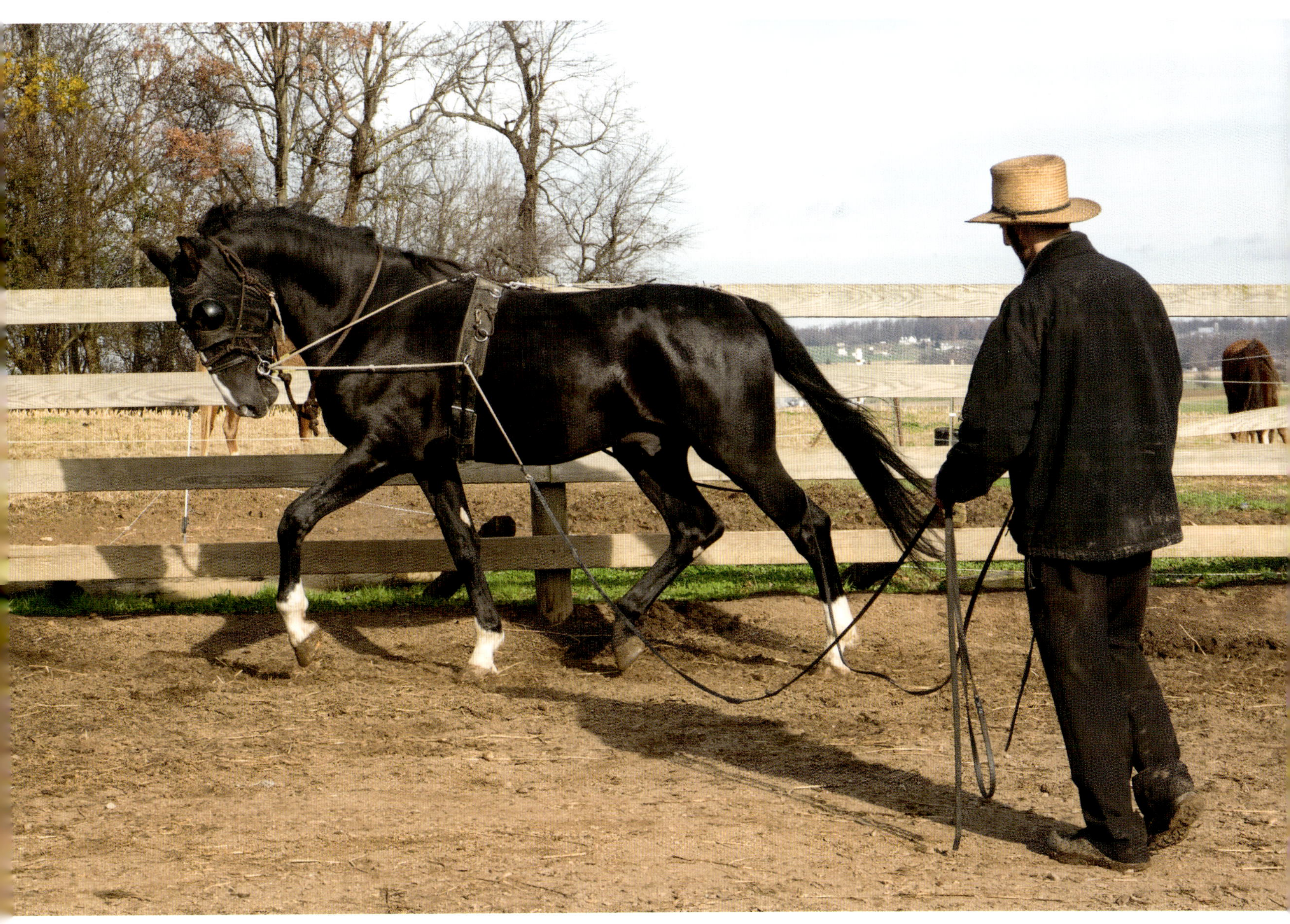

“Horses need to be encouraged and supported.”

An experienced horseman—who has observed the mistakes that some owners make—offers these instructions to his fellow buggy drivers:

The checkrein, a line that goes from the back of the horse's head to the shoulder harness, helps keep the horse under control. Set too tight, it pulls the head up too high for comfort. It's better to buy a horse that naturally holds its head high.

Some drivers use a buggy whip occasionally to redirect the horse's attention, especially if the horse is just learning. Using a whip repeatedly to encourage more speed is poor horsemanship. Providing better care, including plenty of food and extra vitamins, may improve a horse's performance. But don't expect more than your horse has to give. If speed is important, buy a faster horse.

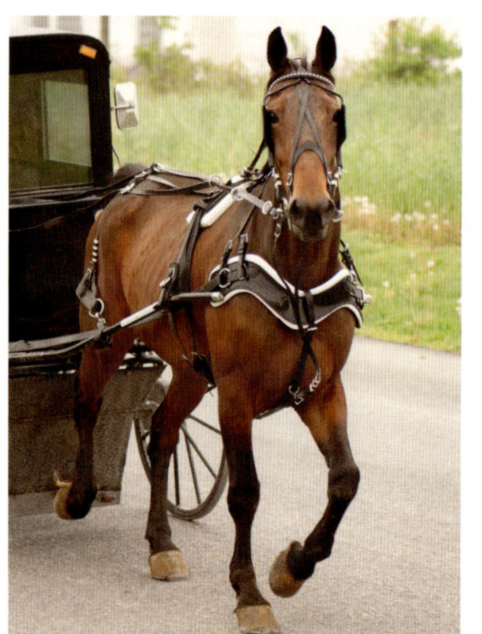

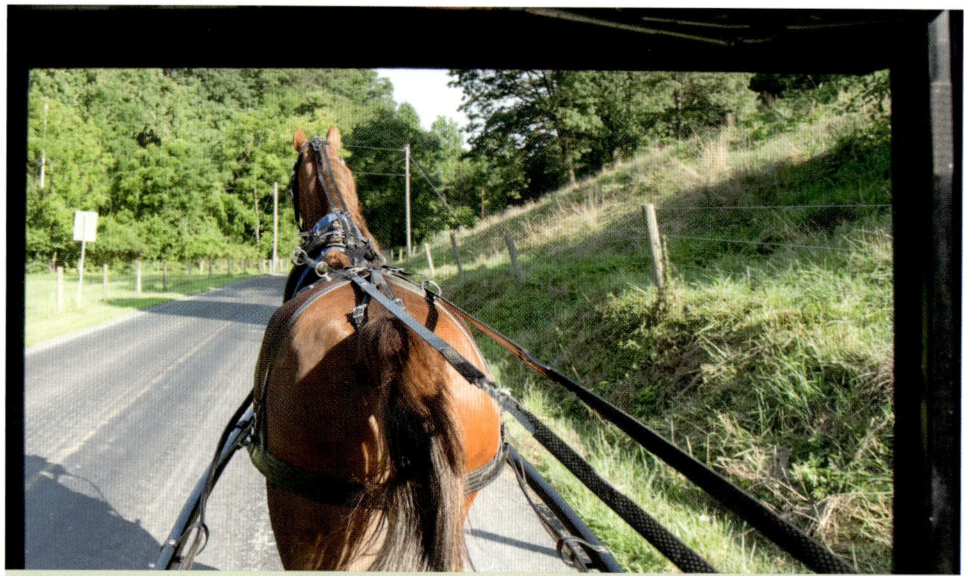

Why drive from the right?

In the early days, there was no standard for driving from the right or left side of the seat. People simply did what was logical to them. Since most people carried the whip in their right hand, it would have been impractical to lean across a passenger to use it. The brake was typically on the right too.

In 1792, Pennsylvania established a turnpike from Lancaster to Philadelphia and mandated that travel would be on the right side of the road. Drivers sat on the right side so they could ensure that their buggy or wagon didn't run into the ditch.

Cars initially had steering wheels on the right as well, but they moved to the left following the design of the popular Ford Model T in 1912. Drivers of horse-drawn vehicles, however, continued to sit on the right.

Lancaster County carriage and wagon drivers carry on this long-held tradition. Junior explained why he sits at the right when he drives his buggy: "My wife sits to my left, beside my heart."

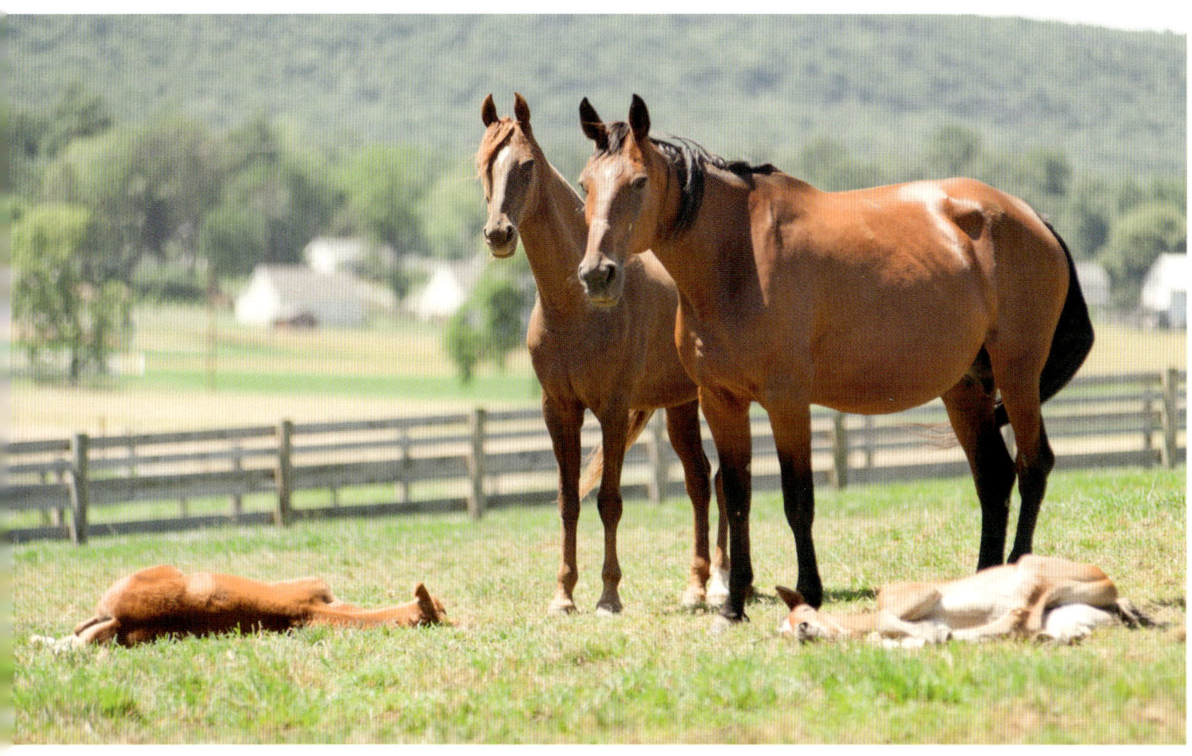

It's not unusual to see foals stretched out on the ground sleeping, all tuckered out from frolicking, while their mamas keep watch.

Adult horses sleep standing up, though they sometimes lie down for a few minutes in the sun. If they have plenty of space and good bedding, they will also flatten out to sleep in their stalls. Horses sleep for only three hours total in a twenty-four-hour period, usually for a few minutes at a time.

Horses are social creatures that enjoy being with others, equine or human. They develop bonds through mutual grooming with their stable or meadow mates and regularly connect by nuzzling and nipping each other or just standing close.

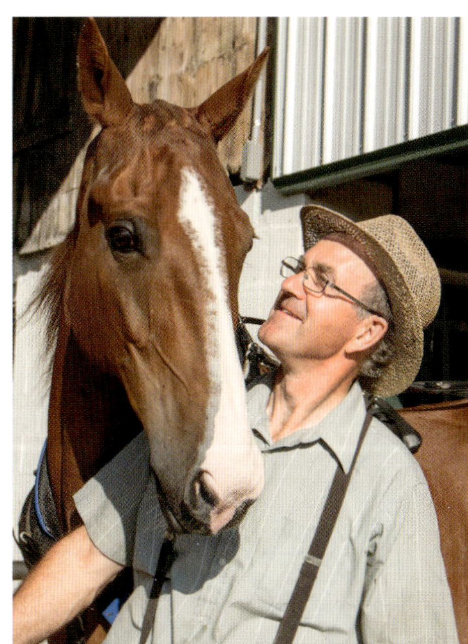

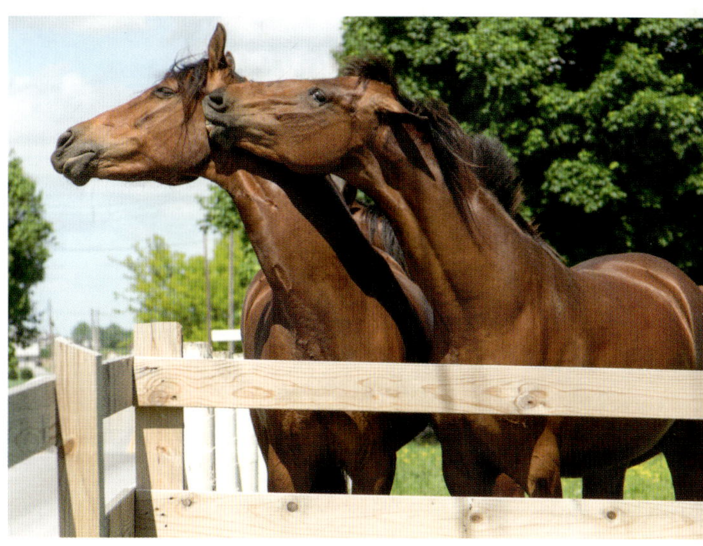

Unlike cars, which can be parked and forgotten, horses need attention regardless of whether they're working. Routine horse care includes daily food, water, and exercise, along with regular grooming, dental check-ups, and hoof upkeep.

Young horses are taught early on to cooperate when their feet are lifted. It's much easier to begin the lesson with a 300-pound foal than a 1,200-pound adult.

A buggy horse has its hooves trimmed and shoes replaced every eight weeks or so, more often if there are injuries or weaknesses in the hooves. The correct kind of shoe and padding results in a good gait and contributes to overall good health.

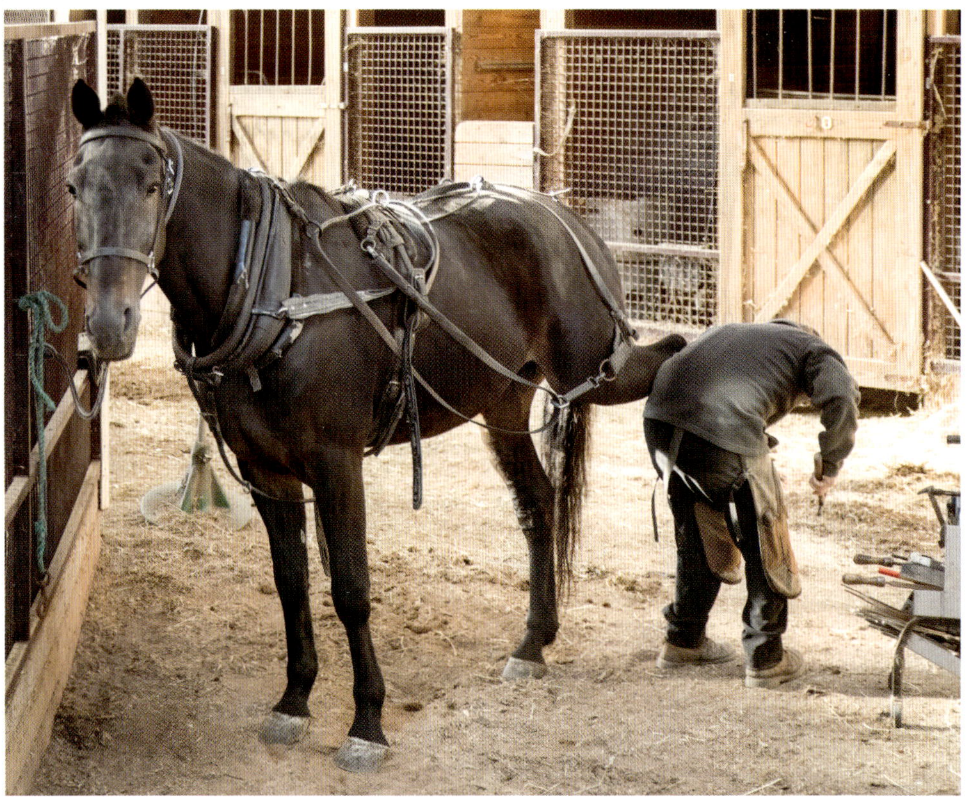

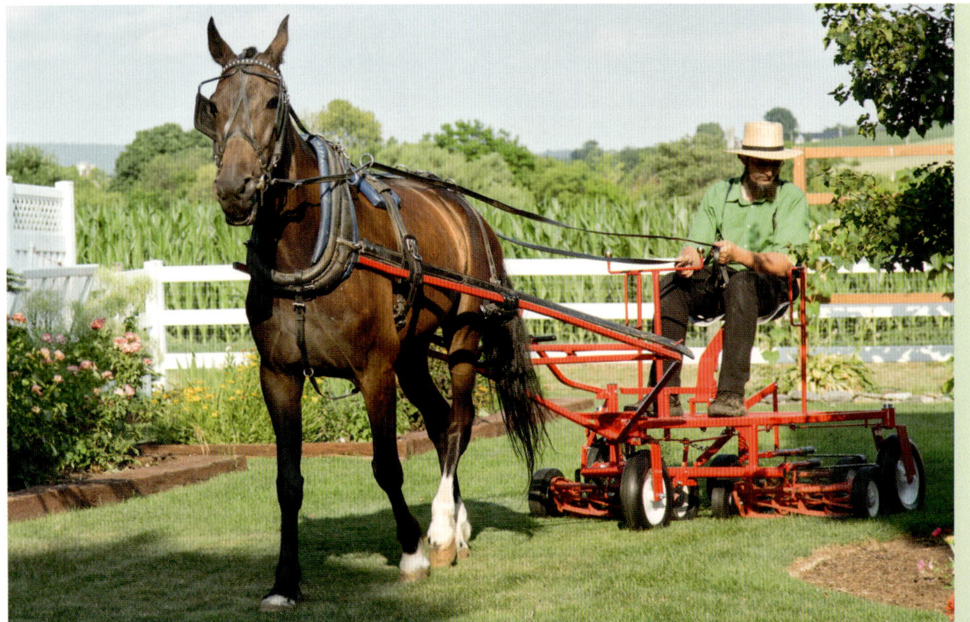

Versatility

The family carriage horse can be called into service for more than transportation. Sporty, a tame and agreeable Standardbred gelding, pulled a three-gang reel mower around the yard.

Owners hitch buggy horses to wagons to haul everything from groceries to seed corn to flats of flowers.

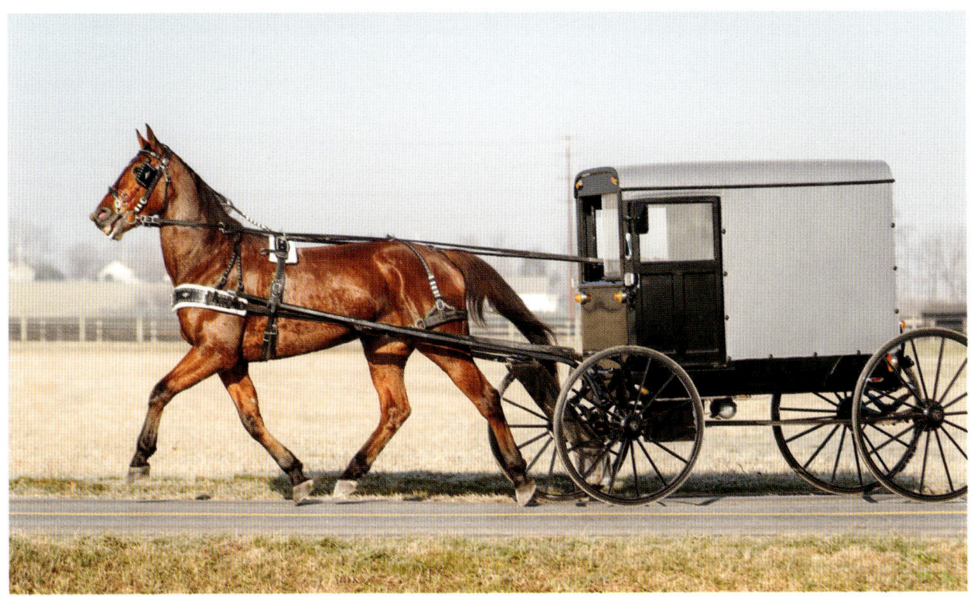

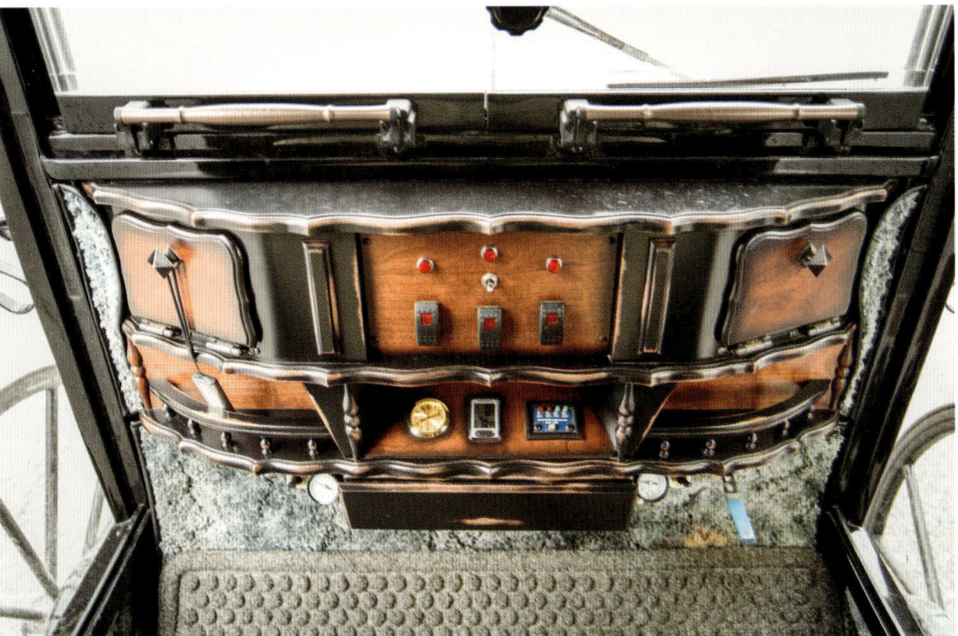

The purchase of a horse is a considerable investment; prices vary depending on the breed, age, and condition. A high-quality carriage horse that is sound and attractive costs around $6,000 to $10,000. One of merely passable quality can be had for much less, perhaps under $1,000. And there are many options in between.

A new closed carriage costs $10, 000 or $12,000 and an open buggy around $3,000 or $4,000.

A carriage shop's woodworker creates wooden dashboards that fit the 36-inch interior width of the buggy. Switches and buttons operate battery-powered flashing hazard lights, head lights, and turn signals. The driver operates the windshield wiper and opens the windows by hand. Reins are threaded through slots under the front window or through the window when it's open. The main brake is on the floor, and the parking brake is on the floor or below the dash.

The interior of a carriage built in 2016, *shown at the left,* clearly belongs to a young man. It's a little fancier and has more buttons and dials than an older man might find necessary: "All you really need is reins, lights, and brakes."

It may not all be strictly necessary, but a clock and speedometer come in handy on the road. Small glove boxes and shelves corral possessions, while sculptured shag carpet insulates and decorates.

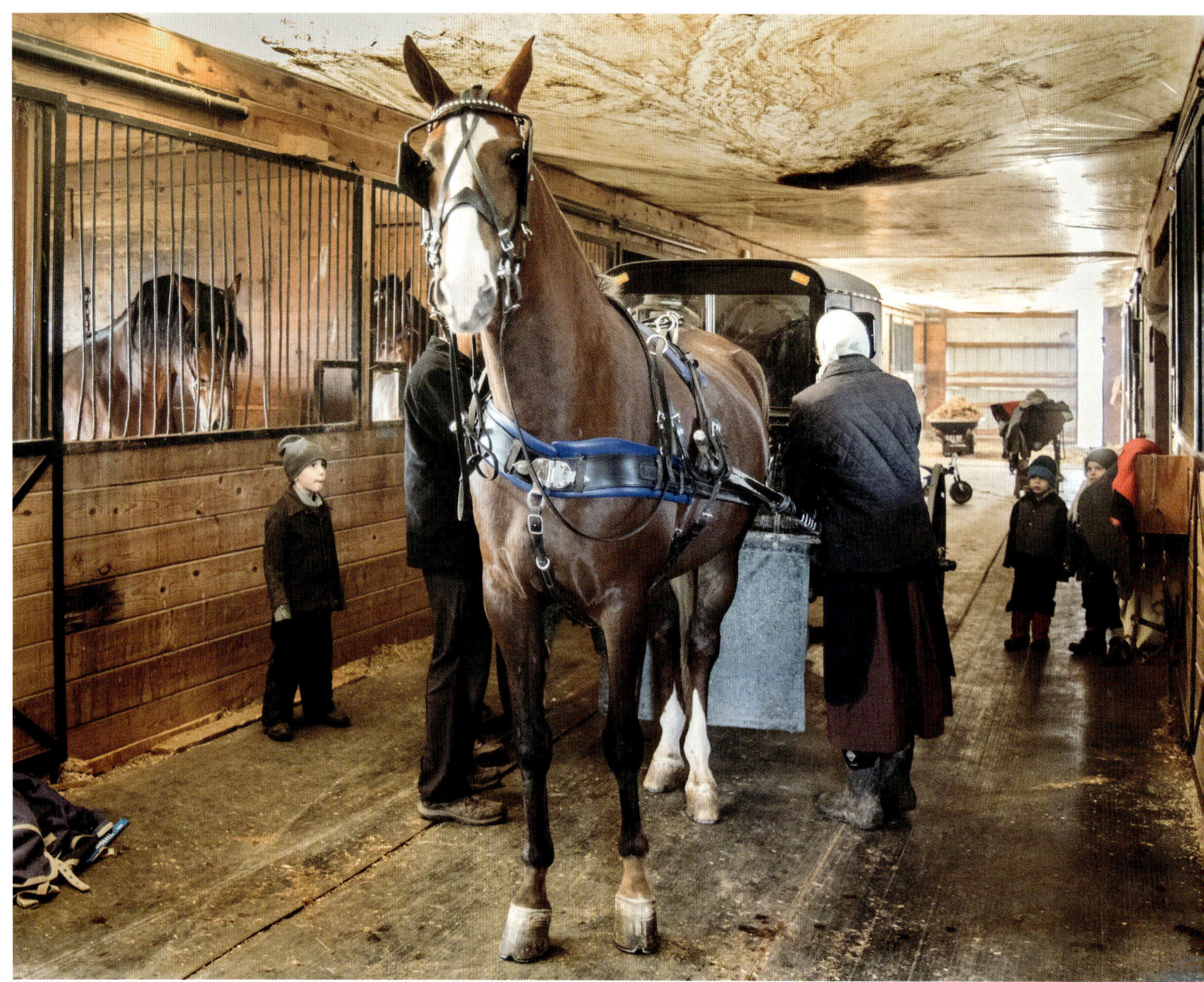

Barbie and her husband, *left,* harness their carriage horse in the stable. The children stand well out of the way until told to climb into the buggy.

The best way to teach youngsters how to handle horses safely and treat them well is for adults to model that behavior. Toddlers sitting on mom's lap often like to pretend they're driving the horse by holding the tail ends of the reins.

If they live on a farm, children help in the field and have chores involving the draft horses. Most families have a miniature horse or pony for the children to drive and care for. At early elementary age, the youngsters can hitch up and drive the pony cart around the farm. Children in middle elementary school may drive a pony cart the short distance to school. Boys at age ten or twelve, and girls a little older, help harness the buggy horse.

Depending on if traffic is heavy or not, children in their early teens may drive while sitting beside a parent. Dad and Mom constantly stress safety. Since cars routinely whip around buggies to pass them on the left side, one dad tells his kids repeatedly to always "watch the left side when you make a left turn. Cars will pass on the left even when your turn signal is blinking and obvious."

A boy at fourteen and girl at fifteen might begin driving a buggy on their own. They start with short trips and work up to more traffic and longer trips.

One young lady remembers three key instructions from her grandmother: keep your reins tight, stay on your side of the road, and stay out of the gutter.

Driving safety is included in the Old Order school curriculum. Fourteen-year-olds work their way through a manual created by an Amish publishing company. The lessons include stories, quizzes, and worksheets that teach them how to safely share the road with cars. Along with practical advice, students are reminded: "Being respectful and courteous on the road is an excellent opportunity to be a light to the world."

Driving a buggy is more than just directing a horse. It's cooperative. Horses are quick to apply what they've learned. They gather clues to where they're going on the basis of who is driving, which way they go at the end of the drive, the turns they take on the way, and even how their driver smells.

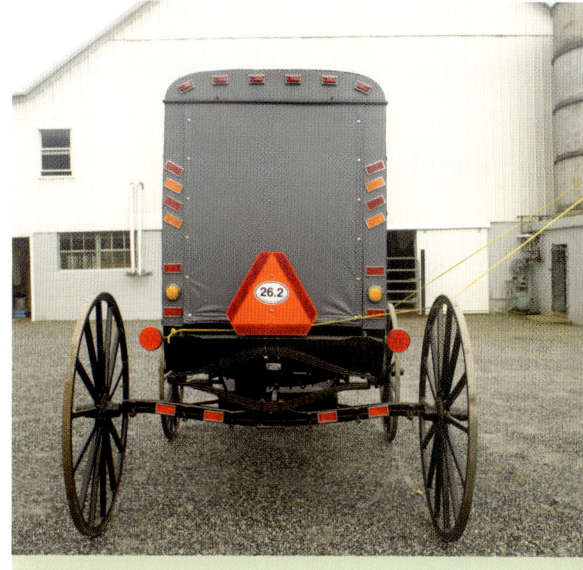

Long Distance

Though John relies on his Morgan mare for transportation, he is an experienced marathoner who was two minutes from qualifying for the Boston Marathon in his last race. The yellow ropes attached to his parked buggy anchor the volleyball net used by young people setting and spiking on a break from school.

> "Keep your reins tight, stay on your side of the road, and stay out of the gutter."

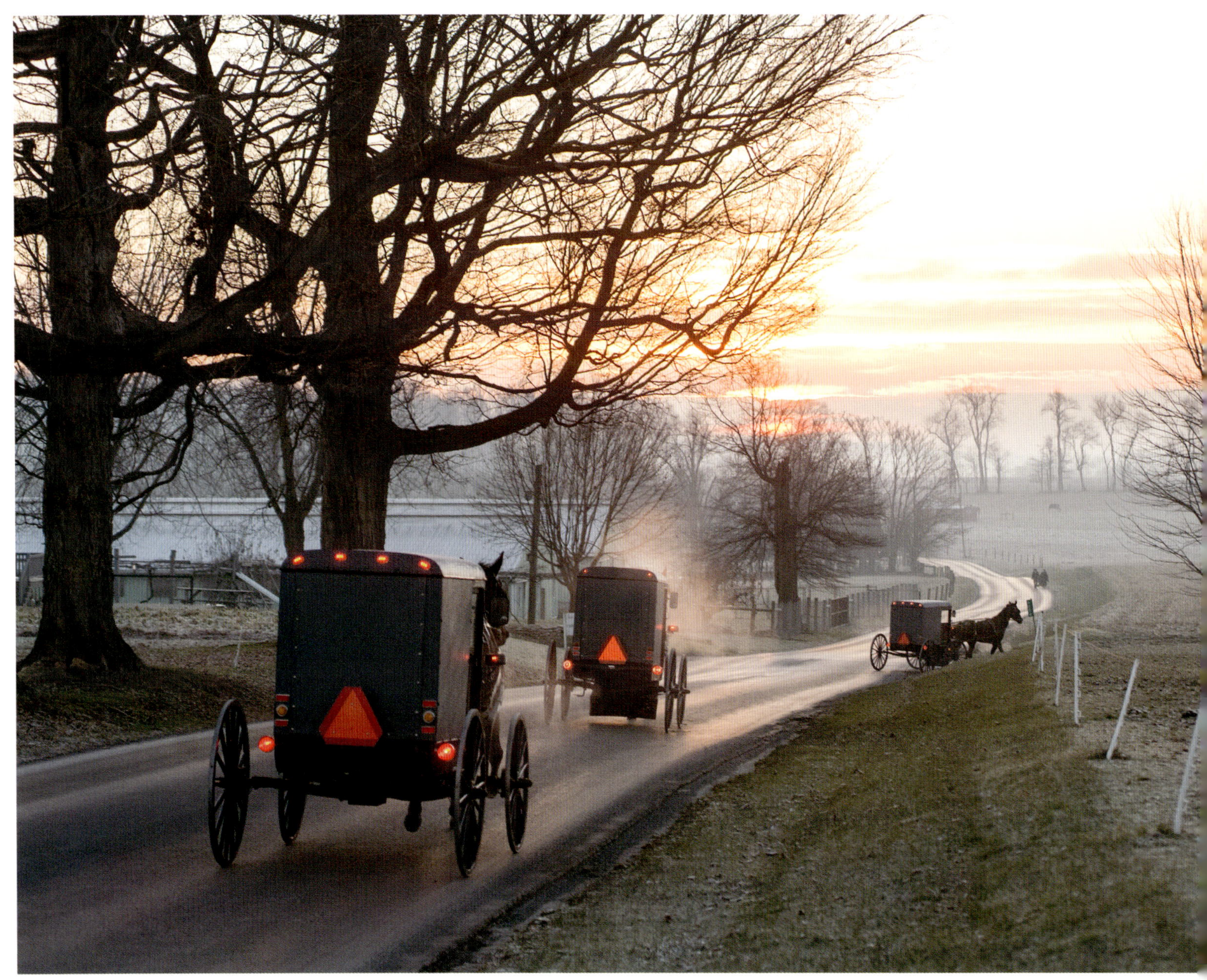

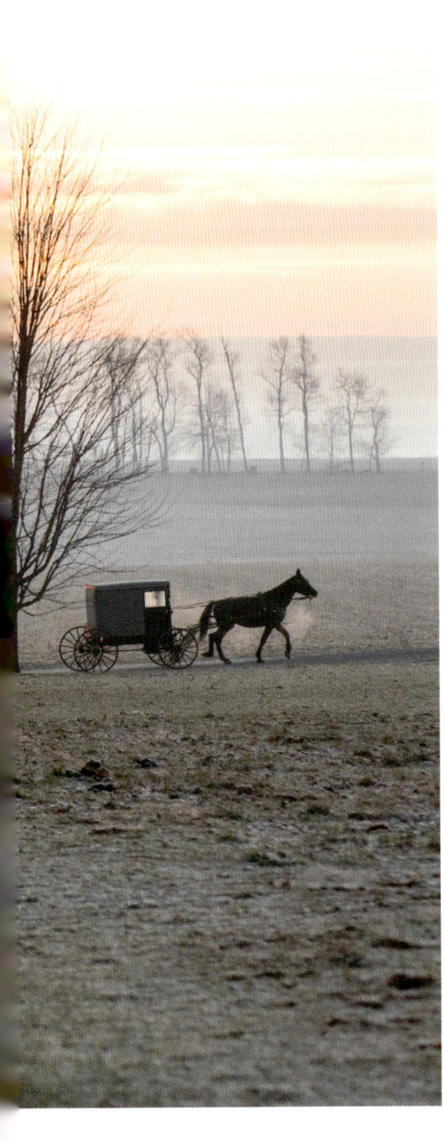

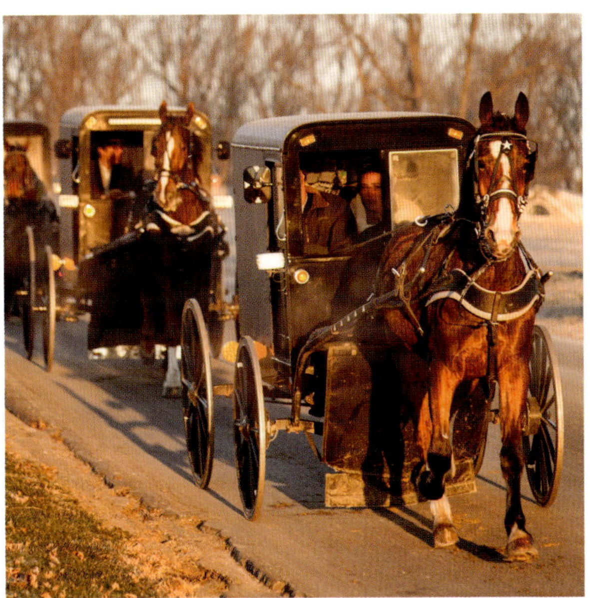

At a recent wedding, the parents of the bride hosted over 500 guests at the all-day affair. Siblings, aunts, uncles, cousins, and friends had worked for months planning and making the food, scrubbing and polishing everything in sight, and clearing out and cleaning the equipment barn to accommodate everyone for the church service and two meals.

Guests came from as close as the next farm or as far as several states away. Most arrived by horse and buggy, some by Amish taxi. They poured in early that December morning, happy to celebrate with the bride and groom.

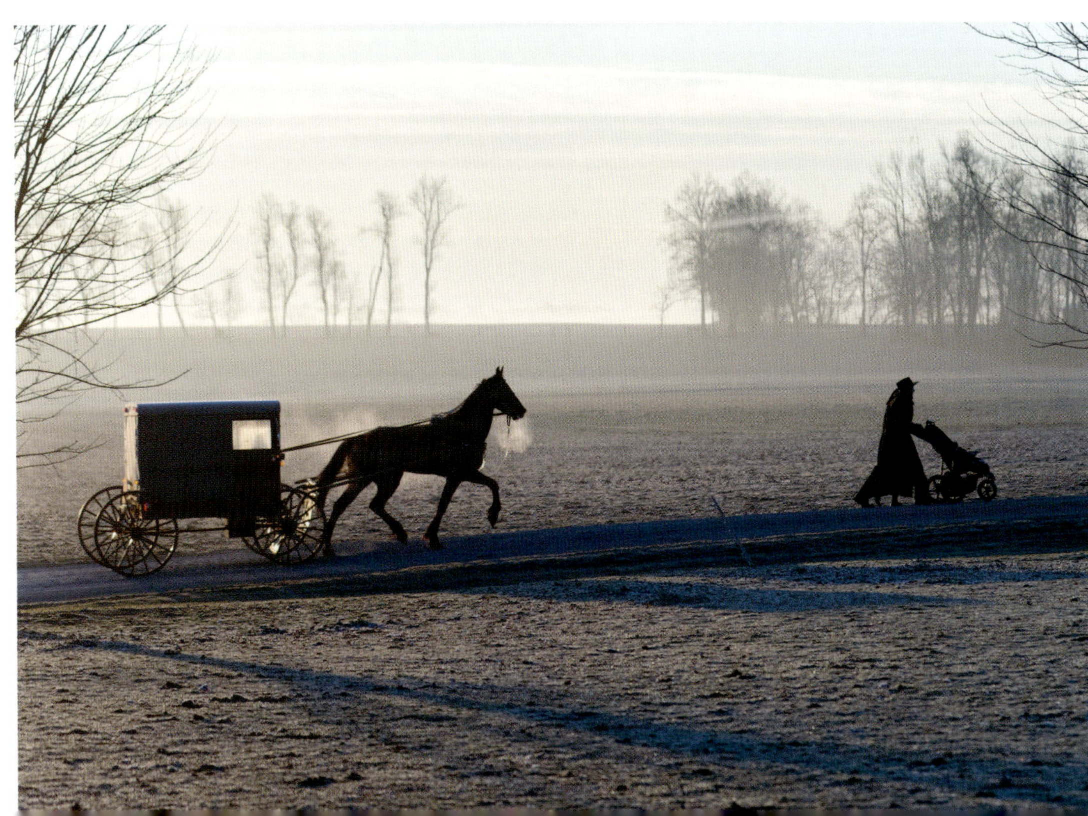

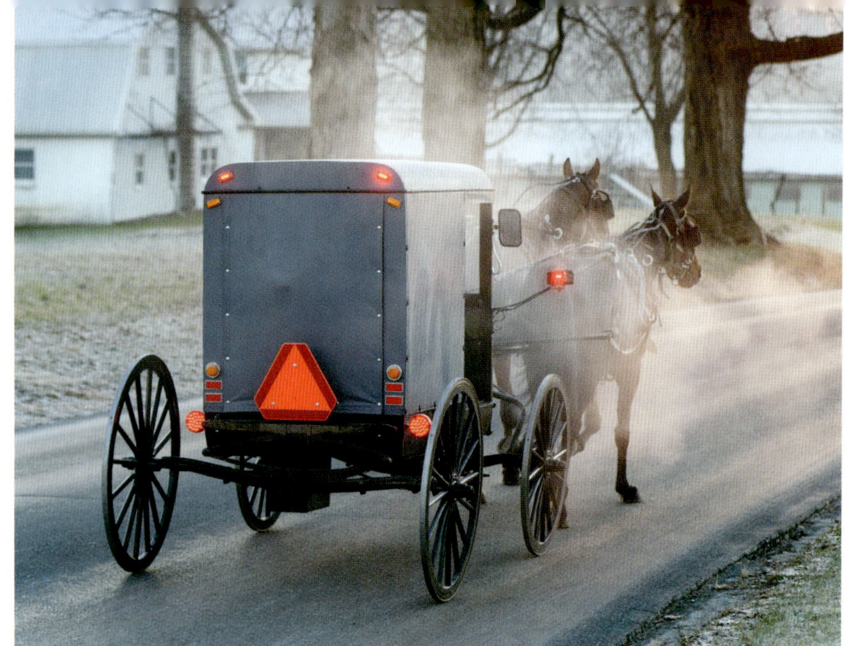

Some guests who traveled a long way hitched two horses together so as not to exhaust a single horse.

The week before the wedding, the bride's father cleared space for the visitors' 120 horses by transferring the hay from his barn to his brother's barn. The morning of the wedding, he moved the draft horses from their stalls to the meadow.

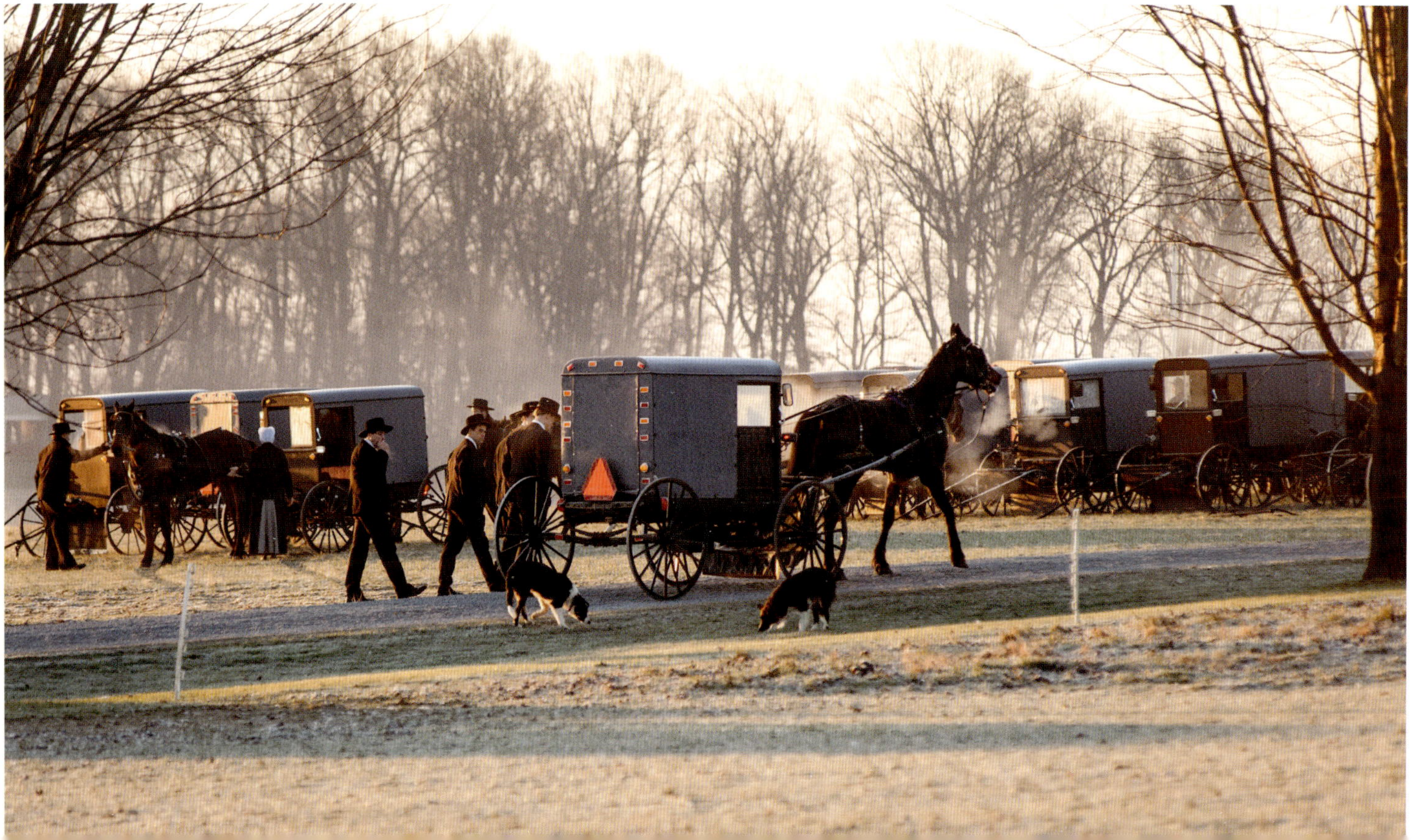

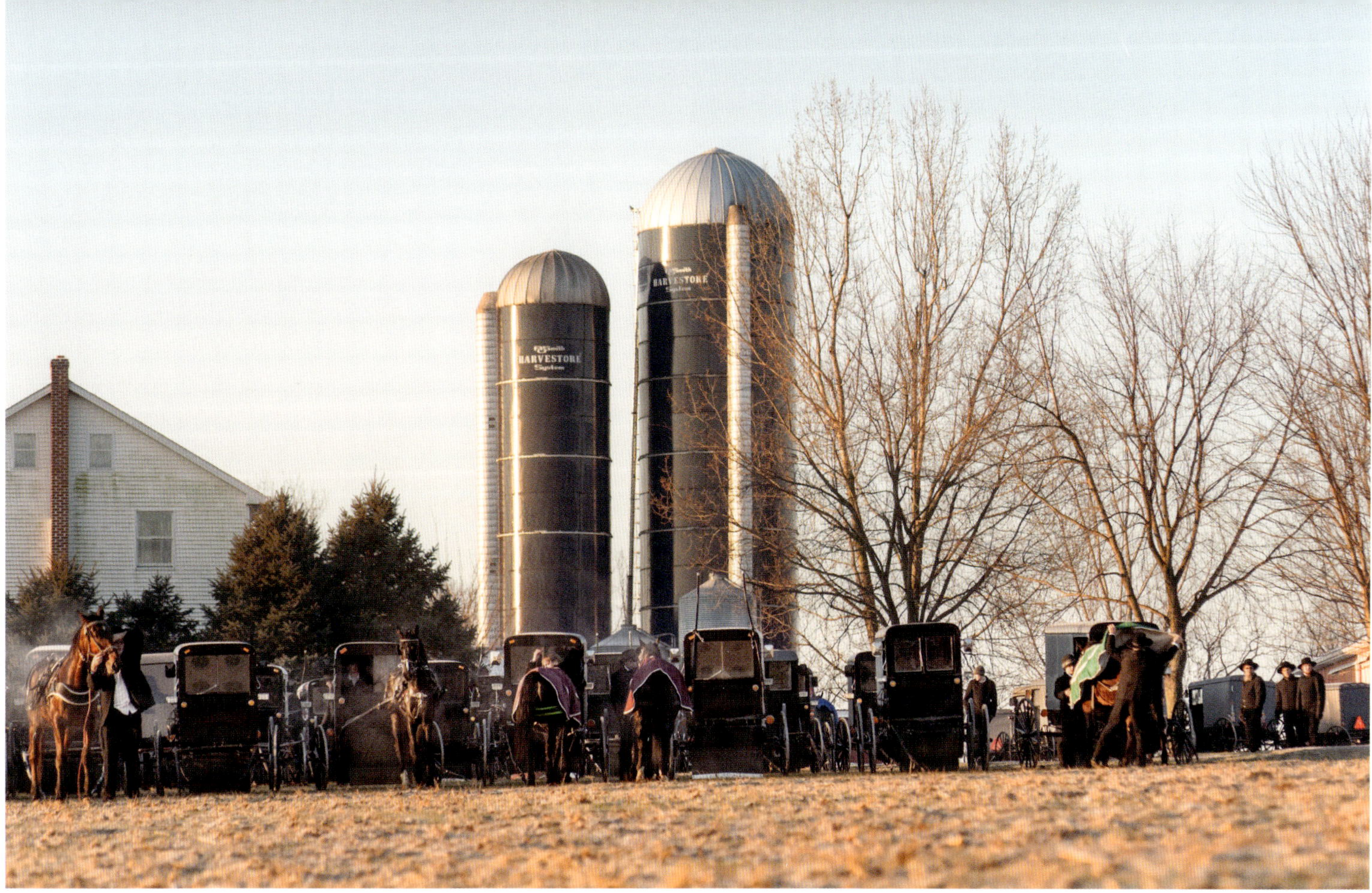

Five men were tasked with helping visitors park their buggies. A dozen young men worked as hostlers, helping unhitch and blanket the horses and leading them to the barn. Seventy horses went into box stalls that held seven to twenty horses each, depending on the size of the stall. Sixty horses were tied around two hay wagons parked in the barn's upper level. The hostlers fed and watered the horses at noon and kept an eye on them during the day.

Even though they spent the day in close quarters, the horses were well mannered. Their owners stopped in throughout the day to check out each other's horses and check on their own.

When it was time to leave, the men retrieved their horses and took them to the buggies, where their wives met them to help hitch up for the trip home.

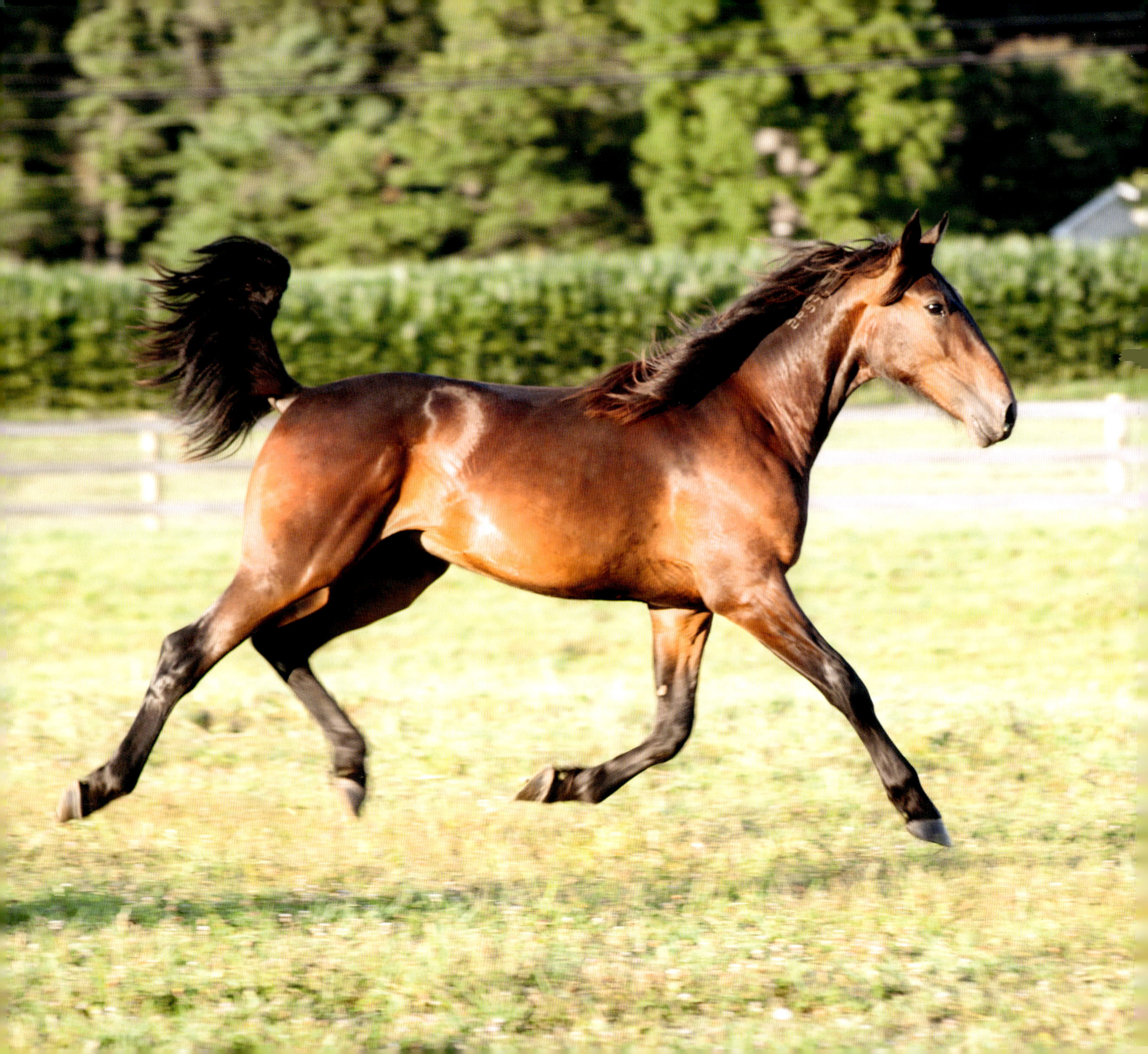

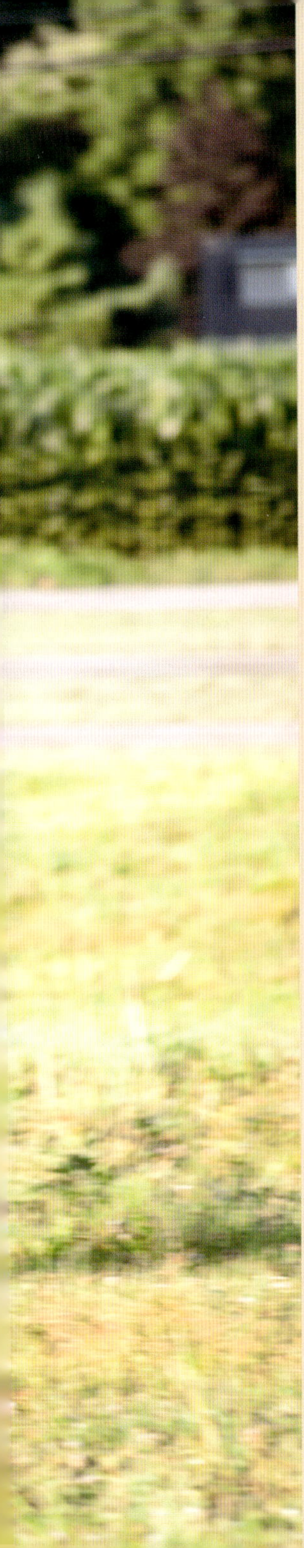

Standardbred

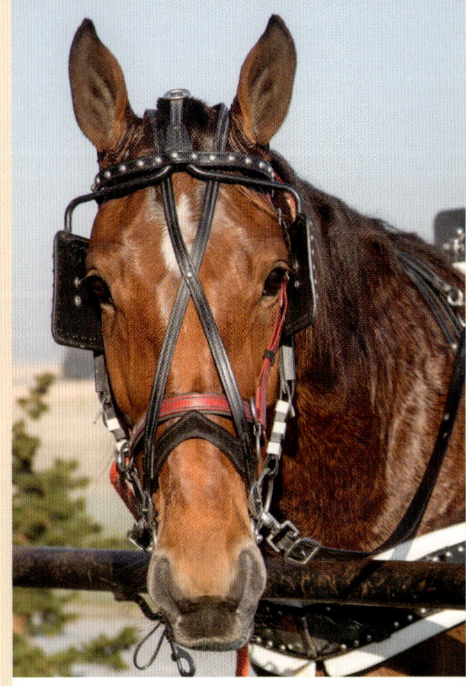

Origins: English Thoroughbred stallion, 1788

Height: 15–16hh or more

Weight: 900–1,200 lbs

Colors: usually solid bay, brown, black

Three fillies tore around the meadow with wild abandon, leaping and kicking, their coats gleaming in the late afternoon light. In the adjoining field, a yearling colt raced from one end of the pasture to the other, his gait streamlined, his body suspended midtrot.

Eli leaned on the fence and watched. He breeds Standardbreds to be sold for the racetrack. When Eli sells a horse for harness racing, there is a chance, depending on its success on the track, that the same horse will be back at an auction in Lancaster County in a few years and offered as a fine buggy horse. Eli has an eye on a filly he sold last year and hopes he can buy her back to use as a brood mare when she retires from the track.

The Standardbred horse is really the standard in Lancaster County. It is the breed most commonly used to pull carriages, and the breed to which other buggy horse breeds are compared. A Saddlebred is described as being more spirited than a Standardbred, a Morgan smaller and tougher, a Dutch Harness stronger and more stylish, a Friesian prouder and sturdier.

"Standardbreds are a good combination of sensitive and sensible."

Every birth is exciting, but that of a potentially high stakes race horse can be particularly nerve wracking. Eli's veterinarian had carefully stitched a sensor in place in each mare. When the birth begins, an alarm is triggered to alert Eli. It always seems to happen at night. Eli rushes to the stable to assist or, if needed, call the veterinarian.

An increasing number of Old Order horsemen in Lancaster County are getting into the breeding business. The most-important factors in raising a successful racehorse are good bloodlines and top-quality care. When they are yearlings, the young horses are sold at auction.

"Right after they're born the foals can run around the pasture."

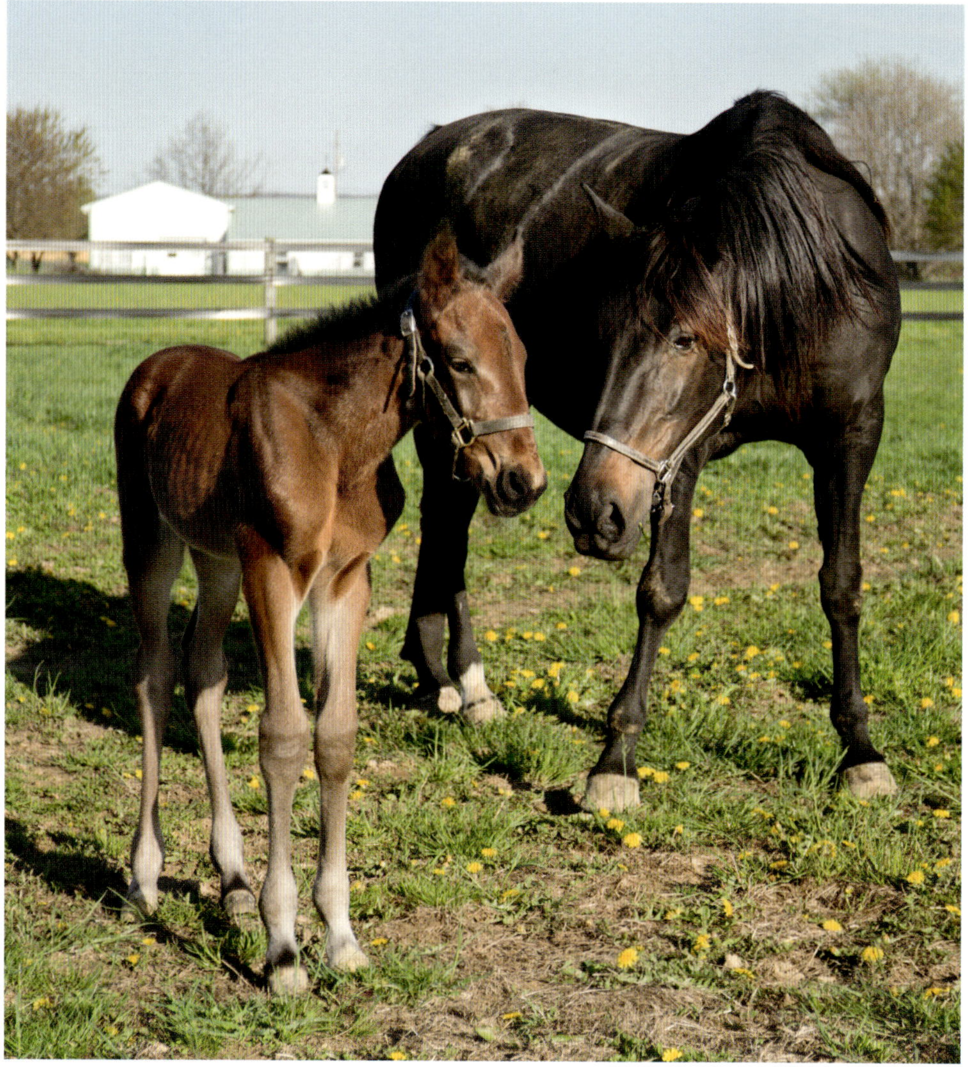

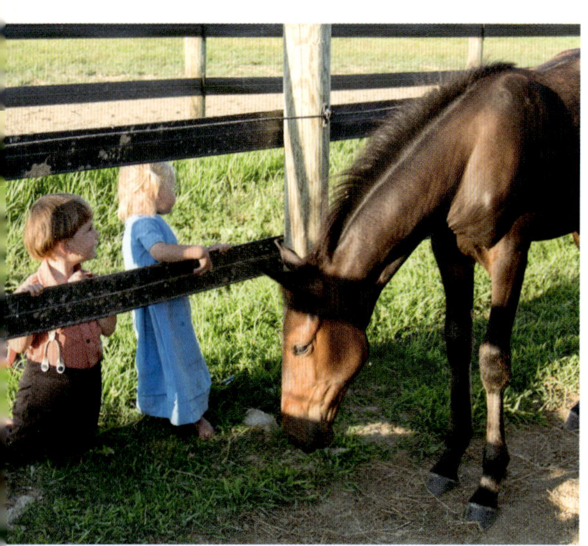

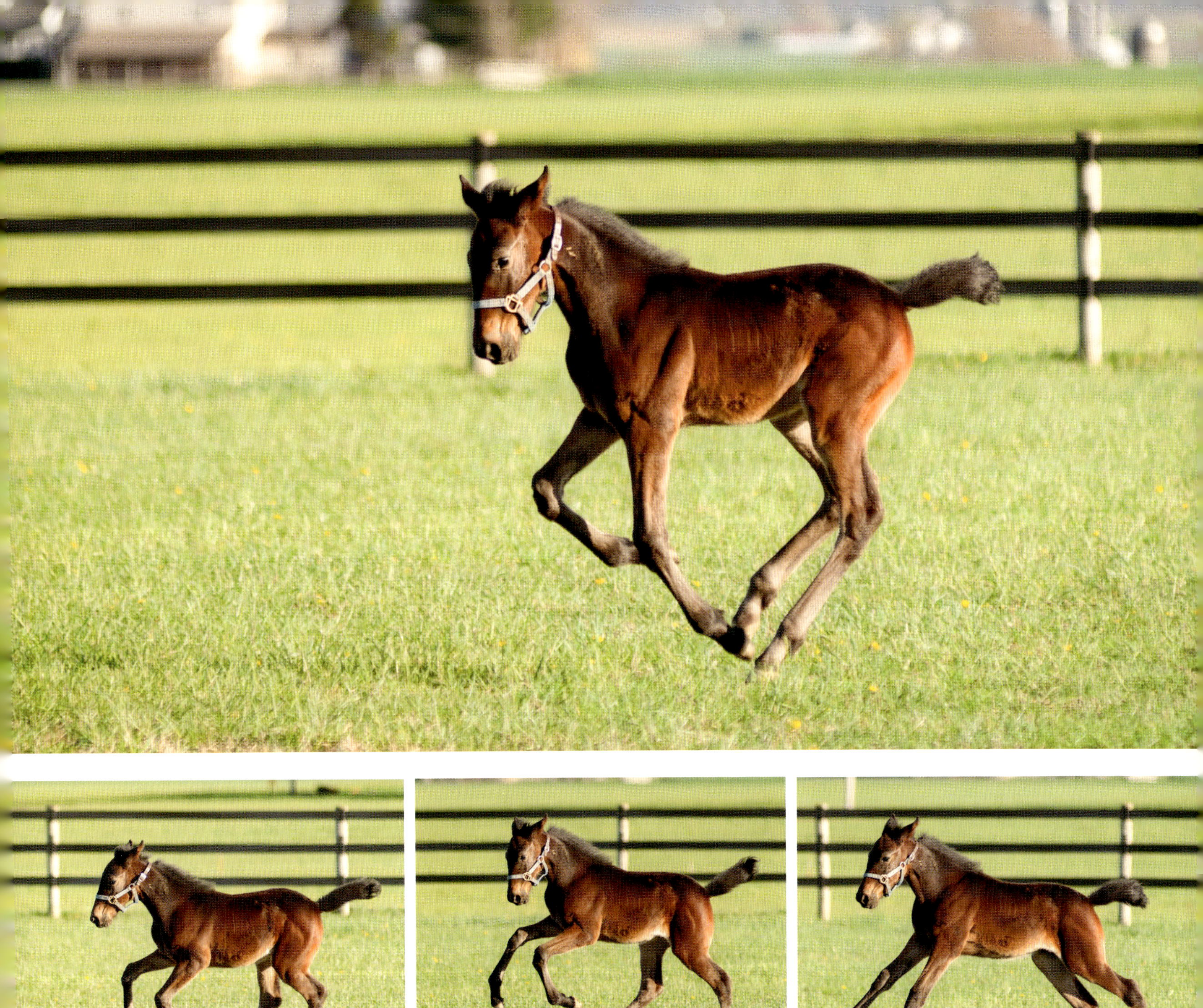

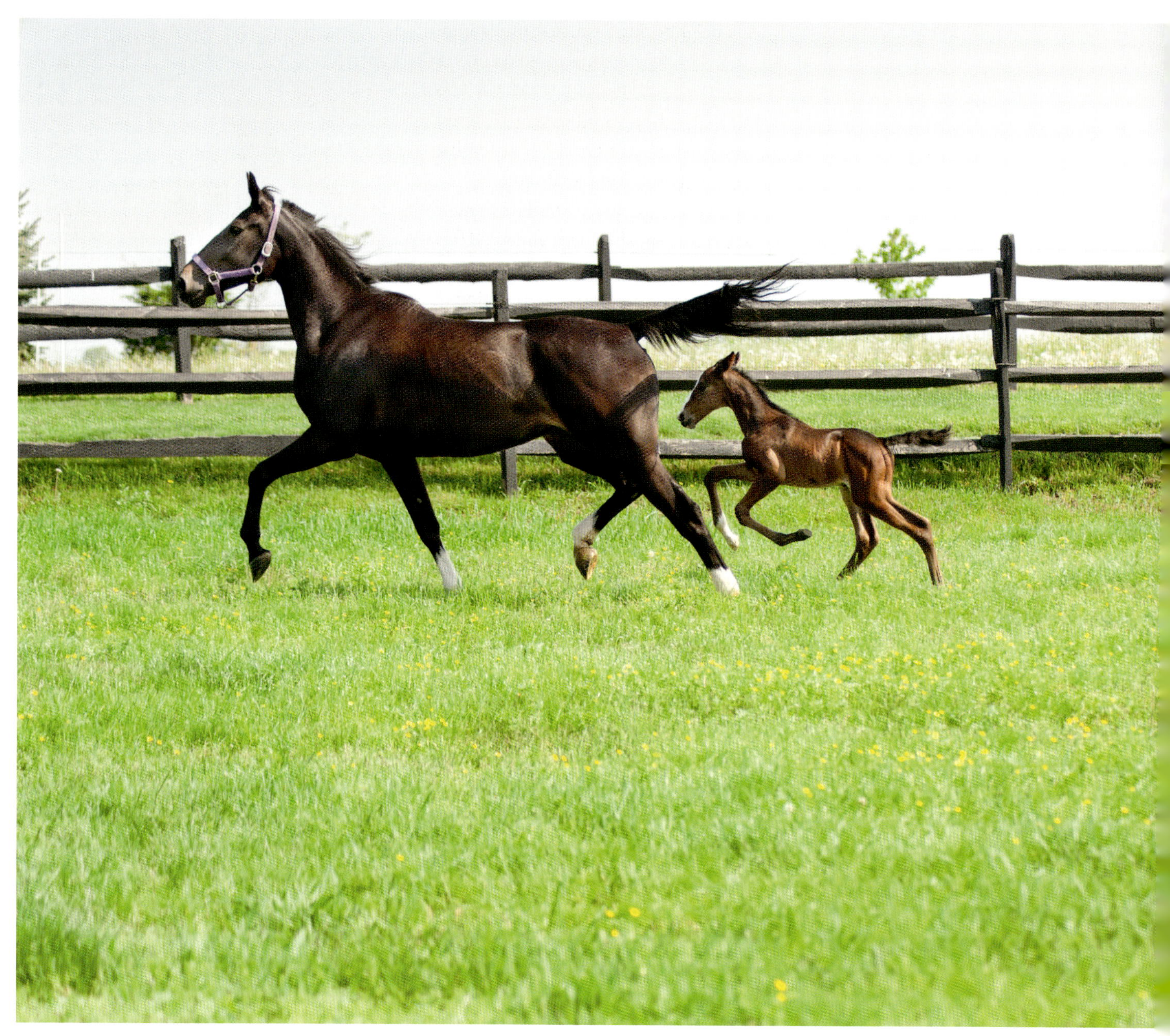

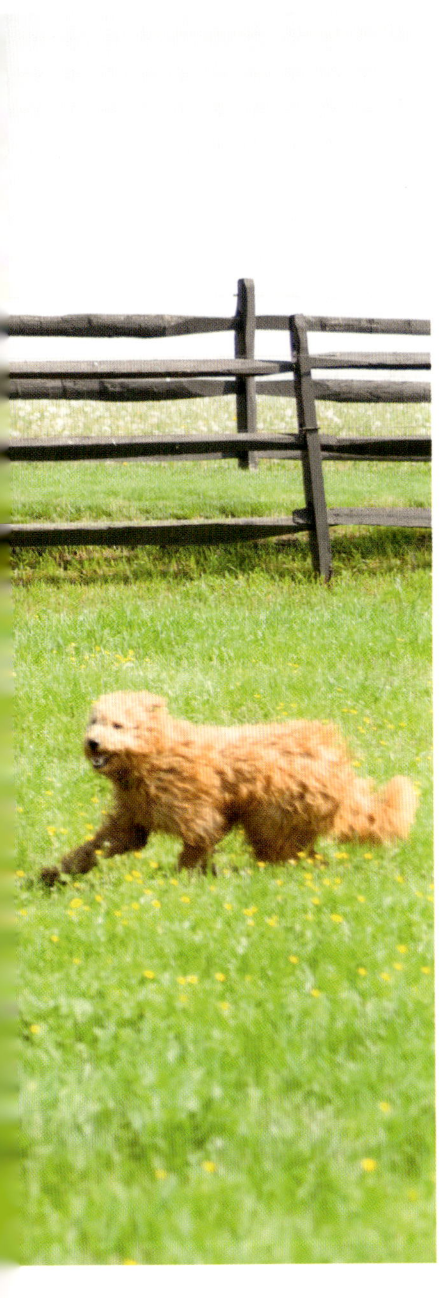

At a neighboring farm, first-time mom, Stardust took to motherhood well and was quite protective of her filly, Sunshine. At six days old, Sunshine raced to keep up with her mom in the meadow, *left,* joined by a Keisha, the family's goldendoodle.

Five weeks later when Stardust went back to work, Sunshine was unnerved to see her mother, *right,* wearing all those straps and pulling a strange contraption.

Sunshine didn't know quite what to do with herself. At one point, she was so alarmed at how her mama looked in harness that she nearly ran to the pasture to join the pony.

Finally Stardust's harness was removed and the pair was allowed to return to their stall; all was right with the world again.

At six months, Sunshine, *right,* had completely lost her baby coat, showing the dark color she will carry into adulthood.

Sunshine's owner isn't sure whether he'll sell her as a yearling or keep and train her to pull a carriage.

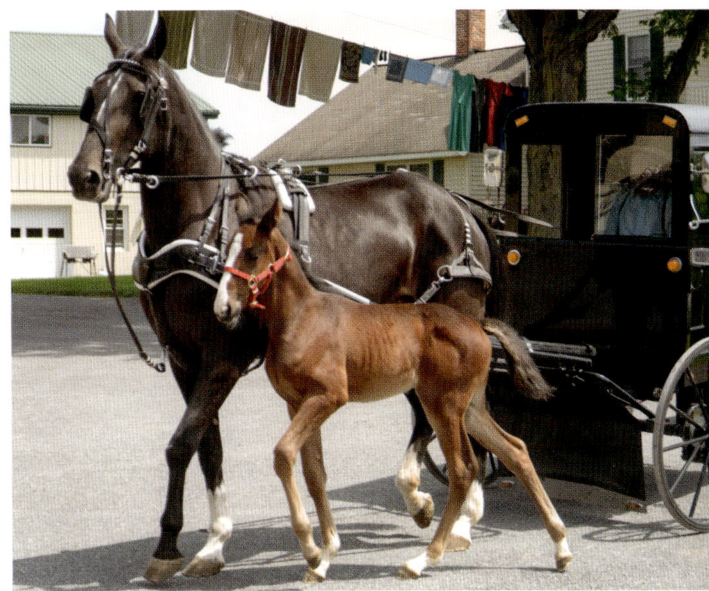

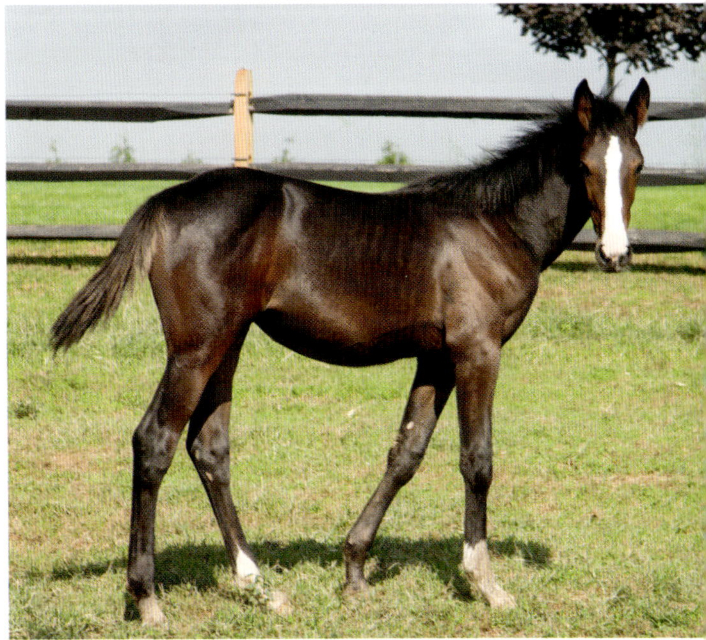

Fans of the Standardbred, and there are many, consider Standardbreds the perfect blend of grace, speed, and efficiency. Most of county's working Standardbreds have come from the racetrack.

Depending on a horse's success, its racing career is over by age three to five, though some race until age fifteen. And while they are well trained to the harness and have experienced raucous crowds, these former track horses must be acclimated to the road.

New training includes building muscle by gradually increasing travel distances. Short trips at first also allow the horse to grow comfortable sharing the road with cars and trucks.

Rather than going 30 miles an hour in two minutes on a mile-long track, the Standardbred pulling a buggy typically travels at 12 miles per hour on a 10-mile trip. A 15-mile journey is reasonable if the horse can rest for two or three hours before the return trip. A 20-to-25-mile trip requires a four-hour rest before return.

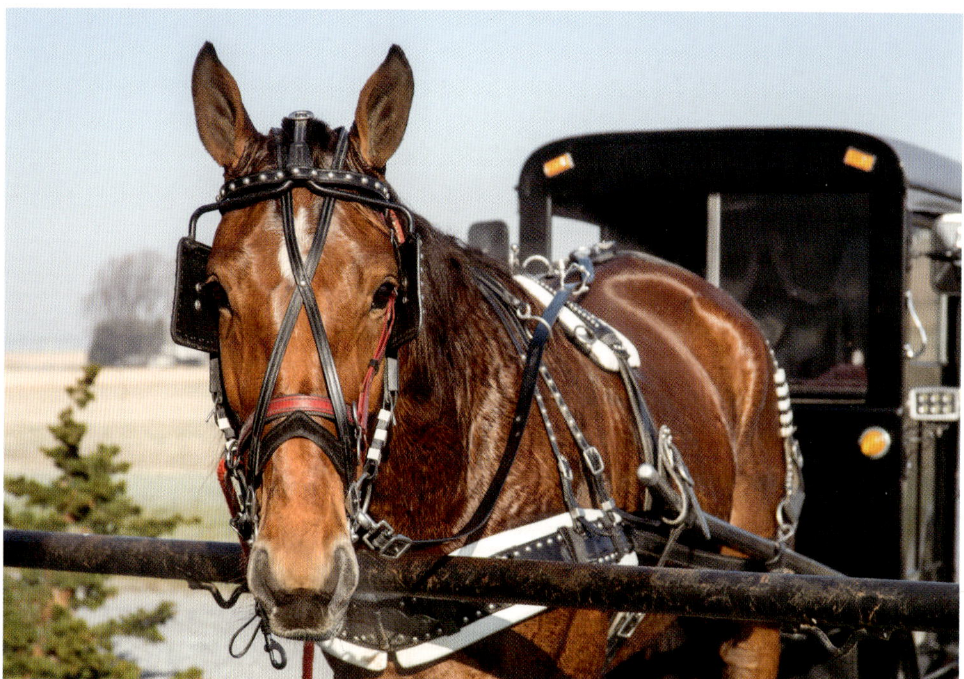

David's uncle, a fan of Standardbreds, helped him find a horse when it was time to buy one. They researched what was available, then went to an auction to see the horses in the flesh.

Super, *above and right,* caught their eye with his good looks and performance. A former racer, he had excellent bloodlines. David went ahead with the purchase and has been pleased. Super has plenty of zip, and David loves the challenge.

Buggies look alike to the untrained eye. However, there are a few indications that David's buggy belongs to a young man.

Alternating black and white blocks decorate the sides of the bridle and backstrap. An older, more sedate driver would likely use black padding on the harness rather than white. And at night, purple glow lights under the buggy lend an air of mystery.

"It takes muscle and concentration to drive a spirited horse."

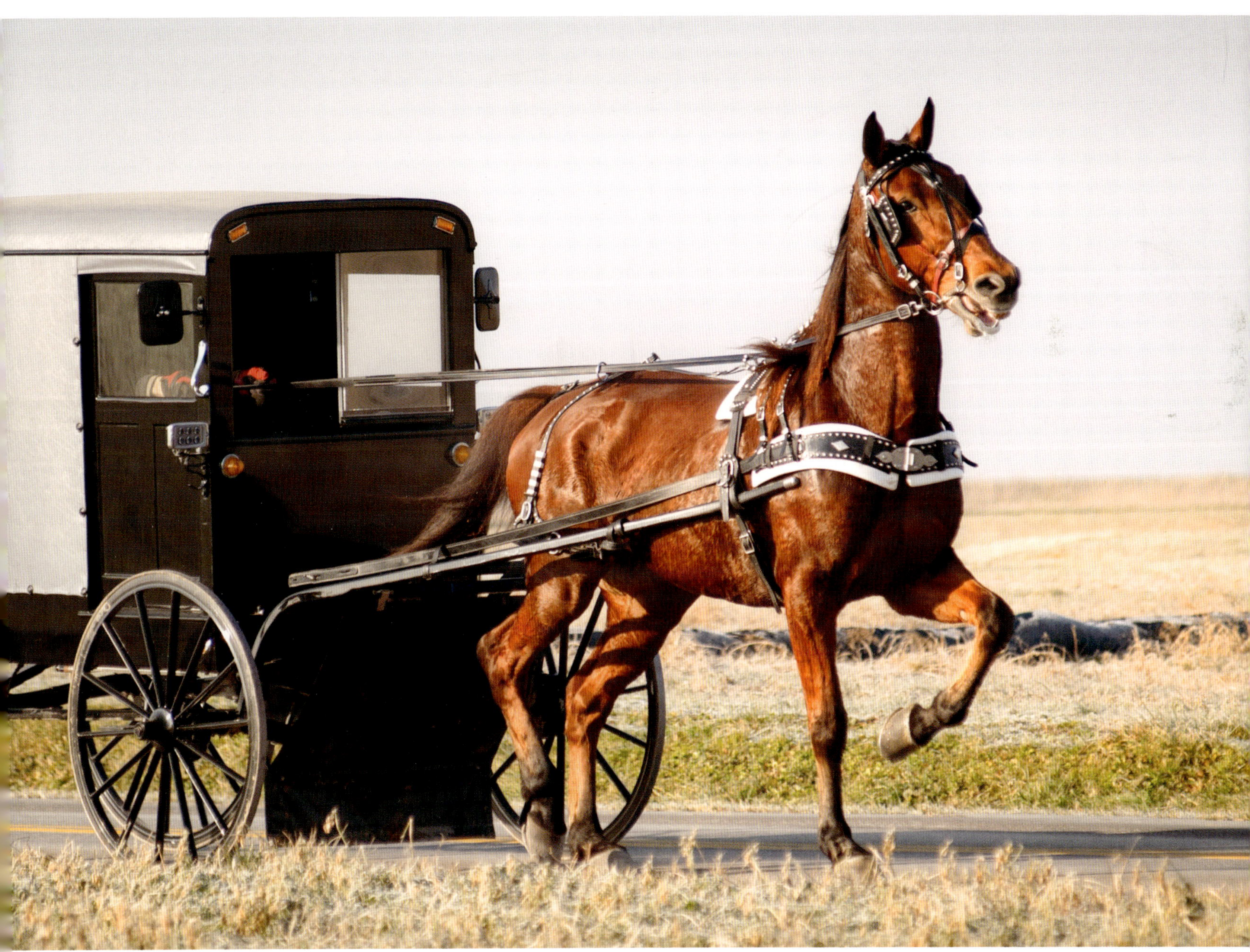

Three-year-old Tina stepped out briskly, settling into a lively trot, *facing page,* with Eli at the reins. Her experience as a harness racer made her comfortable being driven, and the jogging sulky gave a familiar pull as she covered the miles.

Now that Tina is retired from driving, Eli anticipates using her as a brood mare with hopes of coming up with a winning foal. Tina's half sister just sold for a high price in an exclusive auction in Kentucky; her good performance on the track will raise the value of Tina and her offspring.

Even though performance, not color, counts in a race horse, there seems to be a preference for black horses. Some buggy drivers also choose black horses, and are willing to pay more for one. A dappled look also appeals to buyers.

"She's a very smart mare and is aware of everything around her."

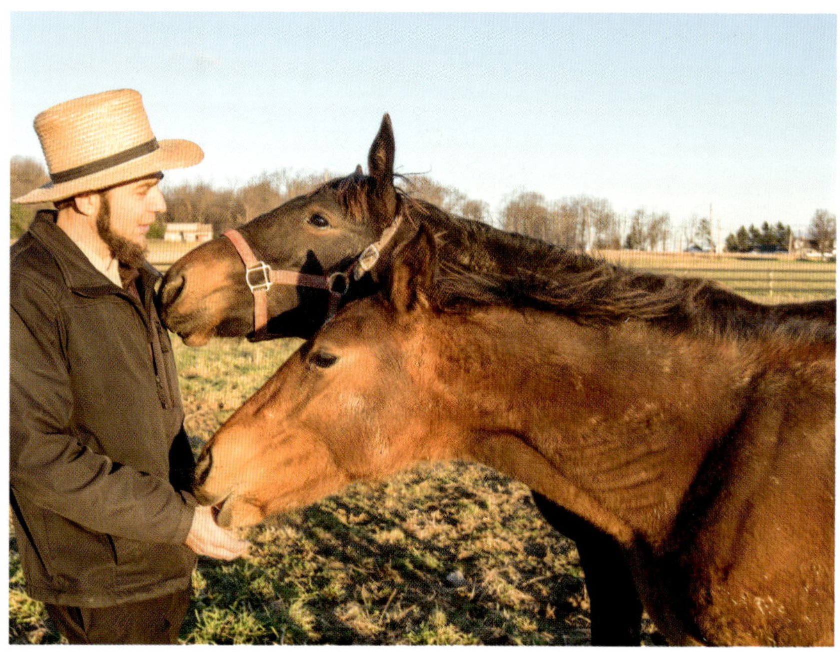

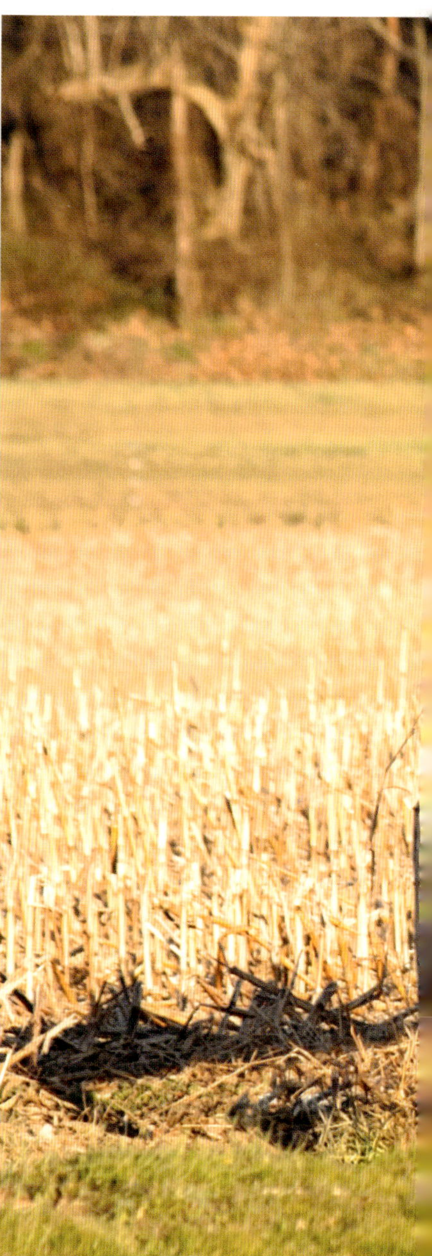

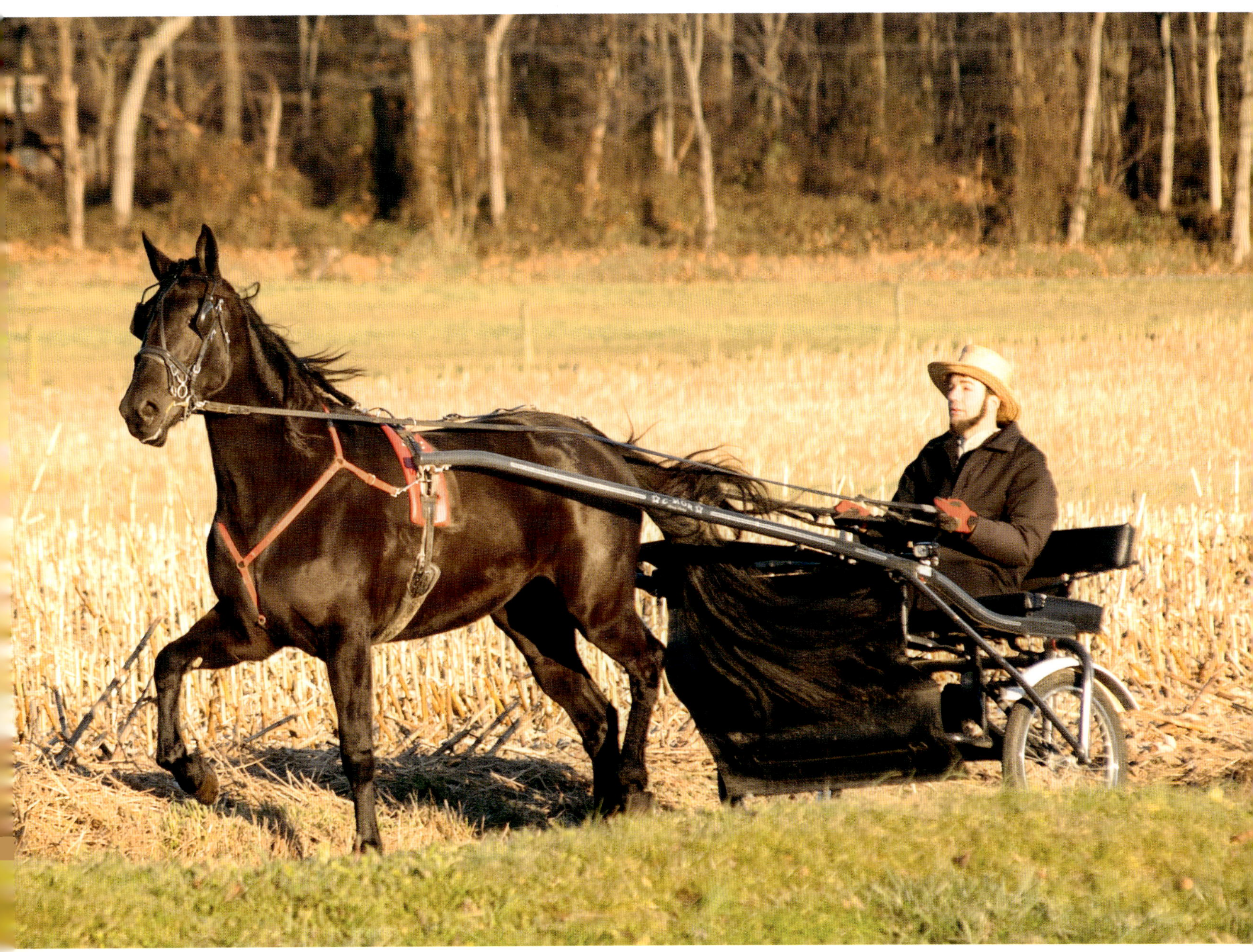

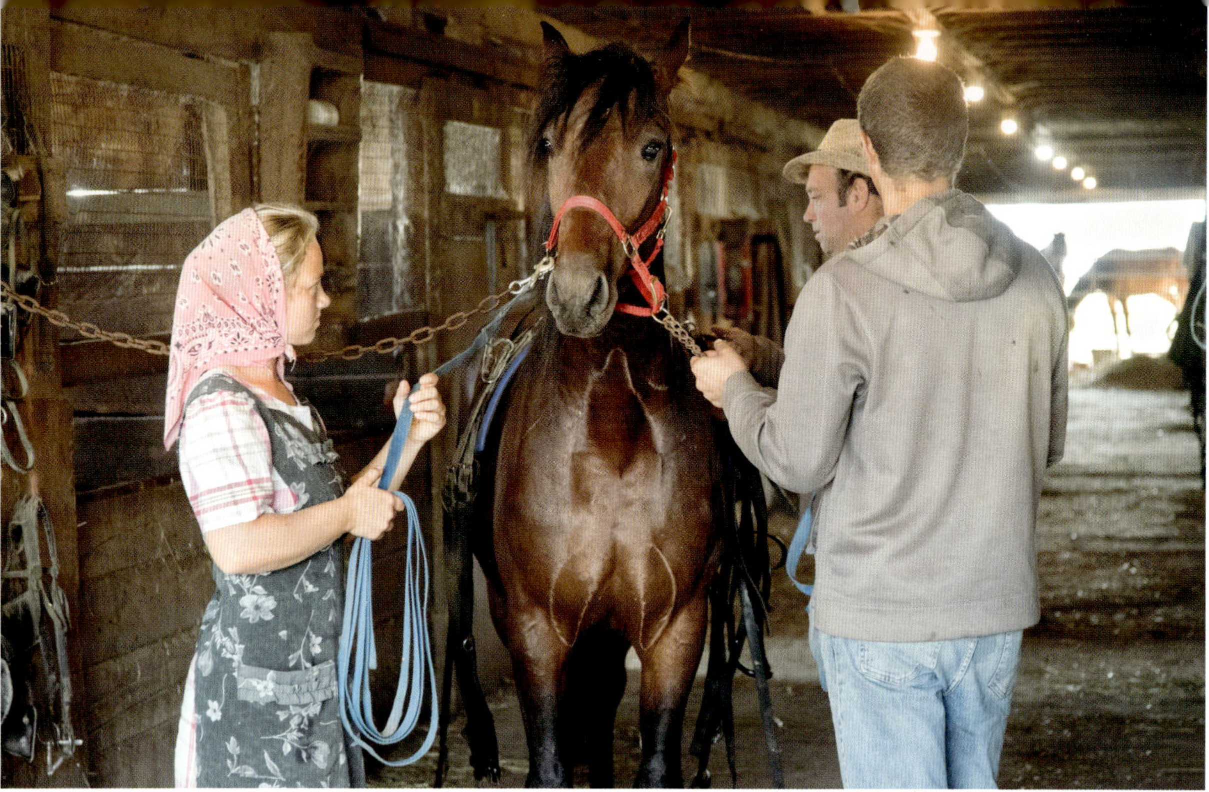

Glen's father built a half mile track on the family farm in 1970. He was hoping to supplement his income from crop farming by training young Standardbreds for harness racing. His investment paid off, and the exercise and training business is now carried on by his son, daughter-in-law, and grandchildren.

Young horses are brought to the stable for training; some return to the owners when ready to enter the racing circuit, while others stay and race out of the stable. Sharon, twenty, and Anthony, twenty-two, help their dad the most, though other siblings and their mom are sometimes called in to exercise horses when the census is high.

Sharon and Anthony clipped leads to both sides of Stormy's halter while their dad carefully strapped a simple harness around his middle, then slipped the bit into his mouth and bridle over his head. It was Stormy's first experience with a bridle and a harness, and he was nervous. Calmly and slowly, Sharon and Anthony walked Stormy outside to the track, keeping the tension even on the two leads. Glen walked along behind, plying the reins with an a very light touch.

Stormy's first walk in harness lasted only ten minutes, then was repeated the next day. On the third day, Glen hitched him to a cart, again with Sharon and Anthony leading on both sides. When Glen guided Stormy into a trot, the kids jumped onto the cart with their dad and Stormy completed a loop.

The pattern of incremental challenges, each met with success, would continue until Stormy was gliding confidently around the track.

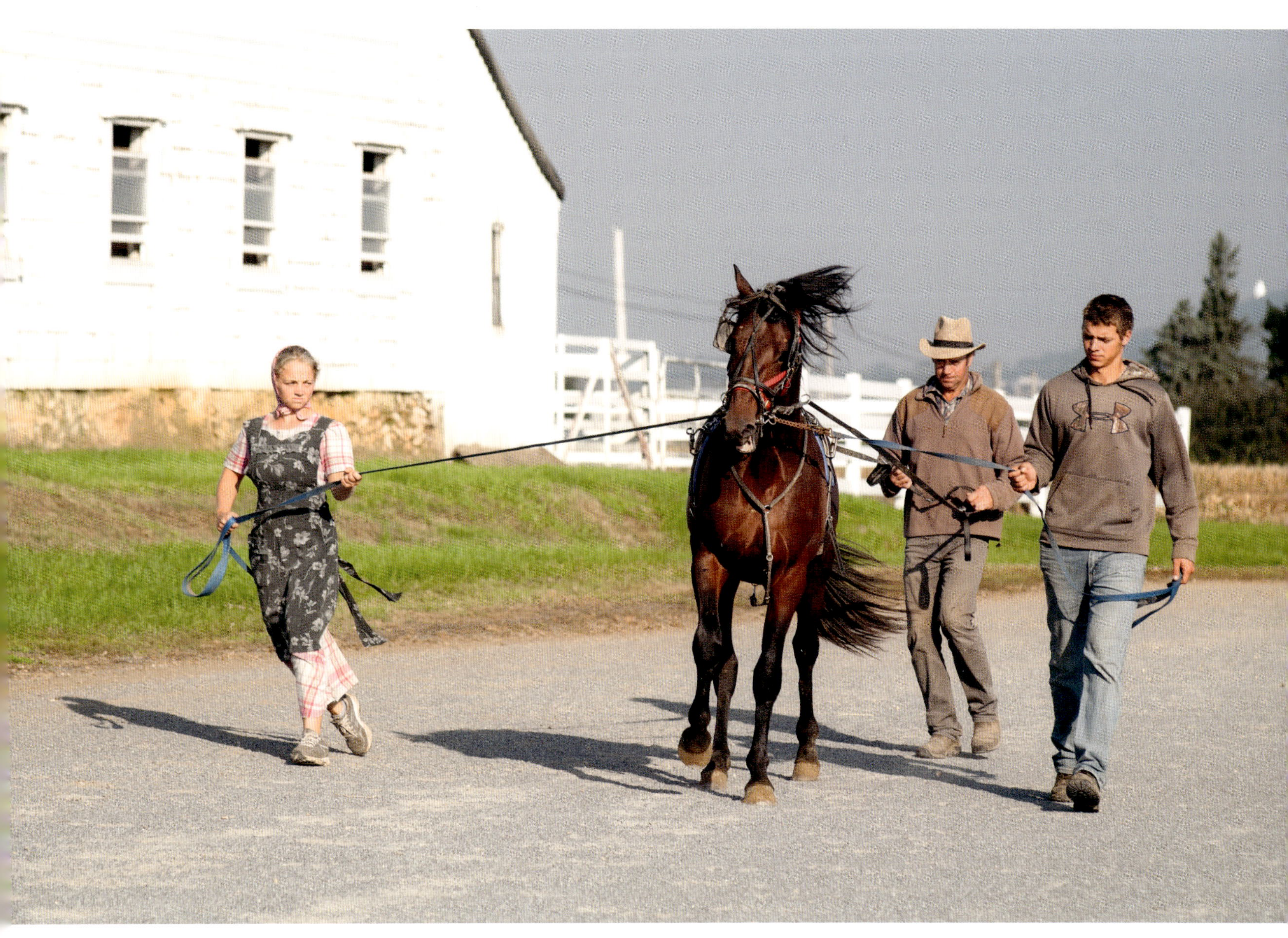

"We came up with a couple of good ones."

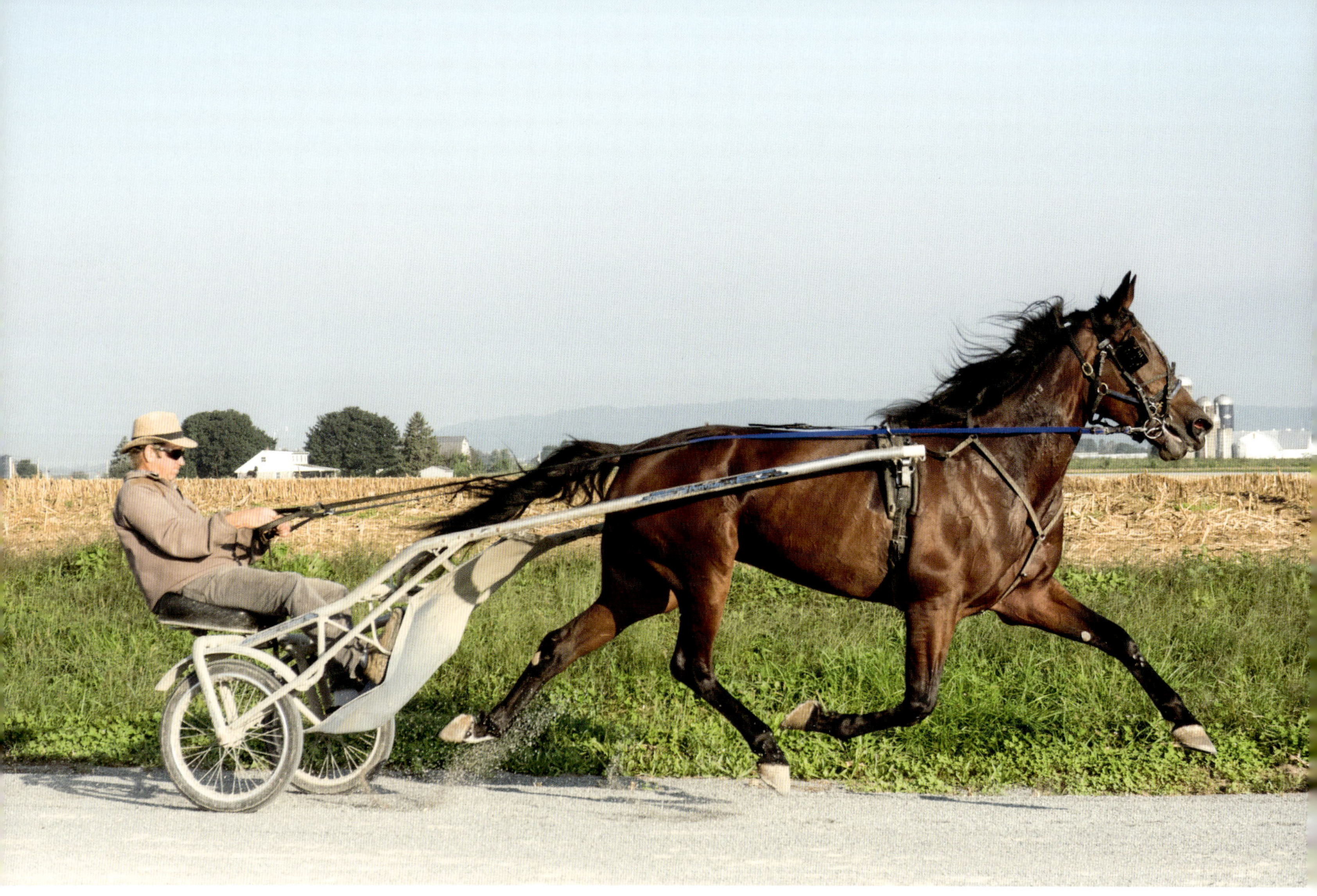

The corn in the infield of the track had just been harvested and there was a nip in the air. The number of young horses in the stable was growing as owners brought their two-year-olds to begin training. Glen kept careful records for each horse, charting details of exactly where they were in training and what came next.

Anthony, Sharon, and their dad worked all the horses on the roster. As soon as one training circuit was completed, they unhitched and stabled the horse and went on to the next. Routine training and conditioning takes place six days a week. For the first few months, each horse is driven eight times around the

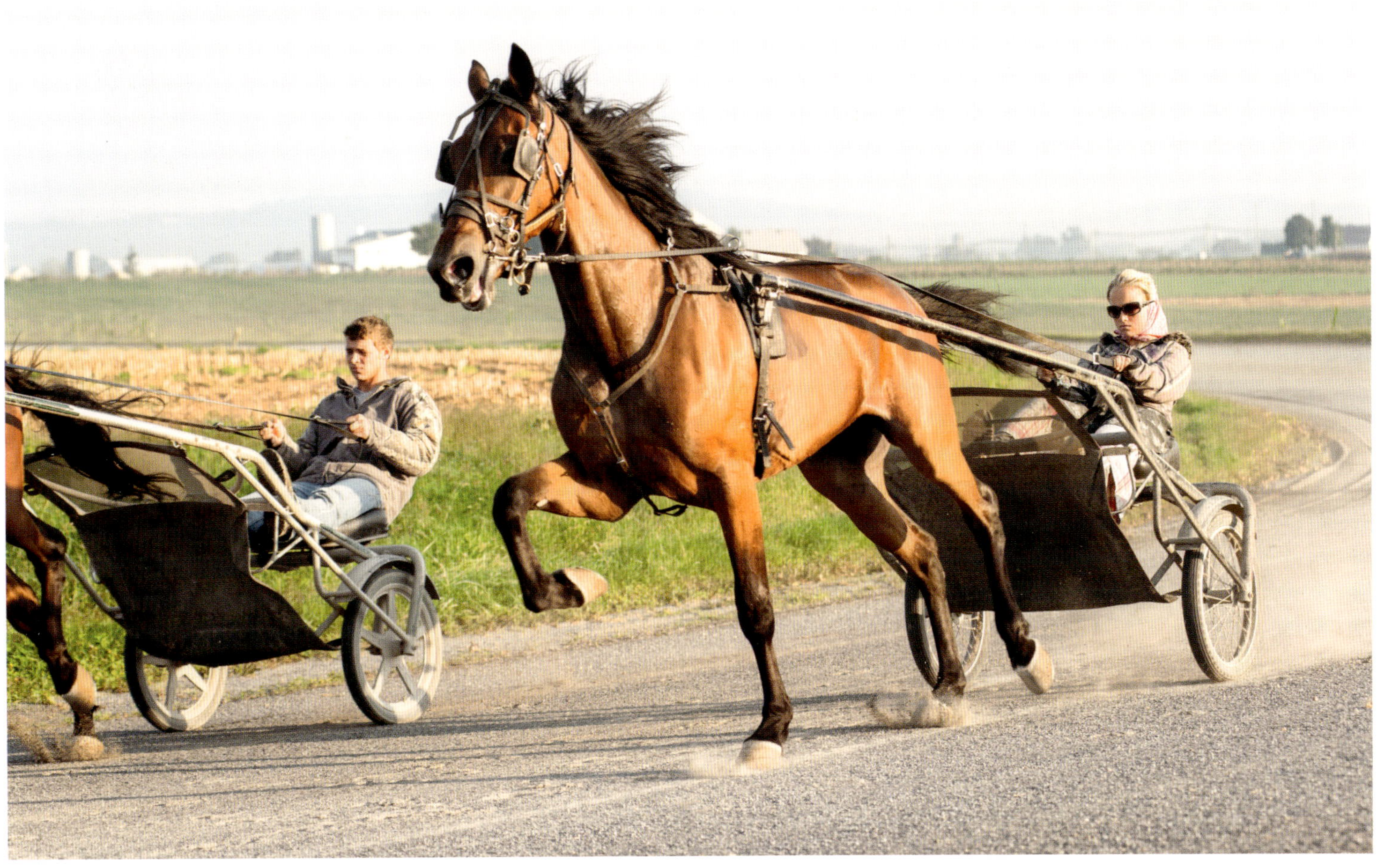

half-mile track to total 4 miles. The first five times around are at a slow jog, the sixth and seventh times are fast, and the eighth is a slow jog to cool down. Later in training, each horse is driven four times around at a jog, then turned in the opposite direction on the track and trotted at top speed for a training mile (which should take less than three minutes).

The drivers sit upright during the slow jogs. By the time the horses are moving at a fast trot, the drivers are nearly prone in their seats, legs braced against the metal stirrups, reins taut in their hands.

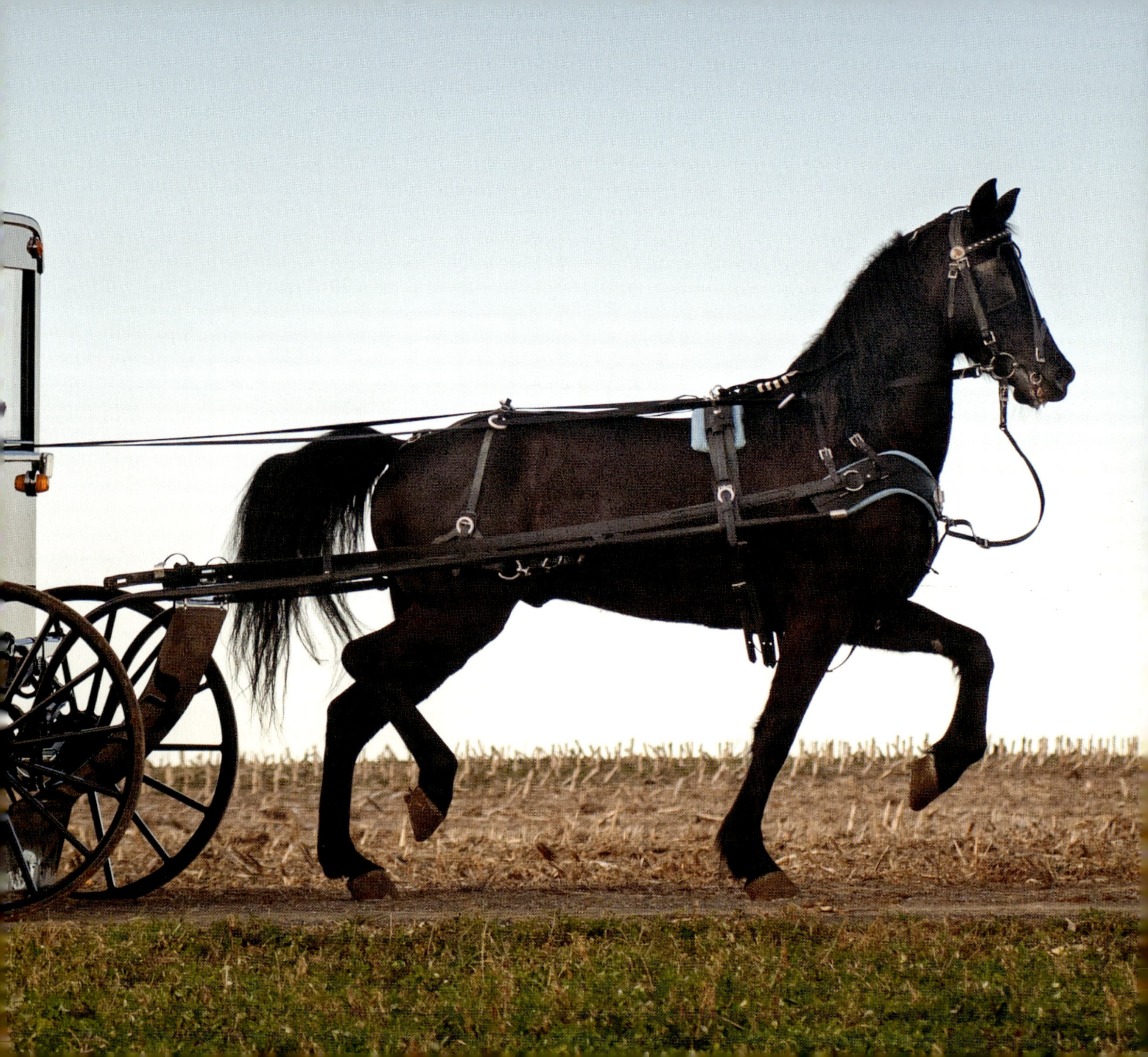

Morgan

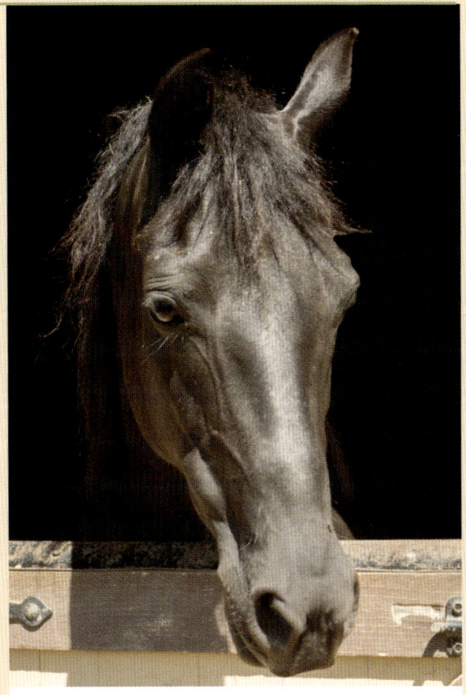

Rambo, an eleven-year-old black Morgan gelding, has the proud carriage and beautiful gait common to the breed. His owner is Stoltzfus, who loved horses and driving even as a toddler. He would sit on a cart for hours holding lines that led to a pretend horse. At age eight he could harness a pair of mules, hitch them to the forecart and to a wagon, and take them out the field to his dad. He stood on a hay bale to throw the harness onto the 16- or 17-hand mules, then moved each mule to the water trough so he could stand on the trough to reach the mule's head to put the bridle on.

Now an adult, Stoltzfus works all day as a farrier and helps with the farm chores when he gets home. He talked about Rambo in the barn while his father and brothers milked the family's herd of Holstein cows.

What is so special about Rambo? Stoltzfus likes the extra little spring in Rambo's step when he pulls the buggy and the way he can take all kinds of miles. Rambo won't be replaced anytime soon.

"He goes mile after mile . . .
he fills my two hands.
He's just fun to drive!"

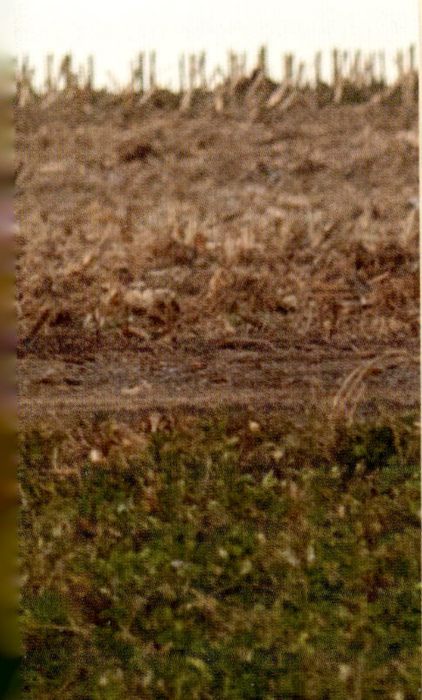

Origins: First documented American breed

Height: 14.1–15.2hh

Weight: 904–1201 lbs

Colors: generally bay, black, or chestnut with very little white

Zach, *right,* is a handsome young horse with a proud stance. Even at two weeks old, his high head and tail and sturdy, compact body identify him as a Morgan. Five months later, he was named the champion weanling in a prestigious national competition.

Morgans are known for much more than their good looks. They may be smaller than the typically buggy horse, but they are strong and spunky, brave and eager to please. There is often a powerful bond between owners and their Morgans.

Known as easy keepers, Morgans are long lived and require less grain and grass than a larger horse.

Compared to Standardbreds, Morgans are smaller and tougher. They may require a little more finesse to handle but make up for it with loyalty and affection. Beautifully animated, the Morgan holds its head high like a Saddlebred, but it is not as high-stepping.

The yearling and two-year-olds in the adjoining pasture, *facing page,* will be sent out for training shortly. They will be prepared for cart or saddle, depending what strengths the trainer sees as he puts them through their paces.

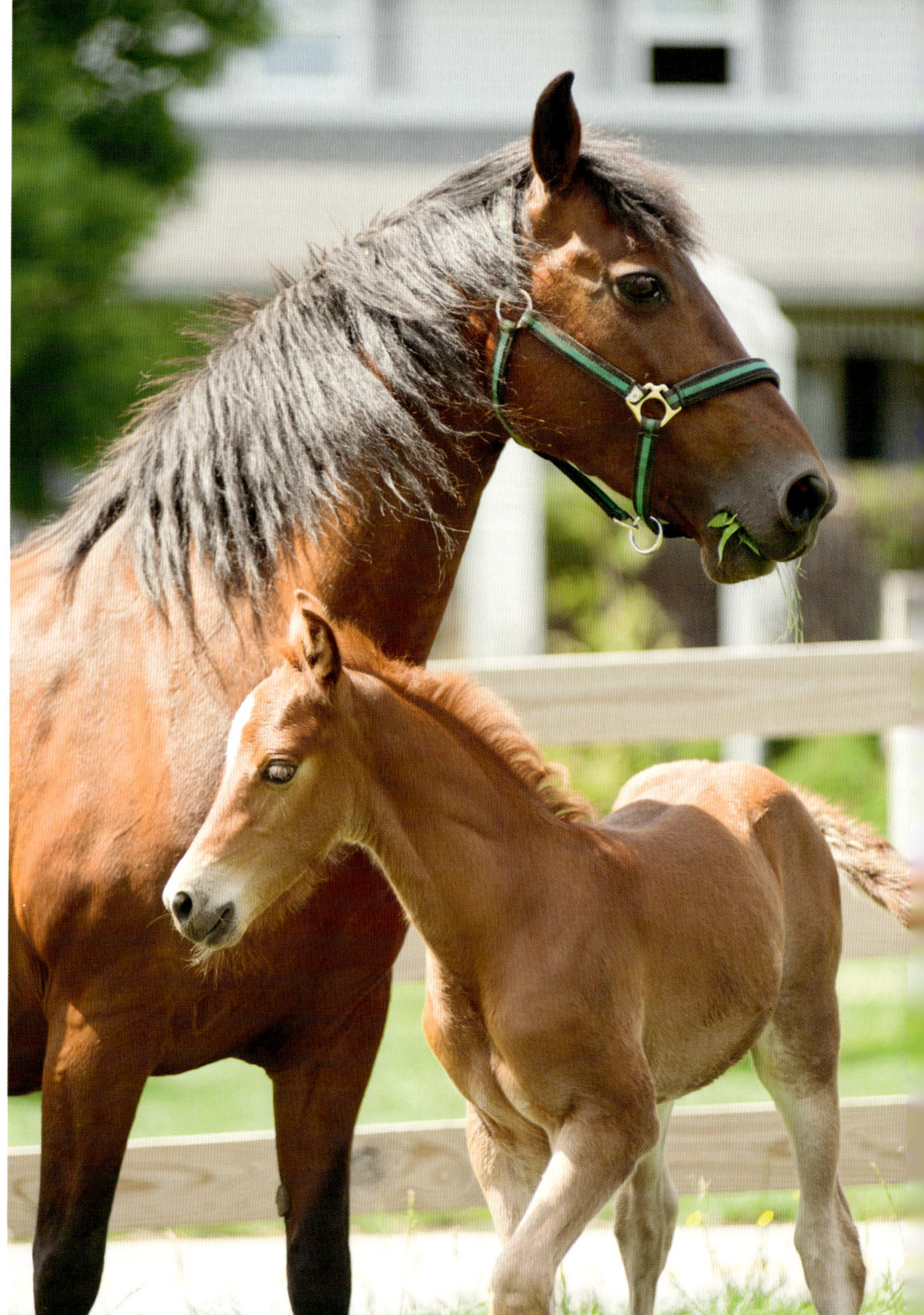

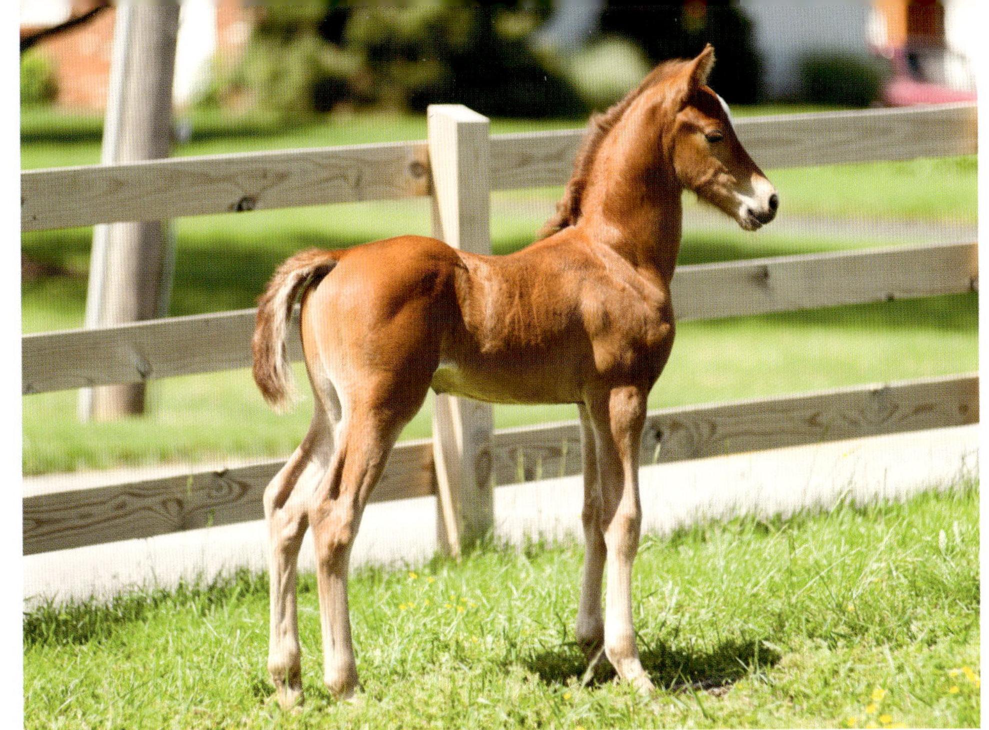

"Zach looks good. His head is up, he looks proud and stylish."

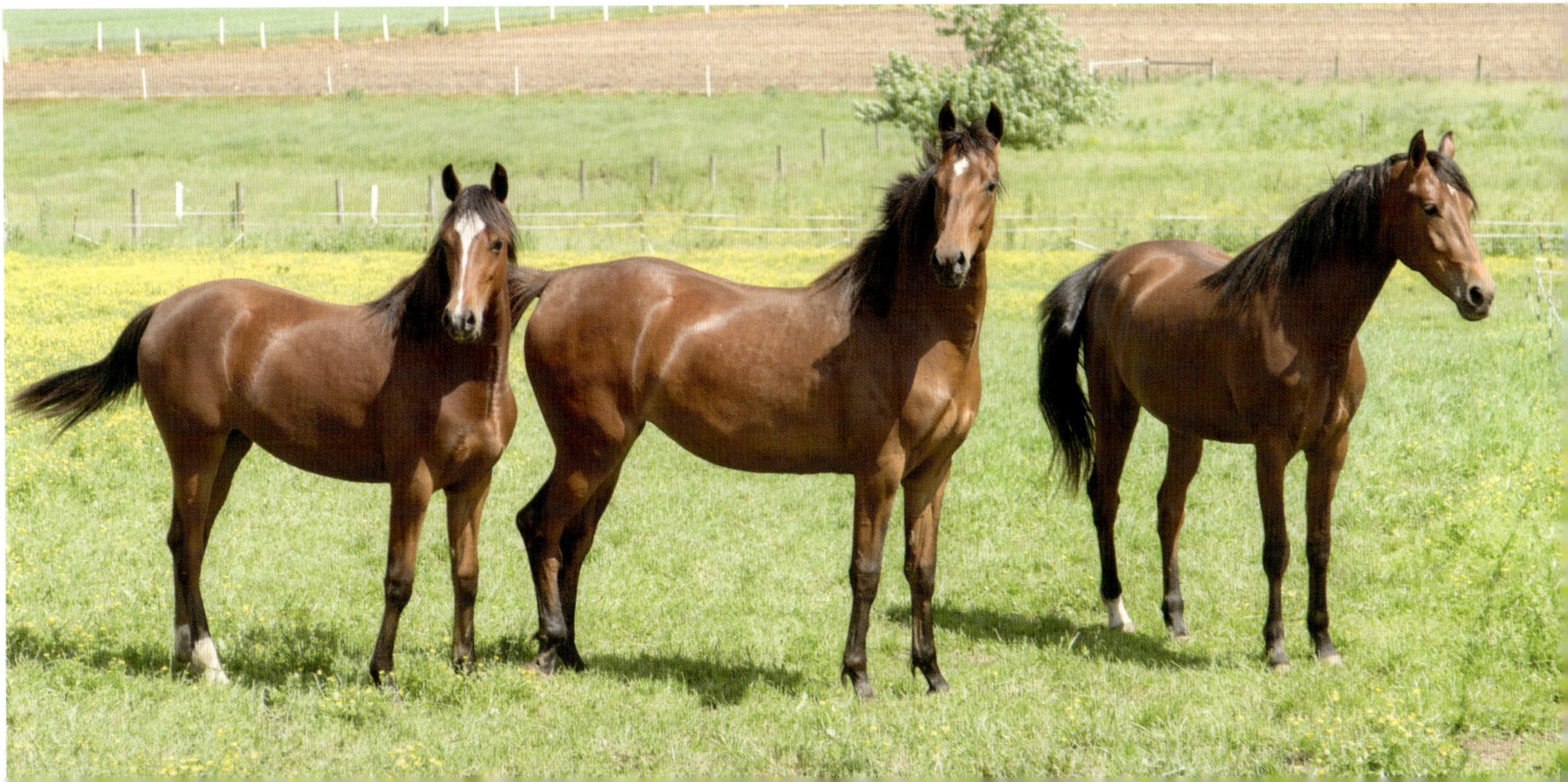

One of Fisher's uncles breeds Dutch Harness horses, while others favor Standardbreds. His cousin farms with Belgians and Percheron–Dutch Harness crosses. After owning and driving three or four other horses over the last few years, Fisher thinks Lightning, his six-year-old Morgan gelding, is the best. He bought and trained Lightning three years ago and has driven him ever since.

"He's my favorite horse."

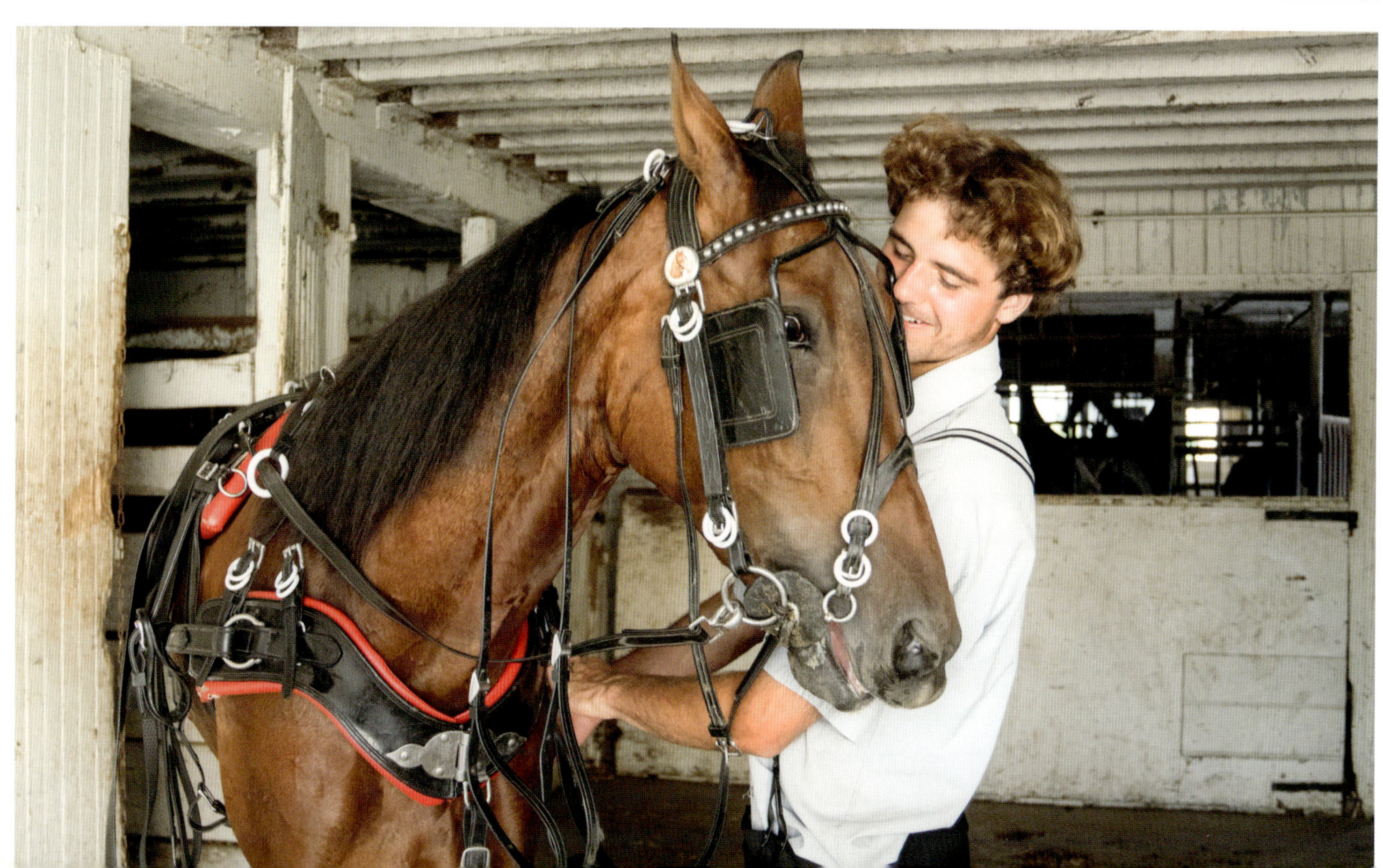

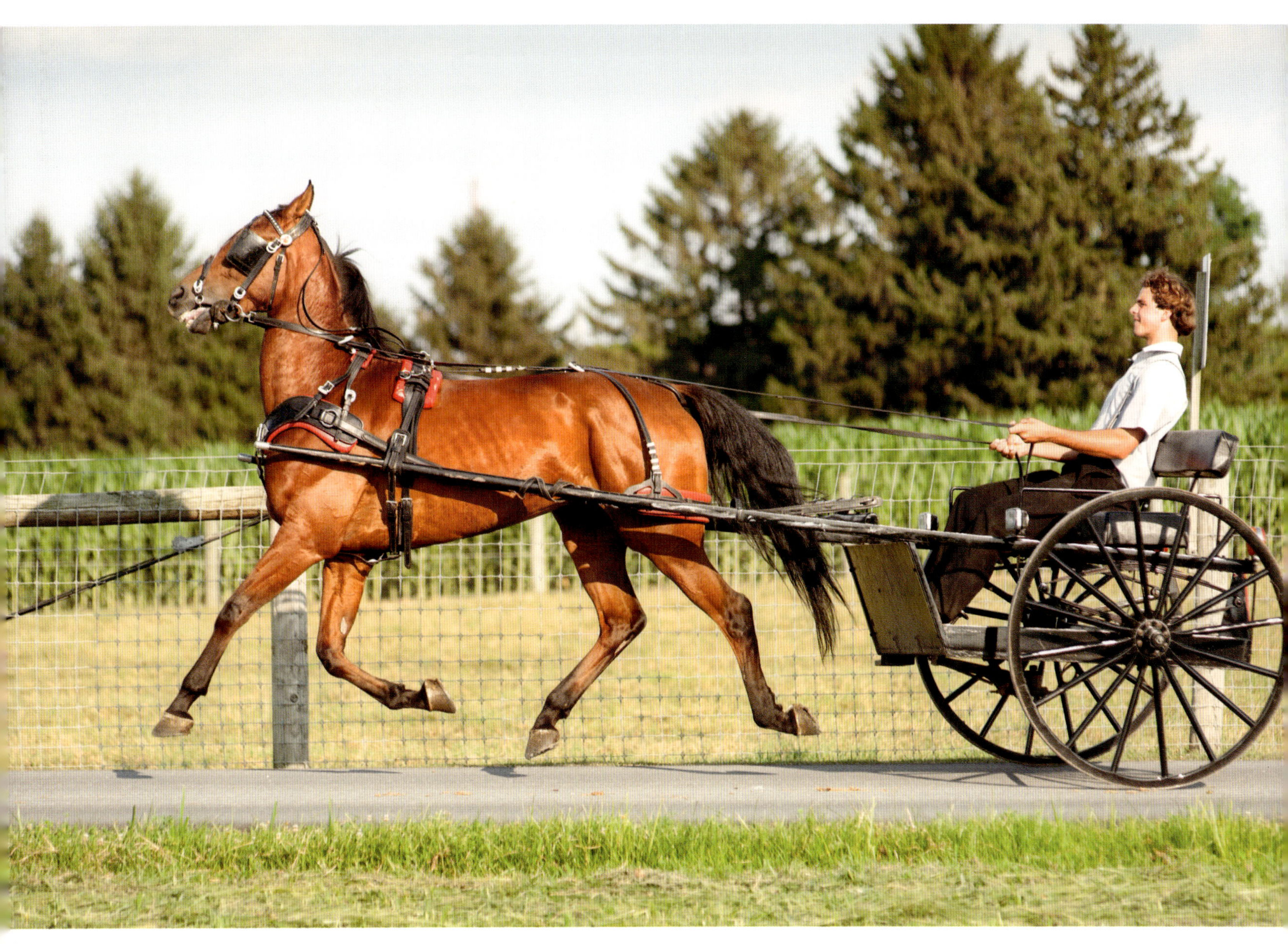

“Lightning may look small, but he’s big in the harness.”

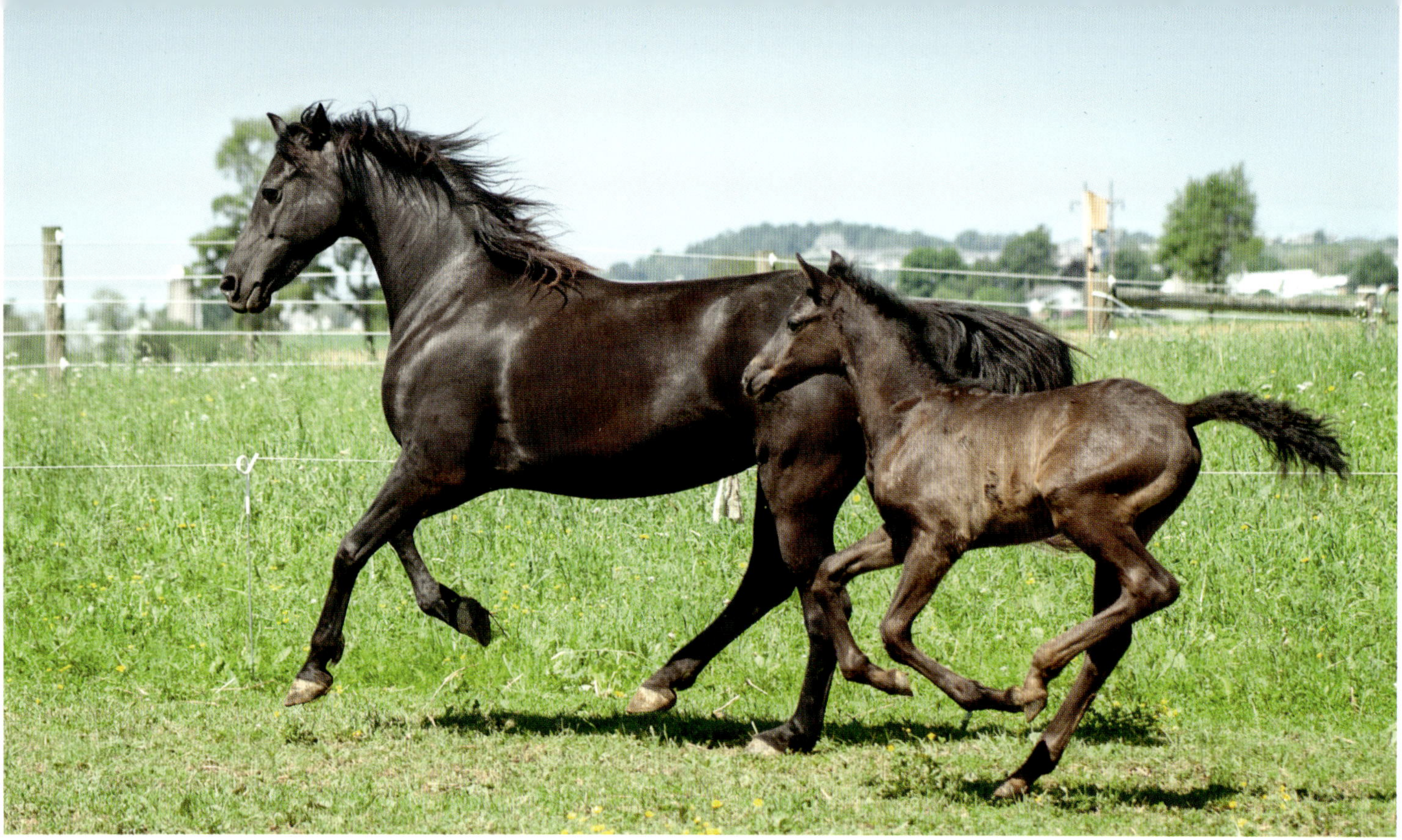

At another farm, one-month-old Ranger, *above,* shows the build and style he inherited from his mother, Holly. Like her, he may make a good carriage horse when he grows up, though his owner is considering keeping him to breed at three years old.

Morgans have great personalities, says Andrew, who trains them for show. He finds them fun and sporty, more "awake" (perky and responsive) than other horses, as well as uniquely sensitive. Three-year-old Abbey, *right,* is a good prospect to show this year.

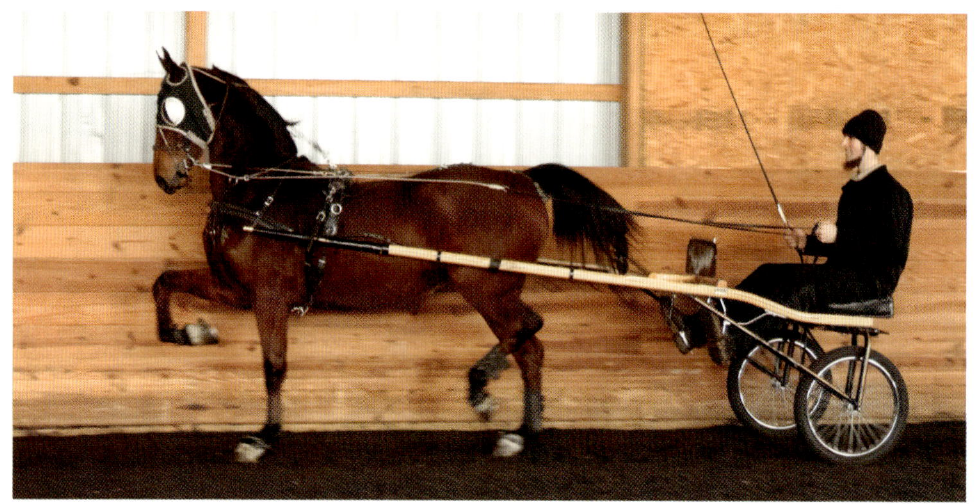

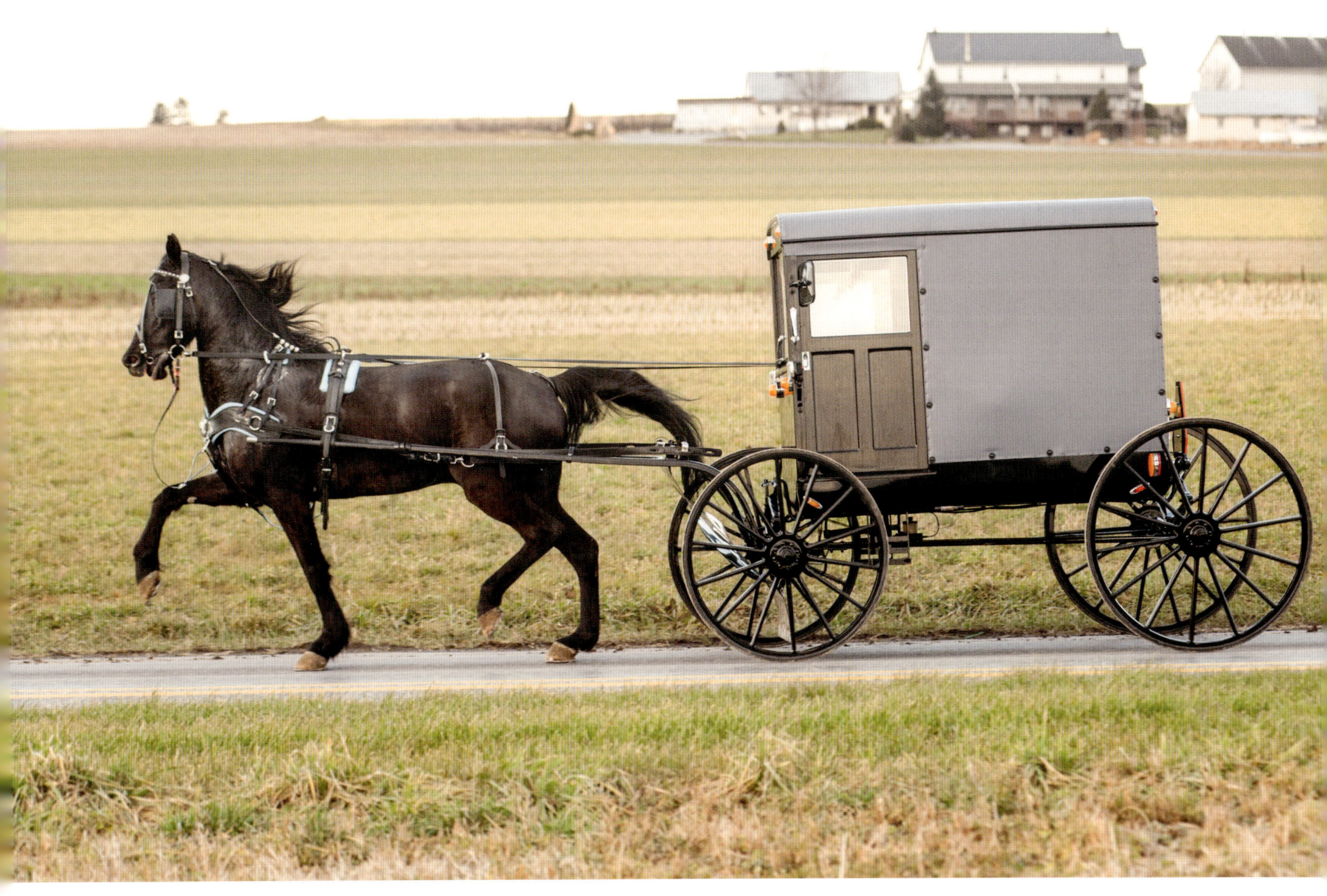

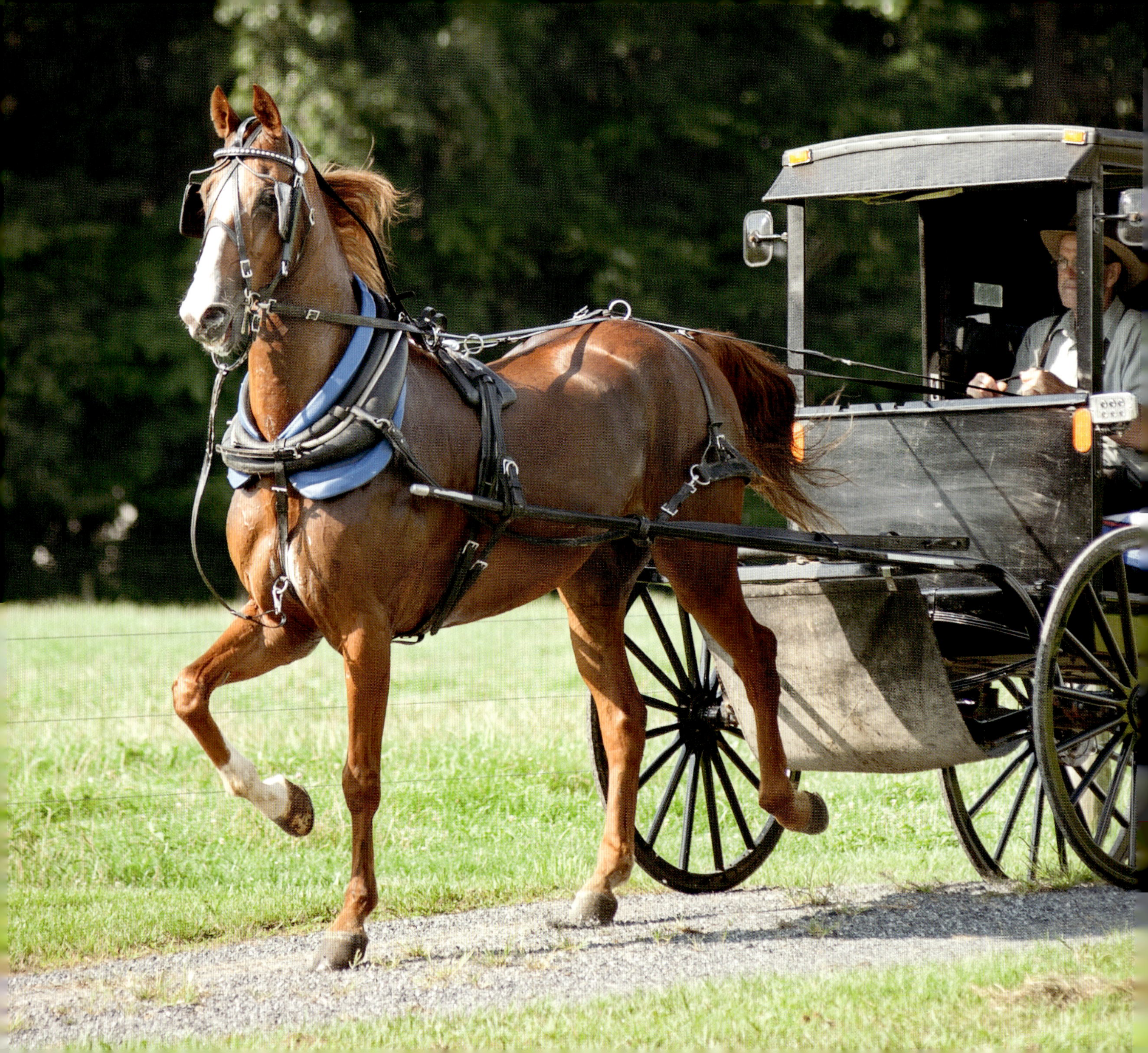

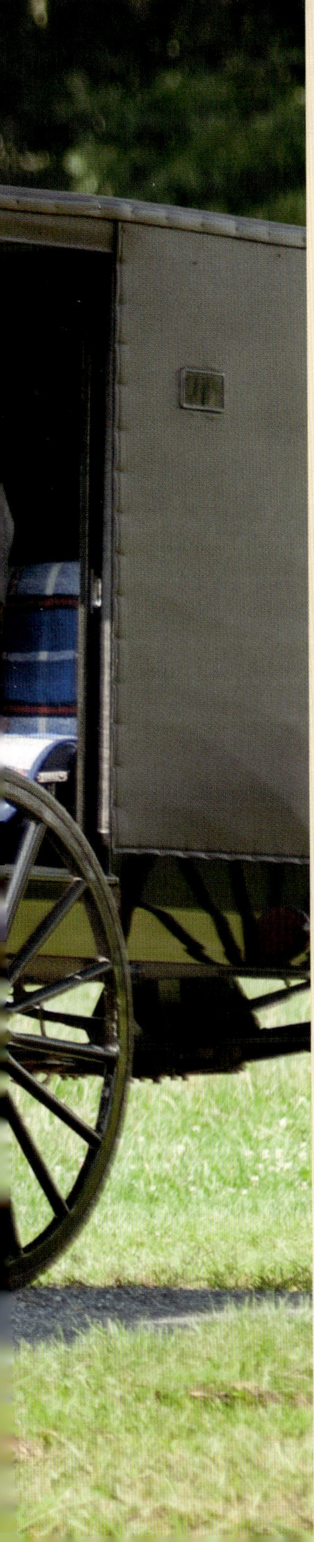

American Saddlebred

Amos delights in all kinds of horses, but he is a particular fan of the American Saddlebred. Though not as popular as the Standardbred, Saddlebreds have staunch supporters, and are a favorite to cross with other breeds. Amos is encouraging this enthusiasm in the next generation. He has offered to breed his prize mare, Goldie, to the stallions his two daughters and son choose.

Old Order Mennonites and Amish value the spirit and athleticism exhibited by Saddlebreds. When hitched to a buggy, the Saddlebred brings strength and a willing attitude to its stylish looks.

But there is indication that the Saddlebred population in the County is waning, however, possibly because the breeding priority has become refinement for show at the expense of practicality on the road.

Depending on where he is going, Amos determines which of his two carriage horses is best to drive. When he will be in heavy traffic, he hitches up Sparky, *left,* a gelding with a calm temperament. When he is up for a challenge, Blondie is his choice. She has a good bit of energy and keeps Amos on his toes.

"My dad bought me my first horse—a Saddlebred—and we just clicked."

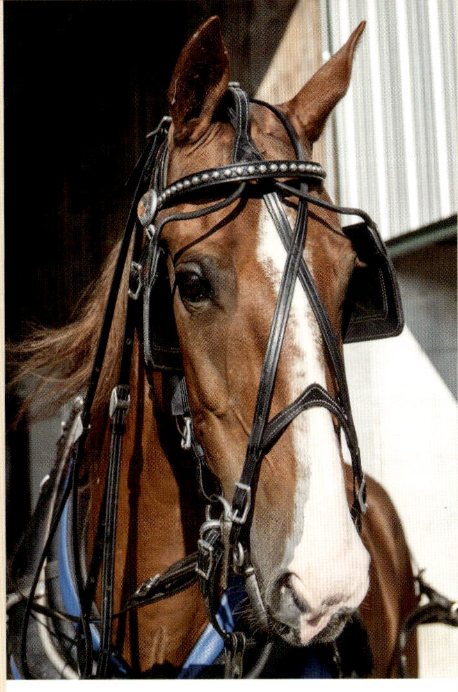

Origins: British and Irish colonists in 17th century

Height: 15–16hh

Weight: 900–1,000 lbs

Colors: all

The American Saddlebred is admired for its proud carriage and smooth gait.

Founded on horses the colonists brought to the Americas, the "American Horse" was developed by crossing Thoroughbreds with pacers. The result was a saddle horse that combined the best of both foundation breeds. Saddlebreds grew in popularity, even carrying Civil War generals into battle.

Today the Saddlebred is known for its versatility—for pleasure and show, dressage and driving.

Amos's son-in-law is allergic to horses, which can be an issue when members of your church travel by horse and buggy. When Amos offered to breed his Saddlebred mare to the stallion of Andy's choice, Andy chose a Bashkir Curly, which is thought to be hypoallergenic. The foal that resulted, *left,* does seem to have fewer allergens, and Andy is pleased.

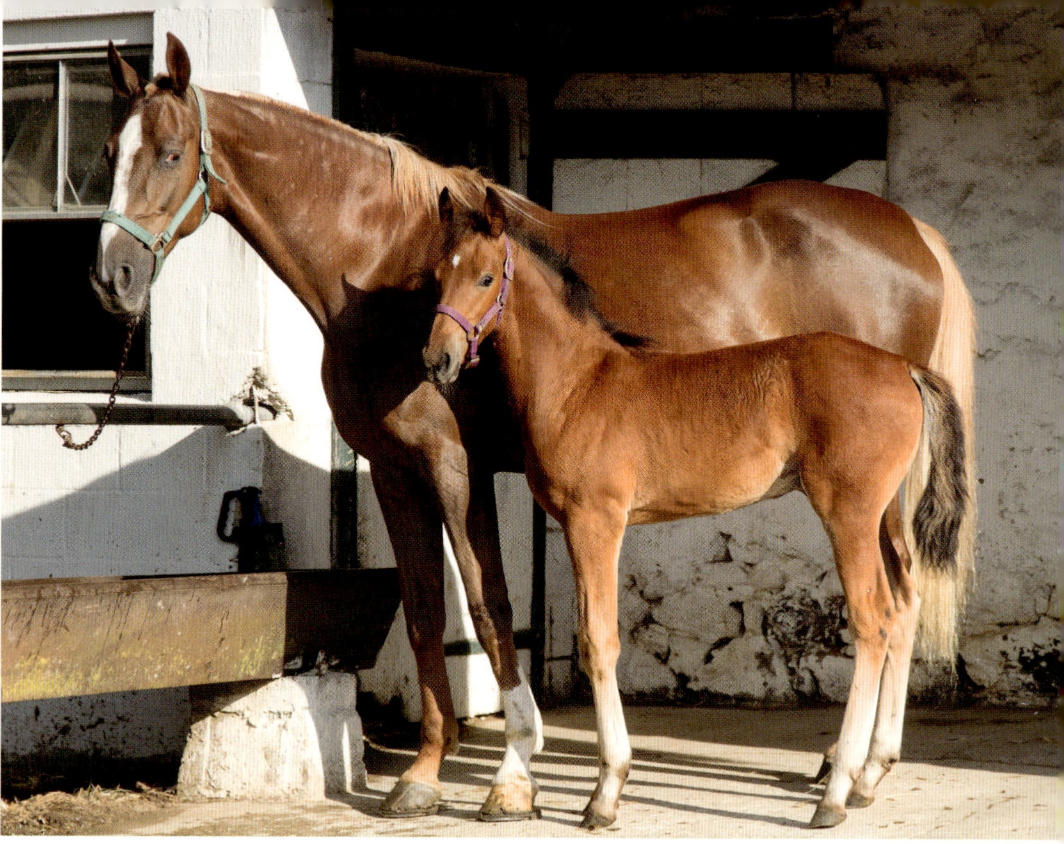

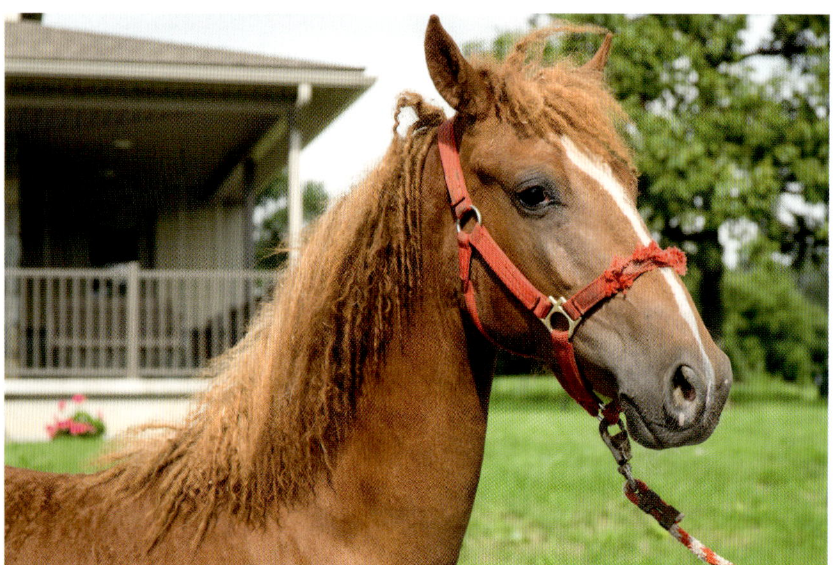

The next year, Amos crossed his Saddlebred mare with a Friesian stud for his son. The resulting foal, *above,* is a little more docile than a pure Saddlebred but still spirited in head and step.

Mixing it up a little more the following year, his younger daughter chose a Friesian-Standardbred cross stud to breed with her dad's Saddlebred mare. She's anticipating a just-right mix of good looks and stamina.

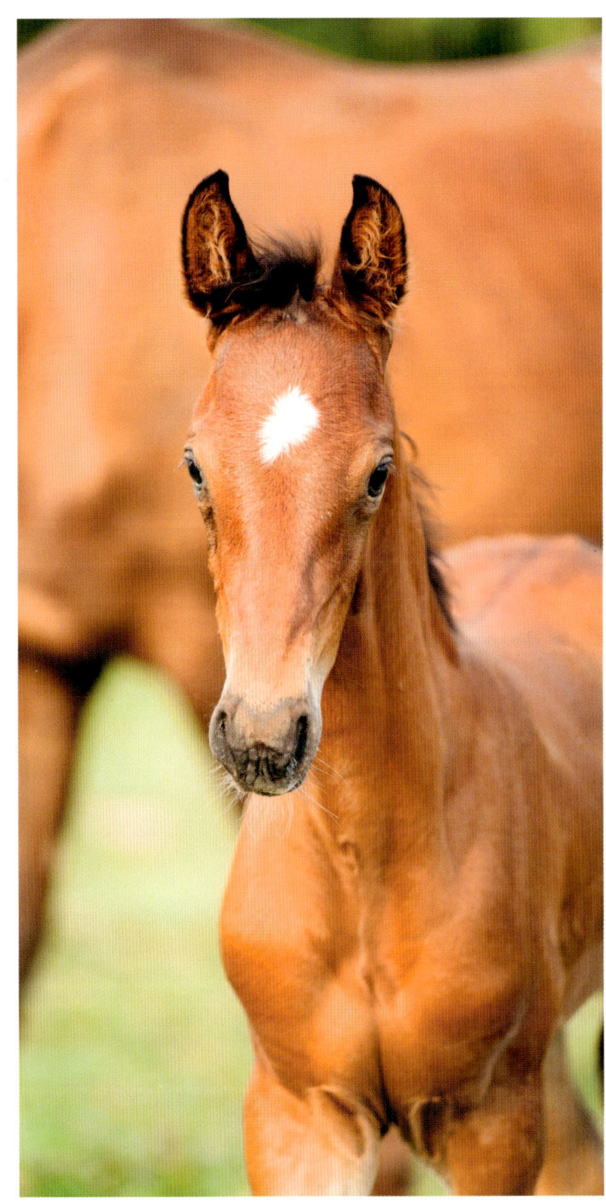

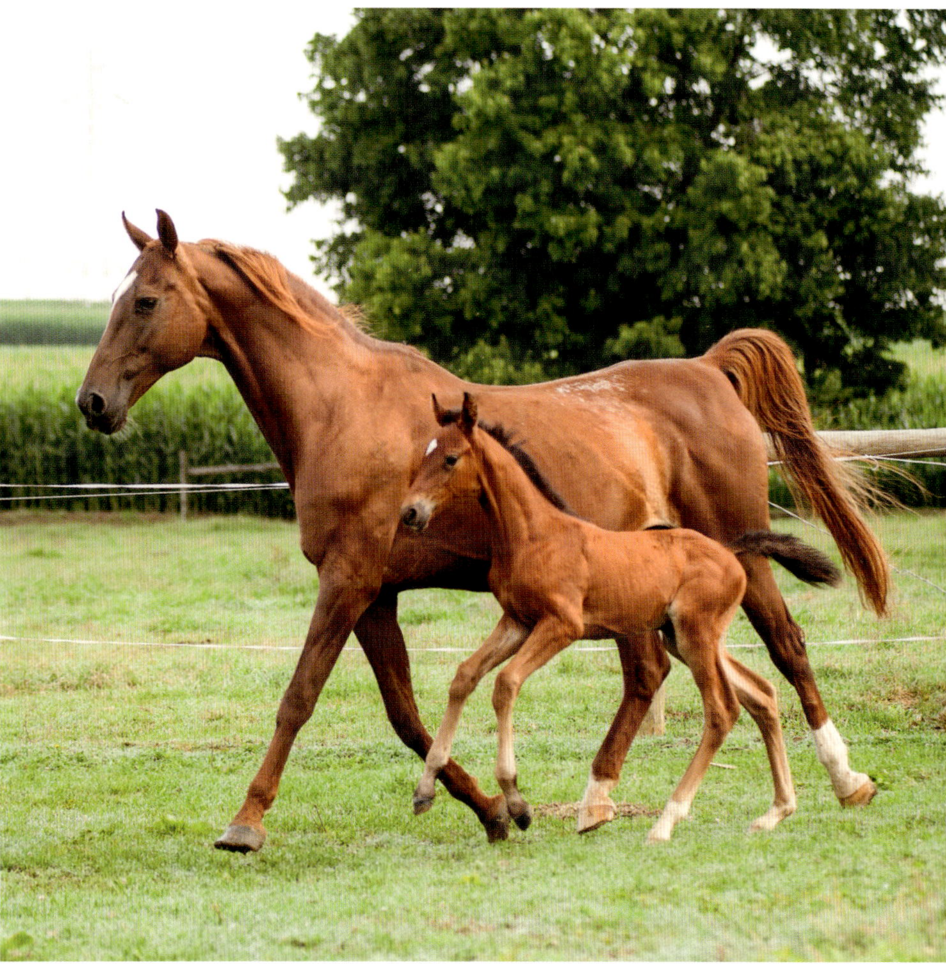

A bay-colored three-week-old foal shows the proud head; long, elegant neck; and spirit that characterize a Saddlebred. Compared to the more common Standardbred, a Saddlebred is lighter weight and slimmer with a smaller head. A Saddlebred's head and tail are held high and its step is high and showy. Sometimes a bit skittish, they are friendly, intelligent, and gentle.

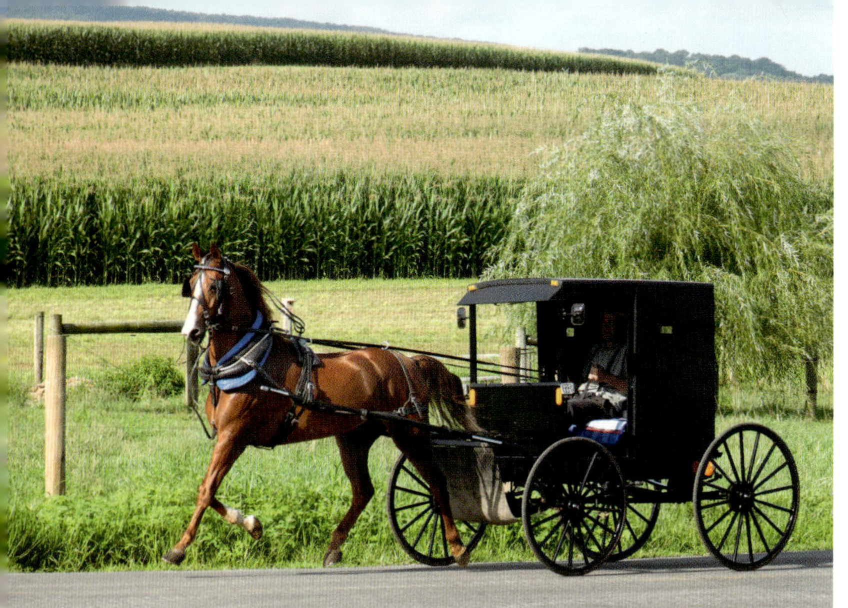

The initial training of a horse to pull a cart or wagon is the same whether the end goal is a carriage horse or a show horse; every driver wants an attractive horse that is also responsive and reliable.

After a horse adjusts to the feel of a bridle and harness, a trainer works it on a long line. Put through his paces by a trainer, Bellview's Rodger, *right,* a four-year-old liver chestnut, smoothly performs a trot, canter, and flat walk on command.

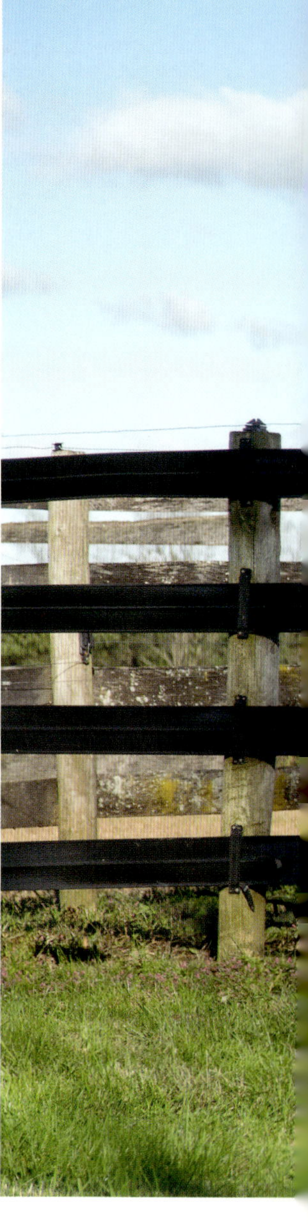

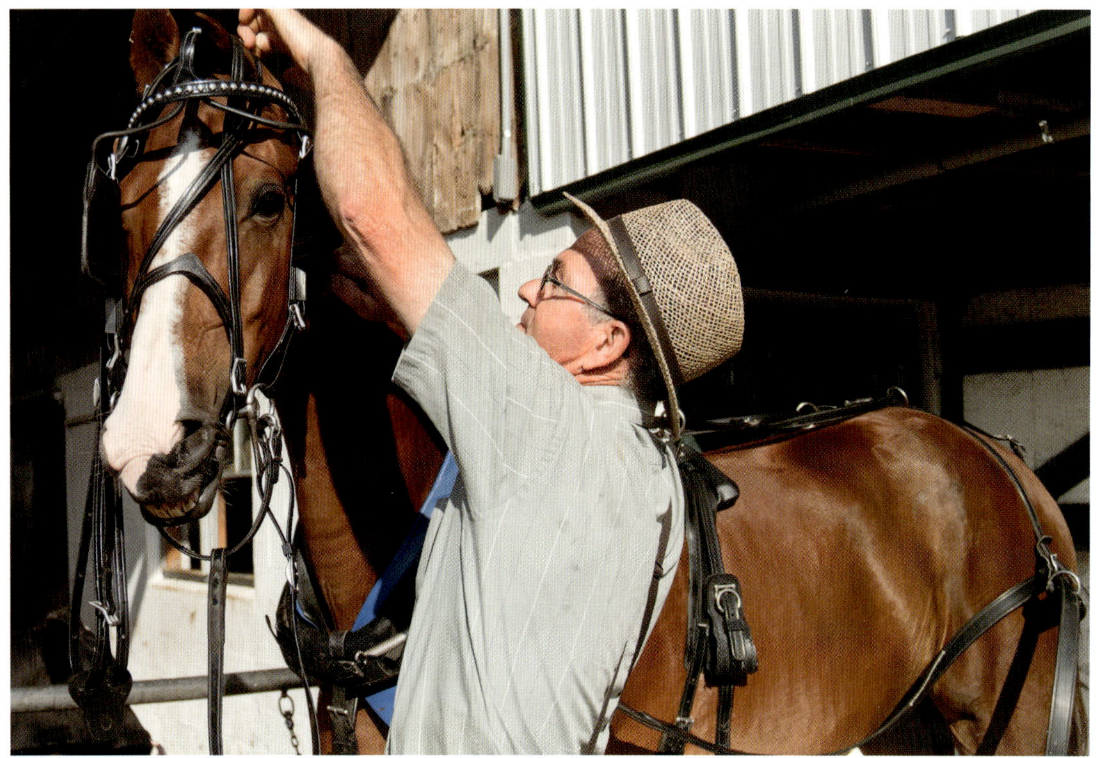

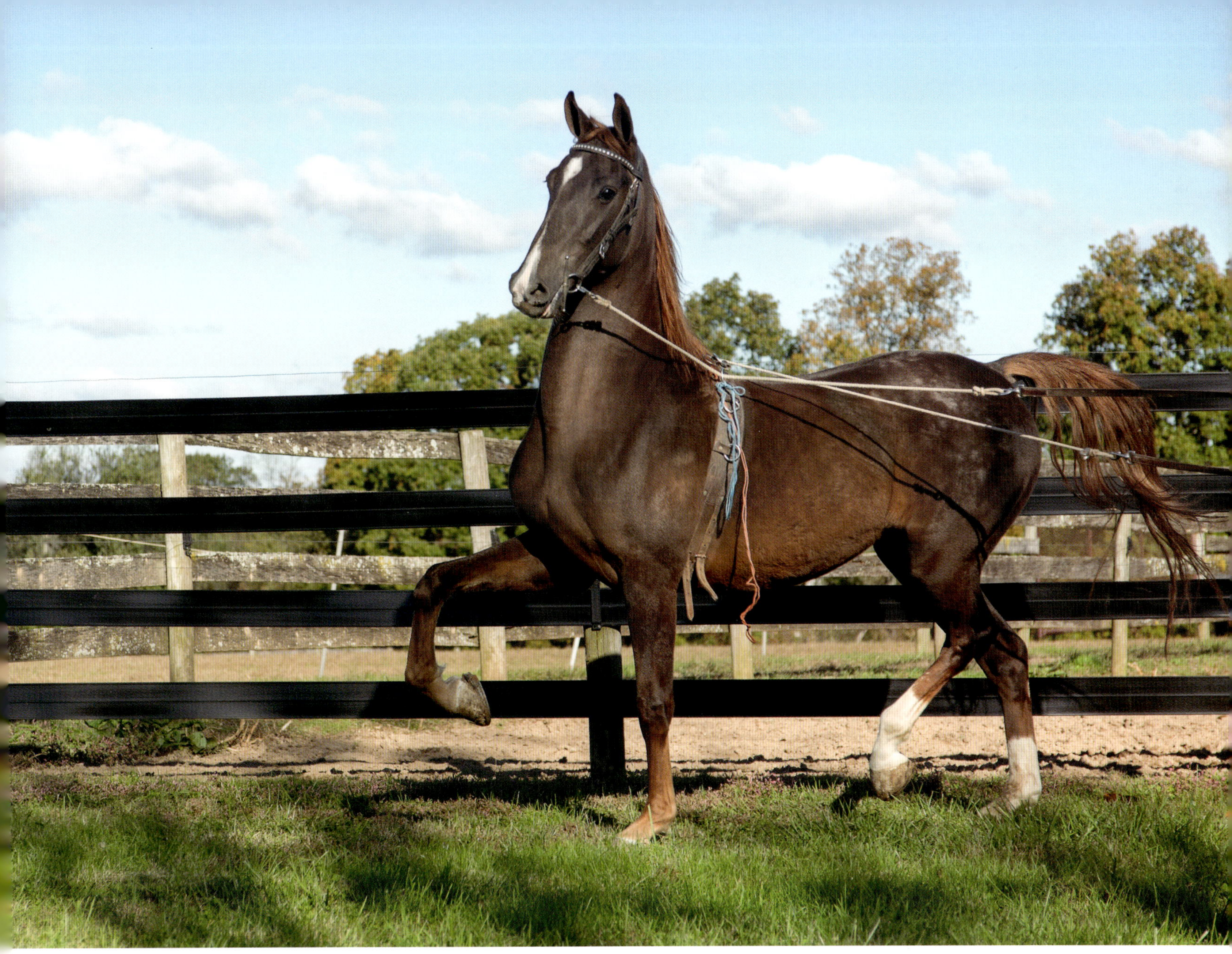

“The horses talk to me about how it’s best to train them; it’s not my choice.”

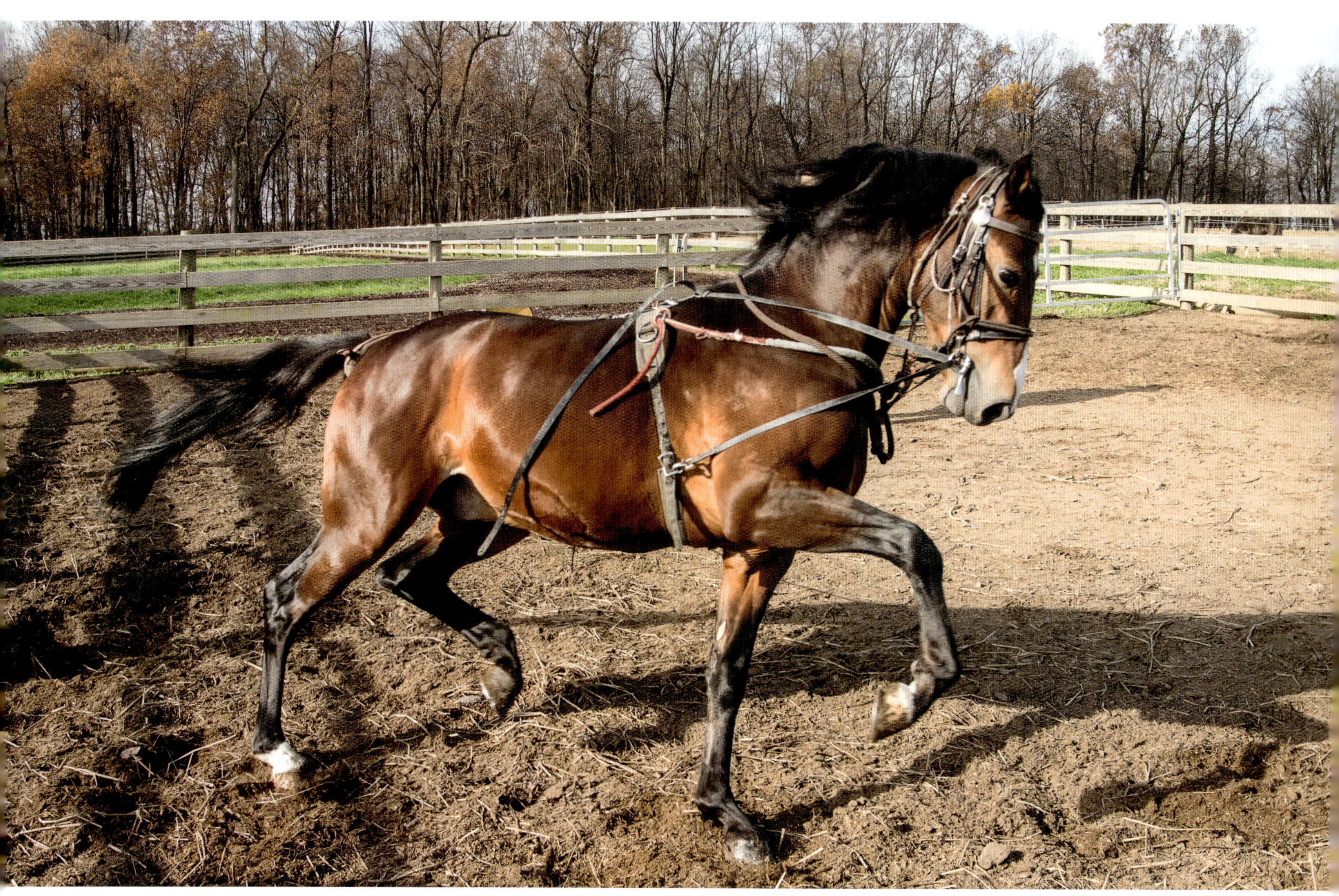

"Fire has great talent. His neck is strong, his body has nice conformation. He's a bouncy mover."

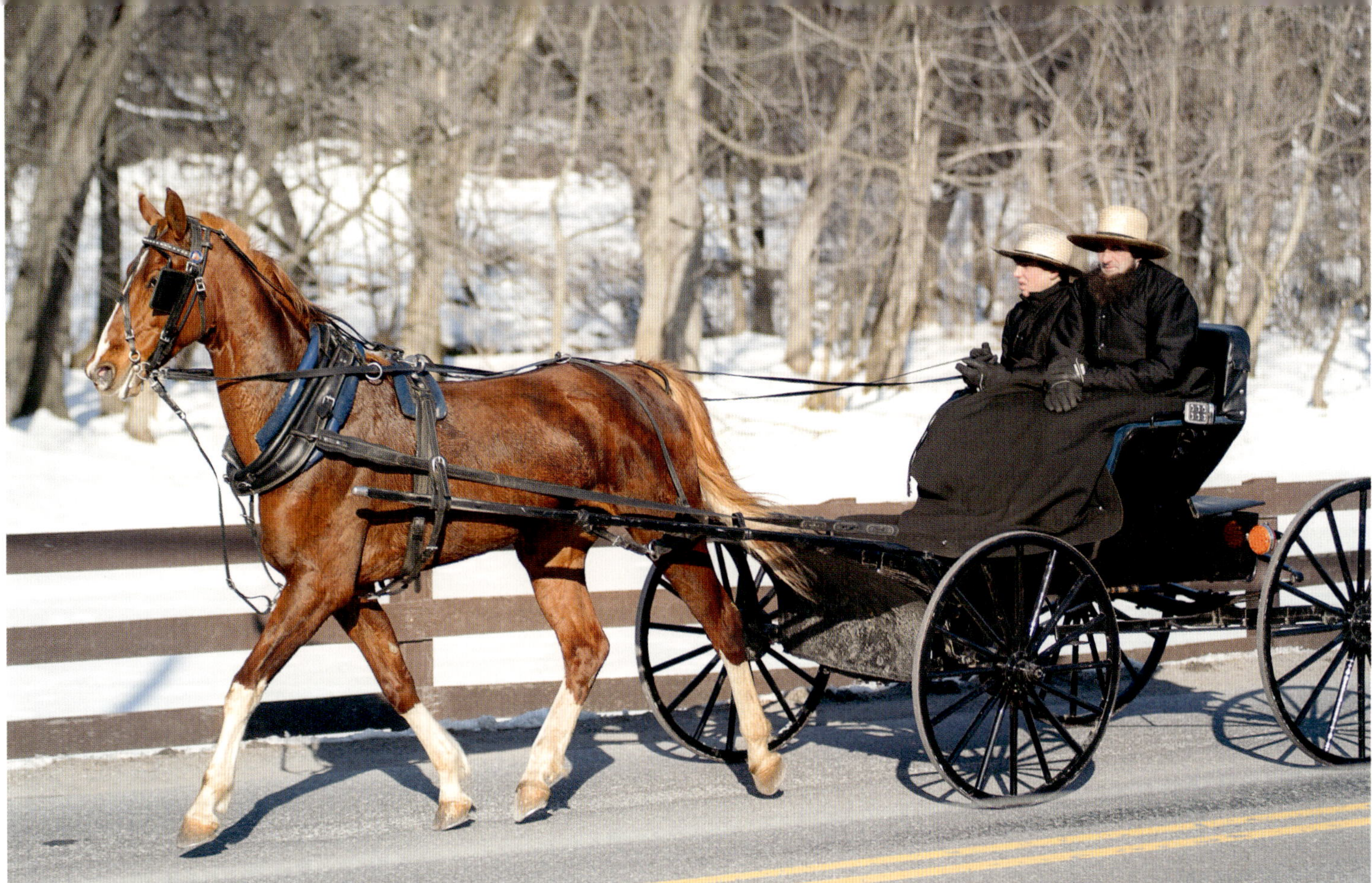

There is a bright future for Supreme Fire, *left,* a three-year-old Saddlebred with good bloodlines. Fire's physical assets—strong neck and nice body conformation—were obvious early on, enhanced with that elusive "sparkle" a successful show horse must possess. Fire's training includes working on bit management and building muscles so that he carries his weight evenly and trots with a precise elegance.

Though there's a difference between workaday Saddlebreds and those carefully bred and groomed for show, the same proud carriage and good looks are evident. A dad and his teenage son, *above,* braved the cold in an open carriage and drove their seven-year-old Saddlebred gelding, Stormy, 9 miles from home to an auction. When they arrived, Stormy joined the other driving horses blanketed and tied outside while his owners went inside to look at the mules being offered for sale.

Bellview's Dancing Fort, *right,* is a popular stud that has sired champions. His owner's stable offers stud service for a variety of stallion breeds, training for riding and driving, mare care, and farrier services.

Also offered is teeth floating. Unlike human teeth, a horse's teeth continue growing throughout its life. Wear on the teeth is frequently uneven, which results in difficulty grinding food and sharp points that irritate the horse's mouth. A file called a "float" is used to smooth and contour the teeth, resulting in a better bite and a healthier horse.

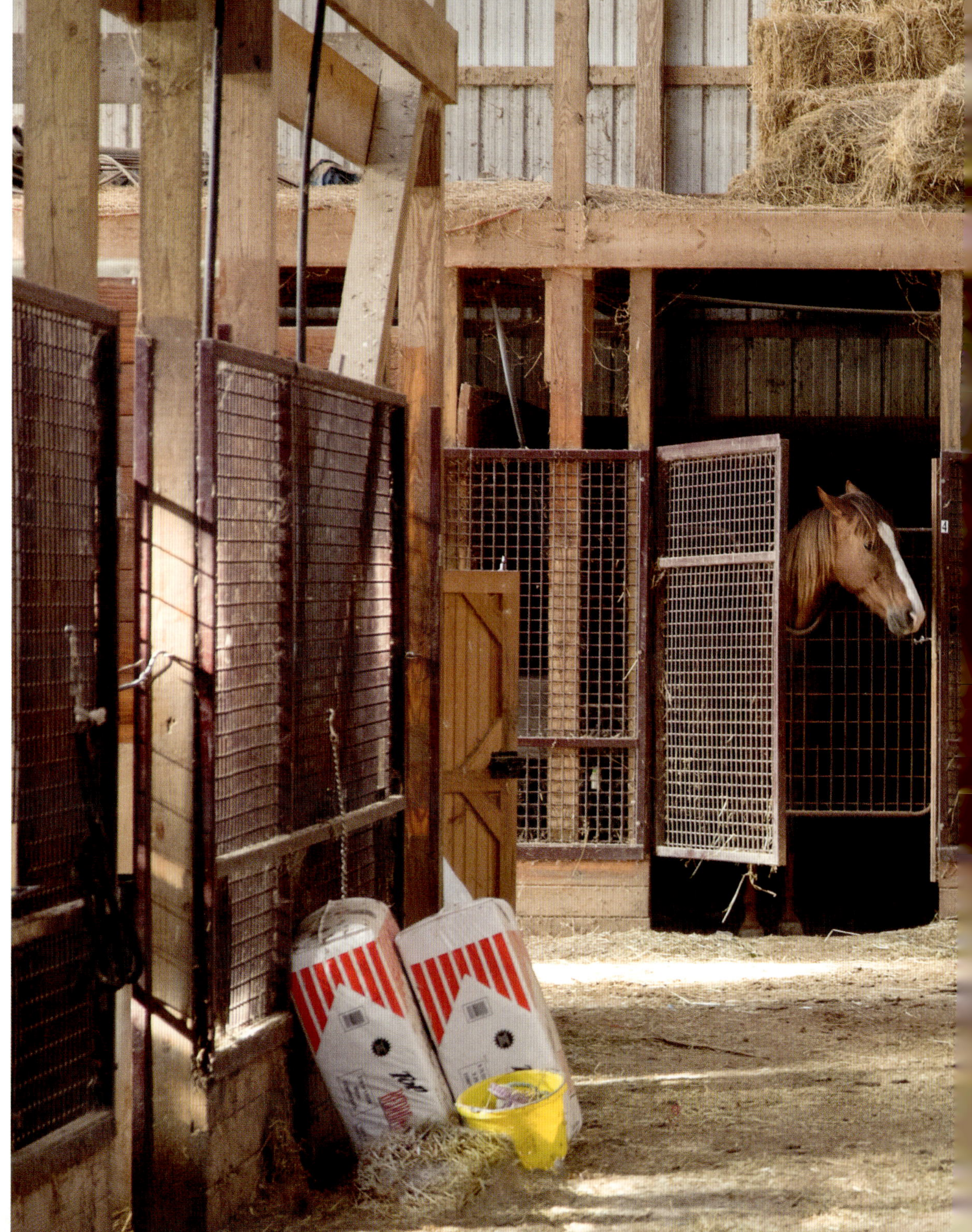

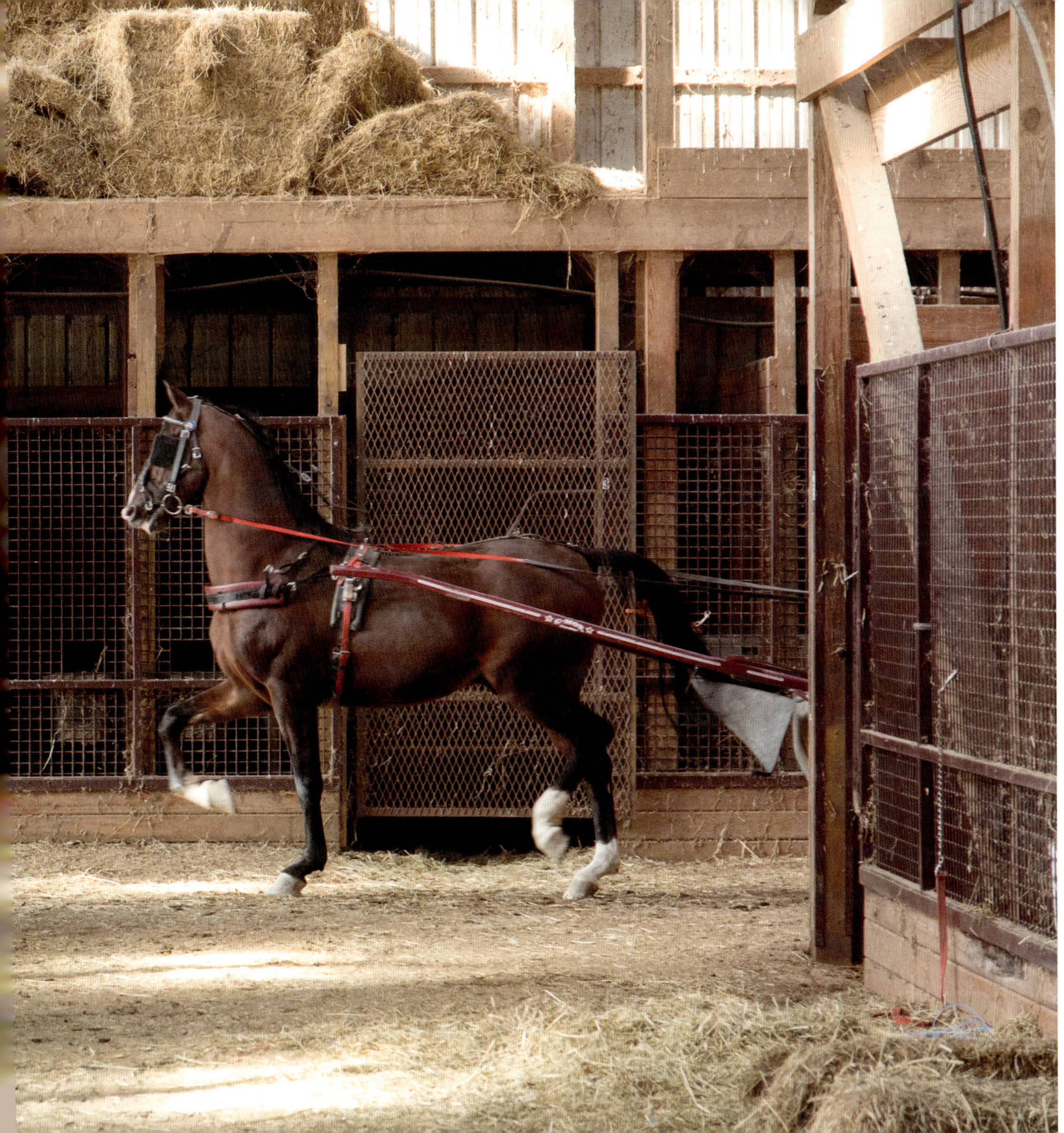

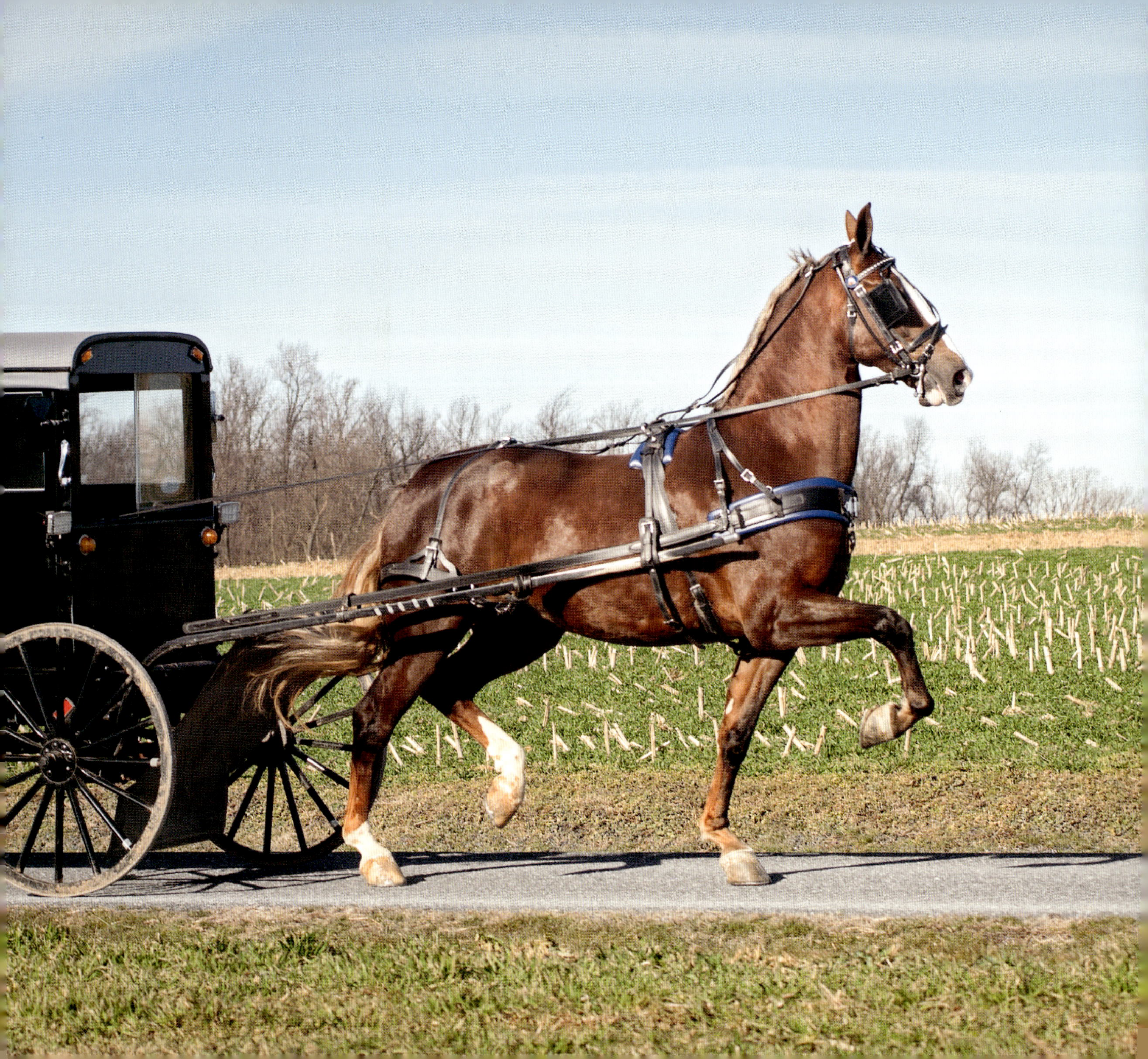

Dutch Harness

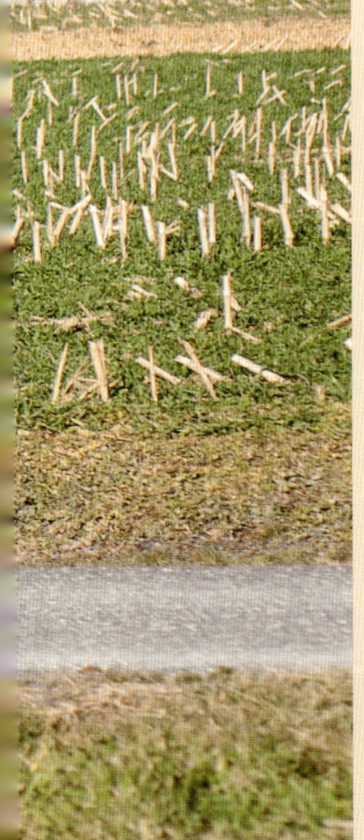

Steven's older brother introduced him to the Dutch Harness breed when Steven was a boy. Dutch Harnesses were new to the United States from the Netherlands in the first few years of this century and showed a size and flash not typically seen in a buggy horse. Steven was drawn to their beauty and elegance. But the size and temperament of these new imports did not easily bend to the needs of the buggy driver. Local breeders found that crossing the Dutch Harness with other breeds resulted in a horse better suited for the road than is a full Dutch Harness.

Steven trains a variety of horses and breeds, from a young crossbreed being trained for the buggy to a full Dutch Harness being prepared for fine harness competition.

For transportation, he uses a Dutch Harness–Saddlebred cross, *left*—an ideal combination of style and practicality.

"People like Dutch because they have looks and spark."

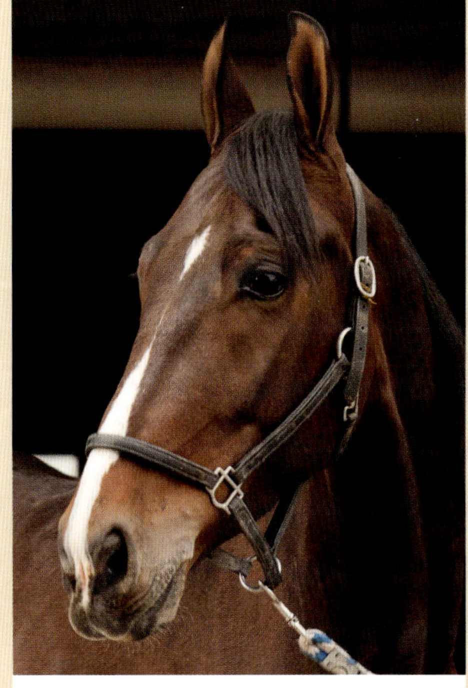

Origins: Netherlands

Height: 15 –16.2hh

Weight: 1,050 lbs

Colors: chestnut, gray, bay, black, roan, pinto, cream dilutions; white socks are often desired

The first wave of Dutch Harness imports, though beautiful, proved to be heavier and slower than was ideal to pull a carriage. It also took more feed to maintain a bigger horse. So breeders turned to careful crossbreeding. When they crossed the Dutch Harness with the Standardbred, a bit of speed may have been lost, but strength and style was added. Crossing a Dutch Harness with a Saddlebred brought attractive coloring and added power to the Saddlebred's narrow body.

Later imports from Dutch breeders and a strong US breeding program improved the American stock and resulted in purebred Dutch Harness horses with a more refined look, especially beneficial for horses that would compete in the show ring. Dutch Harness horses with the lighter build also proved to work well pulling buggies on the road.

Conversely, breeders found that a Dutch Harness of more-sturdy origins crossed with a Percheron resulted in a small draft horse that found favor with produce farmers working in their smaller fields.

Two young Dutch Harness-Saddlebred crossbreed foals, *left and below,* enjoy the spring sunshine. Showing an innate style and spark, *opposite page,* a three-day-old full Dutch Harness colt frolics beside his mother.

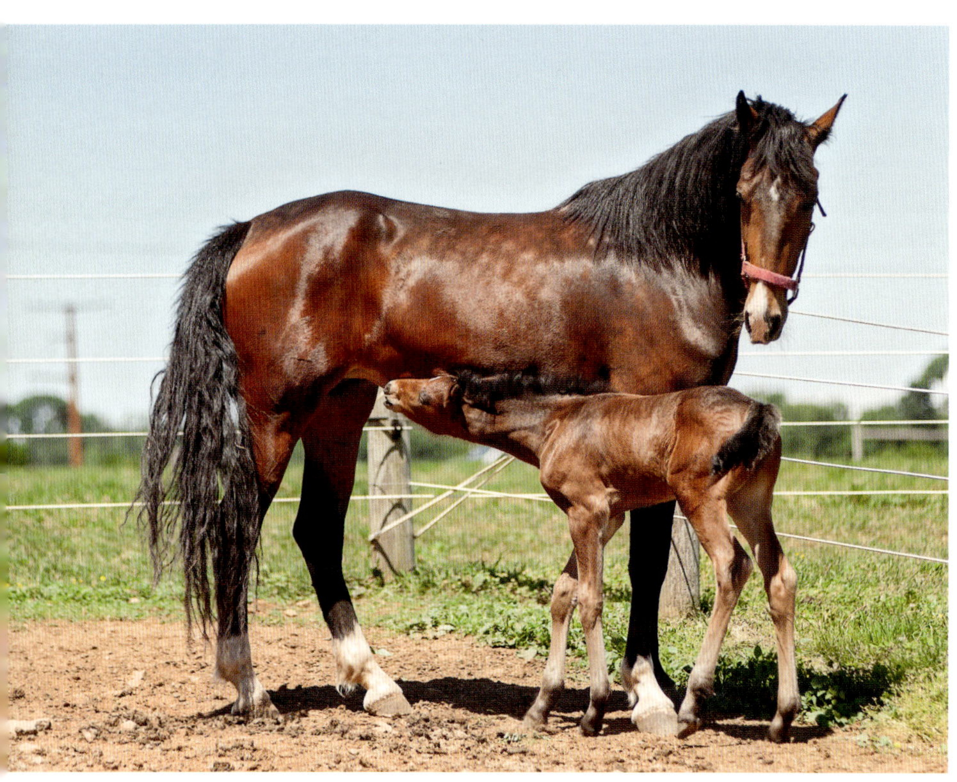

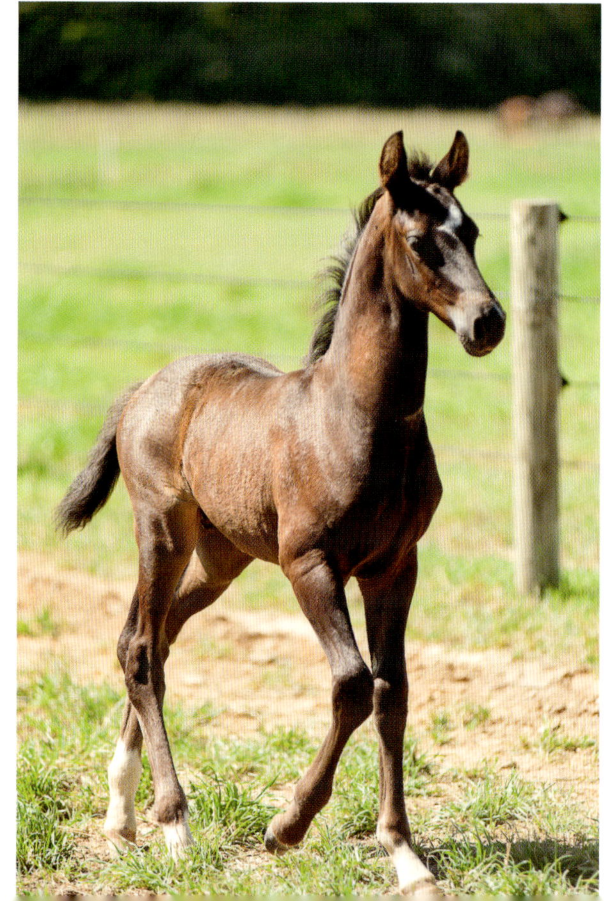

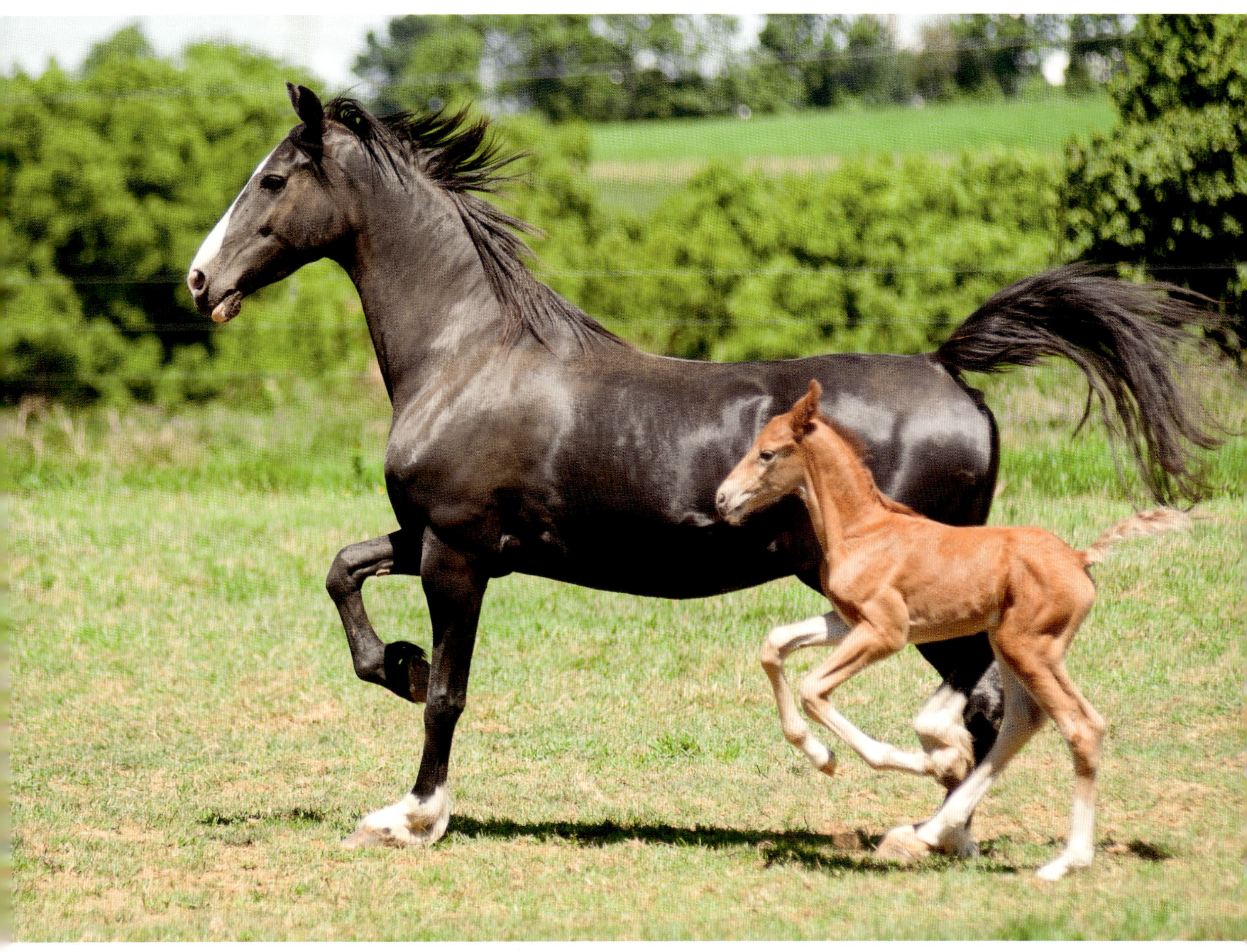

Though a young horse's buggy training can be completed in three months or so, training a show horse takes far longer. Much more care and time goes into the specifics of conditioning, muscle building, bit management, and refinement of gait and carriage. Skills and fitness must also be maintained in the off-season. Some high-level trainers such as Steven also show their clients' horses in competitions.

Dutch Harness horses that Steven trains for show are typically shown in hand or in fine harness pulling a viceroy (a lightweight four-wheeled show buggy) or a bike (two-wheeled cart). Some classes are restricted to specific breeds; others are open to all.

Horses in training often wear a soft mesh training mask. The mask with built-in blinders is easier to fit over a bridle than switching to a bridle that incorporates blinders.

As prey animals, horses have peripheral vision that allows them to monitor what is happening all around them and stay alert for danger. Blinders do not "blind" a horse; they simply narrow the field of vision to block out distractions and focus the horse's sight forward.

"A Dutch Harness is more hot-blooded than some horses."

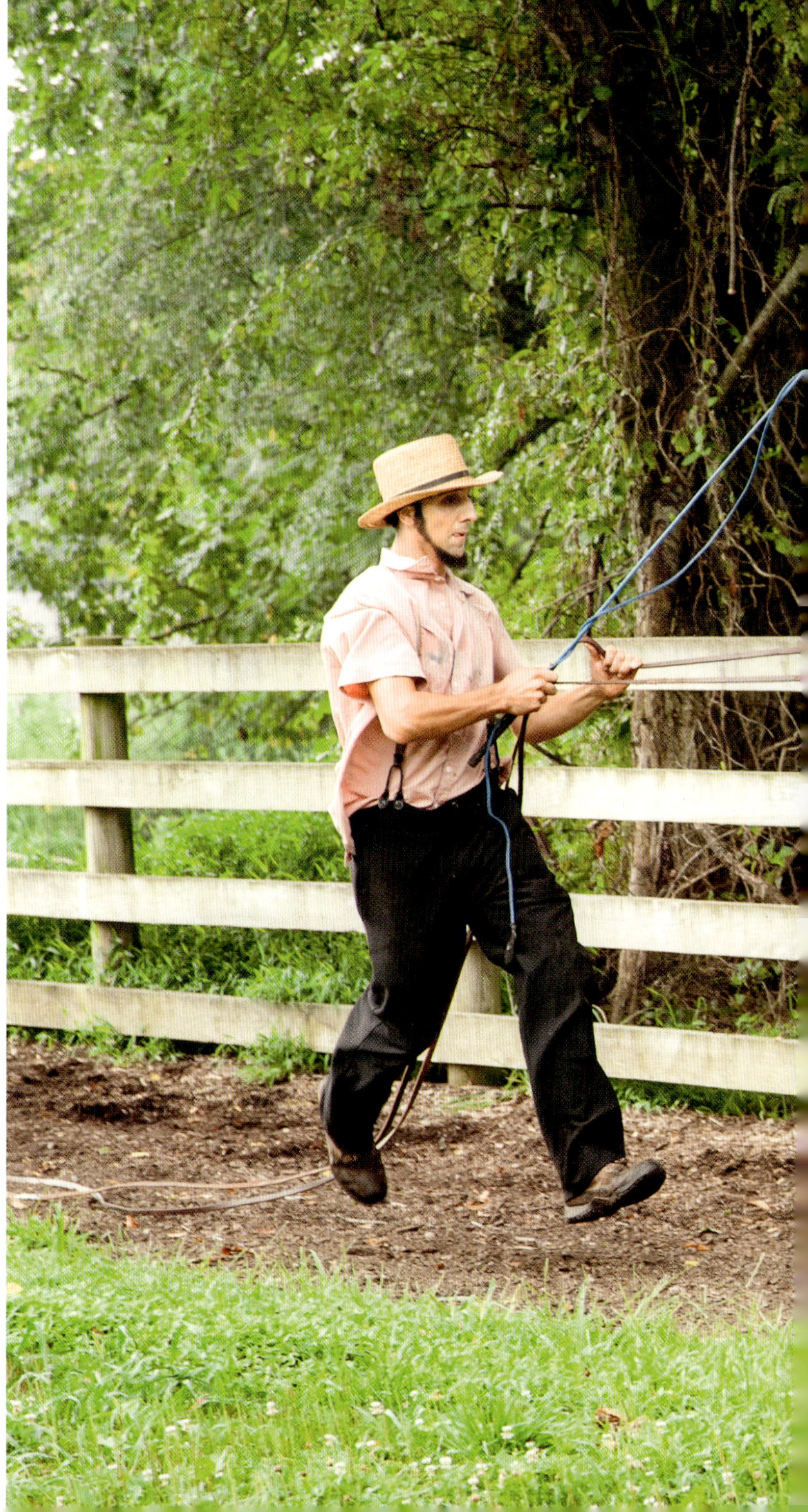

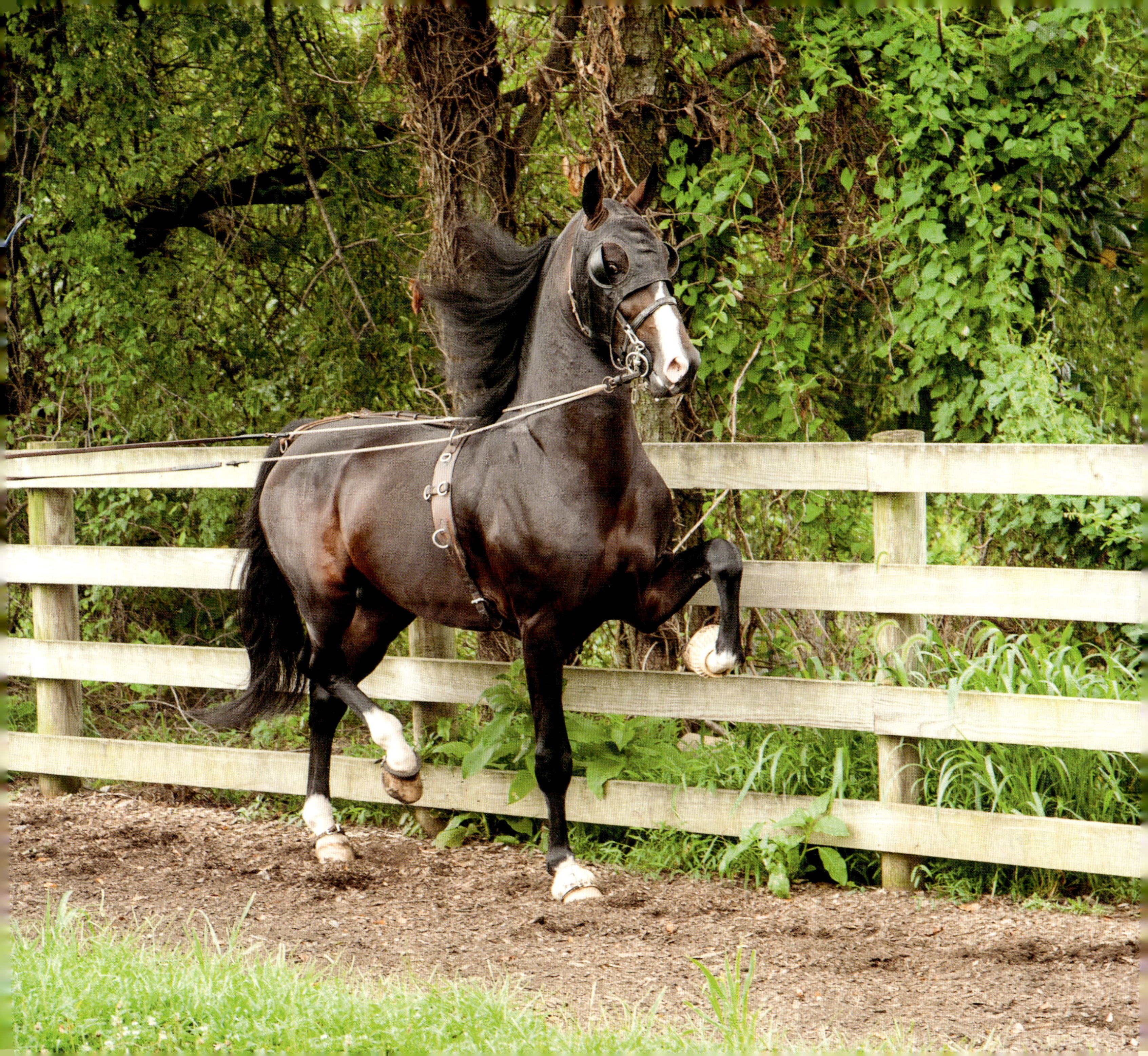

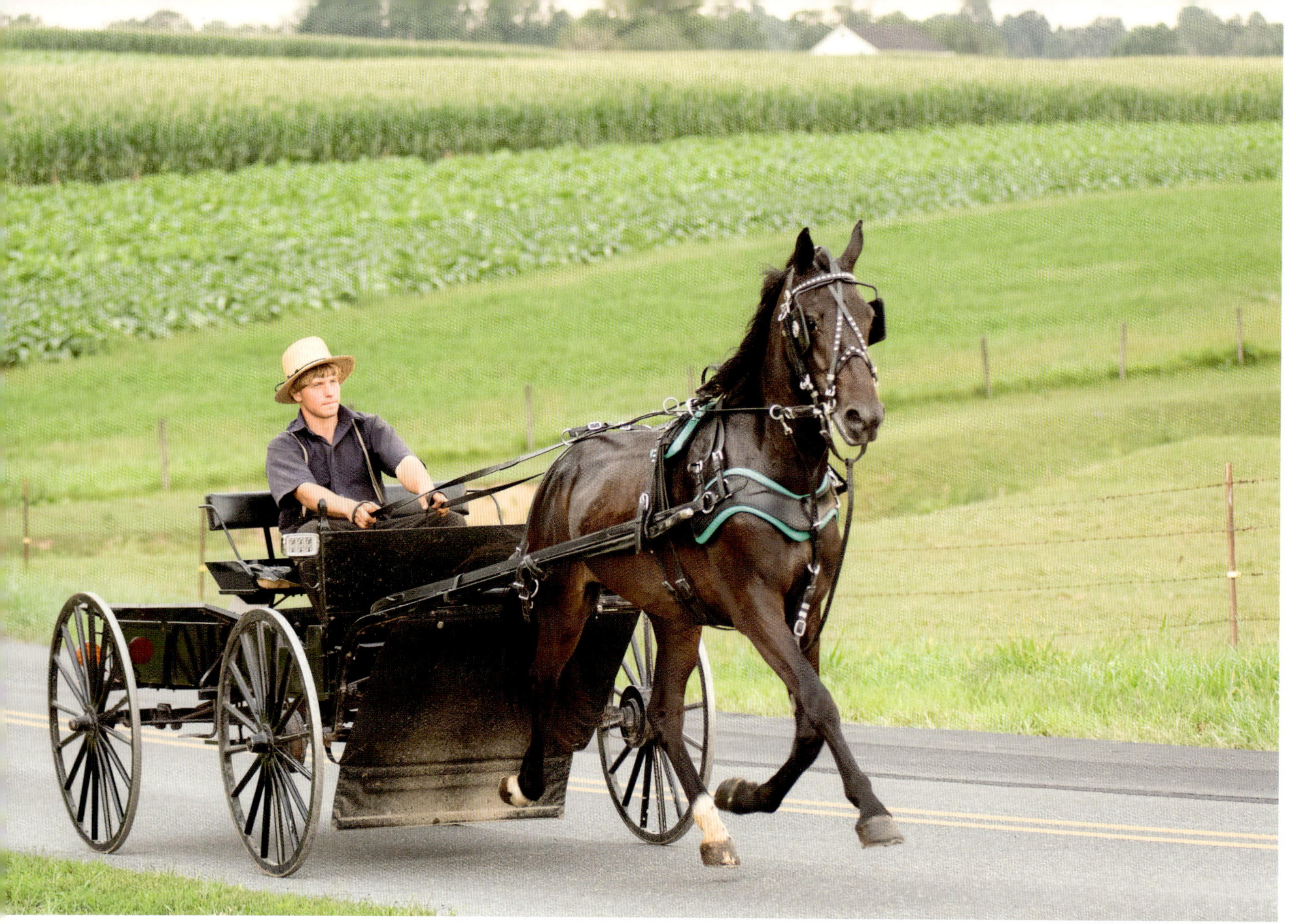

Stoltzfus is delighted with Rhonda. He bought the slim, two-year-old full Dutch Harness horse six months ago and is training her to pull his buggy. Since she is still learning, he drives her on short trips with a light vehicle, like the spring wagon above.

If she fulfills the promise Stoltzfus sees in her, Rhonda will see him through marriage in a few years. She could produce handsome foals as well as provide transportation for him and his family over the next fifteen years or more.

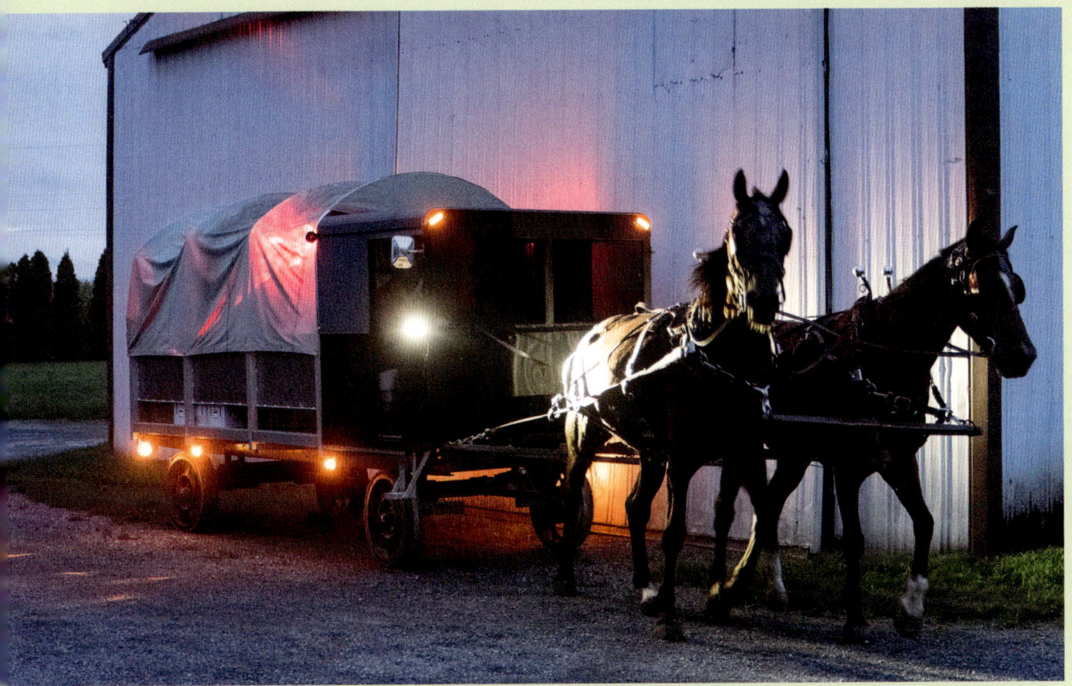

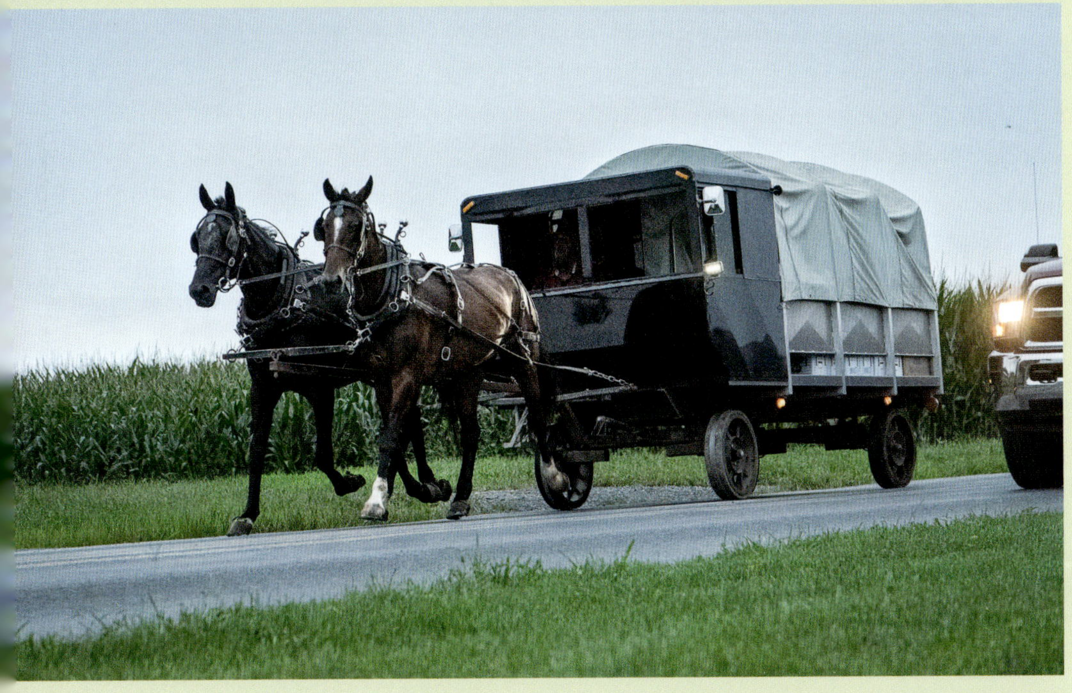

Produce Express

Up well before dawn on a hot August morning, King washed and prepared vegetables for sale at a local produce auction. He harnessed his two carriage horses for the 5-mile drive. Made several times a week in summer and fall, this was a routine trip for Diamond and Tracy, Dutch Harness–Standardbred crossbreeds. Today they hauled a half ton of eggplants, carrots, string beans, lima beans, and red beets.

Most farmers haul goods in open wagons; however King created a hybrid wagon/buggy that brings to mind a covered wagon. The team leaned forward and dug in to get the wagon going. As they pulled out of the farmyard, bright flashing lights illuminated the way and alerted other drivers of their slow-moving progress.

King is hyperaware of automobile traffic. He keeps Diamond and Tracy trotting at a constant pace as far to the right of the roadway as is practical. His steadying hands on the reins keeps them calm and under control, even when cars and trucks come up close behind, then move swiftly around and cut back in front of them.

Carriages are generally pulled by single horses, although two horses are called into service when pulling a heavy load or going a long distance.

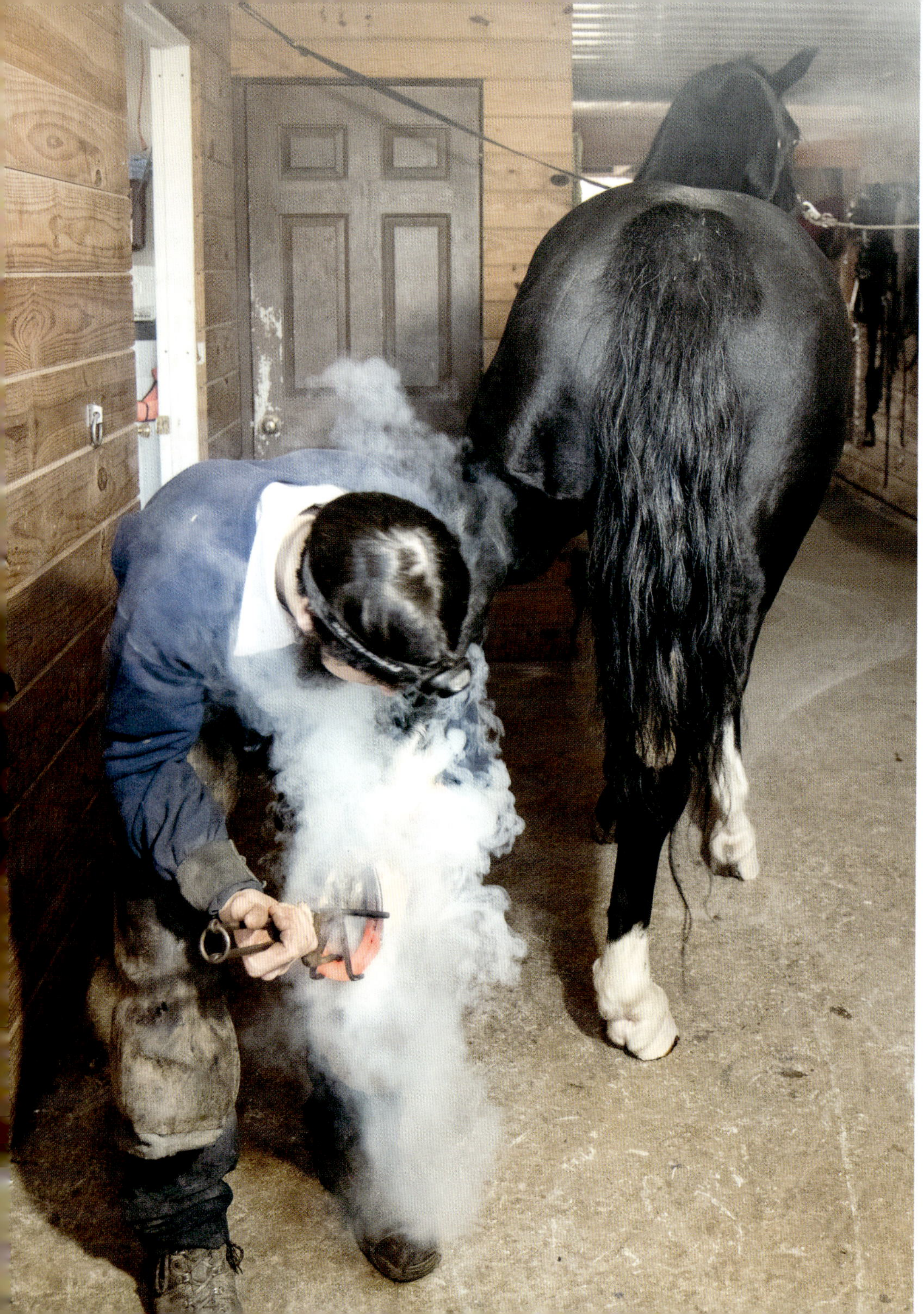

The farrier hot-fitted five-year-old Dutch Harness breeding stallion Izzy, *left,* with new shoes. Hot fitting is often the preferred shoeing method. It creates a smooth fit between the hoof and the shoe, sealing the hoof wall and protecting from over-drying or too much moisture in extreme conditions.

A good fit is vital, whether the horse is in the ring or pulling a buggy. The correct shoeing for a show horse helps build muscle and contributes to a well-balanced trot. Jantz wears his work shoes (*at right*) but will switch to show shoes when the season begins.

Steven's son Benji, a young trainer-in-training, accompanied his dad in the cart when he took Jantz for a spin. The four-year-old Dutch Harness stud showed the beautiful muscle definition and high-stepping action that won him awards in the show ring. A four-wheeled cart is used to train driving horses at all levels, from a young buggy horse to a high-level competition horse.

Steven values plenty of bounce in a horse, but not so much that it "bounces around like a golf ball." The energy needs to be contained and directed.

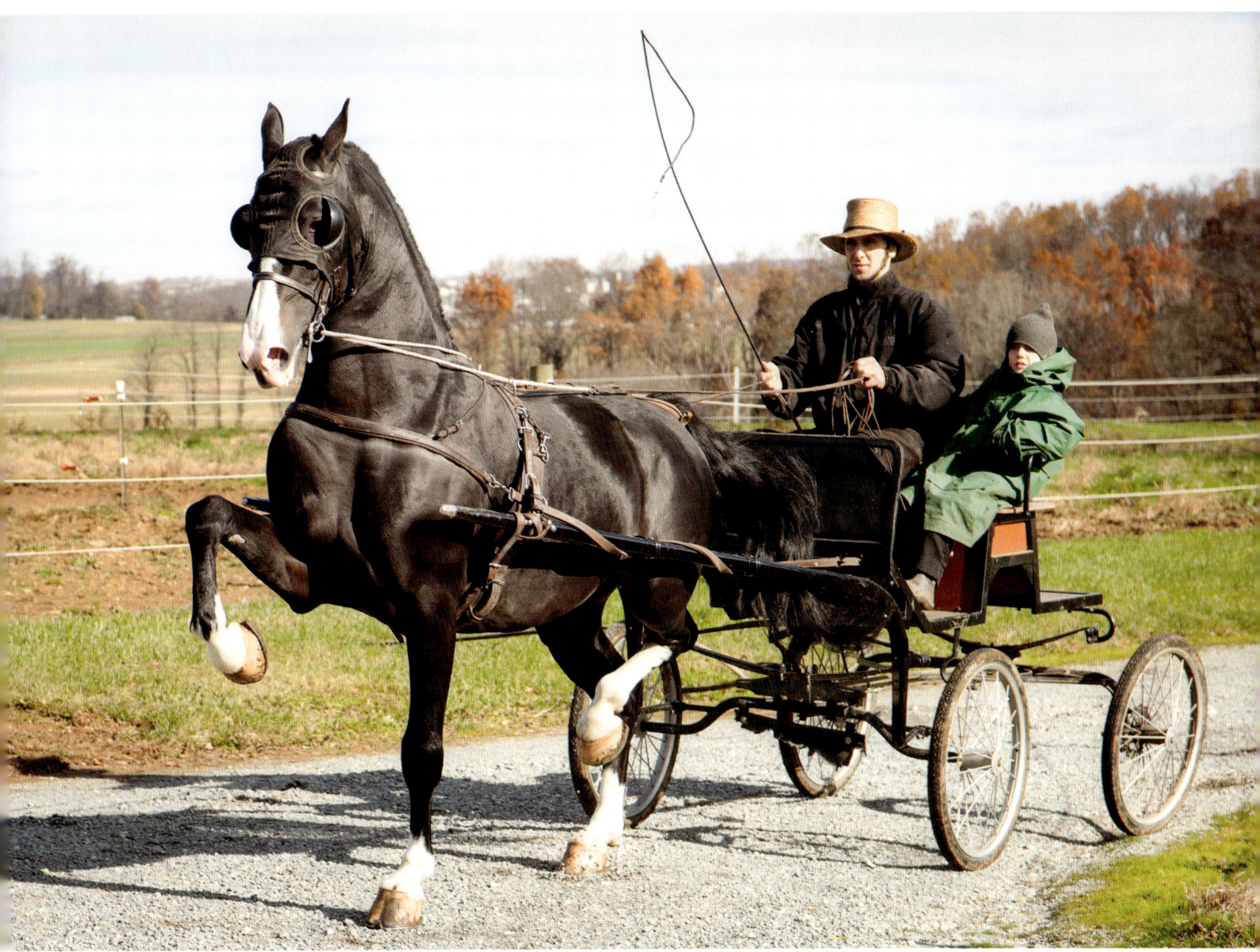

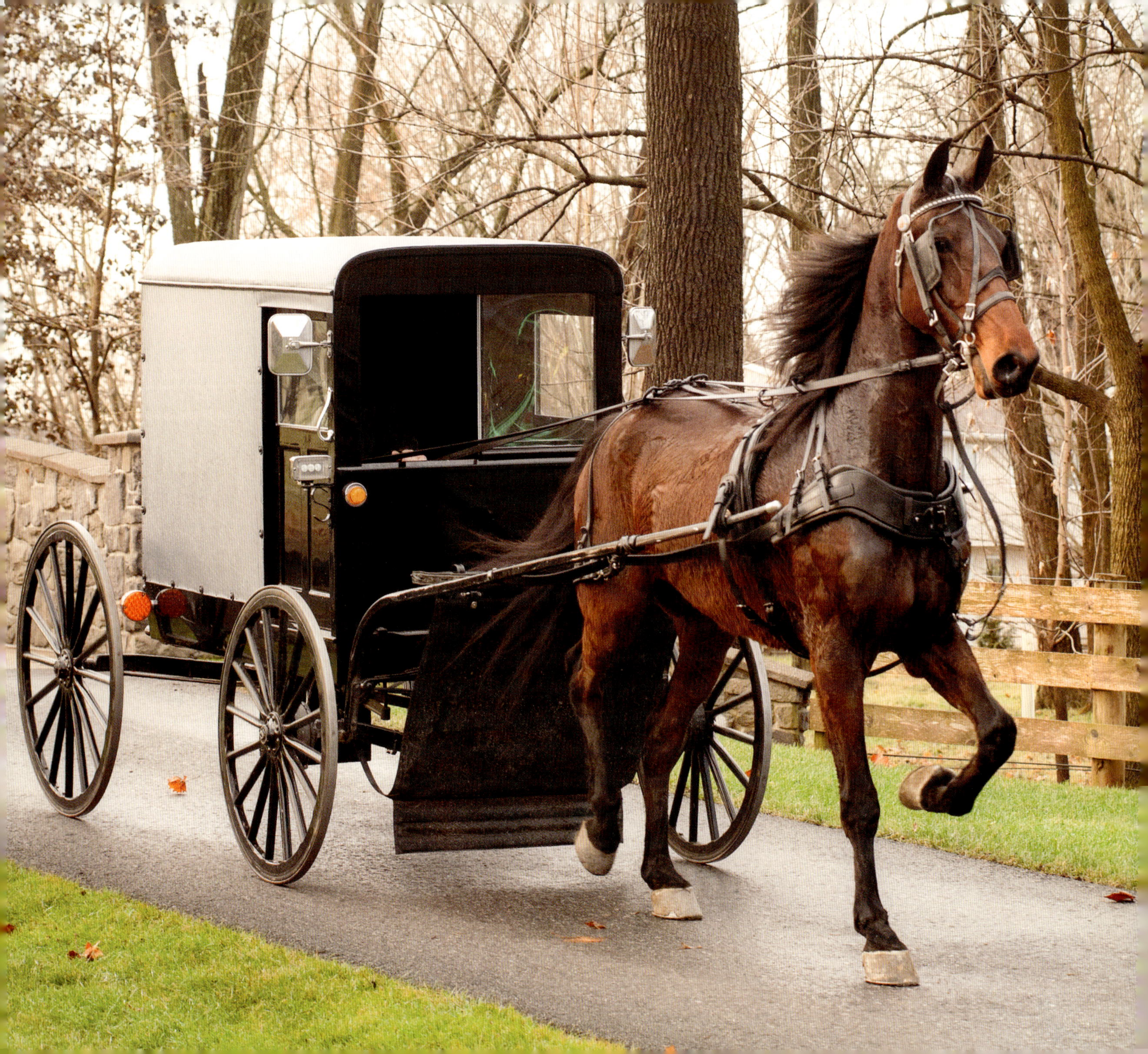

Friesian

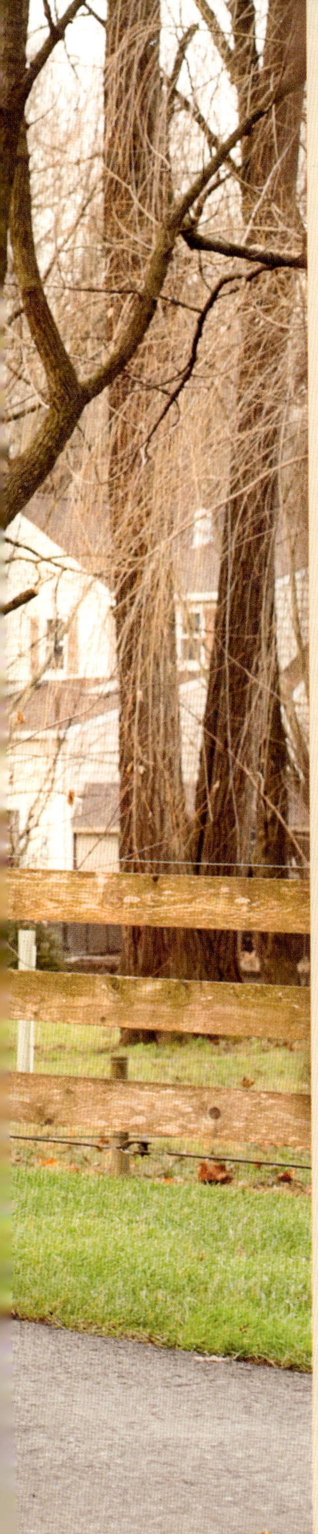

Melvin's father helped him buy his Friesian stallion, and his younger brother helps with his modest breeding business. The Friesian's build is a little sturdier and it's trot a bit slower than the typical carriage horse, but its proud appearance and flowing mane and tail make it an attractive option when cross-breeding to produce a driving horse.

Although Melvin is committed to a cross of Friesian and Standardbred for driving, he also breeds Friesians for show. Their strength, beauty, and refinement make them especially popular for dressage—and Melvin has taught himself the elementary moves from books to make his young horses more attractive to buyers.

Melvin's choice of driving horse puzzles some of his friends: "My friends laugh and tease me when I'm driving my three-quarters-Friesian cross (*right*) and they pass me driving their Standardbreds. But I say, 'You laugh now, but I'll be right behind you.' Their Standards can't keep up their fast pace while my Friesian cross just keeps going steady long after their horses tire out."

Fellow Friesian enthusiast Elam drives Benson, *left*, a Friesian-Standardbred cross. Five-year-old Benson shows elegance and high action on the road.

"My Friesian cross just keeps going steady long after others tire out."

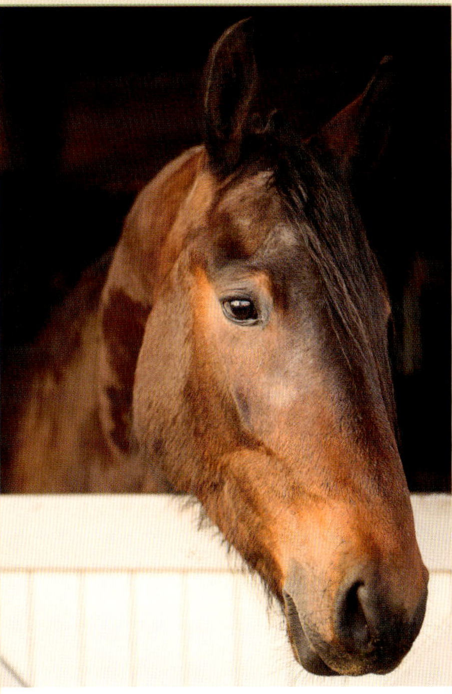

Origin: Friesland, Netherlands

Height: 15.2–16hh

Weight: 1,300+ lbs

Color: black, bit of white acceptable if it's above the eyebrows

The Modern Friesian is descended from the heavy warhorses of the Middle Ages that were later crossed with Spanish Andalusian horses. They worked farms, pulled carriages, and carried riders.

Often noted for their flashy appearance and movement, these Friesians are also known for their intelligence. Shown in the ring under harness or ridden in dressage competitions, they demonstrate a willingness to learn and a readiness to perform.

In the stable, Lucie turned her head slightly and nuzzled Melvin's cheek as he fitted her bridle in place behind her ears. She stood patiently while he buckled the harness and adjusted the crupper under her tail. When Melvin hitched up the sulky, Lucie, a full-breed Friesian, was ready to step out. Melvin settled in the seat and gave her the go-ahead. She trotted out briskly, her black coat glistening in the sunlight.

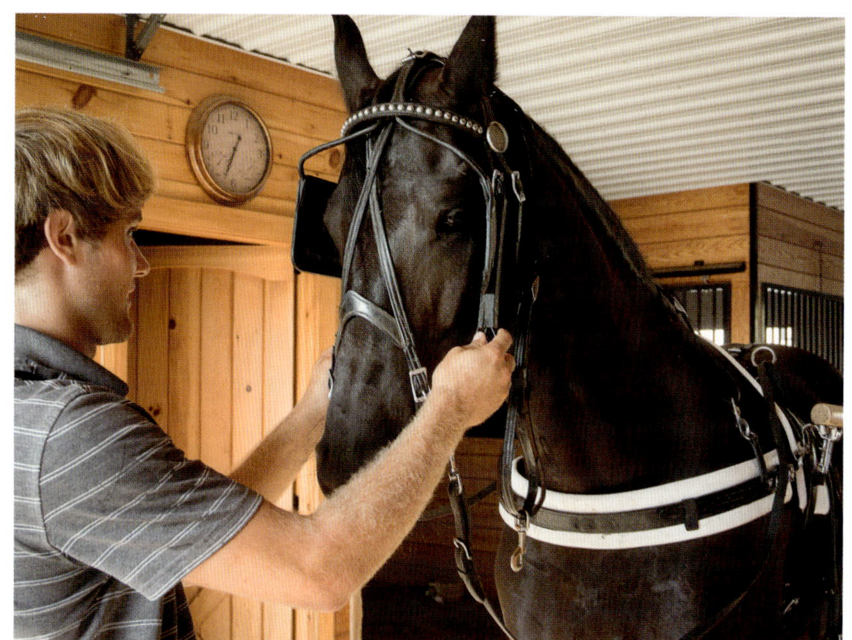

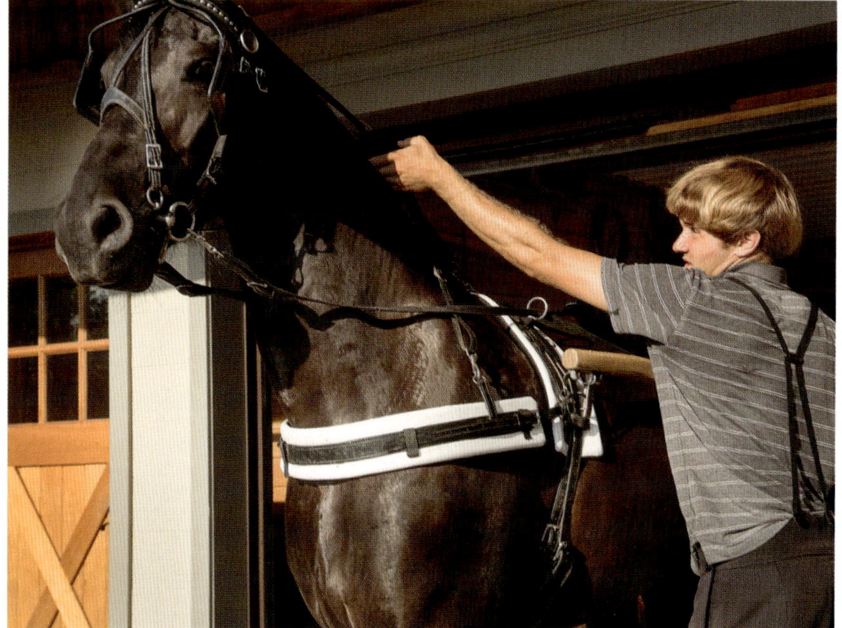

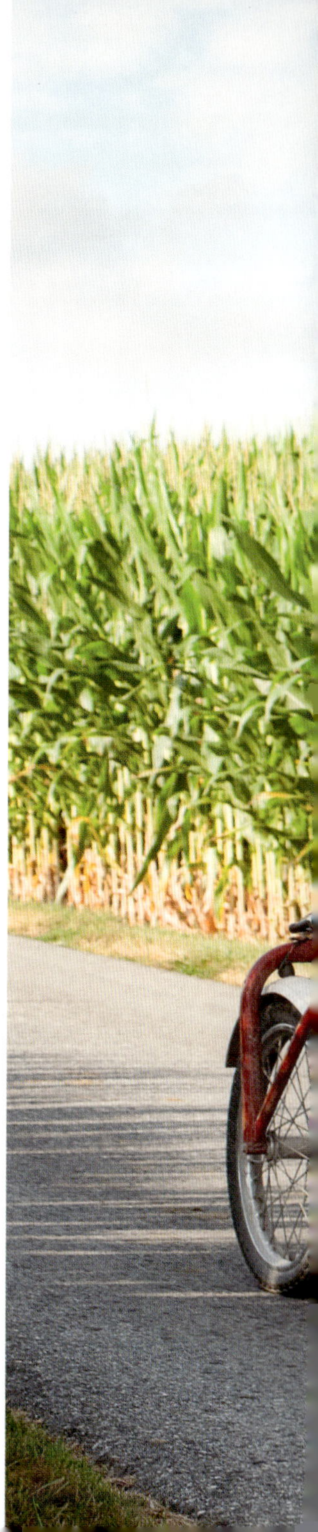

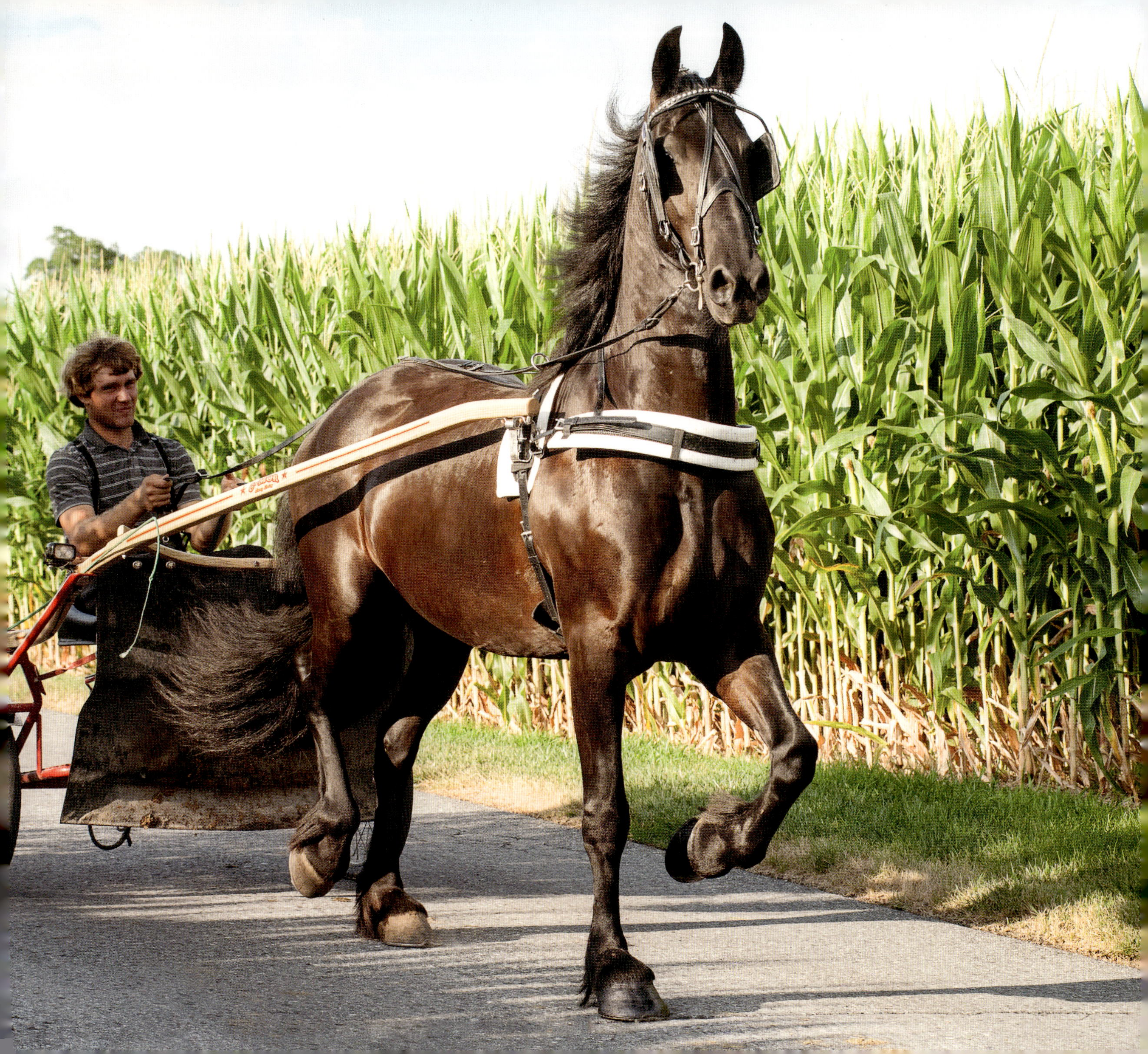

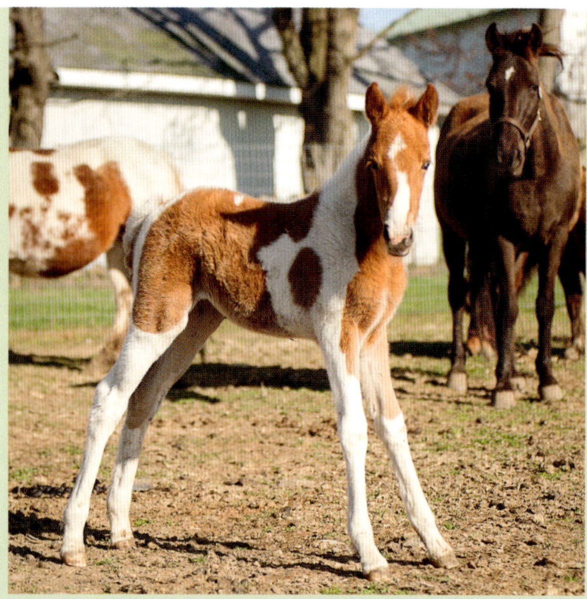

Adele the spotted Friesian

Adele's coloring was a bit of a surprise to her owner. She is the three-week-old offspring of a solid chocolate-colored Rocky Mountain mare and a coal black Friesian stallion. Despite her chestnut spots on white, the Friesian influence in the proud set of her head was obvious right away. Her long cannon bones predict feet lifted high in action and good endurance.

Since Adele's coloring makes her an unlikely dressage candidate, the younger children in the family may benefit. In a few years they will have outgrown their miniature horse and will need something more substantial to pull the cart. They've already begun training Adele to the halter and expect to begin working with her in harness when she's two.

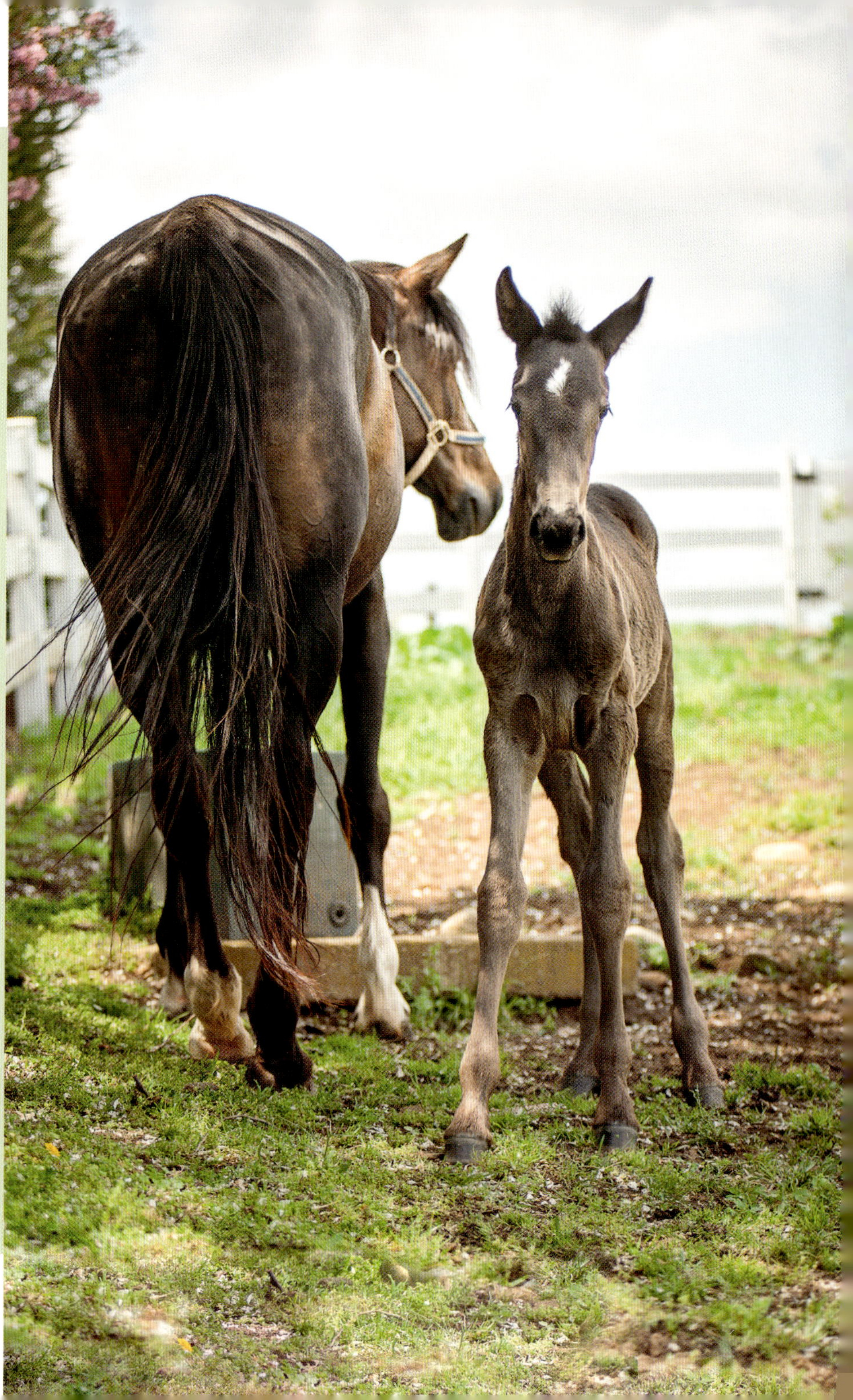

Standardbred mare, Elaine, *left,* gently tended her young Friesian-Standardbred cross foal. The young filly faces the world proudly, with a healthy mix of trepidation and curiosity.

Four-month-old Captain, *below,* offspring of a Friesian sire and a Percheron-Morgan mare, shadows his mother, Princess, in a trot around the pasture. He's starting to lose his baby coat and the dark coloring on his head shows the color he will be as an adult.

Captain's solid build and pleasant temperament can be attributed to his Percheron and Friesian parentage. Though perhaps too "drafty" to use primarily as a carriage horse, he may be a good multipurpose choice for a small farm.

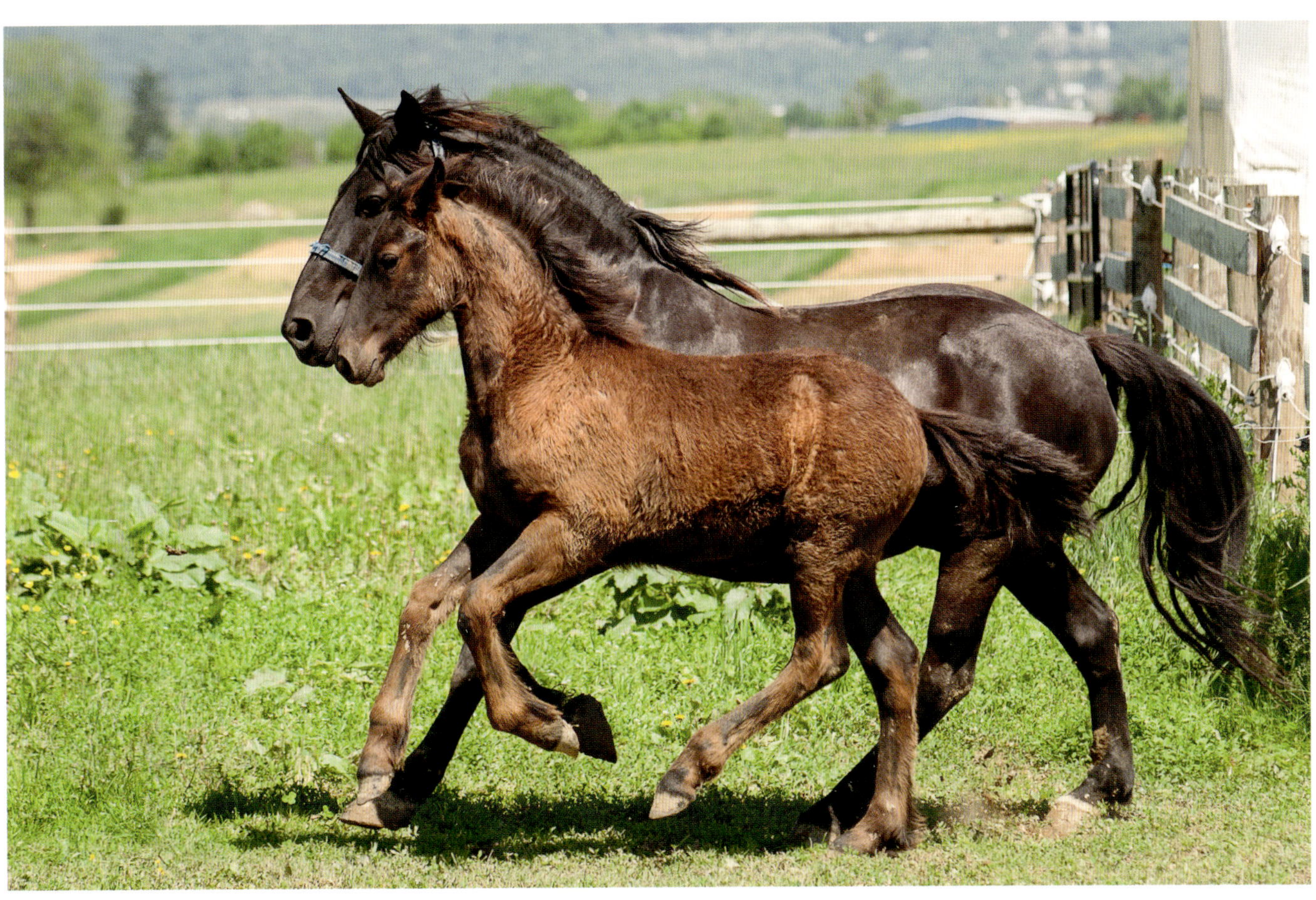

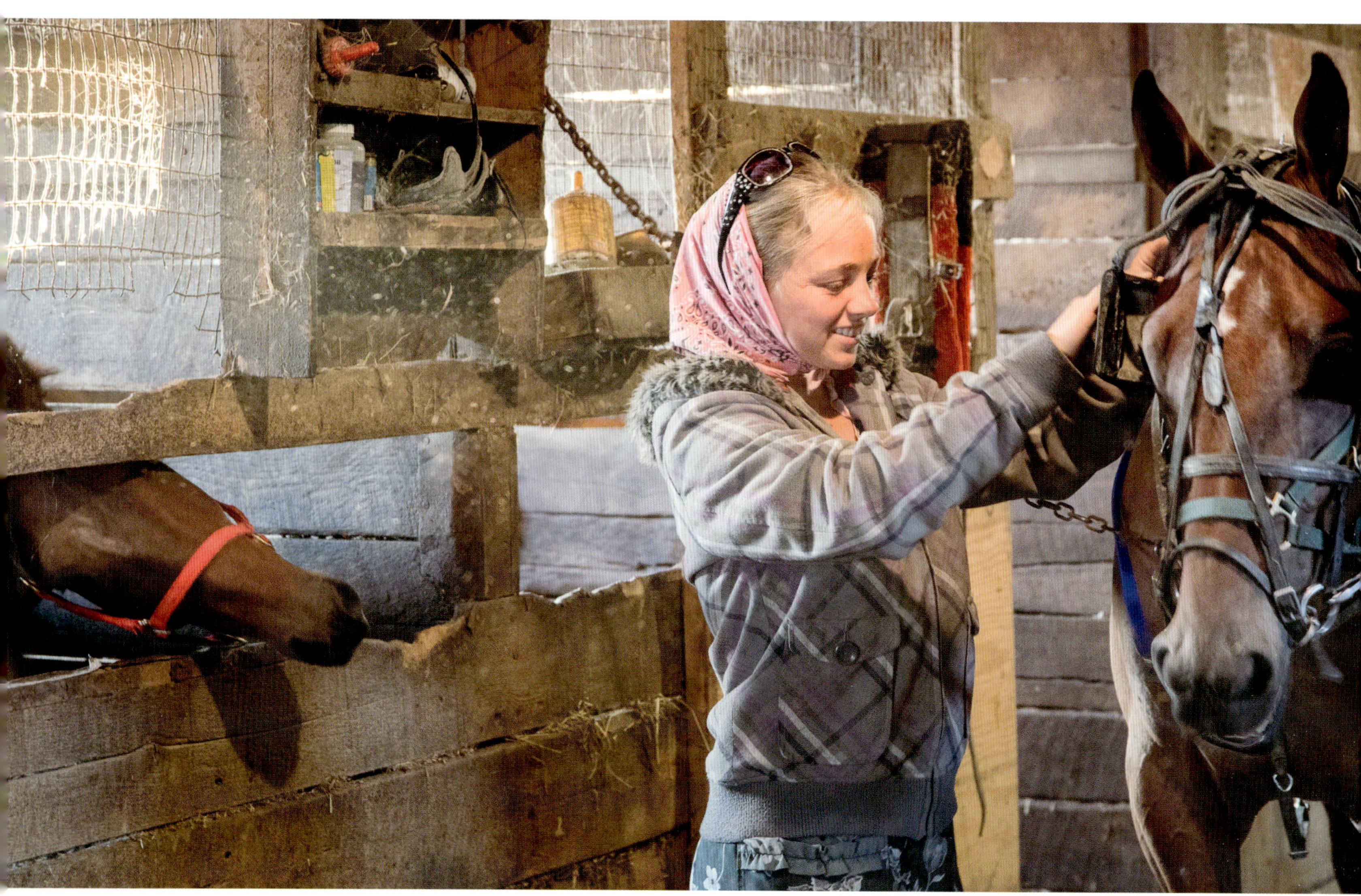

Acknowledgments

We are grateful to the many people, some unnamed, who have shared their love of horses with us. They've allowed us to follow them as they went about their work, spiffed up their horses to be photographed, answered our many questions, and connected us with others.

Frank M. Abel, VMD, Quarryville
Amos and Ruth, Narvon
Belmont Acres Belgians
Amos Beiler, Mt. Joy Acres Percherons
Andrew L. Beiler, Sunrise Stables LLC, Gordonville
Bellview Stables and Equine Services, Oxford
Breezy Trees Farm, Kinzers
Jason R. Brubacker, Brubacker Haflingers
Daniel, Bird-in-Hand
Elda GTA, Quarryville
Christian F. Esh, Center Square Harness Shop
Allan Fisher, Alpha Star Morgans
Elam Fisher Jr., Intercourse
Fisher Acres
Jacob Glick, New Holland
Steven Glick, Quarryville
Jacob, Quarryville
Abner S. King
Isaac K. King, Wateredge Belgians, Lititz
Jacob King, Belmont Acres Belgians, Quarryville
Jacob L. King
Levi S. King
Landis Valley Village & Farm Museum, Pennsylvania Historical & Museum Commission
Elam Lantz, Little Stream Friesian Farm, Gap
Paul H. Martin Jr., Spotted Fever Farm, New Holland
Mascot Sharpening and Sales
Enos Miller, Leola
Jacob and Abner Riehl, RRA's Equine
Rocky Ridge Belgians, Quarryville
Rocky Ridge Stables, Narvon
Dale K. Stoltzfus, Log Cabin Horse Farm, Leola
Eli Stoltzfus Jr., Red Well Stables, New Holland
Stoltzfus, Bird-in-Hand
Stoltzfus, Quarryville
James Z. Stoltzfus, New Holland
Levi Stoltzfus Jr., Le-Arie Farm, Parkesburg
Mark Stoltzfus, Paradise
Melvin Stoltzfus, Homestead Equine, New Holland
Glen Zimmerman, New Holland
Jason K. Zook, Parkesburg

"I love everything about horses, including the smell. But I don't crave it, like some people."

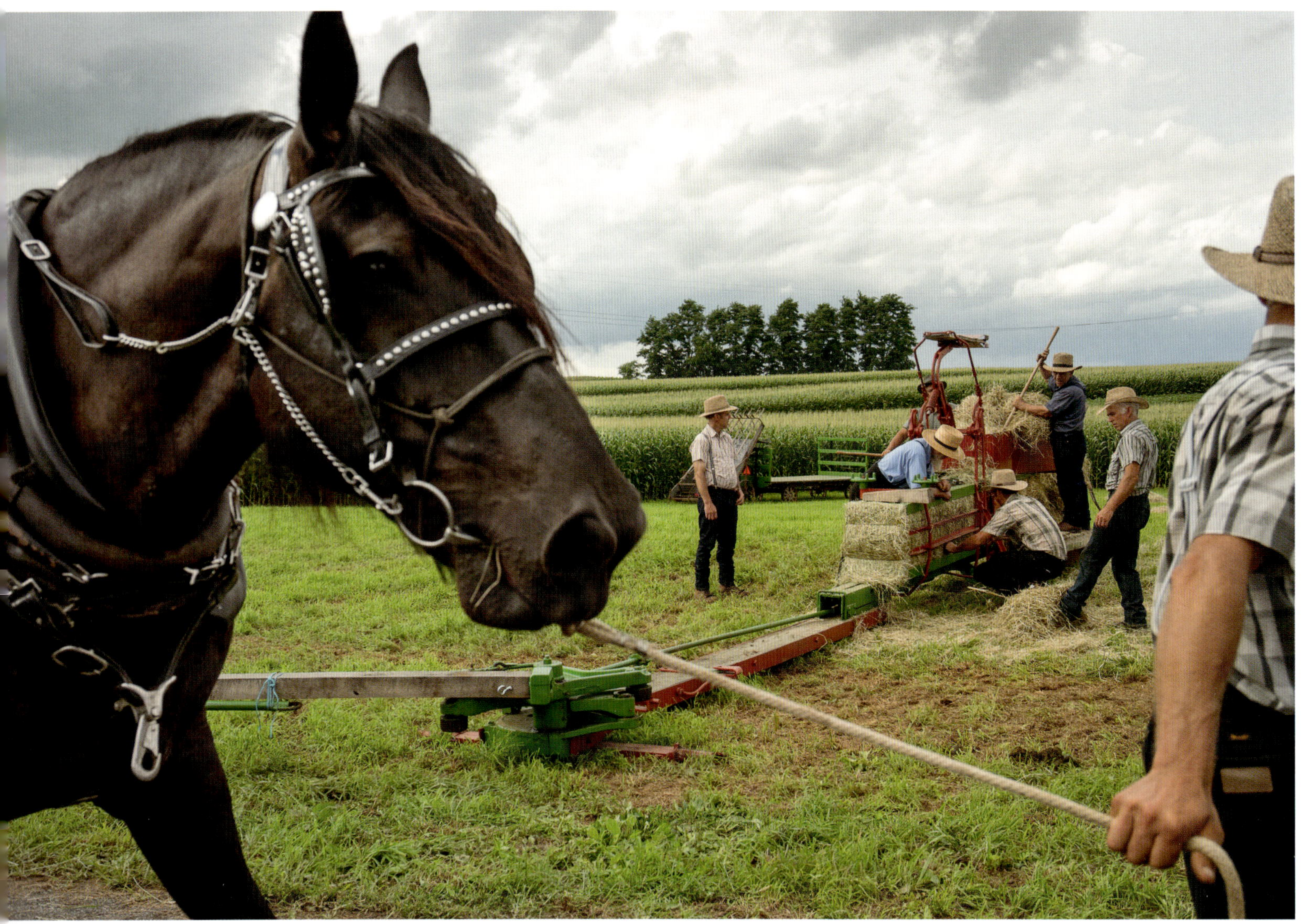

Sources

Books

Damerow, Gail, and Alina Rice. *Draft Horses and Mules: Harnessing Equine Power for Farm & Show.* North Adams, MA: Storey, 2008.

Fitzpatrick, Andrea. *The Ultimate Guide to Horse Breeds.* Edison, NJ: Chartwell Books, 2007.

Holderness-Roddam, Jane. *The Horse Companion: A Comprehensive Guide to the World of Horses.* London: Quarto, 1997.

Kraybill, Donald K. *The Amish of Lancaster County.* Mechanicsburg, PennsylvaniaA: Stackpole Books, 2008.

Nentle, Jerolyn Ann. *Draft Horses.* Mankato, MinnesotaN: Crestwood House, 1983.

Pitts, Gill, and Kaiya Shang, eds. *The Horse Encyclopedia.* New York: Dorling Kindersley, 2016.

Telleen, Maurice. *The Draft Horse Primer: A Guide to the Care and Use of Work Horses and Mules.* Emmaus, PA: Rodale, 1977.

Weaver, Sue. *The Donkey Companion: Selecting, Training, Breeding, Enjoying & Caring for Donkeys.* North Adams, MA: Storey, 2008.

Publications

East Coast Equestrian
www.pennsylvaniaequestrian.com

Equus Magazine
https://equusmagazine.com

The Draft Horse Journal
https://drafthorsejournal.com

Rural Heritage
https://ruralheritage.com

LNP
https://lancasteronline.com

Reports

Mumma, Tracy, program specialist. *Draft Animal Power for Farming.* Butte, MT: National Center for Appropriate Technology, 2009. **http://attra.ncat.org/attra-pub/viewhtml.php?id=259**

Urbanchuk, John M., project dir. *Impact of the Equine Industry on the Economy of Southeastern Pennsylvania.* Doylestown, PA: Delaware Valley University, October 10, 2017. **www.pfb.com/images/stories/counties/chester-del/Summary.pdf**

Machinery Cost Estimates for Amish Farms **www.joe.org/joe/2004october/rb8.php**

Events and Sites

Horse Progress Days
https://horseprogressdays.com

Keystone Draft Horse Sale
www.keystonedhs.com

Landis Valley Village & Farm Museum, Pennsylvania Historical & Museum Commission
www.landisvalleymuseum.org

Farmers, *left,* forked loose hay into the 1-horsepower hay baler at a demonstration of historical farming methods. Percheron gelding Rudy walked in a circle, turning an arm that provided power to pack the hay into bales.

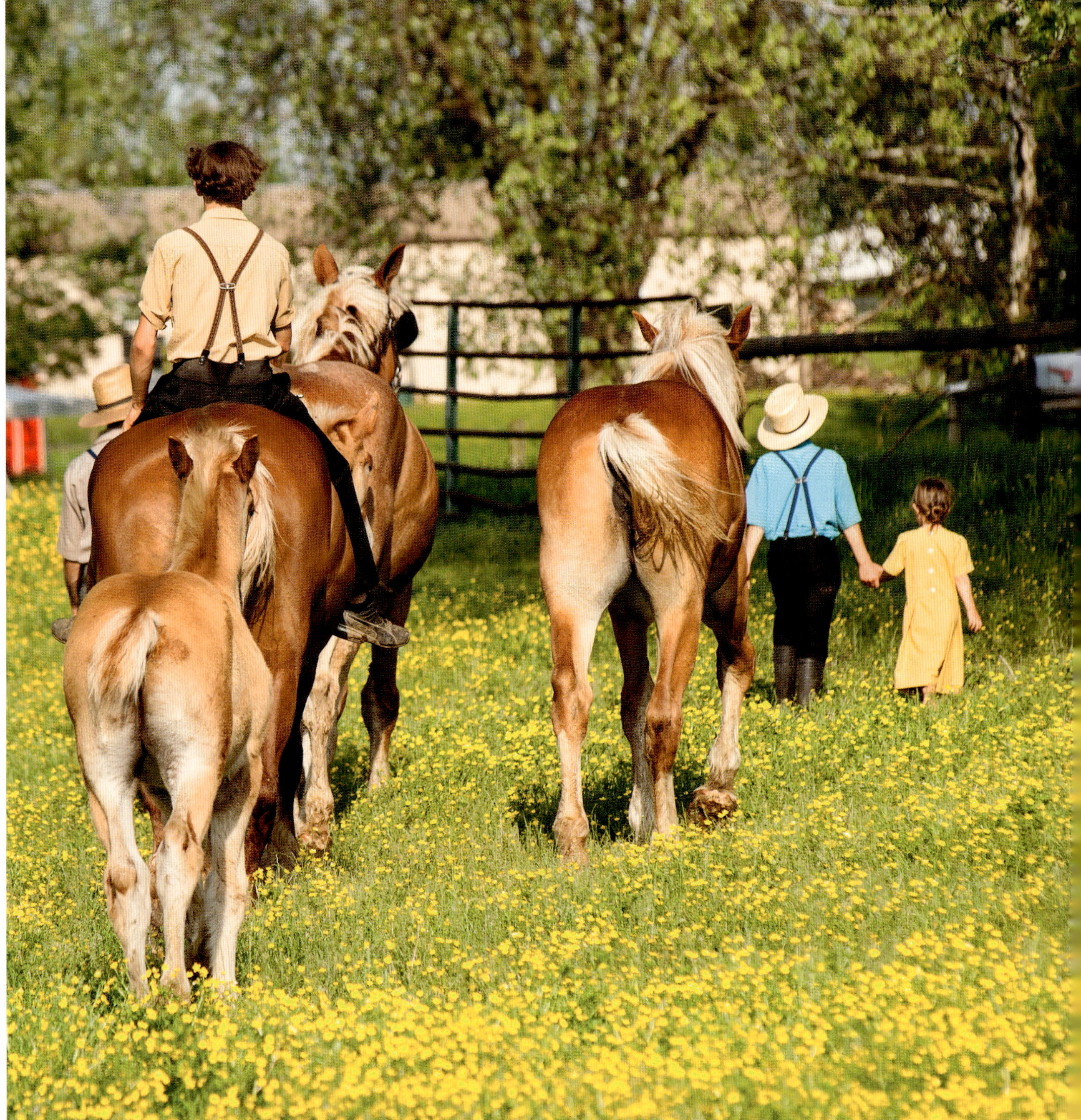

Websites

American Horse Council
www.horsecouncil.org

American Mule Museum
www.mulemuseum.org

Draft Animal-Power Network
www.draftanimalpower.org

The Equinest
www.theequinest.com/breeds

Equestrian and Horse
www.equestrianandhorse.com

Highway History
https://www.fhwa.dot.gov/infrastructure/right.cfm

Pennsylvania Draft Horse and Mule Association
https://padhma.org

The British Mule Society
https://thebritishmulesociety.blogspot.com

Horse Breeds Pictures
www.horsebreedspictures.com

KWPN North America
https://kwpn-na.org

The Livestock Conservancy
https://livestockconservancy.org

Lucky Three Ranch
www.luckythreeranch.com/lucky-three-ranch-training/mule-facts

Belgian "Brabant" Draft Horses
www.trekpaard.net

New Vocations Racehorse Adoption Program
www.horseadoption.com/standardbred-training-tips

The Young Center for Anabaptist and Pietist Studies at Elizabethtown College
www.etown.edu/centers/young-center

Pennsylvania Equine Council
https://pennsylvaniaequinecouncil.org

The Spruce Pets
www.thesprucepets.com

US Equestrian
www.usef.org

Breed Associations

The American Brabant Association
www.theamericanbrabantassociation.net

American Bashkir Curly Horse Registry
www.abcregistry.org

American Donkey & Mule Society
www.lovelongears.com

American Dutch Harness Horse Association
https://adhha.org

American Haflinger Registry
https://haflingerhorse.com

The American Mammoth Jackstock Association
https://americanjackstock.org

The American Morgan Horse Association
www.morganhorse.com

American Saddlebred Horse Association
https://asha.net

American Shire Horse Association
https://shirehorse.org

American Suffolk Horse Association
www.suffolkpunch.com

The Belgian Draft Horse Corporation of America
www.belgiancorp.com

Clydesdale Breeders of the USA
www.clydesusa.com

Clydesdale Horse Society
clydesdalehorsesociety.com

Friesian Horse Association of America
www.fhana.com

The International Curly Horse Organization
www.ichocurlyhorses.com

The North American Spotted Draft Horse Association
https://sites.google.com/site/naspotteddrafthorseassn

Percheron Horse Association of America
www.percheronhorse.org

Spotted Draft Horse Registry
https://spotteddraftregistry.eaph.com

World Percheron Congress
www.worldpercheroncongress.us

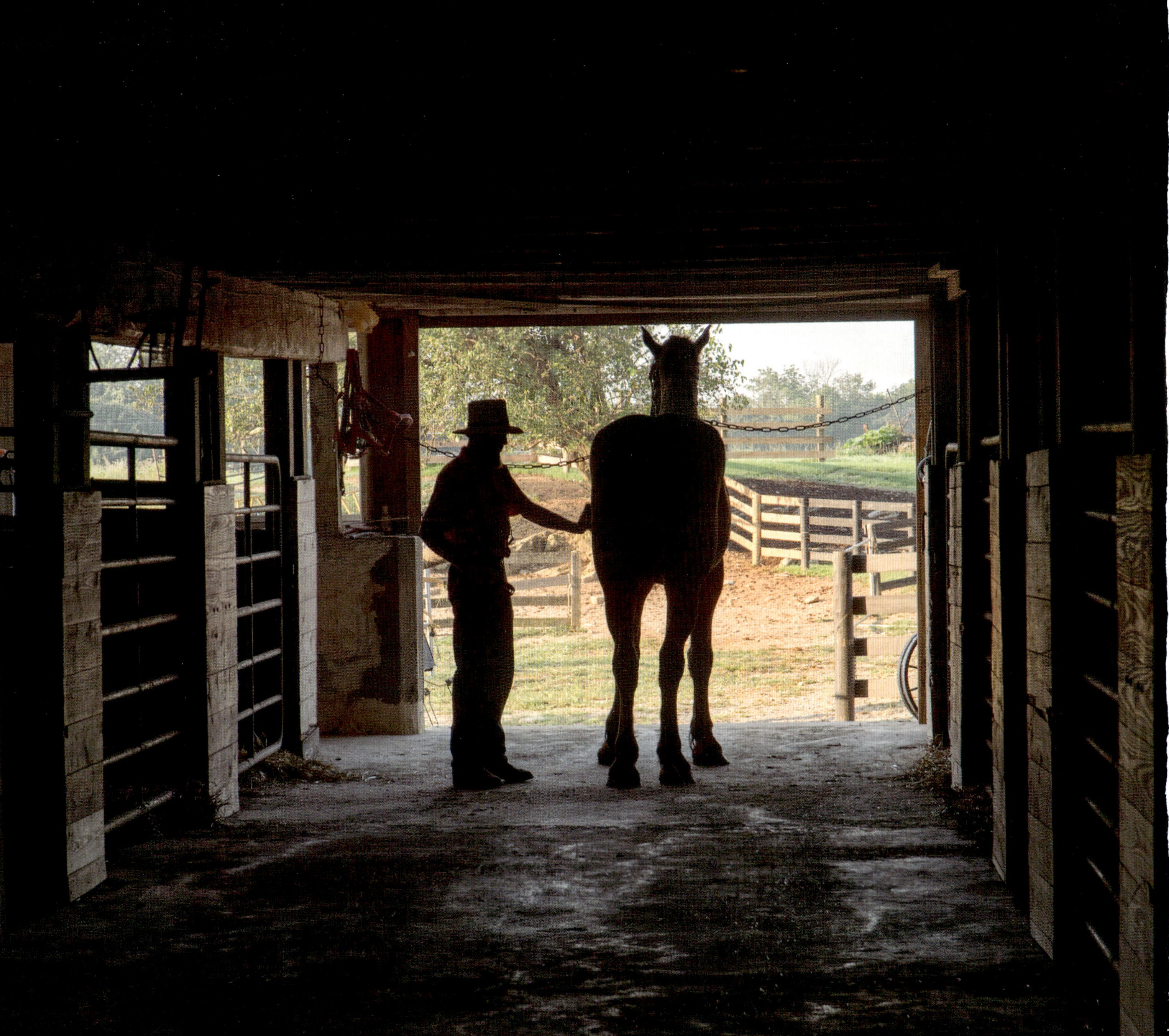

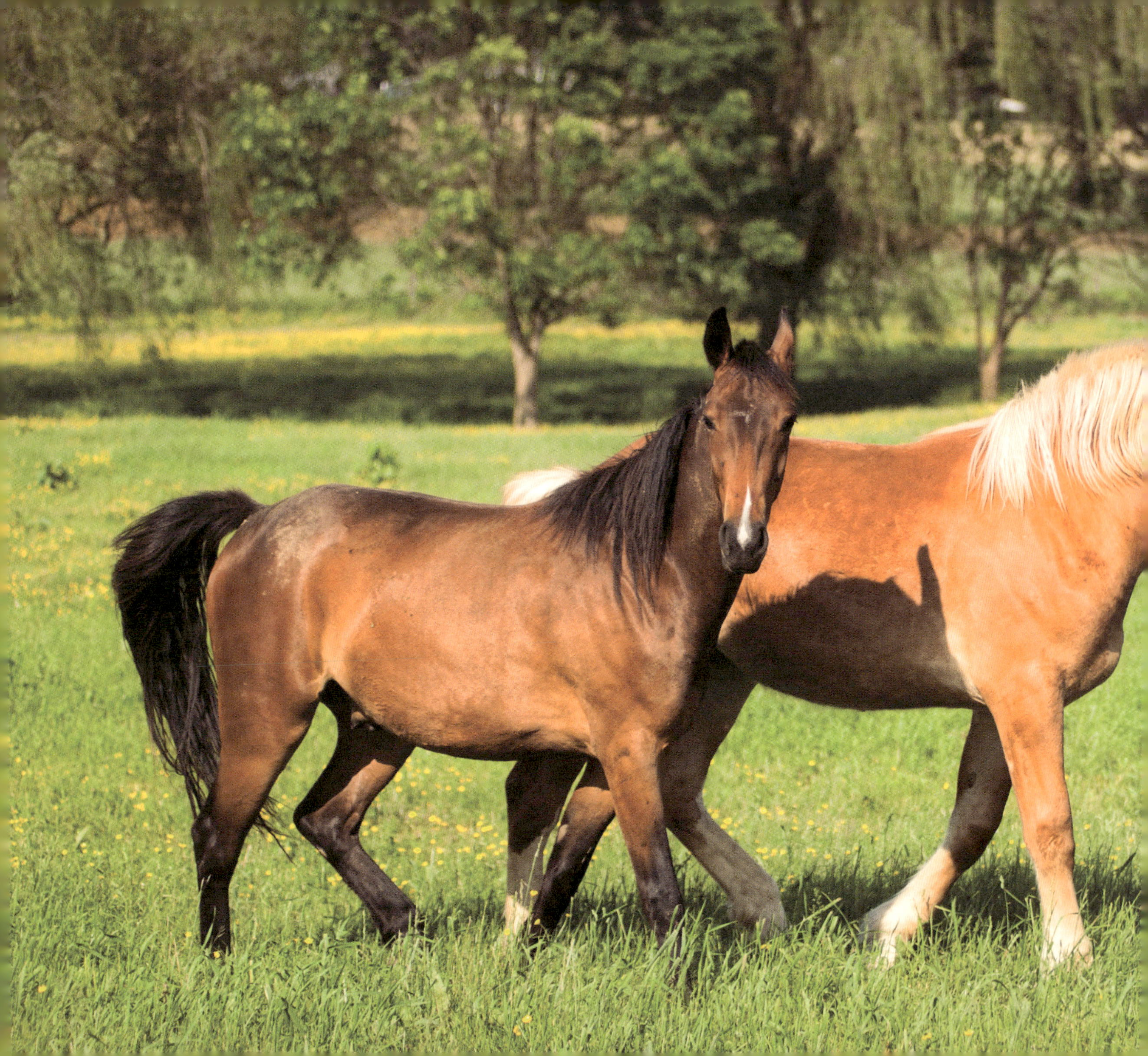